Pencil sketch of General
Washington - from life, taken
by Chas. Willson Peale 1777

George Washington's Momentous Year

Twelve Months that Transformed the Revolution

VOLUME I

THE PHILADELPHIA CAMPAIGN,
JULY TO DECEMBER 1777

GARY ECELBARGER

WESTHOLME
Yardley

Facing title page: "Pencil sketch of General Washington from life, taken by Chas. Willson Peale 1777." See page 143. (*Historical Society of Pennsylvania*)

Westholme Publishing, LLC
904 Edgewood Road
Yardley, Pennsylvania 19067
Visit our Web site at www.westholmepublishing.com

ISBN: 978-1-59416-422-4
Also available as an eBook.

Printed in the United States of America.

To the memory of my father,
Elvin J. Ecelbarger
The Best of the Washington Men

Contents

Illustrations

MAPS

Preface

While major cities of every state in America celebrated Independence Day on the Fourth of July in 1777, no available evidence suggests that George Washington acknowledged the first such anniversary. Yet, one year later, Washington not only was recognizing the second anniversary of American independence, he was hailing that event with a glorious display of military pageantry remembered by veterans fifty years later as distinctly as they recalled any battle. *George Washington's Momentous Year* examines the twelve months between those "Fourths," and in doing so explains the contrasts that set those anniversaries apart.

This two-volume history can be best described as a single-year, military campaign biography of General George Washington that guides the reader from the summer of 1777 to the summer of 1778—a year highlighted by the Philadelphia Campaign, the six-month Valley Forge encampment, and the Monmouth Campaign. Numerous books and monographs have detailed these iconic events, but not persistently from the perspective of

George Washington, his headquarters, and his interactions with other army personnel.

Washington usually stands front and center in histories addressing the Philadelphia Campaign, Valley Forge, and Monmouth. However, since publication more than seventy years ago of volumes four and five of Douglas Southall Freeman's magisterial seven-volume biography, no book-length treatment has emphasized these critical events chiefly from His Excellency's point of view. Given the sheaves of primary documents unearthed since Freeman's research in the 1940s and the subsequent updating across more than half a century of interpretations of Revolutionary War decisions, movements, and battles, a fresh focus upon Washington during this critical year is long overdue.

George Washington's Momentous Year strives to achieve that goal by explicating Washington's direct and indirect role in the war between July 4, 1777, and July 4, 1778. The Commanding General's antipodean responses to those anniversaries bookend the twelve months chronicled, explaining Washington's wondrous change of attitude toward the Fourth of July. That this transformation occurred before the halfway point of the Revolutionary War enhances the drama.

Two volumes, their timeframes nearly equal, tell this compelling story. Volume One places the reader in Washington's headquarters tents and houses and follows the General's bootsteps as well as his horses' hoofprints through the Philadelphia Campaign, beginning in early summer and ending near the start of the 1777-1778 winter season. The autumn campaign around Philadelphia has garnered considerable historiographical attention; seeking to drill more deeply into that vein, this volume covers the summer and fall months from Washington's perspective and in "real time," contemporaneously studying his decisions and actions and analyzing what he said and did. The volume presents new sources and fresh analyses regarding Washington in the battles of Brandywine, at White Horse Tavern, and at Germantown and Whitemarsh. Likewise, the narrative recasts Washington's generalship between these battles.

In similar manner, Volume Two of *George Washington's Momentous Year* illuminates his military life from departing camp at Whitemarsh on December 11, 1777, through to Independence Day along the Raritan River on July 4, 1778. The primary events examined in Volume Two are winter and spring at Valley Forge and June's Monmouth Campaign. Volume Two will appeal to the full spectrum of readers of history—from novices trying to grasp command decisions during the Revolutionary War to those well versed in the era's literature. Of note to all will be a revised interpretation of the Valley Forge experience informed by latter-day revelations regarding that encampment's previously underappreciated population and the gripping story of the pursuit of Crown forces through New Jersey, culminating in the last great land battle of Washington's career.

Army headquarters—the brain center of the campaigns of this 1777-1778 slice of the Revolutionary War—is the point of emphasis in these volumes. The reader follows headquarters operations during days of encampment, days of movement, and days of battle. Those duties are performed in all instances by Washington and his military family, a closely bonded retinue of aides, secretaries, adjutants, department heads, and numerous volunteers dedicated to The Cause and to the General. Their routine and unusual behind-the-scenes machinations—usually relegated to mere mentions or none at all in traditional campaign histories—are brought forward from the first pages and remain throughout these volumes to add fresh perspectives to even the most recitable events of this period.

Each volume stands alone. Neither of these books indulges in hagiography, presenting as they do Washington at his best and his worst across four seasons. His poorest day as a commander in 1777-1778 is not the date of a lost battle, and his most satisfying day is off the battlefield as well. If readers of one or both volumes frequently pause to think "I never knew that!" and upon finishing declare, "That was a unique story," then the author has accomplished his chief objectives.

CHAPTER ONE

USA

July 4, 1777

Two weeks after the summer solstice of 1777, George Washington rose before that Friday's sun to begin his third year at the head of the "Grand Army," the main force of Continental soldiers operating in the United States of America. Washington was most commonly identified in conversation and correspondence as "His Excellency" and "the General." Both references proved apt; he certainly looked the part. Handsome, with reddish brown hair and blue-gray eyes, Washington was of a size that distinguished him from every other officer and most every other colonial American. A contemporary referred to him as "a large, heavy man." Considered *in toto*, portraits of him suggest a man whose weight could fluctuate, but during the summer of 1777 the odds favored a mass close to his only recorded wartime weight of 209 pounds.[1] Whether viewed at his heaviest or lightest, Washington was blessed with more visible muscle than bone or fat, but it was his height that dominated most of the era's descriptions of him. Fully dressed, George Washington stood six feet, three inches, a measurement that lofted him a head above most subordinates and civilians.[2]

At forty-five, Washington was beginning to show the responsibility of his position and the stress of war in his graying hair and aging face. (Artists powdered his hair to neutralize the former; Martha Washington cajoled portraitists into concealing the latter.)[3] Longer-term imperfections had been blemishing other parts of him for decades. Washington had a permanent tooth pulled for the first time during his twenties and began to have trouble with his gums much earlier than his contemporaries. He did not sit for any life portraits in the first half of 1777, so his most recent image at this time was a work by Charles Willson Peale for which Washington had posed in the late spring of 1776. The scar on Washington's left cheek did not escape Peale's portrait; it was believed to have resulted from an abscessed tooth. Peale did not include on his subject's visage faint but visible smallpox scars, left when he contracted that illness on Barbados a quarter of a century earlier. Those pockmarks were evident to any who got close enough; very few dared to comment about them.[4]

The General's most unusual physical flaw never appeared in any painting of him and remained hidden from infrequent face-to-face visitors at headquarters or in the field. A portraitist bluntly characterized the anomaly: "the General has a remarkable dead Eye." A delegate to the Continental Congress said he had been startled to hear the artist's comment about Washington's eye, which he said "did not strike me in either of the three or four times when I saw him." In a rare moment of public candor regarding her husband's imperfections, Martha Washington confessed (as related by an aide to His Excellency) "to the Languor of the Generals Eye—for altho' his Countenance when affected by Joy or Anger is full of expression—yet when the Muscles are in a state of repose, his eye certainly wants animation."[5] This "languor" could not have escaped the notice of those who frequently interacted personally with Washington, yet these witnesses so effectively guarded the secret that the affected eye was never identified as being the right or the left.

By the early summer of 1777, the name "George Washington" ranked nearly equally with "King George III" among the most recognizable on Earth. A biblically minded comparison imagined Washington as David battling the British Empire's Goliath. Like David's stone stunning his gigantic foe, what Washington had accomplished during the previous six months shocked the world.

After a disastrous struggle to defend New York City during the summer and autumn of 1776, early that December General Washington and his remnant of the Continental army retreated to the Pennsylvania side of the Delaware River. In three months of fighting, the army, devastated by battlefield losses, prisoner taking, and desertions, had been ground down to less than a third of its original strength. Washington made the best use of his reduced manpower. Racing an end-of-year deadline that would see his Continentals' enlistments expire, he recrossed the ice-choked river on Christmas night and marched several wintry miles to Trenton, where the next morning he surprised and thoroughly routed an outnumbered outpost of Hessians. Persuading enough of his soldiers to extend their enlistments to parry the British reaction to the American victory at Trenton, Washington expertly arranged his force behind Assunpink Creek and on January 2 withstood several attempts by Redcoats to dislodge his troops. An audacious decision that evening envisioned a rapid overnight march away from Assunpink Creek to the northeast. At Princeton, he surprised and clashed with rearward British regiments, so swiftly and decisively defeating them on the morning of January 3 that Washington and his force were able to escape northward, eluding a rapidly arriving relief force of British infantry.

Start to finish, these three American victories occurred in slightly over eight days. Beginning a few days after the Battle of Princeton and continuing for four months Washington and his army nestled in and near Morristown, New Jersey. The Watchung Mountains surrounded the town and shielded the Continentals from the British army as both forces hunkered in winter quarters. He had marched into Morristown in early January with no more than 3,500 Continentals, a count that by mid-March had shrunk to 2,500 armed men.[6] That winter and spring Washington tapped into his organizational skills to fulfill Congress's third establishment of the Continental army by building a force capable in manpower—but not yet honed to martial precision and able to confront Crown forces. To avoid the mass departure of troops at the end of 1776 triggered by single-year enlistments, Washington proffered to new recruits three-year enlistments. Men who signed on were to receive a $20 bonus and a new suit of clothes. Recruits signing on for the duration got the same cash and clothing—plus, if the war went beyond three years, one hundred acres of land to be granted at the end of hostilities.

While Washington was building his new army, his veterans and militia remained active. All winter and into early spring, he assigned bands of Continentals to aid New Jersey militia against British reconnaissance and foraging parties, resulting in fifty-eight skirmishes in eighty-four days. Collectively, these engagements became known as the Forage War. Whether in the field or in camps, Washington's new army got preventive medical care in the form of inoculations against smallpox to protect them against a fourth deadly outbreak of the disease during the 1700s in America. Smallpox killed fifteen percent of its victims in the first wave of 1721; the 1775 outbreak lasted seven years.[7]

With congressional approval, obtained late in 1776, Washington reorganized his army with the focus on the brigade over the battalion as the unit of basic battlefield maneuver. He renamed each regiment by its state of origin rather than the generic "Continental." He attempted to recruit seventy-five thousand men to fill out the eighty-eight Continental regiments established by Congress. He intended to form these men into brigades, each consisting of four regiments and led by a brigadier general. In turn, he intended to organize three brigades into a division commanded by a major general. This goal proved unattainable, but by the time Washington broke his winter and spring encampment at the end of May 1777, he was leading a force approaching ten thousand infantry officers and men in forty-three regiments, arrayed in ten brigades forming five divisions. This truncated organization reduced divisions to two brigades instead of three. Adding artillery and cavalry and anticipating the arrival of detached troops, including an independent infantry brigade from North Carolina, brought Washington's force in early summer to nearly twelve thousand—a figure that grew as more bodies of troops joined them over the next several weeks.[8]

In estimates that summer, British newspapers bloated Washington's strength, putting it at forty thousand—a wild overestimation. Although adversarial, the British press did not universally demonize Washington; on the contrary, snippets of respect crept into dailies and weeklies serving Great Britain. The *Ipswich Journal* reported that "the only decent" costume at an early July masquerade ball was one which was part clerical and part military, the latter touches notably Washingtonian. The *Newcastle Courant* printed a rumor that he had been killed. "If General Washington be dead, as reported, it is clear that the American rebellion will not long survive him," surmised the paper, "His character as a humane, brave, and skillful officer, has done more to keep the Provincials under arms, than all the hypocritical invocations of the whole republican Congress put together." The *Public Advertiser* in London carried prideful anecdotes about the American: "The Warwickshire Patriots in London boast much of having General Washington for their Countrymen. They say their Country has produced the greatest Poet, and the greatest General in the World—Shakespeare and Washington."[9]

Washington's nation-saving victories at Trenton and Princeton, as well as his continuous dominance in the Forage Wars, lifted top American officials' spirits in early summer. Financier Robert Morris acknowledged from Philadelphia that the British "will look with longing Eyes at this City but they will look (I hope) in vain. Genl. Washington is watching their motions & you may depend he is a powerful & dangerous Foe to them." Morris also considered Washington the "Great Banker" whose successes had solidified the new nation's credit with the financiers of Europe. Morris confidently stated that "appearances are more favorable now than ever and I have not despaired at any time." Noting that General William Howe, commander of Crown forces in America, remained seemingly inactive in New York, North Carolina delegate Thomas Burke declared, "General Washington with a superior army is ready to oppose him whichever way he moves." The New York delegation assured that state's Council of Safety, "General Washington's regular forces are much better appointed and, in all respects, superior to any he ever commanded." Charles Carroll of Carrollton, a Maryland delegate to the Continental Congress, wrote to his father that "The Secretary to our board returned yesterday from Camp; he says the men are healthy & in spirits and he thinks the army, tho' much smaller than what Gen. Washington commanded last Summer & fall, [is] much more formidable."[10]

Patriotic Americans spoke respectfully, even reverentially of "the General." "Please to insert the following accrostic on General Washington in your next," a worshipful reader urged the editors of the Boston *Independent Chronicle*; "though it falls infinitely short of his unparrelled character." The paper granted the request early in July:

> G enuine production of the God's above,
> E merg'd from Heav'n on the wing's of sovereign love,
> O ver COLUMBIA's Host to take command,
> R egain her freedom, and defend her land;
> G reatness of language can't his praise express,
> E clipses but his fame and makes it shine the less.

W isdom and knowledge all his deeds inspire,
A nd his vast soul warm'd with angelic fire;
S tatesman accomplish, hero BRAVE and BOLD,
H is matchless virtues like the Stars untold;
I n utmost perils calm and most serene,
N or over flath'd when he's victorious been;
G odlike his mind's from common changes free,
T urns o'er the fate of nations and their end does see;
O f all the heroes, history doth record,
N one ever were so great, so free from vice, or so well serv'd the Lord.[11]

Departing his winter quarters at Arnold's Tavern in Morristown at the end of May, the General advanced most of his army thirty-five miles in a crescent-shaped line of march around the protection of the Watchungs—formidable heights when viewed from the northeastern New Jersey landscape—retracing that route to return to Morristown on July 3. Half a day later, on the first Friday of July 1777, Washington maintained the early-morning routine that had marked his five weeks in camp. With the help of William Lee, twenty-seven, his enslaved valet, the General washed and shaved, brushed his hair, and donned his blue and buff uniform, then worked at his desk as dawn was arriving. He took a brief break to consume a light breakfast.

Probably before 8:00 A.M., most of Washington's headquarters staff had coalesced at his headquarters marquee, one of a trio of heavy linen tents raised for his use. The General conducted business in a red-and-white-striped shelter; the others were a larger dining tent and a baggage tent.[12] The headquarters tents stood six hundred yards north of his previous winter and springtime quarters at Arnold's Tavern. The marquees were raised on Benoni Hathaway's property while most of the army encamped between headquarters and the Whippany River, three hundred yards east.[13] Washington chose the setting for its proximity to a road leading north to New York's Hudson River, almost exclusively called the North River, and southwest to the Delaware River, sometimes called the South River, near Philadelphia. Howe's eventual destination would likely be one of those locales. Washington needed that road to cut Howe off or confront him.

The Continental army's growth increased its leader's duties. That summer, Washington oversaw six regional departments in North America. (In 1776, a seventh department incorporating Canada had gone defunct when the humbled Americans had to quit that region.) Washington personally commanded the Grand Army, also called the "Main Army," within the Middle Department, which spanned New Jersey, Pennsylvania, Maryland, and Delaware. Most of the remaining five departments were commanded by major generals; Washington oversaw all their defenses and operations. These included Brigadier General Robert Howe's Southern Department (Virginia, both Carolinas, and Georgia); Major General Philip Schuyler's Northern Department (most of New York outside New York City except for a sliver of Hudson River Valley defenses called the Highlands Department, assigned to Major General Israel Putnam); Major General William Heath's Eastern Department of four New England states; and Brigadier General Edward Hand's Western Department, covering the territorial regions northwest of Virginia as well as western Pennsylvania.[14]

To address these burdens, Washington sought to establish a superlative staff, enhanced in talent and in numbers. In addition to authorizing an adjutant general, a chief quartermaster and staff, and commissary department personnel, in 1775 the Continental Congress had authorized Washington to have a military secretary and three aides de camp, all ranked lieutenant colonel. Halfway through 1776, the government approved an assistant clerk reporting to the secretary and a fourth aide. Traditionally, headquarters aides had been inexperienced officers assigned rudimentary headquarters duties, mainly delivering orders to and from the general. Washington revolutionized this group's nature and functions. Aide de camp was now a multi-purpose position whose duties included converting a commander's outlined themes into daily dispatches. Washington required his aides to be "ready Pen-men."[15]

This arrangement proved unstable from the first appointment early in July 1775. Two years later, no fewer than twenty officers had cycled through six positions, but signs of stability had finally become evident. An aide unexpectedly died as Washington was breaking his winter encampment, to be replaced within weeks. Regardless, Washington could now claim to have the most experienced cadre of personnel at army headquarters working for him.[16]

Two of Washington's military family were thirty-something Maryland natives now more associated with their adopted states. Washington's most seasoned staff officer, Lieutenant Colonel Robert Hanson Harrison, thirty-two, was a Virginia attorney who by July 1777 had logged twenty months at headquarters. Harrison had started with Washington as an aide de camp and accepted a promotion to military secretary, tripling his monthly salary to $100.[17] The other Marylander, who drew no salary, had become Washington's most prolific penman. At the outbreak of the war while a merchant in Philadelphia, Tench Tilghman had captained a Pennsylvania militia company. He joined the headquarters staff as a volunteer aide during Washington's failed defense of New York. In April 1777, Congress promoted him to lieutenant colonel, but three months later he still was laboring unpaid, drafting twice as many pieces of correspondence for the commander in chief that July as any headquarters aide de camp on the payroll. Tilghman's self-sacrifice allowed Washington to maintain five aides; Congress had salaried four.

Aide George Johnston's startling death from an undetermined cause at the end of May left Washington with three paid aides and Tilghman. The longest serving salaried aide, John Fitzgerald, had emigrated from Ireland to Virginia a few years before the war. He knew Washington as a neighbor and business associate in the port town of Alexandria and had served "The Cause" (a common patriot phrase) as a major of the 3rd Virginia Regiment before joining the General's staff in November 1776. Aide Richard Kidder Meade, staggered by the deaths of his wife and their three children before the war, had served as a captain in the 2nd Virginia Regiment in the conflict's early months. He turned thirty-one in July 1777, having served on Washington's staff for four months.[18]

Washington's youngest aide de camp mysteriously portrayed himself as three years younger than his actual age of twenty-three. As several fellow staffers had, before joining the headquarters staff he had fought in the field as a captain of artillery. His official appointment date was March 12, 1777, but he had started work at headquarters nearly two weeks before. Born and raised on the Caribbean islands southeast of Florida, he was ambitious, with talent and prospects to match; he had turned down requests to serve on the staffs of two Continental generals before accepting Washington's offer at Morristown late in the winter of 1777. His name was Alexander Hamilton.[19]

Captains Caleb Gibbs and George Lewis also served as penmen, but primarily functioned as officers of the commander in chief's guard, commonly identified as the "Life Guard." Gibbs, twenty-eight, was a Rhode Islander who had relocated to Massachusetts in 1775 entering military service there in the 14th Continental Infantry. Lewis, twenty, had been a captain in the 3rd Continental Light Dragoons. He enjoyed a stronger tie to his commanding general than his compatriots; he was Washington's nephew, the son of His Excellency's sister. Both Gibbs and Lewis essentially performed double duty as aides and Life Guard officers.[20] Gibbs was officially designated "Captain Commandant" of the Life Guard in 1776.

The Life Guard was Washington's creation, formed in the spring of 1776 by recruiting four men from each of his infantry regiments, handpicked as being "handsomely and well made," known for "sobriety, honesty and good behavior," and standing between five feet, eight inches and five feet, ten inches tall. Their primary function was to protect the General's baggage and military records. When the army changed encampments, the Life Guard chose the site for Washington's latest headquarters. Life Guardsmen fought in battles during the horrendous New York summer and perhaps at the Battle of Trenton, embodying the motto "Conquer or Die" adorning their emblem.

Gibbs's command entered the Revolution with 180 men, but by the time the army was at Morristown for the winter that complement had withered to less than a third of that strength. The attrition traced to tough campaigning in the latter half of 1776 and re-enlistments in a freshly formed company of dragoons commanded by newly promoted Captain George Lewis. Recruits slowly swelled the Life Guard ranks as Washington restricted recruitment to American-born soldiers at least five feet, nine inches in height. Washington instructed his nephew's dragoons to operate as part of the Life Guard when called upon—and for Captain Lewis to continue as an aide de camp when needed. Washington revitalized his Life Guard during the first half of 1777, dressing them in blue and buff uniforms topped with leather helmets sporting blue-tipped white plumes. Even Life Guard uniform coat buttons stood apart from those worn by the rest of the Continental army. They were not stamped with a numerical designation or a tell-tale design, but with three interlocking capitalized letters that formed an acronym which spoke volumes: "USA."[21]

In addition to Washington's aides de camp and secretary, headquarters included a colonel serving as Adjutant General, another position marked by high turnover. The preceding three holders had accepted explicitly temporary appointments during 1777-1778. The fifth and newest adjutant general was Colonel Timothy Pickering, thirty-one. The Salem, Massachusetts, native and Caleb Gibbs were the only New Englanders on Washington's eight-member staff. Pickering could claim less than three weeks of experience as the senior officer within the commanding general's suite . He was assigned to supervise outposts, secure the safety and organization of army correspondence, and transmit Washington's orders. He loved his job. "His secretaries and aides-de-camp are gentlemen of education, and of the most polite, obliging manners," raved Pickering in his first letter to his wife since joining headquarters. "I am very happy in the General's family."[22]

After breakfast that Friday, Washington, as usual, convened his secretary and aides for a meeting at his headquarters marquee. The staff dissected daunting stacks of correspondence, with penmen assigned to draft responses. Everyone working on the General's letters and orders had at least four months' experience adapting to his pointedly economical style. Washington laid out the theme of each response and the assigned aide carried it through. On this day, Hamilton formulated a mild rebuke to Major General Charles Lee—the British army's prize captive these seven months—for speaking about issues beyond his expertise. Secretary Robert H. Harrison was assigned to update Major General Heath of the Eastern Department, stationed in Boston, on the military situation in New York and New Jersey. Tilghman took on the crafting of Washington's instructions to Major General John Sullivan, commander of his detached division; he also wrote to the Southern Department's Major General Robert Howe in Charleston, South Carolina, to assure him that Washington seconded his urging against a southward expedition against St. Augustine and responded to Pennsylvania's militia commander, Major General John Armstrong, regarding affairs relating to Armstrong's command.[23]

General Orders—circulated daily while the army was encamped—commanded the most attention from General Washington. Tilghman wrote out these orders, working closely with the General to draft what usually was the day's lengthiest document. Washington began by announcing his approval of sentences imposed on eight soldiers tried by courts martial two days earlier. Only two of the accused were acquitted. Most of those found guilty were to be punished with thirty-nine lashes; a deserter who had attempted to escape from two different regiments was to receive 150 lashes.

Washington next addressed preparedness ("that every thing be held in the most perfect readiness") as essential to being able to march at a moment's notice. Officers were to shed all excess heavy baggage and to arrange storage for it in Morristown. In a change of pace, the General decided to end his morning General Orders abruptly with an announcement that "After Orders" would follow later that day.[24] He needed to make time to produce specific instructions facilitating a quick and efficient advance. Clearly, Washington placed a premium on a rapid response to his chief adversary, Crown forces commander General William Howe, currently in New York City.

Headquarters staff handled the morning General Orders while Washington and Tilghman worked on that afternoon's "After Orders" (not a routine follow-up but deemed necessary to construct this day). The Major General of the Day—designated in the previous day's orders—arrived at Washington's tent to relay orders to Colonel Pickering, who prepared the written orders after consulting with the major general. Before noon, Pickering called for a meeting of aides to brigade and division commanders; most of those summoned held the rank of major. Pickering dictated the orders to these men, who reproduced them, then departed to relay the orders to their respective commands, sometimes slightly modified. Per the army's formal style, orders were written into brigade orderly books.[25]

Washington's morning usually included a ride to view his Continentals. But headquarters being adjacent to the summertime Morristown encampment and given the matter of the day's After Orders, Washington likely remained tethered to his red-and-white marquee, reviewing and editing drafts. The aides had become decent mimics, over time adopting Washington's style. Once the documents met Washington's approval, he signed them and sent them on, often responding to an originator by the same rider who had delivered the message to him.

Washington's favorite part of the daily encampment schedule came at midafternoon when he and his staff gathered for the principal meal of the day in the eighteen by twenty-five foot dining tent, the largest of the three marquee enclosures, which could accommodate fifty. This reliably grand affair could last hours as diners worked through several courses. Chairs there were only folding camp stools made of walnut with leather seats and studded with brass nails, but little else about the meal was rudimentary, from the finely woven tablecloth to the ornate flatware and dishware. Several dishes of meat and poultry buttressed with an impressive variety of vegetables comprised the first course, followed by a pastry course of pies and puddings. Washington did not sit at the head of the table. Instead, on a rotating daily basis an aide de camp held that honor, which was more a duty since it fell to the holder to serve the dishes and distribute bottles of Madeira and Bordeaux. Several rounds of toasts punctuated the meal. Once the formal courses had been dispatched, the dishes were cleared, the tablecloth removed, and platters of fruit—usually apples—and "enormous bowls of nuts" made for post-prandial snacks. This final and least formal of the meal's courses was usually marked by Washington cracking nuts between his weak teeth while he conversed.[26]

Washington took great pleasure in this daily event, not only because it involved a meal reminiscent of dining in good company at Mount Vernon but for the quality of conversation it afforded. The repartee with and among his staff and their guests was a highlight of his day. That particular Friday no guests attended but after accepting an invitation to dine seven weeks earlier a visiting Virginia colonel's wife observed:

> Colo Fitz Gerald and [*sic*] agreable broad shouldered Irishman . . . Colo Hamilton a sensable Genteel polite young fellow a West indian—Colo Meade—Colo Tillman a modest worthy man who from his attachment to the Genl vollenterly lives in his family and acts in any capacity that is uppermost without fee or reward—Colo Harrison Brother of Billy Harrison that kept store in Petersburg & as much like him as possible a worthy man—Capt Gibbs of the Genls Guard a good natured Yankee who makes a thousand Blunders in the Yankee stile and keeps the Dinner table in constant Laugh—These are the Genls family all polite sociable gentlemen who make the day pass with a great deal of satisfaction to the Visitors.[27]

The unremarked-upon constant at midday meals and around the marquees was the roster of household servants who toiled long hours each day at every Washington headquarters throughout the Revolutionary War—black and white, male and female, young and elderly, free and enslaved. These included Washington's manservant, William "Billy" Lee; his housekeeper, Elizabeth Thompson, seventy-three; his washerwoman, Margaret Thomas; and his cooking staff, including a Black man known as "Isaac." These servants were here because they were considered hard-working and reliable; their steward, or overseer, was not. Patrick Maguire, an Irishman, had been overseeing the servants since April, but Washington had come to distrust him. He considered Maguire insolent and too fond of liquor.[28]

That Friday's headquarters meal went by without comment in a journal, a letter, or a memoir, but it was memorable nonetheless for its date: July 4, 1777—the first time Americans celebrated Independence Day on the Fourth of July. Nearly a year earlier—on July 8, 1776—the one-ton Liberty Bell had tolled from the State House tower to summon Philadelphians to the first public reading of the Declaration of Independence, ratified by the Continental Congress four days earlier. The reading set off a city-wide celebration and started a national tradition.

With only two days of preparation, Philadelphia celebrated American Independence in fine style in 1777. Cannoneers aboard warships aligned in a row on the Delaware River shook Philadelphia with a *feu de joie*—"fire of joy," a running barrage echoed around the city by the interval firing of muskets by British deserters converted into a battalion of Georgia infantry. The festivities ran all day with dinners, music, sermons, and toasts—thirteen of them, one for each newly independent state. The first known Fourth of July parade commenced in Philadelphia late in the day with a march by Maryland and North Carolina soldiers, many of them barefoot, their ranks punctuated by rolling artillery pieces and buoyed by fifes and drums and cheered by patriotic citizens crowding either side of the procession. When the proud soldiers reached their camp at the edge of town, they fired another thirteen-gun salute.[29]

The first anniversary of Independence Day reverberated beyond the capital. In Portsmouth, New Hampshire—350 miles north of Philadelphia—one ship captain invited "all true friends to American Independency" to board his frigate, *The Raleigh*, at noon. The New Hampshire celebrants ate a light lunch and then downed toasts to "prosperity, freedom & independency to the thirteen united states of America." At 1:00 P.M. thirteen-gun salutes boomed from the frigate, followed by similar volleys from a nearby French ship and then from a Portsmouth private ship. Throaty cheers emanated from *The Raleigh*, were repeated twice, then answered by onlookers aboard other vessels. The infectious harbor celebration extended to the citizenry crowding wharves. According to the *New Hampshire Gazette*, "their joy & approbation on this ever memorable day which ought never to be forgot, by all true lovers of liberty."[30]

Newspapers reported extensively on Fourth of July festivities. Boston—the hotbed of Revolution prior to the war and the first contested major city in 1775—observed the anniversary with a resonating discharge of brass cannons as part of an afternoon of martial display followed by fireworks that evening on the Common. At the Coffee House in Boston, thirteen selected dignitaries drank thirteen toasts, including "Liberty to those who have Virtue to defend it," and "May the Union of the American States be as lasting as the Pillars of Human Nature."[31]

Celebrations spanned southward. American colors adorned all the ships, forts, and batteries in Charleston Harbor. South Carolina militia and a company of artillery assembled on the parade ground to be reviewed by the Privy Council. At 1:00 P.M., gunners fired three volleys drowned out by seventy-six symbolic discharges from cannons protecting the city's forts, including Fort Moultrie on Sullivan's Island. After an elegant dinner, Charleston dignitaries announced and drank thirteen toasts—each marked by a thirteen-gun salute from two field pieces manned by very busy gunners "with admirable regularity." The subject of the toasts varied from "The Free, Independent and Sovereign States of America" to the American army and navy, to the state of South Carolina, as well as to the opposing themes of "Liberty triumphant" and "Confusion, shame, and disgrace to our enemies." Only the third toast celebrated an individual—George Washington, whose name emanated from Americans' lips and thoughts more than any outside their respective families.[32]

Washington did not celebrate the Fourth of July on its first annual anniversary. He never specified it in that day's orders or those issued the day before, never wrote about it privately, nor mentioned it publicly. If it was mentioned or even discussed during the day's grand meal under the dinner marquee near Benoni Hathaway's house in Morristown, no one present recorded that anyone there took note of the date. The man who beginning in 1775 set aside his wealthy and comfortable livelihood and risked his life to lead an insurgent coalition of colonies-turned-states most certainly paused to reflect on how important early July was to him. But the anniversary he routinely marked invoked his "grateful remembrance of the escape we had at the Meadows," referring to his July 3, 1754, battle at Great Meadows in western Virginia on which Fort Necessity stood.[33] "I did not let the anniversary of the 3d . . . of this Instt pass," he had previously written to a fellow officer in the Virginia Regiment, a reflection that he likely marked again in 1777. But July 4 at Fort Necessity was a day he preferred to forget. That was the day he led his men out of the fort in defeat after he was reduced to signing a surrender document to his French foes.

Back then he was Colonel George Washington, a Provincial officer in his first organized battle, leading a regiment fighting for the British in a war he had intensified against the French over land ownership in North America. Now he was General George Washington, a seasoned combatant commanding a professional army of over ten thousand men while nominally in charge of twice that many American soldiers around the United States of America. He had been formally titled by Congress as "General and Commander in chief."[34]

Washington not only looked the consummate leader of men, in the minds of most he had earned the part as the new nation's top general. For the first half of 1777, George Washington had performed masterfully in a string of front-line and behind-the-lines successes. Although his new army was inexperienced, its exponential increase in numbers fortified Washington's philosophy, which was to seek avenues of assault against his adversary. This desire ran counter to the perception on both sides of the Atlantic that

Washington was the "American Fabius."[35] The sobriquet derived from the name of the third-century BCE Roman general who survived against Hannibal, despite leading a vastly outnumbered force, by employing a delaying strategy which favored small, short engagements and avoided set-piece battles. Admirers called him "Fabius" out of respect, but Washington never embraced the tag, despite the positive image it conjured of a cunning commander, at times of fewer than three thousand men, who survived between December 1776 and April 1777 by frequently winning short contests.

Washington's army grew fivefold through late spring and early summer. Fabian strategy no longer was considered admirable—at least among detractors spoiling for the new Continental army to fight. "Europe and America seem to be applauding our Imitation of the Fabian Method of carrying on this War," derisively noted Massachusetts delegate Samuel Adams in May. Adams despaired that General Howe, who had wintered behind the Raritan River in Brunswick, New Jersey, was likely to get stronger with reinforcements from England, while Washington posed no threat to him. "Would Fabius, if he were his enemy, pursue the Method he took with [Hannibal]?" queried Adams. "Would he not rather attend to the present Circumstances, and by destroying the Army in Brunswick prevent as much as possible the Enemy increasing in Strength even if reinforcements should arrive or putting a total End to the Campaign if they should not?"[36]

Washington's mindset aligned with that of the bellicose Adams, even before May saw his ranks swell. He had one of his division commanders draw up a multi-pronged attack plan at the end of April, then queried six subordinate generals about the feasibility of a full or even a partial attack.[37] Although the war council unanimously discouraged a full attack, they did agree about the feasibility of a partial assault—a tactic Washington rejected. The leading Continental officers well understand their roles in The Cause. Writing to Samuel Adams, among the leading firebrands in the Congress, one subordinate in particular expressed the sentiments Washington most assuredly expected of him:

> I agree with you that it is the business of the army to fight, the temper and the disposition of the people at large require it. . . . The unsettled state that Government is in throughout the Continent is the strongest argument for fighting that can be given as the hands of administration will be strengthened in proportion to the success of the Army. Altho I am not fond of fighting, I am ever ready when commanded. I hope soon to give the Enemy an opportunity if they please.[38]

That opinion, voiced unhesitatingly, came from Major General Nathanael Greene. At thirty-five he was ten years Washington's junior. Through 1777 Greene was the General's ranking subordinate while Sullivan remained detached from the Grand Army with his division in New York State, Major General Charles Lee stayed imprisoned in New York City, and Major General Horatio Gates wallowed in Philadelphia without a field command. Greene's availability served him well as His Excellency's chief counsel.

The fourth of six surviving sons of a Rhode Island spiritual leader of a Quaker meeting, Greene, motherless since childhood, had abandoned the Society of Friends the month the war began in April 1775. He walked with a noticeable limp, a result of one of many ailments that marked him for life (an acquaintance maintained that "one of his legs was shorter than the other"). The limp cost Greene a lieutenancy in the militia company he had raised to join the war. Fortune smiled upon him in May 1775, when the Rhode Island General Assembly plucked Private Greene from the ranks and—in a decision as stunning as it was mysterious—voted him in as a brigadier general leading an "army" of 1,500 militiamen. A commission to convert him to a Continental army general followed in June, and a year later, in August 1776, Nathanael Greene was promoted to major general.[39] That same month fevers temporarily kept him from the front at Long Island, perhaps sparing him from being one of that costly battle's casualties.

Washington's reliance on Greene's judgment damaged both men and The Cause on November 16, 1776. Greene persuaded the General to hold Fort Washington rather than abandon that bastion as others were urging. The Manhattan fort fell at a cost of upwards of three thousand American casualties, a disaster the generals helplessly watched unfold from across the Hudson. Washington stood by Greene, and for eight months America celebrated success in the field as Washington's dependence on the Rhode Islander intensified. In addition to contributing to battlefield victories, Greene served the commander in chief as a liaison between the Grand Army in New Jersey and the Continental Congress in Philadelphia. A visit by Greene to the capital in late March resulted in extensive but unsuccessful meetings to obtain money and materiel for the army, improve the prisoner exchange system, and—prior to Colonel Pickering's hiring—persuade Horatio Gates to return to headquarters for a second stint as adjutant general.

While in Philadelphia Greene came to believe that the city was indefensible. Studying its forts and fortifications, he decided they were "quite insufficient for the purpose without a very strong opposition." Closely reconnoitering the capital and the approaches to it persuaded him "that it cannot be fortified to advantage. The approaches may be made so many ways that it would take a greater number of Troops to defend the Works than would be prudent to shut up in the City."[40] Four months later he still felt the same. Greene preferred military efforts to be placed elsewhere.

Aware that in his suddenly large army only one soldier in five had any appreciable experience with campaigning, marching, and fighting, Washington well understood on July 4, 1777, that his new Continentals were little more prepared to face the Redcoats in New Jersey than they had been a year earlier in New York. No matter how many new recruits he acquired, General William Howe's army—British, Hessian troops from the fief of Hesse-Cassel and other Germanic states, and Provincial and militia Loyalists—could field more soldiers with experience in the Revolutionary War than Washington could count in his entire force. Crown troops had deep experience with arduous marches, frontal assaults, and flanking attacks. They had parried American offensives, in 1776 accumulating an outstanding battlefield record against the Continentals—but Washington wrong-footed them with three momentum-altering victories in the nine days closing 1776 and inaugurating 1777.

In early July 1777, Washington was unsure what his adversary intended. "Our situation is truly delicate and perplexing," he confessed. His aides concurred, Hamilton more bluntly: "Our present situation is embarrassing."[41] Except for foraging and reconnaissance parties, Howe had abstained from campaigning throughout the winter and spring of 1777. When, as summer was beginning, the Briton appeared to withdraw his army from eastern New Jersey to Staten Island, Washington had moved his army out of its strong defenses in the Watchungs to harass the vulnerable rear of Howe's column. But Howe appeared to be trying to lure Washington into a trap. His Excellency divined Howe's game and pulled back into the mountains, leaving one division in appropriately named Short Hills, a locale about fifteen miles west of Elizabeth, New Jersey, to slow the British advance. In a spirited engagement the morning of June 26, that lone division escaped a very close call, surviving an action that inflicted a total of 110 casualties, including heatstroke, with the Americans suffering greater losses. Crown troops managed to wrest three cannons from the Americans. British ire at not achieving something more substantial showed in the trail of eleven thousand destroyed items of personal and public property marking the path of their return to Perth Amboy at the mouth of the Raritan River and Sandy Hook Bay.[42]

The British army had crossed to Staten Island on July 2, quitting New Jersey after nearly eight months of occupation. Washington and his headquarters personnel boiled their situation down to five essential questions: Why did Howe relinquish the shortest route to Philadelphia? What was he going to do next? When? How? And, most important, where would Howe strike? Among answers under consideration—such as shipping Crown forces by armada to Charleston in an attempt to complete the unfinished business of 1776—the likeliest options were a stab at Philadelphia by sailing up Delaware Bay and investing the city from the south and a march north along the Hudson to complete a three-pronged campaign meant to isolate New England from the rest of America by establishing unassailable British control of the river.

Howe appeared to be inclined to choose the Hudson gambit, which threatened the armies Washington oversaw or directly led. That threat was made real when in late June and without Washington's awareness a British force exceeding seven thousand Regulars and Hessians under Lieutenant General John Burgoyne descended from Canada into New York State. The foe, aboard several dozen ships, gunboats, and bateaux, swept toward American-held Fort Ticonderoga at the southern tip of Lake Champlain. Defending Ticonderoga was an overmatched Major General Arthur St. Clair (pronounced "Sinclair"), serving in the Northern Department directly under Major General Philip Schuyler. St. Clair's 2,500 Continentals and several hundred militia were about to be overwhelmed. Nor was the American high command aware that a second prong of Crown force attackers led by Lieutenant Colonel Barrimore "Barry" St. Leger (he was breveted a brigadier general for this operation) had advanced from Montreal to Oswego, New York, from where his Crown troops would threaten Schuyler's defenses from the west and the Mohawk Valley.[43]

Burgoyne's operation was approved not by William Howe, commander of Crown forces throughout North America, but by Lord George Germain, Secretary of State of the American Department of the cabinet of the Prime Minister of Great Britain, Lord Frederick North. This complicated hierarchy did not hamper Burgoyne's early efforts as he descended upon Ticonderoga ahead of schedule during the earliest weeks of summer.

Once Burgoyne captured Ticonderoga, he planned to extend British control of the Hudson by descending the river southward, by land, toward Albany. As he approached the city, he expected cooperation from General Howe's armies in New York City to advance up the Hudson to join Burgoyne at Albany and thus effect complete control of the North River to isolate the New England states—considered the hotbed of the Revolution—from the rest of America and conquer each separated faction of the country in detail, culminating in the diamond prize of Philadelphia to end the war.[44]

Washington knew Burgoyne's plan and had been working with Congress's approval to reinforce the Northern Department with men and commanders. The third prong of the British invasion of the Hudson River valley had yet to materialize but was indeed expected by Washington and his subordinates. This northward thrust could be accomplished by a large detachment of Howe's command under General Henry Clinton advancing from British-occupied New York City, a more equitable split of Howe's force, sending nearly half of that complement (including Clinton) northward up the Hudson Valley, or the full weight of Crown forces in America committed to the third prong of the Burgoyne operation, led by Howe himself.

As much as Washington's headquarters anticipated a move north by Howe, His Excellency could never ignore Philadelphia. On July 4 an American who had escaped from a British prison ship in New York Harbor entered camp. The former prisoner reported that preparations were being made on a grand scale to load transports with soldiers on Manhattan as well as Staten Island. A witness to this testimony wrote the next day, "He further adds, that on board the ship he was, Delaware River, was said to be the place of destination."[45]

The need for the speediest possible mobile response to Howe's moves and Washington's recollections of the deficiencies recently on display in his army on the march prompted his "After Orders" of July 4, 1777. That document provides a rare postscript to the daily general orders and illuminates why the General was unable to let his guard down to celebrate the anniversary of American Independence. In his mind's eye, if he lagged in countering Howe, there would be no second anniversary.

The 1,200-word "After Orders" constituted a startling de facto admission by Washington that his new army needed step-by-step instruction in how to relocate en masse, additionally illustrating the premium he placed on every detail being followed to the letter. "When the order is given to march," began the orders, "and the men are paraded for that purpose, the rolls are to be called; and the commanding officer of each corps is to see that his men are all present, or know with certainty where, and why they are absent." Officers were to keep the men in ranks. "If either of the Major Generals, in their respective divisions, should see any apparent cause for a halt, before the time, or place, designed for it," explained the General, "he is to send an Aide-de-Camp to the commanding officer, with his reasons for it, who, if he judges it expedient, will order it accordingly." Washington specified drumbeats for marches after halts, the number and type of personnel to serve as wagon guards, and exactly where those wagon guards were to position themselves ("on the sides, but as far back as the tail, of each waggon, that if any thing falls out, they may discover, and pick it up"). Washington even included adjurations applying to civilian camp followers: "That no women shall be permitted to ride in any waggon, without leave in writing from the Brigadier to whose brigade she belongs."

The After Orders dug deep and spoke unblinkingly. "None but spare arms, and such as belong to sick and lame men, shall be suffered to go in waggons, as they are almost certain of receiving some injury: Or if any drummer presumes to put his drum into a waggon, unless under similar circumstances—The soldier or drummer so offending, shall be immediately flogged by any officer commanding the baggage guard of such waggon." Washington explained how to care for cooking implements: "To prevent the enormous abuse and loss of kettles, by slinging them to waggons, from which numbers fall, the General positively orders that each mess in turn carry their own kettle; as usual in all armies, and can be little burthensome in this."

Private property was to be spared, according to the General, who forbade impressing horses and cattle, taking fence rails, or destroying farmers' fields. His subordinates were to lead by example:

> And as it is impossible that good government and order can be preserved, unless every officer will take his share of duty, and be attentive to the discharge of it—The Commander in Chief directs, that upon a march, the Major Generals do not quit their divisions; the Brigadiers their brigades; the Colonels their regiments; nor other officers their respective divisions; unless it be in cases of absolute necessity, by order, or with leave; each watching with a careful eye, the conduct of all those under his command. It is unreasonable to expect regularity and good order in the common soldiers, if the example is not set by the officers; nor can an officer with propriety punish a soldier for a disregard of any order, which he dispenses with himself—It would be a happy pride, and a most laudable ambition, to see the commanding officers of corps vieing with each other in discipline and good behaviour.[46]

The devil was in the details—not those that Washington knew but those a commander in chief did not know. In an ironic turn, as he was adjuring his division and brigade generals "to not quit" their commands, the Continental Congress was receiving letters of resignation from his most senior active division commanders, Major Generals John Sullivan and Nathanael Greene, as well as from his chief of artillery, Brigadier General Henry Knox. Congress was contemplating approving those worthies' threats to leave the army.

If those resignations were accepted, Washington's and America's quest for success would be dealt a devastating blow.

CHAPTER TWO

"An Army of Observation"

July 5 to August 1, 1777

"Our army still continues in high Spirits," reported a soldier on July 5. A comrade echoed the sentiment a few days later: "Our troops are healthy; and I can, with infinite satisfaction, assure you, that the spirit of subordination and discipline makes great and daily advances among us."[1]

Upper-echelon officers of the Grand Army did not share that optimism. On July 9, Washington was blindsided by reading Greene's, Sullivan's, and Knox's letters of resignation, dated July 1 and sent not directly to the General but to John Hancock, President of the Continental Congress. Hancock forwarded copies to Washington, along with Congress's resolutions on the subject.[2]

A single factor had triggered the resignations: the impending appointment of a pretentious Frenchman to major general in the Continental army. Philippe Charles Jean Baptiste Tronson du Coudray, thirty-nine, was an artillerist and engineer, well connected in European courts and well regarded for his expertise, as well as his intelligence, energy, and confidence. He also was blessed with excellent timing. In September 1776 in Paris he had met with Silas Deane, a former Connecticut delegate to Congress. Deane had been sent by Congress first as a secret envoy assigned to persuade the French government to lend the new nation financial aid. Later that year he also worked overtly with American diplomatic delegates, including Benjamin Franklin and Arthur Lee, to obtain from France formal diplomatic recognition as well as financial and military support. In both roles, Deane recruited officers by issuing commissions and promising appointments for four hundred Europeans ranging from proven officers to soldiers of fortune and freedom fighters. Coudray came out of his meeting with Deane with the rank of major general and the promise of horses, carriages, ten staff officers, an adjutant, aides—and a pension. Deane's deal with Coudray also stood to generate massive conflict at home. Henry Knox was the Continentals' chief artillery officer, but Coudray was to be "General of Artillery and Ordnance" with "the direction of whatever relates to the Artillery and the Corps of Engineers."[3]

Coudray also was given to florid displays of vanity often repugnant to Americans. After his arrival in Boston in May, Coudray reached Philadelphia in June. He rode out to Morristown in July for a brief visit with Washington, escorted by a bloated entourage of eighteen officers and ten sergeants that was three times the size of the commander in chief's own staff. "I dare say his expectations are high," Washington noted afterwards. "Congress will undoubtedly make a genteel and honorable provision for him; but I hope it may be done in such a manner, as not to give disgust to any of the general officers in our army."[4]

French officers seeking American commissions in Philadelphia were inundating the Continental Congress. "The City swarms with French Men," railed a delegate.[5] Several members fretted about Coudray's lavish deal and its effect on American army commanders. When Congress heard from Greene, Sullivan, and Knox early in July, delegates responded in anger—not at Coudray, but at the three generals who intimated that Congress had ratified the Deane-Coudray contract, backdating the Frenchman's appointment to rank his commission above Sullivan's and Greene's commissions. Neither imputation was true; the debate over and resolution of Coudray's appointment lasted through July.[6] The generals' letters disrupted Congress and generated much ire, but as the Coudray imbroglio dragged on Washington neither condemned nor condoned his generals' collective gesture.

Also dragging on was the idleness of Washington's army, still hunkering on the outskirts of the region where headquarters had been established through the preceding winter and waiting for a signal as to Howe's next move. "Their ships give them a vast advantage," Hamilton wrote in early July, "and we shall probably be much puzzled when they begin their operations again." In this private letter the aide went on to say he expected Washington to "act cautiously" when he ordered the army to march. "We are anxiously waiting for northern intelligence," he added.[7]

That intelligence arrived Thursday morning, July 10, and the news was awful—so much so that Washington admitted, "I fain flatter myself it is not true." St. Clair had been forced to abandon Fort Ticonderoga on July 6, leaving the bastion to Burgoyne, who had anticipated a long and costly fight but instead bloodlessly won a gift. The British advance from Canada was proceeding at an alarmingly swift rate.[8]

The fall of Ticonderoga broke the deadlock. Washington consulted his officers. All agreed "that Howe will push against the Highland passes, to cooperate with General Burgoyne." He ordered the army to head north from Morristown; the march began Friday, July 11. "We are now properly an army of observation," declared Major Persifor Frazer, "the Movements of the Enemy will determine our Rout."[9] The route led northeast toward the Hudson, a commitment reflecting the General's confidence that Howe was going to move his fleet to link with Burgoyne's army or position his men to provide support. Either way, the British presence on the Hudson would be dominating. Washington needed to prevent or neutralize that outcome.

Coudray's relationship with George Washington began badly and continued to brew ill. The Friday that the army departed Morristown, Washington received and opened Coudray's week-old assessment of his army's artillery arm. The letter, riddled with mistaken assumptions, showed Coudray to be attempting to assert authority over the artillery corps's structure, which stirred Washington to correct him. "You seem to have misunderstood," noted the General in response; "You also misconceived . . . I am at a loss to conceive how you could imagine . . . You are even mistaken as to the fact of . . . ." Washington swiftly tamped Coudray down. "I am not as yet authorised to consider you as giving advice or direction in an official capacity; since Congress have not instructed me in what light I am to view you," Washington wrote. "For this reason, it would be irregular to interfere with any arrangements General Knox has made with my approbation, in compliance with those you propose."[10]

Two days of heavy, persistent rains held the American troops at Pompton Plains, New Jersey. They proceeded on July 14 and marched for two days. After crossing from New Jersey into New York, Washington stayed five nights at Suffern's Tavern near the hamlet of Ramapo, thirty miles by road northeast of Morristown. On July 20, informed that Howe's fleet had been sighted near the entrance to Long Island Sound, headquarters proceeded eleven miles through a narrow north/south pass in the Ramapo Mountains known as the Clove. The headquarters complement fetched up at the northern end of the pass in the most rustic headquarters imaginable—a simple log house serving as a tavern and owned by a man named Galloway. Rather than erect the tents, Washington and cohort crowded into the house. "The General lodged in a bed," Colonel Pickering noted, "and his family on the floor about him."[11]

"We have been under great embarrassments respecting the intended Operations of Genl Howe, and still are, Notwithstanding the utmost pains to obtain intelligence of the same," Washington wrote with chagrin during his Clove stay. Perceiving a threat to Boston, Washington had moved north through the Clove as the first step in a planned advance to New Windsor, New York, to oppose Howe's landing on the Sound with a subsequent advance toward Boston from there. At Galloway's tavern Washington learned the information about Howe and the Sound was wrong. Spreading his army out on both sides of the northern entrance to the Clove, Washington retraced his steps southward through the pass and relocated his headquarters at Ramapo on Wednesday, July 23.[12]

Although he had overreacted to bad intelligence, Washington remained resolute. Nathanael Greene distilled the plan in a letter to his wife shortly after returning to Ramapo. "Our future motions will depend entirely upon General [Howe's] motions," Greene explained. "If he goes into N England we shall follow him, If he goes to Philadelphia we shall go there." Greene expected a very rapid march for his division if the British general's destination materialized as Philadelphia.[13]

Howe's intent became clear the same Wednesday evening when Brigadier General David Forman of the New Jersey militia observed the enemy's armada departing Sandy Hook and heading not northeast but southwest. Apprised of this valuable intelligence, Washington immediately sent a flurry of dispatches ordering all detachments to make for Philadelphia. General Orders had been drawn up that day detailing the march in all facets except direction. Given that more than thirty hours had passed since Howe's departure from "The Hook" by the time Washington learned of it, Greene's prediction of a rapid march was about to come true.[14]

One key commander would no longer be serving directly under Washington in this campaign. Washington sent a dispatch to Major General Benjamin Lincoln ordering him to get to the Northern army and report to Major General Philip Schuyler. Washington's experiences with tetchy militia from New England dating to summer 1775 had taught him the importance of placing the right leader in charge of them. "My Principle view of sending you there," Washington told Lincoln, "is to take the Command of the Eastern Militia, over whom I am informed you have influence and who place confidence in you."[15]

Another prominent Revolutionary separated from the army at the same time. Major General Thomas Mifflin, Quartermaster General of the Continental army, thirty-four, agreed to head directly to Philadelphia to assist in his hometown's defense. Although young, the Quaker merchant turned major general had headed the quartermaster department for two years and had served respectably as a fighting commander in the Battle of Princeton. His patriotic service had earned him a great deal of respect. An apparent agreement between him and Washington sent Mifflin to Philadelphia with quartermaster duties in the field going unofficially to Mifflin's deputy and fellow Philadelphia Quaker Clement Biddle, who owed his skills in that realm to experience in the Pennsylvania militia. Biddle had donned a second hat in July as Commissary General of Forage. He and Mifflin were familiar with headquarters duties as well—Mifflin as a former aide de camp to General Washington, Biddle formally as General Greene's aide.[16]

As Mifflin was riding to Philadelphia, the Pennsylvania Supreme Executive Council was reacting to news of the enemy fleet heading south out of Sandy Hook. The Council sent a Philadelphia physician to Egg Harbor on the New Jersey coast to look for the fleet, determine its direction, count the vessels, and, by way of hired express riders loyal to The Cause, report his findings to the Council. The Council also formed committees in preparation for Howe's potential passage up the Delaware. These included a "Committee for Driving off Cattle" as well as a "Commission to Search For and Seize County Records."[17]

The mass American movement commenced on Friday morning, July 25. Washington completely reversed his steps of the previous week as headquarters backtracked southward from Ramapo to Pompton that day. By the time he settled in for the night, having read a clearly bogus letter ostensibly meant by Howe for Burgoyne but really composed to be captured and mislead the Americans, Washington was more inclined to think Howe was indeed bound for Philadelphia. The message informed Burgoyne that Howe intended to surprise and rapidly capture Boston and from there join Burgoyne to defeat Schuyler's army and control the Hudson River. American high command saw through the ruse, intended to gull Washington into diverting his focus from Philadelphia to Boston and the Hudson. Discerning the fakery, Washington was persuaded "more than ever, that Philadelphia is the place of destination."[18]

By Saturday afternoon the army was at Morristown for the second time since its winter encampment there. On Sunday night troops bivouacked fifteen miles from the Delaware River. Washington and companions awoke in a tented encampment four miles east of Flemington, New Jersey, on Monday morning, July 28. The General spent most of the day at headquarters processing paperwork. One of his first tasks that morning was to compose a letter to Mifflin responding to new intelligence regarding Howe's whereabouts. Mifflin had barely arrived in Philadelphia when an express rider delivered a report from the physician turned covert agent at Egg Harbor, seventy miles away. On Thursday afternoon the doctor had counted seventy ships sailing south off the Jersey coast, halfway between Sandy Hook and the mouth of Delaware Bay, a vicinity known as the Cape or the Capes. Seventeen hours after that, Mifflin jotted a summary of the intelligence that he packaged with corroborating evidence from another observer and sent to Washington's headquarters, a half-day, fifty-mile ride away. In the meantime, Mifflin was informing other Philadelphians "that the enemy are coming around to our Cape."[19]

Hamilton drafted Washington's response. "I last night received your favor of Yesterday morning," the letter read, "if it does not amount to a certain proof that their design is against Philadelphia, is at least a very strong argument of it." Noting Mifflin's concern that Howe could sail up the Delaware River at any moment, Washington assured him that his army would concentrate in time to defend Philadelphia.

Washington's vow was not true for Sullivan's division and was overly ambitious for a division of New Jersey and Pennsylvania Continentals commanded by Major General William Alexander (universally referred to by Americans as "Lord Stirling," reflecting his persistent claim to the Scottish title "Earl of Stirling," denied by Great Britain).

In his letter to Mifflin, Washington also hinted at additional reinforcements sent from Major General Israel Putnam's Highlands Department ("his best remaining brigades"). The commander in chief assigned Mifflin to reconnoiter locales at which the enemy would likely land and to map all main and secondary roads and terrain between Wilmington and Philadel-

AMERICAN FORCES
BRITISH FORCES
0
10
20
SCALE IN MILES
PENNS.
Delaware River
SUSSEX
Sussex Court House
NEW JERSEY
NEW YORK
Ringwood Iron Works
Ramapo
Haverstraw
King's Ferry
Peekskill
A
Hackensack River
North River (Hudson)
Fort Lee
G
New York
Paulus Hook
Bergen
BERGEN
RAMAPO MTNS.
MORRIS
Pompton Plains
Parsippany
Morristown
START JULY 3
Chatham
MTNS.
Aquackanonk
Hackensack
Newark
ESSEX
Elizabethtown
Basking Ridge
Vealtown
Bedminster
Pluckemin
Germantown
Philipsburg
Passaic R.
WATCHUNG
1
2
3
4
5
6
7

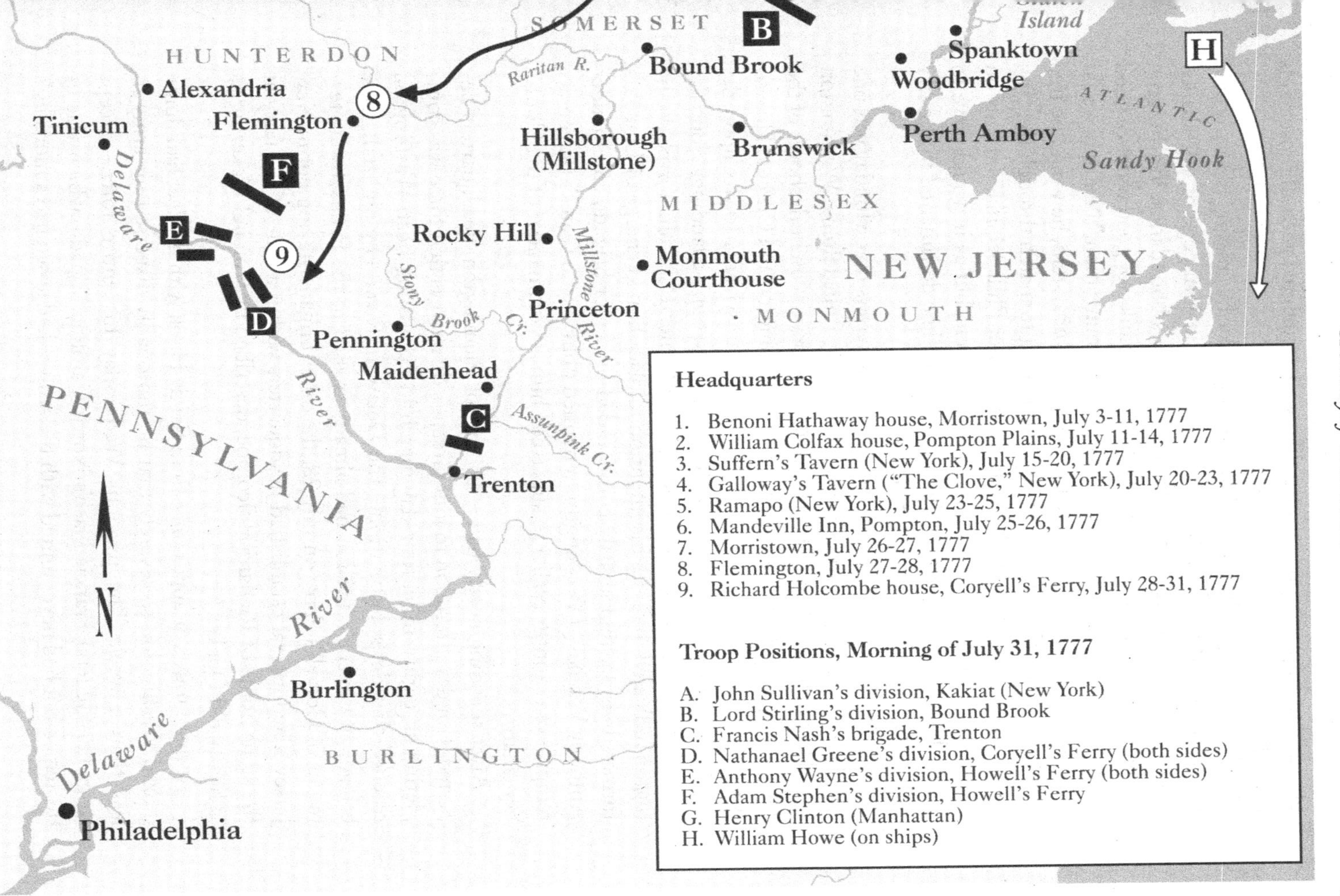
Island
SOMERSET
B
H
HUNTERDON
Alexandria
Tinicum
Flemington
8
Raritan R.
Bound Brook
Spanktown
Woodbridge
Perth Amboy
ATLANTIC
Sandy Hook
Hillsborough (Millstone)
Brunswick
MIDDLESEX
Delaware
F
E
9
D
Rocky Hill
Millstone River
Monmouth Courthouse
NEW JERSEY
MONMOUTH
Stony Brook Cr.
Princeton
Pennington
Maidenhead
River
PENNSYLVANIA
C
Assunpink Cr.
Trenton
N
River
Burlington
BURLINGTON
Delaware
Philadelphia
Headquarters
1. Benoni Hathaway house, Morristown, July 3-11, 1777
2. William Colfax house, Pompton Plains, July 11-14, 1777
3. Suffern's Tavern (New York), July 15-20, 1777
4. Galloway's Tavern ("The Clove," New York), July 20-23, 1777
5. Ramapo (New York), July 23-25, 1777
6. Mandeville Inn, Pompton, July 25-26, 1777
7. Morristown, July 26-27, 1777
8. Flemington, July 27-28, 1777
9. Richard Holcombe house, Coryell's Ferry, July 28-31, 1777
Troop Positions, Morning of July 31, 1777
A. John Sullivan's division, Kakiat (New York)
B. Lord Stirling's division, Bound Brook
C. Francis Nash's brigade, Trenton
D. Nathanael Greene's division, Coryell's Ferry (both sides)
E. Anthony Wayne's division, Howell's Ferry (both sides)
F. Adam Stephen's division, Howell's Ferry
G. Henry Clinton (Manhattan)
H. William Howe (on ships)

phia and to employ "good trusty guides well acquainted with all those roads and paths."

Washington said he planned to form a defense by crossing his army over the Schuylkill River. The Schuylkill was the western edge of a V-shaped river system constituting most of Philadelphia's boundaries. Washington predicted his encampment would be suitable thanks to "good water & good ground and because it has a free and open communication." Not only would he avoid being squeezed inside the V of the river system, he would be free to do all he could to keep his army from having to march through the city: "I would not by any means have the troops enter Philadelphia, not only on account of its being pent up between two Rivers, but as it would serve to debauch them and introduce disease and would be detrimental to the city and disagreeable to the inhabitants."[20]

Among other letters streaming from headquarters that Monday was one to Major General Horatio Gates, stationed in Philadelphia. Washington urged Gates to assist Mifflin in surveying all avenues on both shores of the Delaware, particularly at and across from Wilmington and Chester. He also instructed Mifflin to assist the Council of Pennsylvania to "fix upon the most proper places to encamp Bodies of men" to oppose landings along the river. Already regretting having sent Major General Lincoln north, Washington indicated to Gates his intention to place him in charge of Lincoln's former division, temporarily commanded by senior brigade commander Anthony Wayne.[21] (Washington remained oblivious to Gates's brazen attempt seven months earlier to supersede him as commander of the Continental army.[22])

After spending nearly half a day east of Flemington, headquarters departed Monday afternoon to join Greene's division as that force was completing an eighty-mile, four-day march in exhausting heat. Washington reached that day's destination—the Delaware River—by nightfall. One brigade of Greene's division had already crossed to the Pennsylvania terminus of Coryell's Ferry on July 28, the other brigade staying put in New Jersey. The General established headquarters within a mile of the ferry at the stone home of Richard Holcombe, described by Colonel Pickering as "a hearty old Quaker."[23]

At first Howe's disappearance from Sandy Hook with his fleet had flummoxed Washington so severely that he thoroughly dispersed his army in less than a week. The previous Wednesday his entire force—except Brigadier General Francis Nash's North Carolina brigade, which was in the region but had never united with the army—had awakened a morning's march to the Hudson across from Peekskill, with all divisions operating within a day's march of the main body. Five nights later, each of Washington's five divisions was isolated from the others and the force was separated by ninety road miles—from Kakiat in New York, where Sullivan had his division, to the Pennsylvania side of Coryell's Ferry, where hunkered part of Greene's division.[24] Under reasonable circumstances, Washington would need a full week to unite all five divisions of the Continental army.

Howe had not materialized at the Capes when his presence was feared most. "This delay makes me suspicious that their real intentions are yet a secret to us," a wary Washington surmised. He refused to pull all his eastward divisions out of striking distance of the Hudson, fearing that Howe might fake a lunge along the coastline in an effort to lure him into doing just that. Washington was not going to fall for a feint. Headquarters remained at Holcombe's property for three nights, with several white tents and the distinctive headquarters marquees popped up adjacent to the Quaker's home to accommodate nearly twenty men. Four miles above them at Howell's Ferry, Major General Adam Stephen's Virginians nestled behind Wayne's Pennsylvanians, all encamped on the east bank of the river except for one of Wayne's brigades, which crossed to the Pennsylvania side of the ferry route on July 29. Although the artillery and most of the dragoons were close to these three infantry divisions, Washington's remaining infantry remained deeper in New Jersey and even in New York, isolated and now well apart from the rest of the army. Stirling's two brigades had encamped at Elizabeth and were on the march to Bound Brook with his endpoint roughly established at either Coryell's or Trenton. While most of Washington's army was proceeding to three crossings on the Delaware above Philadelphia, Sullivan's division stayed within a day's advance to the Hudson.[25]

The interlude pleased Greene and his division. The two full days of respite served his brigades well; the men were, Clement Biddle noted, "in fine spirits; after great fatigue."[26] But Greene was not convinced Howe had the Delaware in his sights. He firmly maintained that the Hudson was Howe's true objective, terming the appearance of a partial fleet off Egg Harbor a ruse. "I think it an object of the first importance to give a check to Bourgoyne," said Greene, endorsing his current location. "Our position in the Jerseys was calculated to cover the North River and Philadelphia and afford protection to the State of New Jersey."[27]

Notwithstanding Greene's preference, Washington prioritized Howe over Burgoyne, but was determined not to cross his troops into Pennsylvania "till the Fleet actually enter the Bay." His Excellency found himself writing daily to Gates. On Tuesday he notified his former Adjutant General that he had redirected a newly arrived French engineer, Antoine-Jean-Louis Le Bègue de Presle Duportail, from Coryell's Ferry to Philadelphia to assist Gates and Mifflin in preparing defenses on the Delaware. Washington advised Gates to keep Duportail and countryman Major General Coudray out of one another's way ("I perceive there is a jealousy between them"). The next day, Washington notified Gates, "As I shall pay no regard to any flying Reports of the appearance of the Fleet, I shall expect an account of it from you the Moment you have it ascertained to your satisfaction."[28]

Washington failed to follow his plan. At 9:30 A.M. on Thursday, July 31, at the Holcombe house, an express courier from Philadelphia handed the General a letter from John Hancock; also enclosed was a communique from Caesar Rodney. In 1776 the intrepid Delaware delegate had ridden all night to Philadelphia to vote for declaring independence from England. Now the heroic Rodney had sent Hancock a letter, written on Wednesday, chronicling the sighting of Howe's fleet at the mouth of Delaware Bay with winds favorable to speed the armada upriver toward Philadelphia.

Washington reasoned that his army was within two days' march of Philadelphia. But that was true only for men on the Pennsylvania shore; thousands in New Jersey would need three days to get to Philadelphia. Howe had the inside track not to Philadelphia but also Wilmington, a Delaware River port a mere twenty-five land miles from Philadelphia. Howe could reasonably reach Wilmington by August 2, disembark his army, and deploy it toward Philadelphia, fielding at least four thousand more Crown forces than readily available Continentals on the same day that Washington's men could enter Philadelphia from the north.

At 10:00 A.M. the General sent a batch of dispatches distributing orders to consolidate his men, cross the river, and proceed to Philadelphia. Meantime, he told Hancock, he had decided to ride "off for your City." That afternoon, he departed Coryell's Ferry, crossing the Delaware from New Jersey to Pennsylvania. The same Durham boats he and his men had used the previous Christmas at McConkey's Ferry, nine miles south, would have been the preferred and most available vessels used at Coryell's by Greene's and Stirling's divisions (the latter having rerouted from his previously intended route to Trenton). At about the same time, Stephen and Wayne were able—with some difficulty—to cross their divisions and artillery above Coryell's by fording the shallows at Howell's Ferry.[29] Before the Coryell's crossing was complete, Washington set off southwest, accompanied by two hundred dragoons, twenty-one headquarters personnel, and twelve free and enslaved servants, all on horseback. He and his party traversed Bucks and Philadelphia Counties, a forty-mile ride, dismounting in Philadelphia at the renowned City Tavern at 10:00 P.M.[30]

Sitting down for a late meal in City Tavern's dining room, Washington and his staff encountered dignitaries offering greetings as he made his first appearance in Philadelphia since spring 1776, when he had visited to sit for portraitist Charles Willson Peale. Washington took special notice of one such well-wisher, a Frenchman one month shy of his twentieth birthday: Marie-Joseph Paul Yves Roch Gilbert du Motier, Marquis de Lafayette, known as "Lafayette" or "the Marquis."

Lafayette had arrived in Philadelphia from France four days earlier, completing a four-month journey whose final six hundred miles by land had consumed the final month. After disembarking near Charleston, South Carolina, and bearing a letter of recommendation from Benjamin Franklin and a commission as a major general from Silas Deane, Lafayette had traveled north in a three-carriage caravan accompanied by Johann de Kalb, fifty-six, a German-born French brigadier general bearing a major general's contract from Deane. Supported by a retinue of aides, advisors, and servants, Lafayette and his countrymen, all of whom were seeking commissions, had that day learned from members of the Continental Congress that their predecessors—especially Major General Coudray—had irritated American politicians who did not welcome the Frenchmen and did not grant appointments Deane had promised them.

Lafayette did his best to propitiate Congress, agreeing to serve The Cause while adhering to a series of special contingencies to preserve his rank of major general. Congress agreed to this, awarding him a sash to signify his rank with the understanding—according to one of the other French officers seeking a command in the American army—that Lafayette was to serve with "no claim to a command, no salary, a pension, or any of the prerequisites of that rank." When he entered City Tavern that night, nobody had to tell him which officer was Washington. Lafayette later wrote, "Although he was surrounded by officers and citizens, the majesty of his figure and height were unmistakable."[31]

Washington knew nothing about Lafayette. Given his interactions with numerous and often pretentious French officers, Washington likely had low expectations regarding the young Frenchman. He was mistaken. Lafayette was engaging if not disarming. His enthusiasm was infectious. On his voyage he had taught himself a rudimentary form of English that he could test on Washington and his dinner guests; Colonel Hamilton likely translated to convey what Lafayette could not. No record exists of the pair's discussion at City Tavern, but the outcome was that Washington invited Lafayette to join him the following day while he inspected defenses along the Delaware. Of course, Lafayette accepted.

Lafayette would naturally have been one of twenty companions who ate breakfast with Washington the following morning. Before departing to view the defenses, Washington fired off a short letter ordering Greene to march the army from its bivouac twenty-five miles north of Philadelphia to a selected campground at Germantown. Howe's position was unknown that morning, but Washington must have realized that the seven and a half infantry brigades with roughly one thousand dragoons and artillerists under Greene's temporary command totaled barely nine thousand soldiers of all arms currently in Pennsylvania.[32]

Departing City Tavern, the General and party, including the Marquis, rode forty miles on Friday, August 1. They first dropped southward to Fort Mifflin, crossed over to New Jersey to inspect Fort Mercer and Fort Billingsport, then ferried back to the Pennsylvania side of the river. They proceeded southwest to Wilmington, Delaware, inspecting the region by heading down the river along its western bank. By evening they had doubled back to Chester, Pennsylvania, finishing the day near Marcus Hook, a promontory adjoining Chester near a creek by the same name. Washington and his staff established headquarters, apparently at the Pennsylvania Arms, a three-story tavern within six hundred yards of the Delaware's bank.[33] His Excellency and penmen Harrison, Tilghman, and Hamilton spent the evening initiating and responding to correspondence, with Lafayette along for the experience. Hamilton would have aided further to enhance communication with Washington and the newest member of the family.

Headquarters thinking focused on holding the Delaware River against Howe's massive fleet by defeating or at least stalling or rebuffing the armada. That intent wavered at 10:00 P.M. that Friday night when a new message arrived from Hancock in Philadelphia. He was forwarding a report written at Cape May at the mouth of the Delaware. On Thursday morning, Cape May coast watcher John Hunn had observed 190 vessels—which he incorrectly determined to have been Howe's entire fleet—reverse direction eastward out of the bay, disappearing beyond the horizon. After those ships had been out of view for three hours, Hunn decided they may have permanently left the region. "I am now of opinion they are making a feint," he wrote, "if so, they have a fresh wind at S.S.W. which will carry them to the Eastward very fast." Hunn's report had left Cape May around noon Thursday with a courier. Traveling eighty miles, the report reached Hancock Friday at 7 P.M., and soon was en route to Chester.[34]

Washington accepted Hunn's assessment that the British commander was attempting a feint. Were the General to continue to call in all his peripheral forces and with the main body bring them southwest of Philadelphia along the Delaware near Chester and Wilmington, he might find to his chagrin that Howe had reappeared on Long Island Sound and that he was marching his men up the Hudson to help Burgoyne cut off New England from the rest of the states. If so, the Continental army would be helpless to buttress Schuyler against the dual threat because the fifteen thousand Americans massed near Chester would be 120 miles by rough colonial roads from the Hudson. It would take at least three days to alert Washington and another week to march an army the size of the young country's third largest urban population from the banks of the Delaware to the banks of the Hudson—arriving far too late to stop Howe and Burgoyne. Howe's ten-day head start would be catastrophic to The Cause.

A sheaf of letters left headquarters warning all detachments from the Grand Army to suspend any operations that might be moving toward Philadelphia and revert to the original plan to defend the Hudson. General Sullivan was ordered to proceed to Peekskill, about one hundred miles downriver from Albany. "This surprising event gives me the greatest anxiety," Washington told General Putnam, "and unless every possible exertion is made, may be productive of the happiest consequences to the enemy, and the most injurious to us." Knowing Greene had advanced four infantry divisions and most of the artillery to Germantown, Washington sent orders to Greene to provide the men with two days of rations and to hold them in readiness to march northward as soon as ordered to do so. One of the final messages Washington sent that night was directed at George Clinton, New York's new governor: "I shall return again with the utmost expedition to the North River."[35]

CHAPTER THREE

"Irksome State of Suspense"

August 2 to August 24, 1777

Philadelphia, which marked its ninety-fifth anniversary in 1777, was named by William Penn, who chose a Greek term translating literally to "beloved brother," though more colloquially meaning "brotherly love." Philadelphia's layout deviated drastically from Penn's notion of a country town occupying a grid with widespread houses and abundant green space in the form of gardens and orchards. Vestiges of Penn's plan had been realized but certainly not his grand design. The third year of the Revolutionary War found the city still matching a description written a generation before, during the Seven Years' War:

> It is situated upon a tongue of land, a few miles above the confluence of the Delaware and Schuilkill, and contains about 3,000 houses, and 18 or 20,000 inhabitants. It is built north and south upon the banks of the Delaware, and is nearly

two miles in length, and three quarters of one in breadth. The streets are laid out with great regularity in parallel lines intersected by others at right angles, and are handsomely built on each side there is a pavement of broad stones for foot passengers; and in most of them a causeway in the middle for carriages. Upon dark nights it is well lighted, and watched by a patrole: there are many fair houses and public edifices in it. The [State]-house is a large, handsome, though heavy building; in this are held the councils, the assemblies, and supreme courts; there are apartments in it also for the accommodations of Indian Chiefs or Sachems; likewise two libraries; one belonging to the province, the other to a society, which was incorporated about ten years ago, and consists of sixty members. . . . The city is in a very flourishing state, and inhabited by merchants, artists, tradesmen, and persons of all occupations. There is a public market held twice a week, upon Wednesday and Saturday, almost equal to that of Leadenhall, and a tolerable one every day besides. The streets are crowded with people, and the river with vessels, Houses are so dear, that they will let for 100 l. currency per annum; and lots, not above thirty feet in breadth, and an hundred in length, in advantageous situations, will sell for 1000 l. sterling. There are several docks upon the river, and about twenty-five vessels are built there annually. I counted upon the stocks, at one time, no less than seventeen, most of them three-masted vessels.[1]

Still taking concrete form, the city was far from completed. Its original grid had been a north-south eight-block rectangle extending two miles from the Delaware River to the Schuylkill River, divided by twenty-three streets, each about a mile long, running north and south. The developed Philadelphia of 1777 hugged the Delaware and stretched more than a mile from the shore, with most of its population residing therein, roughly resembling a sideways pyramid. The Schuylkill side of Philadelphia more closely hewed to Penn's concept, being a less populous town separated by large stretches of woodland, including the impressive Penn's Woods. Though narrower than intended, Philadelphia was colonial America's largest city with upwards of twenty-four thousand inhabitants housed in 3,681 dwellings wedged into the urban grid and fourteen thousand more in the adjoining region.[2]

Philadelphia's wartime importance traced to fewer than sixty individuals comprising the government of the United States of America; to wit, the Continental Congress. Save for a brief sojourn in Baltimore the previous winter, the thirteen states' representatives, to conduct the people's business, mainly waging war, had been relying on a Philadelphia free of imminent threat.

Would the General completely abandon Philadelphia, the locale that he had been prioritizing for ten days since leaving the Clove? Washington had no idea why Howe had sailed away from Burgoyne and the Hudson River in the first place, followed by an approach to, penetration into, and then abandonment of the Capes of the Delaware. His intelligence network was not far reaching enough to apprehend that Lord Germain had unwisely approved two conflicting campaigns: Burgoyne's operation along the Hudson and Howe's effort to capture Philadelphia, the latter outlined in December 1776. Germain believed that Howe could make quick work of the seat of American government and then double back to assist Burgoyne in isolating and conquering the New England states. The undertaking's transition from an overland expedition to an amphibious one had its roots in an April 2 letter Howe wrote—"I propose to invade Pennsylvania by sea"—and sent to the Secretary of State. With the aid of his brother, Vice Admiral Richard Howe, an armada exceeding 260 transports carried seventeen thousand soldiers and an additional 1,500 allied personnel as well as horses, munitions, and other supplies away from Sandy Hook southward to Delaware Bay.[3] One week and 150 miles later, the Howe brothers caught Washington off-guard. With no American troops any closer than forty miles to Philadelphia, the British began to ascend the Delaware River.

Aboard his flagship, HMS *Eagle*, William Howe had on July 30 received—and believed—erroneous claims that Washington was wise to his scheme to invest Philadelphia by water and had a sizeable force approaching Wilmington to contest him. Howe's informants also wildly oversold Philadelphia's river fort defenses. The misinformation rattled the British leader such that he feared the cost of attempting to capture Philadelphia by attacking the forts at the city's southern outskirts or landing within striking distance of the city and having to battle the foe along his line of march. The same day (July 30) Howe pulled his fleet back out to sea, invoking a secondary plan requiring his armada to head below the Capes of the Delaware and beyond.[4]

As Howe was steering his fleet south on an adjusted operation, Washington was planning to head north. After sending orders from Chester on August 1 for his army to advance toward the Hudson, he returned to Philadelphia to stay at City Tavern. Over the next two days he had to rescind those commands. Fresh intelligence from Cape May had Howe's ships again approaching the bay. Washington surmised that the enemy fleet had pulled back to readjust and thread a route through the shoals off Cape May with plans to sail swiftly up the Delaware. Howe's movements were tying Washington in knots. His Excellency well understood on that 90 degree day that "it is terrible to march and counter-march the Troops at this season." His subsequent orders to Major General Sullivan and Brigadier General Nash instructed them to maintain their present positions in a state of readiness to march swiftly toward New England or to Philadelphia if called upon to do so.

Most of the Grand Army benefited from the holding pattern, relaxing in camp since arriving on Friday, August 1. The encampment populated a plateau southwest of Germantown and a mile northeast of the Falls of the Schuylkill which tumbled just above a large bend in the river. During their second full day of enforced leisure, the soldiers enjoyed a visit from a large party of Philadelphia women—"The largest collection of young ladies I almost ever beheld," a soldier recalled.[5]

Washington did not immediately reunite with his army but conducted business for a few days at City Tavern, including informing his former Adjutant General, Horatio Gates, that he was to command the Northern Department, replacing its polarizing and maligned field commander, Major General Phillip Schuyler, demoted to acting Quartermaster General.[6] On Monday, August 4, Washington rode south to inspect river defenses for the second time in three days.[7] The next day, after breakfasting at City Tavern with a party of forty-four, the General rode north to join his four divisions.[8]

He took up headquarters at the home of Philadelphia merchant Henry Hill, who had made Hill's Madeira one of the most recognized brands of the General's favorite wine in the region. While Hill's house was modest, his estate sprawled into two townships. In like manner, the encamped Continental army stretched from Hill's property nearly two miles east. Colonel Daniel Morgan's light infantry had camped there in and around Stenton, a mansion built in the 1720s as a country home for Pennsylvania Supreme Court Chief Justice James Logan, deceased for a quarter of a century in 1777. Morgan learned from Washington that he and his Virginia and Pennsylvania riflemen, about five hundred strong, were to be detached from Washington's command and sent to reinforce the Northern army.[9]

Soon after establishing his presence at the Hill home, Washington huddled with his subordinates, including Joseph Reed, who as a colonel had held the position of Adjutant General for several months after General Gates exited that post. Reed and Washington had been close in 1776 until November of that year when Washington learned that Reed had been carping about Washington's leadership, specifically alleging indecision on the

General's part during the New York campaign. Although not directly confronted by his superior about his private correspondence, Reed resigned from headquarters and gave up his colonelcy in January 1777; four months later he was appointed a brigadier general but in June declined that commission to remain a civilian. Regardless, Washington continued to solicit Reed's counsel.[10]

Apparently, the meeting also included controversial French general Coudray, now exchanging poison-pen letters with Massachusetts delegate and Coudray critic James Lovell. Notwithstanding Lovell's derision, Coudray was considered more an asset than a source of animus in the Continental army. In limbo regarding his official title and rank, he had quietly accepted "that the Congress has decided that the ratification of my treaties with Mr. Deane, their lawful representative, is inconsistent with the honor and safety of the United-States." Overseeing fort defenses on the Delaware downstream of Philadelphia, Coudray carefully avoided overstepping his authority and by late July it appears that Washington had warmed to him, a rapprochement akin to one Coudray had engineered among members of Congress several weeks earlier. "He seems to have studied more the arts & sciences than the Graces," observed a delegate; "yet his plain & unaffected manner, his good sense, & sweetness of temper gains upon us daily."[11]

The meeting mainly sought to assess riverine defenses below Philadelphia at Forts Mifflin, Mercer, and Billingsport. For four days, Washington studied opinions offered at the conclave. The five surviving appraisals, simultaneously thoughtful and thought provoking, represent three schools of thought. Generals Knox and Coudray advocated heavily manning the forts with a total of 1,800 soldiers and as many as thirty-six cannons. Reed and General Anthony Wayne pushed for a dominant land force arrayed at Chester. They believed Howe, rather than challenge the forts, would disembark his army at Wilmington or further downriver and from there attempt a short overland attack on Philadelphia.

General Greene's response was the most forceful and provocative. Perhaps still stung by the November 1776 disaster at Fort Washington on northern Manhattan Island, Greene belittled nearly every aspect of committing quality infantry to the forts. He claimed there were too few cannons to spare for the riverside bastions and that the navigable channel of the Delaware near Philadelphia was too narrow and crooked to accommodate an invading armada. Greene suggested instead emplacing a series of half-moon batteries to annoy enemy ships and augmented by fire rafts whose flaming presence would distract the British from the needed task of removing tangles of submerged *chevaux de frise*—underwater obstacles installed to bar vessels in at least three locales. They traversed the navigable width of the Delaware in a double line near Fort Billingsport and obstructed shipping lanes in segments strategically submerged between islands further up the river. Greene echoed Wayne's and Reed's wish for a dominant land force not compromised by diverting healthy infantrymen to forts. As an alternative means of immediately staffing the forts, Washington ordered the creation of the Invalid Corps, a force whose ranks were to include one-armed or single-legged privates and similarly compromised non-commissioned staff.[12]

American response strategy reset the following week, during which the British fleet disappeared again. Washington grew more and more convinced that Howe's armada was doubling back to the New England states. In his mind's eye this rationale explained Burgoyne's vigorous thrust south into New York. Midsummer "is not only against their going Southward, but there is no object there worth their attention, and it would leave Genl Burgoine to make head against the whole Eastern force and the Continental army up the North River," Washington said. "My opinion therefore is, that they intend either to go round the East End of Long Island into the Sound and land in Connecticut, or stand more Eastward, and make a decent upon Rhode Island, or somewhere in Massachusetts, from either of which places, they may attempt to penetrate and form a junction with Genl Burgoine, who is pushing down the North River with scarce any opposition."[13]

Expecting he would be needing to redeploy near the Hudson, Washington decided to move on. Until Howe's fleet reappeared—it never was seen again at the Capes of the Delaware—he would place his army on the New Jersey side of the Delaware by way of Coryell's Ferry. Including the half day required to cross the Delaware River, this placed the Continental army three days closer to the Hudson River but still near enough to Philadelphia to provide timely succor. No council was held to make this decision, but Greene certainly would have endorsed the idea given his opposition a week earlier to the army getting drawn toward Philadelphia from Coryell's Ferry. Ranking the Hudson as far more important, he claimed on July 31 that "the cry was so great for the salvation of Philadelphia that the General was prevailed to leave Coryell's Ferry contrary to his judgment, and march down to the city."[14]

At noon on August 8, Washington held a formal review of his army. The ceremony started late; by the time the ritual began troops had been under arms for six hours. The temperature surpassed 80 degrees, baking the men from their powdered and dressed hair through their bare, shoed, or booted feet. General Lafayette had ridden up from Philadelphia that morning to join Washington for the next phase of the campaign. Two years later he vividly recalled the General's Continentals as poorly armed and clothed, the latter making them the image of a "motley and naked array. The best garments were hunting shirts, large jackets of gray linen." Lafayette also noted that they were aligned in two ranks, divided by height, with the shorter-statured men in front of the taller ones.[15]

Astride Blueskin, the dappled Arabian he most frequently saddled during the first three years of the war, Washington, with Lafayette in tow, rode past all eight of his available infantry brigades and his dragoon regiments and artillery companies as officers and men saluted. In a moment of candor Washington turned to his protégé.

"We should be embarrassed," the General confessed.

"I am here to learn, and not to teach,"[16] the young Frenchman replied.

The laggard start of the review shortened the planned Grand Army's march toward its next bivouac to an eight-mile trek north to a region called Whitemarsh to camp overnight. The following day, the deputy quartermaster misdirected the troops, who had to tramp a five-mile correction on August 10 to be within a day's march of Coryell's Ferry.[17]

Washington intended to cross at Coryell's on Monday, August 11, poised to head north to the Hudson if Howe was seen moving in that direction but close enough to Philadelphia if Howe doubled back to threaten the city. Shortly after dark on Sunday, a courier handed Washington a dispatch. The envelope's contents led with an explanatory note from John Hancock written four hours earlier. Hancock said he was enclosing information sent three days before by a Maryland militiaman stationed on the Atlantic coast near the Maryland-Virginia border fifty miles south of Delaware Bay. The spotter had sighted a fleet of more than two hundred ships sailing to a southeast wind. Wherever Howe was heading, he seemed unlikely to be supporting Burgoyne's advance on Albany. Washington quickly suspended the march toward the Delaware River and decided to stay on the Pennsylvania side.[18]

The troops knew the camp site; they had spent eleven hours at the locale overnight July 31-August 1. It was called "Crossroads" because it was where the north-south York Road intersected the east-west Bristol Road. Half a mile north of Crossroads flowed a branch of Neshaminy Creek, a tributary of the Delaware River. Washington's headquarters stood on the north side of the creek, east of the York Road and four hundred feet north of the creek bridge. The Life Guard had secured for the general the sturdy, spacious stone home of Catherine Moland, the widow of a prominent Bucks County attorney.[19]

The headquarters complement and allied expenses swelled as more officers joined the General's party. At the Moland house, Washington tallied costs that had accumulated to $6,000 since the end of June: for travel ($1,150), reimbursement to Captain Gibbs ($2,000, likely for lodging and Life Guard bills), summertime secret service expenses ($1,935), outlays from examining the Philadelphia defenses ($146 2/3), a horse bought from Parke Custis ($333 1/3) which apparently succumbed to distemper, inducing Washington to acquire two cheaper steeds ($200) from one of his dragoon commanders.[20] By pausing near Neshaminy Creek, Washington was reducing the day-to-day costs of keeping an army on the march.

Two new aides de camp, volunteers unranked until their appointments were made official by Congress, replaced the reassigned Colonel John Walker and the late Lieutenant Colonel George Johnston. Peter Presley Thornton, twenty-six, son of a pre-war friend of Washington, had signed on at Henry Hill's. He was joined by John Laurens, twenty-two, who came from money—his father was Henry Laurens, an active and highly respected South Carolina delegate to the Continental Congress. Well tutored and worldly, young Laurens spoke fluent French. Early in the war he had been studying law in England. He left his pregnant wife in London at the end of 1776 to return to America and join the fight. At the Moland House he immediately set about learning from more senior aides how headquarters worked. One was Alexander Hamilton, who quickly bonded with Laurens as a contemporary.[21]

Hamilton's and Laurens's linguistic skills were put to the test with the addition of a Polish officer who spoke no English but was fluent in French. Casimir Pulaski, a hero to fellow Poles from his exploits fighting the Russians in the 1760s, had been exiled from his homeland in 1772. While holed up in Paris, he improved his French for at least two years before importuning Benjamin Franklin and Silas Deane for a military appointment in revolutionary America. Both American diplomats armed Pulaski with laudatory letters. Franklin raved about Pulaski as "an Officer famous throughout Europe for his Bravery and Conduct in Defence of the Liberties of his Country against the three great invading Powers of Russia, Austria & Prussia."

Pulaski had first contacted Washington by letter upon arriving in Boston late in July. Besides recommendations from Franklin and Deane he

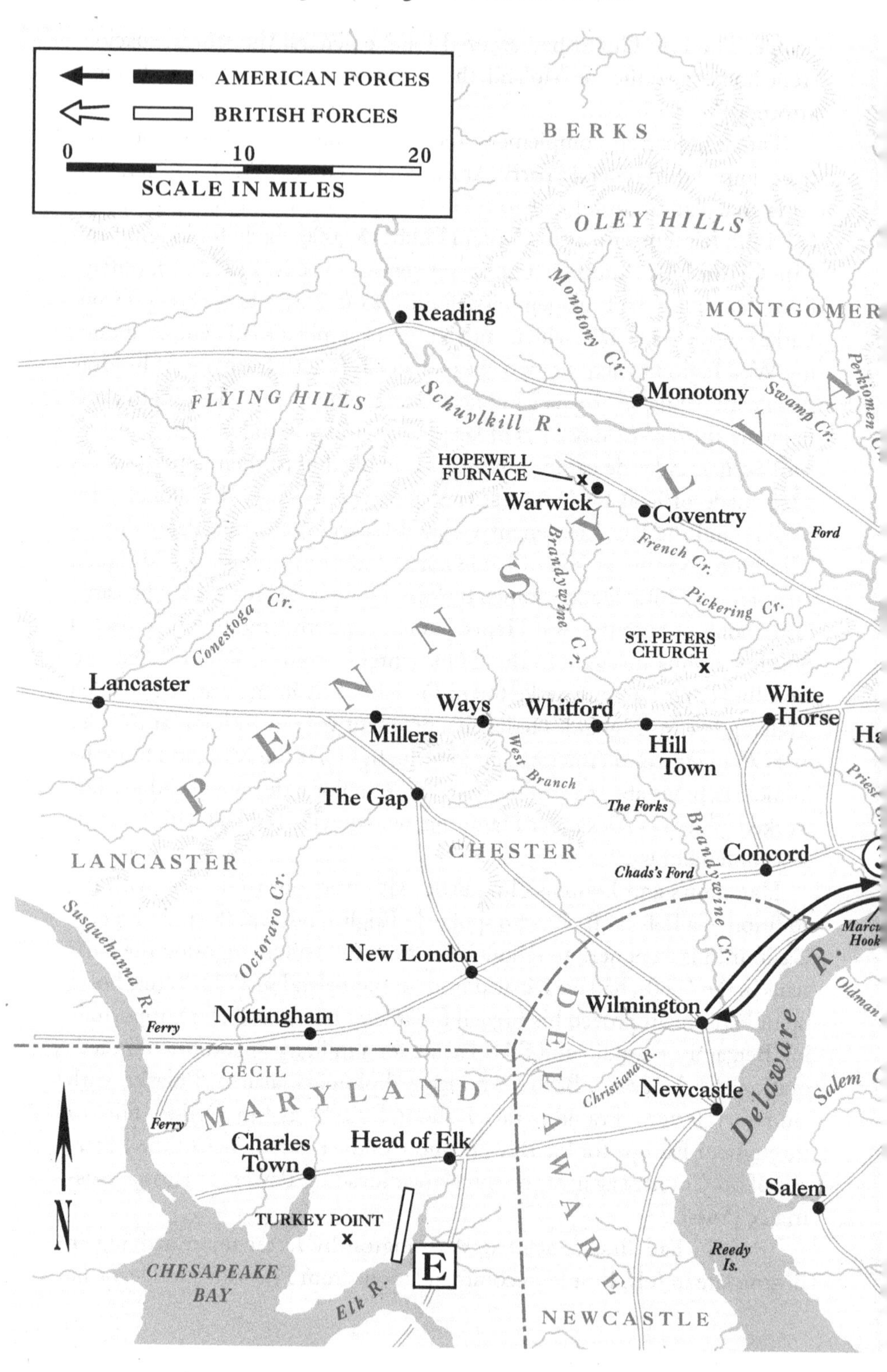
AMERICAN FORCES
BRITISH FORCES
0
10
20
SCALE IN MILES
BERKS
OLEY HILLS
Monotony Cr.
MONTGOMER
Reading
Perkiomen
FLYING HILLS
Schuylkill R.
Monotony
Swamp Cr.
HOPEWELL FURNACE
Warwick
Coventry
Ford
PENNSYLVA
Brandywine Cr.
French Cr.
Pickering Cr.
Conestoga Cr.
ST. PETERS CHURCH
Lancaster
White Horse
Ways
Whitford
Millers
Hill Town
West Branch
The Gap
The Forks
Brandywine Cr.
CHESTER
LANCASTER
Concord
Chads's Ford
Susquehanna R.
Octoraro Cr.
New London
Delaware R.
Wilmington
Nottingham
Ferry
CECIL
Christiana R.
Newcastle
MARYLAND
DELAWARE
Ferry
Charles Town
Head of Elk
Salem
TURKEY POINT
E
CHESAPEAKE BAY
Elk R.
Reedy Is.
NEWCASTLE
N

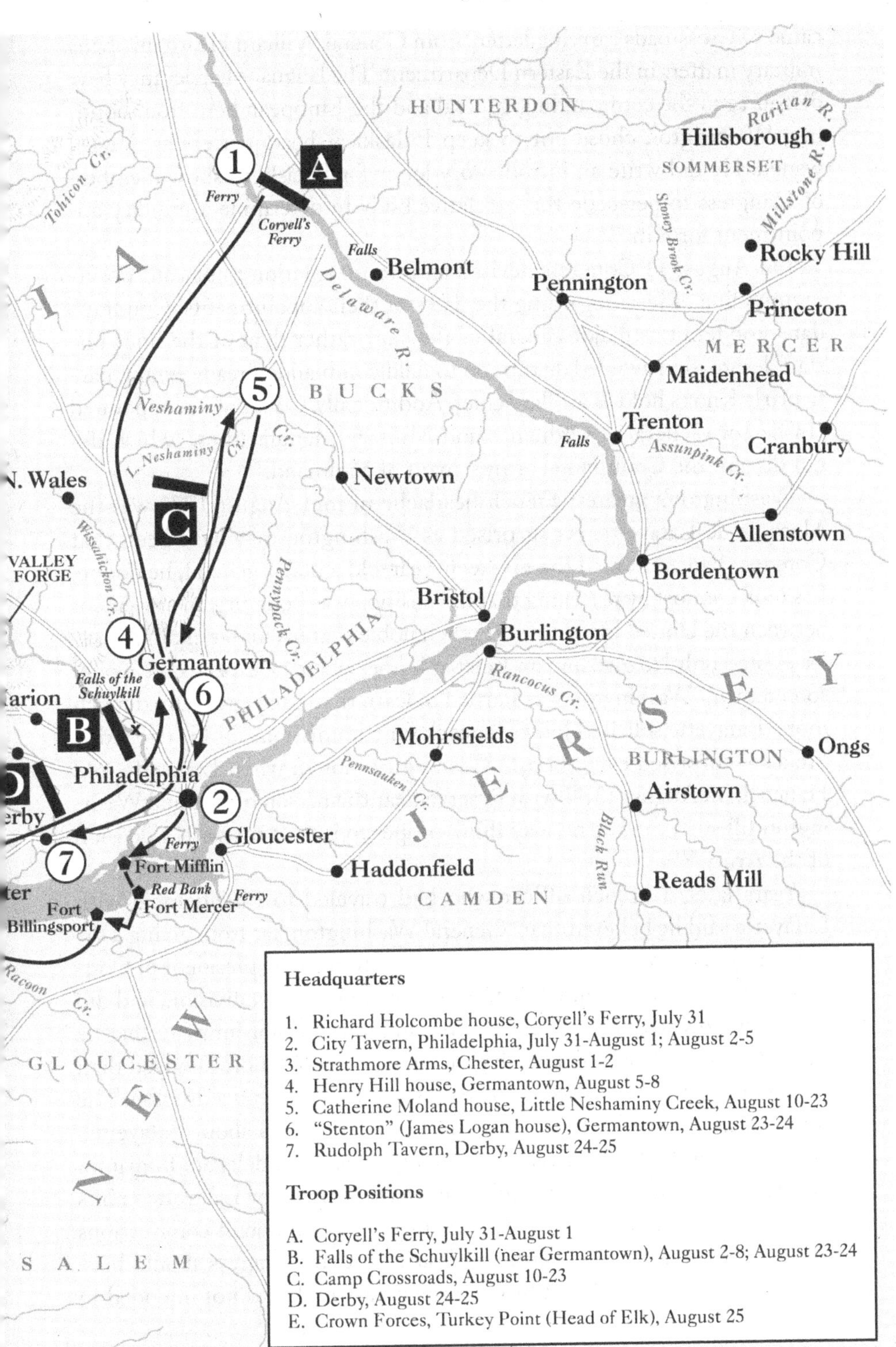
HUNTERDON
Raritan R.
Hillsborough
SOMMERSET
Millstone R.
Tohicon Cr.
Ferry
Coryell's Ferry
Falls
Belmont
Delaware R.
Stoney Brook Cr.
Rocky Hill
Pennington
Princeton
MERCER
Maidenhead
BUCKS
Neshaminy Cr.
L. Neshaminy Cr.
Trenton
Falls
Assunpink Cr.
Cranbury
Newtown
Wissahickon Cr.
VALLEY FORGE
Allenstown
Bordentown
Pennypack Cr.
Bristol
Burlington
Germantown
Falls of the Schuylkill
PHILADELPHIA
Rancocus Cr.
Mohrsfields
Philadelphia
BURLINGTON
Ongs
Pennsauken Cr.
Airstown
Black Run
Gloucester
Ferry
Fort Mifflin
Red Bank
Fort Mercer
Ferry
Haddonfield
Reads Mill
CAMDEN
Fort Billingsport
Racoon Cr.
GLOUCESTER
SALEM
NEW JERSEY
Headquarters
1. Richard Holcombe house, Coryell's Ferry, July 31
2. City Tavern, Philadelphia, July 31-August 1; August 2-5
3. Strathmore Arms, Chester, August 1-2
4. Henry Hill house, Germantown, August 5-8
5. Catherine Moland house, Little Neshaminy Creek, August 10-23
6. "Stenton" (James Logan house), Germantown, August 23-24
7. Rudolph Tavern, Derby, August 24-25
Troop Positions
A. Coryell's Ferry, July 31-August 1
B. Falls of the Schuylkill (near Germantown), August 2-8; August 23-24
C. Camp Crossroads, August 10-23
D. Derby, August 24-25
E. Crown Forces, Turkey Point (Head of Elk), August 25

came to Crossroads carrying letters from General William Heath involving military matters in the Eastern Department. The language barrier may have discouraged the commanding general and the European hero from bonding; Washington chose not to keep Pulaski at headquarters as August waned. He did write an introductory letter for Pulaski to show members of Congress to persuade the legislative body to determine a military appointment for him.[22]

On August 11 Congress devised an interim solution to placate Washington's line officers regarding the dates of their appointments. Coudray's date stood, but as major general of the staff rather than of the line. The staff designation avoided disruption to field commands already extant, particularly Knox's hold as artillery chief. Additionally, Coudray was appointed "Inspector General of Ordnance and Military Manufactures," which did not disrupt the Continental army's chain of command.[23]

Washington's greatest French headache in mid-August 1777 was the Marquis de Lafayette. As surprised as Washington may have been that Congress had appointed the nineteen-year-old a major general, he doubtless took comfort by reasoning that the position was honorary, an agreement between the United States and a French noble that his high rank in America existed only "to give him an Eclat at home, where he expected he would soon return." Washington was startled to learn that Lafayette wanted much more. Lafayette solicited John Hancock for commissions for his two aides. He also "surprised every body," Washington noted, when Lafayette told Hancock on August 13, "I wish to serve near the person of General Washington till such time as he may think proper to intrust me with a division of the Army."[24]

Years later, a French officer who had traveled to Philadelphia with Lafayette said he believed that "General Washington, far from giving a division to Lafayette . . . had complained about him to the president of Congress, said he was tormented by the latter's requests for a division, and did not know how to get rid of him."[25] Washington did not intimate that he wanted "to get rid of" the French general, and seemed more annoyed than "tormented" by the adolescent noble's request to command a division. The commander in chief did complain directly to Congress about Lafayette's insistence that he lead a division, speaking to Virginia delegate Benjamin Harrison as an intermediary to John Hancock. Irritated by Lafayette's hints about getting a division, as well as his overt push to obtain commissions for his aides, Washington vented to Harrison that Congress should have made clear to Lafayette that his major general's rank was not intended to be accompanied by a field command. "If on the other hand," Washington said, "it was intended to vest him with all the powers of a Major Genl why have I been led into a contrary belief, & left in the dark with respect to my own conduct toward him?"[26]

At this stage Washington considered Lafayette a "difficulty," one of "the numberless applications for Imployment by Foreigners." Washington had two infantry divisions without a healthy major general commanding them. Since Major General Lincoln's departure a month earlier, Brigadier General Anthony Wayne, the ranking subordinate, had been leading that unit. Because Major General Sullivan was sick and absent from his detached division, his ranking subordinate, Brigadier General Philippe Hubert, Chevalier de Preudhomme de Borre, was leading that division. Sullivan revealed to Washington that heavy drinking had caused him to suffer a gastrointestinal hemorrhage. "I am extremely apprehensive that I Shall never perfectly Recover. . . . This being the fourth time I have Bled," Sullivan wrote on August 7, shortly after returning to command. He added that his doctor "apprehends That the Bleeding has almost become habitual," and if Sullivan didn't quit the bottle, his intake would "prove Fatal." Washington left those ranking subordinates to continue as division chiefs. He had known Lafayette for merely three weeks and yet saw little in the young upstart to impress him enough to grant him a field command.[27] In no way was the General going to put Lafayette in charge of either division or assign him command of any of those divisions' brigades.

Lolling in mid-August at Crossroads, twenty miles from Philadelphia, the American troops dodged much of the worst of the strength-sapping, sleep-stealing summer of 1777. After a week of moderate heat, the mercury struck the 80 degree mark by 9:00 A.M. daily beginning August 9, preceding a week of afternoons cracking 90 degrees. "These fourteen days in August have all been uniformly and intensely hot," Timothy Pickering noted in his journal, observing that "continual melting-hot weather is unknown in New England." But at least the army was relatively immobile, marching only thirty miles the first three weeks of August, in contrast to July's nearly 150 miles on dusty roads in New Jersey and New York. "It is agreed, by most People, that so long and so intense a Heat has never been known," John Adams wrote to his wife from Philadelphia on August 14. "How we should live through these Heats I don't know." Three days later, a cooling rain temporarily soothed the region.[28] A Continental soldier summed up the weather in a stanza:

Since we came here for to encamp,
Our mornings have been very damp.
But at noonday excessive warm,
And like to do us all great harm.[29]

According to John Laurens, the heat failed to sour troops on Camp Crossroads. "The men are exercised in smaller or greater numbers every day," Laurens reported. "The country people bring in plenty of vegetables, &c.—and we hear very few complaints from those immediately about us of the violations of private property."[30]

Their surroundings did little to comfort American generals struggling to puzzle out the British fleet's whereabouts and destination. Noting that the mystery generated much talk at headquarters, Lafayette nonetheless termed it "the object of many pleasantries." General Greene saw nothing positive about the subject: "This manoevre of General Howe is so strange and unaccountable that it exceeds all conjecture," Greene confessed; "I am totally ignorant yet."[31]

It vexed Washington to be ignorant of Howe's location and intent. "The conduct of the Enemy is distressing beyond measure, and past our comprehension," he vented, describing his men as being in "a very irksome state of Suspence."[32] That August 10 communique about the sighting of the fleet fifty miles south of the Capes of the Delaware was the last news he had received of Howe. Knowing what an extended sail would wreak on army troops, Washington had all but dismissed the notion that Howe was feinting southward as a prelude to making for New England. He wondered if Howe was trying to lure his army deep into southern Delaware, Maryland, or even Virginia, which would allow Clinton to advance his force from New York City up the Hudson unopposed to link up with Burgoyne. Or were Crown forces sailing south to Charleston to complete the mission interrupted in 1776? The only other possibility Washington had entertained was that Howe would come at Philadelphia by way of Chesapeake Bay, but lack of any sighting of the fleet scotched that. "If he is gone to the Southward, he must be gone far that way," surmised the General. "For had Chesepeak Bay been his Object, he would have been there long since, and the Fact well established."[33]

Washington called a council at the Moland house late on the morning of August 21. All four division commanders present attended; among brigade commanders, only Wayne's—both colonels—were absent. Adherence to the generals-only rule at this particular council placed Brigadier

General Henry Knox in the room, along with Major General Marquis de Lafayette, attending his first council.

The meeting likely was brief. Acknowledging that Howe seemed disinclined to attack Philadelphia via the Delaware, the commander in chief queried his generals. What was Howe's destination? The council concluded, perhaps unanimously, that he was heading south, likely for Charleston. That being so, Washington asked, ought they conduct a six-hundred-mile overland trek to parry that assault? Considering the effort and time demanded by such a stratagem, the council turned thumbs down. One option remained, and the council embraced it. "The Army should move immediately" to the Hudson River and operate against Burgoyne.[34]

His Excellency crafted General Orders to that effect Thursday afternoon. Drummers were to rouse the troops at 3:30 A.M. to the drumbeat known as "the *General*," an hour later form up to the beat of "the *Troop*," and step out at 5:00 A.M. But when the document was complete Washington countermanded it.[35]

The reason was an express message from John Hancock. He enclosed two letters whose contents duplicated one another. A week ago, on August 14, a fleet of at least one hundred ships, probably Howe's, had been sighted "directly standing into the Capes" of the Chesapeake. Though not definitive, the news could not be ignored. Had Howe entered the Chesapeake on August 14-15, by now his force could be within range of Head of Elk—less than sixty land miles from Philadelphia.[36]

Washington put off the march to the Hudson. "The destination of the Fleet, if for Chesapeake Bay, must soon be known," he reasoned, "and the Army will remain here, till further intelligence is obtained on the Subject." Washington doubted that Howe had entered the bay, because by now other sources would have flagged that to him. He maintained that the British fleet was at the mouth of the Chesapeake "to amuse and that their designs may yet be against Charles Town."[37]

At the Moland house the General weighed the latest intelligence from Hancock. Those mid-August sightings of Howe's fleet near the entrance of Chesapeake Bay were old news. The absence of confirmatory reports persuaded him that the fleet was bound southward rather than poised to penetrate the bay. Were Howe making a run up the Chesapeake, bringing him closer and closer to Philadelphia, word would have reached Washington, since the news had to travel ever shorter distances to be delivered to him. The coast watcher network's silence implied that the enemy fleet was off North Carolina and bearing south. This assessment and the dire need for over ten thousand Continental infantry, artillery, and cavalry troops to break camp after nearly two weeks convinced Washington to get his men moving by suspending his suspension.

"The army is to march tomorrow morning (if it should not rain) precisely in the time, and manner, directed in the orders of yesterday," he wrote.[38] Their marching destination was New Jersey, by way of Coryell's Ferry. He also issued a series of lengthy General Orders on Friday addressing conflicts with sutlers and multiple courts martial outcomes.

Near sunset, After Orders further amended the plan: "The army is not to march tomorrow morning but remain in its present encampment 'till further orders."[39] Yet again, Hancock had weighed in, this time forwarding intelligence regarding Howe's fleet that left no room for alternative interpretation:

> 4:00 P.M. on 21 Aug. I embrace the earliest moment of giving you the most authentic account of the enemies fleet and their motions since their arrival in Chesapeak bay, the fleet arrived this morning between the hours of seven & eight oclock off Swan Island, which lies directly between Rock hall and the river Potapseco and dropt anchor[.] From the best information we have been able to procure their number is upward of 100 sail. It is uncertain as the tide is strong ebb whether they intend to Baltimore or further up the bay; their number is continually encreasing; there are a great number of cattle which I am afraid must fall into the enemys hands.
>
> 50 minutes past 4 P.M. This moment recd a letter from a gentlemen of veracity & attachment to the country from Swan point 2 oclock P.M., he had just then returned from viewing the fleet, which he is certain is near 200 in number. He says they all came to agst Swan point about 1 oclock P.M. and is certain they will land on this shore to night or to morrow morning as they are very near the land; there is a number of small craft around them and they seem crouded with men[.] Cannon are continually firing at Baltimore[.] Our militia is in a very disordered state our law relating to it not yet executed. Nothing but speedy relief from Congress can save us.[40]

George Washington's reaction to this intelligence became a landmark moment. Howe's commitment to taking Philadelphia by sea dated to an April 2 letter to George Germain in which he named the city as his target.[41] He never deviated from that goal, committing an armada to transport his troops there early in the second week of July. Washington, in contrast, always had had one foot pointed toward the Hudson and the other pointed to Philadelphia. But at about 7:00 P.M. on Friday, August 22, 1777, at the Catherine Moland house near Crossroads in Bucks County, Pennsylvania, Washington committed his effort and his army entirely to defending Philadelphia. For the Americans, what would be called the Philadelphia Campaign began here.

After Orders, issued at 10:00 P.M. Friday, reversed the morning's General Orders. Coryell's Ferry mattered no more. Instead, the march was to be southward toward Philadelphia. Washington set Germantown, five miles north of the city, as the next day's destination.[42]

Two key figures were temporarily excused from the advance. During daylight hours on August 22, as the army was preparing to set off north for New Jersey, General Knox was planning a personal jaunt to Bethlehem, nearly thirty miles from Coryell's Ferry, "to purchase some things for my dear dear Lucy."[43] Knox coaxed Greene—a friend since the New York Campaign—to come along. Greene suggested they travel by carriage, "as the weather is exceedingly hot."[44] The suspension at sunset of the march to Coryell's Ferry and Washington's change of the march's direction set for the following morning made no difference to Greene, Knox, and their determination to shop in Bethlehem.

According to Knox, he and Greene "begged the favor of his Excellency's permission" to travel to Bethlehem on Saturday rather than join their commands en route to Philadelphia. Astoundingly, Washington approved this whimsy, allowing the pair to stay at Crossroads as Washington and twelve thousand Continentals marched south at dawn Saturday morning. Bethlehem sat no less than fifty road miles from Germantown and seventy from Chester, the latter to where Washington ordered Nash to deliver his brigade and apparently where he expected to advance the rest of his army. Greene's absence rippled through his unit's ranks as temporary division, brigade, and regimental commanders suddenly assumed their duties, a factor guaranteed to hobble Washington's largest division until Greene appeared at Chester. This needless state of affairs might persist for three days, particularly since their departure for Bethlehem was marked by a late—4 P.M.—start that Saturday from the Little Neshaminy.[45]

Knox's skewed priorities aside, why did Greene go with him rather than remain in command of his division when he likely knew a clash with Crown forces was imminent? Washington had sent a copy of the tell-tale intelligence to Sullivan the evening of August 22; it would have been most unusual for the General not to have shown Greene the dispatch. But even if that were so, would Washington not have briefed Greene as succinctly as he did Brigadier General Nash ("Howes fleet is high up in the North East part of Chesepeak Bay")?[46]

Greene had been grousing for months about prioritizing the defense of Philadelphia above deployment to the Hudson. He had written about Philadelphia only a week earlier: "It is true it is one of the finest [cities] on the continent, but in my opinion is an object of far less importance than the North River." He had resented how the rush from the Clove toward Philadelphia during a heat wave had sapped his troops' health. He wrote on August 17, "I can assure you I was no advocate for coming so hastily here."[47] Greene likely treated his junket with Knox as a needed respite from the fallout born of an undesired decision by the commander in chief. A days-long absence from command of his division was not immediately ideal for the Continental army, but Greene thought it necessary for him and, over the long term for his men, inasmuch as he believed he would be back on the job well before any clash with the British.

Washington's approval still stands as the most stunning element of this interlude, with Greene's absence second. By accompanying Knox on his joyride, Greene, thanks to the absence of Sullivan's division, shrank the Continental army's command echelon to a mere two major generals—Stephen and Stirling—leading troops, with a third—Lafayette—seeking troops to lead. No evidence has come to light to support a conclusion that Bethlehem had any strategic significance. More likely Washington sensed that Greene needed a break. Greene's headquarters probably stood across the York Road from the Moland house; no doubt the two rode together, ate together, and generally met often through those thirteen days at Little Neshaminy Creek, solidifying a relationship forged in the brutal New York Campaign of a year before. Washington weighed the risk and decided the army could get along for a few days without Greene as it advanced to Philadelphia, and likely beyond.

The army needed Knox on a daily basis less than it needed Greene. With artillery companies attached to each of the eight infantry brigades marching toward Germantown, and others, such as Proctor's regiment at Trenton under General Nash's guidance, detached with independent commands, Knox as chief of artillery had fewer duties than if the artillery advanced on marches as its own entity. Appearances suggest a close bond between Washington and Knox but Knox's own correspondence shows that he was not a member of Washington's inner circle. (Three days after Washington received definitive information on Howe and the Chesapeake, which he immediately sent to General Nash and others, Knox was refusing even to acknowledge the news. "I beleive Philadelphia may be his principall object," Knox surmised to his wife on August 25, "but it is not by the way of Chesepeak, the plain natural way by the Delaware will be his route."[48]) Clearly, Washington did not provide Knox a glimpse of the tell-tale dispatch that had defined the direction of the campaign.

Sometime during the morning leg of that Saturday's march, Washington dictated a message to Lieutenant Colonel Harrison, ordering his military secretary to rush to Philadelphia and deliver that communique to Hancock. Headquarters staff, army officers, and Philadelphians had convinced the General not to bypass the city, as always had been his wont, but instead to march through Philadelphia Sunday morning. Mindful of the August 8 grand review and its morale-building effect—Lafayette was writing about it in vivid detail even two years later—Washington realized that the best way to infuse his army and the local populace with appreciation for and belief in The Cause was to parade his army through the city. Washington reasoned to Hancock that marching through Philadelphia "may have some influence on the minds of the disaffected there and those who are Dupes to their artifices & opinions."[49] Following that spine-stiffening display, the army would march southwest toward the headwaters of the Chesapeake, where he expected Howe to disembark.

The Continentals had marched into Germantown by noon on Saturday, August 23, and camped 2,500 yards east of the spot near the Henry Hill house where they had done so weeks before. The Life Guard directed Washington to Stenton, the late Judge Logan's red-brick home, used by Colonel Morgan earlier that month. Decades later, a witness to Washington's arrival who at the time had been an adolescent vividly described clouds of dust rising at noon that Saturday from a roadbed churned by hundreds of hooves and the multitude of blue and buff uniforms of the Life Guard. He easily recognized Washington, a "grave man who stood apart in deep meditation while the others engaged in merry chaff." He recalled seeing the General's valet, William Lee, and Blueskin, "the great white charger . . . which a black man was tending with such care." A Logan family member's diary entries confirmed the youth's recollection as to the hour, remarked on the presence of numerous officers and servants, and said that "Washington appeared extremely grave & thoughtful."[50]

Once ensconced, the General charted details regarding Sunday's march. Three infantry brigades—Sullivan's Marylanders and Nash's North Carolinians—and their attached artillery would be absent; ergo, Washington deemed it imperative to have his top commanders present at the parade leading their units. To that end, he sent an express courier from Germantown to Bethlehem to demand that Greene and Knox return immediately to the Grand Army. Uncertain if the pair could make it on time, Washington spelled out the route (Front and Chestnut Streets), the order of march (cavalry regiments bracketing Greene's, Stephen's, Wayne's, and Stirling's divisions vanguard and rear), and spacing between units. So that his army would present itself as professionally as possible, he specified that men were not to haul along cooking kettles but were to "carry their arms well and are made to appear as decent as circumstances will admit." Fife and drum units were to center within their respective brigades and when they played a quick step, the men were to march "without dancing along, or totally disregarding the music, as too often has been the case." All baggage wagons, surplus horses, and even the camp women were to bypass the city to the west, rejoining the army at the Middle Ferry. Hancock received Washington's notification in time to get the parade route advertised in Saturday evening's edition of the *Pennsylvania Evening Post*.[51]

Saturday night saw heavy rains that carried into Sunday morning, but, according to John Adams, by the time the army entered Philadelphia from the north at 7:00 A.M. the rain had ceased. Greene and Knox were absent, but no Philadelphians missed them. The army made an impressive show. The Rhode Island delegate must have been too captivated by the "lively smart Step" of Greene's Virginia brigades to notice that the Rhode Island commander was not riding at their head. Washington rode his dappled Arabian ahead of what Richard Henry Lee called "a Gallant army" which "made a fine appearance." John Adams wrote to his wife that he viewed a "fine Spectacle" that lasted two hours. "The Army, upon an accurate Inspection of it, I find to be extreamly well armed, pretty well cloathed, and tolerably disciplined," Adams wrote, hoping soon to see improvement: "Our soldiers have not yet, quite the Air of Soldiers. They don't step exactly in Time. They don't hold up their Heads, quite erect, nor turn out their Toes, so exactly as they ought. They don't all of them cock their Hats—and such as do, don't all wear them the same way."[52]

Colonel Pickering was relieved that the order of march held all along the route through Philadelphia and pleased that the army "was allowed to make a fine appearance." As Washington began to distance himself westward from the city—and likely before the army had completed the two hour-long line of march—he and eleven members of his military family convened at City Tavern. While their horses ate hay and oats at a nearby stable, the dozen guests of Daniel Smith breakfasted on punch and grog,[53] then rode west on Walnut Street. Their destination was the floating bridge over the Schuylkill River at Middle Ferry, constructed for military operations a year earlier and now tested by a large army for the first time in the war.

Amid this panoply Washington might have cast his mind back to the Delaware River on Christmas night, 1776. That crossing from Pennsylvania to New Jersey at McConkey's Ferry led to a series of events, engineered and accidental, that within nine spectacular days saved a nation. Washington yearned for this latest crossing to usher in equivalent good fortune at the headwaters of the Chesapeake and along the Hudson 150 miles behind his right shoulder. That desired sequence of planned and fortunate events would not only preserve the year-old country but also end the Revolutionary War.

CHAPTER FOUR

"If We Behave Like Men"

August 24 to September 5, 1777

Washington's two absent commanders found their way to him an hour after the army passed through Philadelphia that Sunday. The commander in chief was on the western side of the Schuylkill River when Generals Greene and Knox rode in on jaded horses. At 9:00 A.M. that Sunday morning they had arrived in Bethlehem for their shopping expedition, only to be intercepted almost immediately by Washington's express courier, who had beaten them to the town by riding all Saturday night with orders recalling them. Inexplicably, even with this chivvying the wayward generals took their time. Knox later wrote, "We first visited all parts of this singularly happy place, where all the inhabitants seem to vie with each other in humility and brotherly kindness." By Sunday's noon hour, unaware of the army's parade through Philadelphia, the duo rode south to rejoin the Grand

Army, that afternoon completing a circuit to and from Bethlehem of nearly one hundred miles within twenty-four hours.[1]

After the parade, Washington and four divisions of his Grand Army entered Derby (present-day Darby), a crossroads town five miles west of Philadelphia. John Sullivan's two brigades were not expected to unite with them for several days. Washington established headquarters at the Rudolph family residence. He issued General Orders that temporarily divided his force, sending half his infantry toward Wilmington, the rest of his army to follow a day later. Both movements were subject to postponement if rain was falling heavily at dawn. Mindful that only five miles separated troops from the nation's largest city and its beckoning brothels, Washington issued instructions to prevent troops from drifting into Philadelphia and to keep the city's prostitutes from entering the Derby camps.[2]

Washington summoned his officers that evening.[3] Knowing Howe was about to land his armada southwest of Philadelphia and march on the city, he queried his council about the best way to thwart that effort. Generals Lafayette and Conway, backed by two colonels, urged an attack.[4] More than a month at sea—thirty-two days, to be exact—surely had left Howe's British and Hessian infantry, artillery, and cavalry, a total approaching seventeen thousand soldiers, badly out of fighting trim, they reasoned. Howe's infantrymen would never be weaker, individually and collectively, than now, functioning as they were on "sea legs," the pair argued. The same was true of Howe's warhorses, whose condition after weeks at sea likely was even more compromised than that of any human rider or wagoner, at least for the first several days on terra firma. Washington's best chance to deal with the British threat in America, the two declared, was now, or else risk Howe eventually uniting with Burgoyne and Clinton to create an unbeatable force. Wherever Howe landed off the Chesapeake, he would be separated by more miles from every other British army in America than ever before.[5]

Given that his most glorious offensive achievements, at Trenton and at Princeton, dated back only nine months, Washington must have been pleased at the spirited discussion of and enthusiasm for an offensive. Notwithstanding their cogent urgings, however, Washington wanted a defensive battle. The General remembered the Battle of Assunpink Creek, fought the day before Princeton. There, Washington had drawn Lieutenant General Charles Cornwallis into costly and fruitless assaults against a strong infantry line, fortified by Knox's cannons, ensconced on the heights of the banks across the creek from the British. This victory and the lone good day the Americans enjoyed in New York at Harlem Heights in mid-

September 1776 argued for defensive rather than offensive tactics, particularly with three infantry brigades and their respective artillery companies separated from the Grand Army.

The council also discussed a plan to defend against Howe's advance. One general supported defending the heights nearest Wilmington, waiting for Howe to move directly east-northeast to Philadelphia or more northerly to Lancaster and its supply depots. Washington would have also been concerned about Howe moving upon Reading, where the Americans stored munitions. He knew the high ground between Wilmington and the Elk River, through which he had passed several times over the years, including his 1774 journey from Mount Vernon to Philadelphia as a delegate to the First Continental Congress and his momentous 1775 appearance in uniform at the Second Continental Congress. Those and earlier such trips had carried Washington over the Old Post Road, known in 1777 as the King's Road. These travels would have familiarized the sharp-eyed Washington with the waterways between the Elk River and the Brandywine Creek: Christiana River, White Clay Creek, and Red Clay Creek. But these river and creek beds and banks were never analyzed for their potential as positions to align more than eighteen thousand Continentals and militiamen.

The council ended without a decision. Washington left standing the orders for his army to split the following day. Howe had not landed, making any fixed alignment premature.

The commander in chief, his two Virginia divisions, and his cavalry woke before dawn on August 25. This portion of the Continental army continued away from Philadelphia, beginning its march shortly after 4:00 A.M. With Sullivan's division ninety miles away in New Jersey opposite Staten Island, the two remaining divisions of Washington's Grand Army—Stirling's and Lincoln's, the latter commanded by Brigadier General Anthony Wayne—remained with Knox's artillery near Derby with orders to march toward Wilmington, Delaware, the following morning.[6] After breakfasting in Chester, Washington and coterie trotted twelve miles to Wilmington, a path parallel to the southwestern course of the Delaware River. The Virginia divisions had encamped east of the Brandywine by 2:00 P.M. Timothy Pickering's first impression of Wilmington in his journal was of "a pretty town and pleasantly situated."[7]

The Americans' advanced position proved strategically astute. The very day Washington reached Wilmington, Howe landed his army where Washington had predicted he would—twenty-five miles southwest of Wilmington on the west bank of an outpouching portion of the Elk River, four miles from that stream's headwaters, site of the appropriately named town of Head of Elk. By the shortest road network possible, Howe stood fifty-two miles from Philadelphia. This was comparable to the distance from his Raritan River position in New Jersey early in 1777. Howe's inability to sweep into Philadelphia on the Delaware had already proven costly. Could Washington freeze him on the Elk the same way he had done on the Raritan?

Washington and companions reached a tavern at Wilmington early enough to satisfy the General's preference for a mid-afternoon meal. The tavern, never identified, belonged to one George Forsyth. On short notice, he sat twenty-seven people for an abundant meal and more than enough wine, claret, and grog.[8] That night Forsyth hosted a few members of the headquarters staff. When rank and file troops came up short on tents, Washington palliated them with liquor. According to the orderly books, "A Gill of Spirits to be drawn to the men, this to be continued every morning while the men lay out of their Tents."[9]

Washington digested the previous day's council and its proceedings. He had already decided that he personally needed to study Howe's position, as well as familiarize his division and brigade commanders with the lay of the land from Wilmington to Head of Elk. "I propose to view the grounds towards the Enemy in the morning," wrote Washington to John Hancock at 8:00 P.M. "I am yet a stranger to them."[10]

Compounding Washington's ignorance was the absence of any maps to guide him. Quartermaster General Mifflin, assigned four weeks earlier to obtain or create maps of the appointed region, utterly failed to deliver. Congress scrambled, with a delegate promising the General that "a pretty exact Map of the Country" would be forthcoming, but none materialized. Washington hired New Castle County surveyor Jacob Broom to accompany him the next day to map the ground he traversed as he approached the British position.[11]

That ride was no ordinary reconnaissance. Washington mounted Blueskin and rode out of Wilmington with Broom, Lafayette, and several of his household and military staff, including William Lee, Alexander Hamilton, Caleb Gibbs, and others. Timothy Pickering stayed behind. Major Generals Nathanael Greene and Adam Stephen, each with at least one aide, two or three brigadier generals within Stephen's and Greene's Virginia divisions, and four enslaved men, took part. These twenty-three riders were led and surrounded by what Washington called "a strong party of Horse" encompassing three of four dragoon regiments under Colonels Theodorick Bland, Lieutenant Colonel Francis Byrd, and Lieutenant Colonel Anthony

White. The reconnaissance party totaled upwards of five hundred horsemen.[12]

Taking the road to Newport, they diverted southwest to Christiana Bridge, crossing Red Clay Creek and White Clay Creek. Ten miles from Wilmington, the generals and aides stopped in Christiana. At that hamlet Washington and twenty-two others were hosted by one Barnaby Lanigan, who served breakfast—including rum for the servants and "Spirits" for the rest. Washington's admission of unfamiliarity with the vicinity showed in his accepting Lanigan's hospitality; four months later, Barnaby Lanigan was indicted for suspicion of treason in New Castle County.[13]

The reconnaissance resumed southwesterly down the King's Road, crossing the Christiana River over Cooch's Bridge.[14] One mile later they scaled Iron Hill, the easternmost and tallest of three heights forming a triangle from the Delaware-Maryland border. Named for rich stores of subterranean iron oxide, the height began to attract open-pit mining decades prior to the Revolution. By 1777, the area was home to a vast enterprise which deforested the highlands, offering Washington and party a glimpse of British activity ten miles southwest. Apparently, the view from Iron Hill was unrewarding. The generals crossed from Delaware into Maryland and headed up Grey's Hill, three miles from the iron mines. Grey's Hill, although closer, was not as high as Iron Hill. Neither vantage point afforded Washington a decent view—"But few tents," he complained, was all he could discern.

Washington descended from the heights to continue the reconnoiter. "We were down as far as the Head of Elk," wrote Major Robert Forsyth, General Stephen's aide-de-camp (and no relation to the publican in Wilmington). A general in the party claimed the group got as close as four miles to Howe's troops. They learned that Howe had landed all his troops on the northwest side of the river. The Americans had recast Head of Elk as a supply depot a year ago. Whether or not Howe knew it, his force threatened supplies stored near the town. Probably using area militia and his dragoon brigade, Washington spirited the cache away, save for some seven thousand bushels of corn vulnerable to capture by the British and Hessians.[15]

The mission consumed almost every minute of daylight on August 26, despite scouting only twenty miles from Wilmington on horseback. Considering the number of generals on the ride, Washington must have spent considerable time informally conferring with Lafayette, Greene, and Stephen, as well as some of the Virginia brigadiers. If this multi-general mission was meant to determine whether to spring a surprise attack on a physically weakened portion of Howe's army, the discovery that he had disembarked at least five thousand men across from Cecil Courthouse—on the western bank of the Elk—eliminated the shortest option, as an attacking force would have to march an additional eight miles to confront Howe's force on the west side of the river versus the east side, as well as removing the ability to pin surprised troops against the river.[16]

That reality left Washington with primarily defensive options. The best would be to take advantage of the heights closest to the Elk River and fairly lock Howe in position, as at the Raritan River in the first half of 1777. But the heights here were not like New Jersey's towering Watchungs; not a range but isolated hills Howe could skirt.

Washington's more reasonable options for defense were to deploy upon the eastern banks of the Christiana River, White Clay Creek, or Red Clay Creek. These waterways offered prime elevated terrain with natural moats. The monstrous Delaware River also guaranteed Washington ample protection on his left flank. But choosing any of these creek beds ceded nearly fifteen miles to Howe. Not only did this bring Crown forces that much closer to Philadelphia, but it left Washington's right flank vulnerable to flanking. Howe could enter Pennsylvania if desired and pick up other road options to head toward Philadelphia or draw Washington out to him.

As he considered his options, Washington appeared unconcerned about his proximity to Howe's advance. Impending darkness, heavy rain, and, no doubt, hunger pushed the group northeast of Grey's Hill toward Robert Alexander's two-and-a-half story home just off the eastern edge of Head of Elk. Before the war, Alexander, a Baltimore lawyer and member of the Sons of Liberty, had been a delegate to the provincial convention of 1774. On August 26, his home stood seven miles from Howe's landing site. A profusion of Redcoats stretched a few miles closer to Head of Elk.[17]

Some of Washington's entourage lodged elsewhere; Captain Caleb Gibbs stayed at the home of Seth James.[18] Washington, Lafayette, division commanders, and aides dined and stayed at the Alexander home—Washington's decision, notwithstanding protests by Lafayette and others, mindful of Major General Charles Lee's capture, that he was too close to the enemy in unknown and untrustworthy territory. Invoking the ranks of cavalry he had in the region, Washington later told a confidant, "I was equally guarded [against] friend and Foe . . . I was acting precisely in the line of my duty, but not in the dangerous situation you have been led to believe."[19]

According to Lafayette, as Alexander's guests saddled up and rode east in the morning, Washington "admitted that a single traitor could have betrayed him."[20] Washington later learned that a potential traitor had been under the same roof that night. Within days former Son of Liberty Robert Alexander embraced the British and left his patriot wife, eventually moving to England, where, a few years after he was officially branded a traitor by the state of Maryland, he died.[21]

Washington returned Wednesday morning to Wilmington, where he was directed to a new headquarters. The Life Guard had chosen for him the three-story brick home of Captain Jacob Bennett on an impressive height at Quaker Hill, the southwestern part of town. "The situation of this house is very high," a newspaper reported, "and commands an extensive view of the Delaware and Christiana rivers." The Bennett home came with "a pump of fine water." No single residence could accommodate nearly thirty headquarters personnel. Thus, all three of Washington's marquees were erected and at least two more Quaker Hill homes selected to house headquarters personnel. Taverns, tents, and townspeople sheltered the rest. The Life Guard occupied the Friends Meetinghouse one hundred yards north of the Bennett house.[22]

The Head of Elk reconnaissance's extent was illustrated in the headquarters expense account. Nearly $600 was billed for an operation of less than thirty hours, more than double the expense incurred in the four days required to transfer the army from Crossroads to Wilmington. This contrast colored the reconnaissance as a disappointing venture that harvested little intelligence that could not have been obtained from a smaller party on horseback. "I have nothing new to communicate," a chagrined Washington admitted to Congress. The only fruit from the mission was a detailed map of the region by Jacob Broom. Washington retained Broom as a cartographer from this point onward in the campaign.[23]

Washington had barely settled in at the Bennett home when he held his second council of war in three days. His entire army had concentrated near Wilmington except for Sullivan's division, still en route from the Staten Island Campaign. Sharing the intelligence gleaned the previous day, the General solicited his officers' opinions on the best way to contest General Howe. Although remonstrations to attack continued to resonate, the prevailing sentiment was to establish a line of defense behind one of the major waterways traversing the state of Delaware. Having ruled out an offensive against Howe, Washington determined that White Clay Creek would make a decent defensive position. On August 28, Greene's division marched to the Philadelphia side of the creek and aligned in defense there. Pennsylvania militia buttressed their flank at Christiana.[24]

General Greene was apparently not with his division when his men advanced to White Clay Creek because Washington had assigned him to determine the best line of defense the very morning Washington returned to Wilmington. Greene combed the region with General Weedon and scores of Continental dragoons. "This country does not abound in good posts," Hamilton complained regarding defensive options in Delaware. "It is intersected by such an infinity of roads, and is so little mountainous, that it is impossible to find a spot not liable to capital defects." Greene and Weedon concluded that the crossroads at Cooch's Bridge over the Christiana River was the best position, boasting as it had enough open country behind the line to accommodate assistance, if needed. But Iron Hill loomed over this position just a mile west, scotching its defensive utility should British artillery achieve the height and rain iron upon those below.[25]

Greene's separate reconnaissance proved mostly moot. That Thursday, August 28, Washington rode to the White Clay Creek line he had just established, immediately deciding it was not a decent defensive position either. Red Clay Creek, the parallel waterway between White Clay Creek and Brandywine Creek,[26] seemed stronger despite ceding several more miles to Howe and placing him closer to Philadelphia. When Greene protested, Washington explained that Red Clay Creek was the best spot at which to block Howe's advance. Greene countered that Howe would not advance to Philadelphia until he had a good chance of damaging—if not destroying—the Continental army, and that Red Clay Creek was not the ideal place for Washington to counterattack Howe. Greene had clearly not adopted Washington's strategy. "The face of the country is favorable to the Enemy, being very flat and [level]," Greene told his brother. "However I have the greatest hopes if Providence don't think proper to punish us further with the calamities of war to give General How a deadly wound."[27]

Washington did not completely discount Greene's advice regarding the Cooch's Bridge position. He began to align his defense at Red Clay Creek beginning on August 29. The distance between opposing forces now stood at twelve miles. Intelligence from captured British and Hessians troops led Washington to expect an imminent grand advance by Howe; when that move came, he desired it to be closely monitored and contested. He ordered a detachment of his army to occupy the crossroads at the Christiana River. This would be a select force, created to mitigate the absence of Morgan's riflemen. Washington formed "a corps of Light Infantry" from a hundred men from each of the nine brigades in Delaware chosen by their respective commanders, each complement led by a field officer and sixteen company

AMERICAN FORCES
0
5
SCALE IN MILES
Kennett Square
PENNSYLVANIA
New London
White
MARYLAND
Clay
Cr.
Newark
Christia
KING'S
IRON HILL
COOCH'S BRIDGE
3
Head of Elk
GRAYS HILL
Aiken's Tavern
Elk
R.
DELAWARE
N

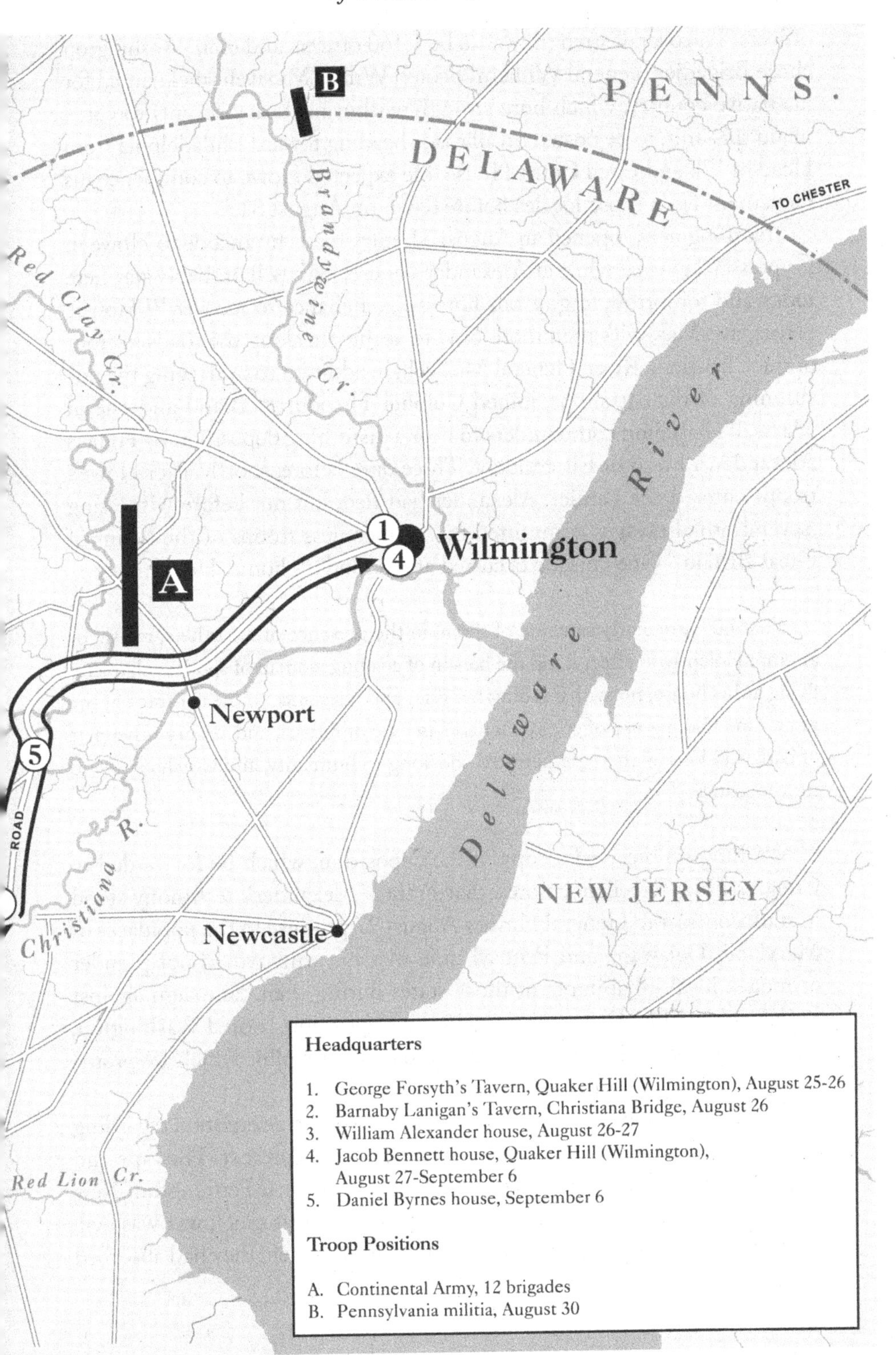
B
PENNS.
DELAWARE
TO CHESTER
Brandywine Cr.
Red Clay Cr.
1
4
Wilmington
A
River
Newport
5
ROAD
Delaware
Christiana R.
NEW JERSEY
Newcastle
Red Lion Cr.
Headquarters
1. George Forsyth's Tavern, Quaker Hill (Wilmington), August 25-26
2. Barnaby Lanigan's Tavern, Christiana Bridge, August 26
3. William Alexander house, August 26-27
4. Jacob Bennett house, Quaker Hill (Wilmington), August 27-September 6
5. Daniel Byrnes house, September 6
Troop Positions
A. Continental Army, 12 brigades
B. Pennsylvania militia, August 30

officers. The overall strength was to be 1,160 officers and men. Washington chose Brigadier General William "Scotch Willie" Maxwell (nicknamed for his native country, which bore strongly within his heavy accent) to command this unit, to be posted on all roads heading toward Philadelphia from Head of Elk and Cecil Court House. He expected Howe to commence his movement from those locales before dawn on August 31.[28]

"Nothing new," opened an August 31 entry made by an aide to Howe in his personal journal while at Alexander's house. "We will probably stay here today and tomorrow to give our horses . . . a chance to recover."[29] Howe's pause gave Maxwell's men more time to acclimate along the roads in front of the Christiana River. General Maxwell, in addition to overseeing the positioning of his battalions, joined Colonel Theodorick Bland and one of Maxwell's battalion commanders to hear a disturbing deposition by Francis Alexander, a Head of Elk resident. Three days before, shortly after Howe's troops entered the hamlet, Alexander had fled, but not before witnessing "several brutal ravages committed by the merciless troops of the tyrant of Great Britain." One episode occurred at Alexander's home. He testified:

> That he particularly saw one of them, in the presence of . . . others, ravish, or attempt violently to effect it, on the person of a young woman of spotless character living at his house, notwithstanding her cries and resistance to the contrary, at the same time making use of severe menaces in case of refusal, and sundry other acts of barbarity he saw there perpetrated shocking to humanity, and which cry aloud for vengeance.[30]

Washington received a copy of the deposition, which he forwarded to Congress. His Excellency noted that Francis Alexander's testimony stood in stark contrast to General Howe's August 27 promise to the populaces of Maryland, Delaware, and Pennsylvania that his army would not plunder or molest loyal inhabitants of those states during their campaign against Philadelphia. "The Facts contained in the Deposition," noted Washington, "seem to be opposed to that regularity and good discipline which are promised by the Declaration."[31]

Washington's low-key written reaction belied his true emotion regarding atrocities laid upon citizens he had been charged to protect. The rape and abuse at Head of Elk in late August echoed events near Pennington, New Jersey, the previous December. War was ugly; war was cruel; war was evil. He knew it and his subordinates knew it. As for the men, they had absorbed rumors of it.

Sullivan's two brigades arrived at Red Clay Creek on September 3, uniting Washington's reconstituted army for the first time in 1777. As August became September, Crown soldiers in the northeastern corner of Maryland and Continentals with Pennsylvania and Delaware militias in west-central Delaware realized the twelve miles between their positions would inevitably disappear. Sometime in September these nearly fourteen thousand American men and boys enlisted as Continental soldiers would battle the foe somewhere east of Philadelphia. Having six months before commanded fewer than three thousand soldiers, Washington must have been relieved—if not satisfied—at his army's numerical strength. The quantity of men he had brought from New Jersey was competitive and advantageous under the best defensive circumstances. But what about the quality of the officers commanding these troops in battle?

Certainly, Washington fretted that some of his most capable and experienced officers were not available. Charles Lee remained a British prisoner in New York; Horatio Gates was in command against Burgoyne along the upper Hudson. Lee and Gates were two of Washington's most capable and experienced major generals, highly effective despite their prickly personalities and tenuous relationship with him. Under ideal circumstances, Washington wanted them together serving under him. Benjamin Lincoln, Benedict Arnold, Daniel Morgan, and a host of others were with Gates and not him. With his new organization of five infantry divisions and eleven brigades—twelve with the ad hoc light infantry force carved from the others—Washington's Grand Army numbered 12,656 Continental infantry officers and men on September 3 (cavalry and artillery adding 1,120 more Continentals).[32] He had achieved his victories at Trenton, Assunpink Creek, and Princeton with mobile fractions of that army. Nine months later, could these five divisions function cohesively and coherently to take the day at this very critical juncture of the War for Independence?

The most experienced Continental division commanders were Nathanael Greene, William Alexander (Lord Stirling), and John Sullivan. Each of these major generals had made suspect, even awful decisions defending against Howe in New York, but each had gained considerable experience from those defeats and had built upon them, and each had led two brigades in New Jersey for nearly a year.

Adam Stephen was the fourth major general in Washington's infantry structure. Appointed like Stirling on February 19, 1777, Stephen had roots and military relationship with Washington during the Seven Years War that uniquely bonded the two Virginians. Adam Stephen had been Washington's second in command in the Virginia Regiment in the previous war and assumed command of it upon Washington's retirement in 1759. Before they united in New Jersey in 1777, Washington and Stephen had written warmly to each other the previous summer, sharing the "grateful remembrance of the escape we had at the Meadows and on the Banks of the Monongahela," referring to the 1754 action at Fort Necessity and to Braddock's defeat in 1755. Washington uniquely opened up to Stephen, revealing his hope that "the same Provedence that protected us upon those occasions will, I hope, continue his Mercies, and make us happy Instruments in restoring Peace & liberty to this once favour'd but now distressed Country." No doubt the two rode together and recounted their shared experiences during the Head of Elk reconnaissance.

Washington and Stephen shared a long adversarial history that preceded their days, current and past, as brothers in arms. They competed to acquire western lands in 1754. Seven years later, Stephen challenged Washington for a Frederick County seat in Virginia's House of Burgesses, a three-way election that Washington won. Recently, Brigadier General Stephen had served under Washington in the Trenton Campaign, during which he nearly jeopardized the operation by instructing his pickets to fire on Hessian sentries, risking alerting the Germans a day before the famous "Crossing of the Delaware." The error turned out not to be costly, but the incident, combined with Stephen's propensity to file, as Sullivan did, purposefully misleading reports on small New Jersey actions during the spring of 1777, doubtless fueled apprehension Washington must have harbored regarding Stephen's ability to handle two Virginia brigades as a division commander on a robustly contested battlefield.[33]

Washington's remaining division, in the absence of Benjamin Lincoln, mainly had been commanded since July by Anthony Wayne (except when Wayne was organizing Chester County militia). He was the only division commander with the rank of brigadier general instead of major general. The Continental Congress prohibited more than two major generals per state, a quota filled in Pennsylvania by Thomas Mifflin and Arthur St. Clair. Wayne was new to division command and regardless of his state of origin would have to prove himself to earn higher rank if it became available. His division was all Pennsylvanians.

After Wayne assumed division command, and Brigadier General William Smallwood was detached to raise and organize Maryland militia, Washington's twelve brigade commanders were mostly unproven commodities, save for Brigadier Generals William Woodford, Charles Scott, and Thomas Conway, who stood out as battle-tested exceptions. Only the brigades of the two Virginia divisions were led exclusively by brigadier generals. The remaining three divisions had at least one brigade led by a regimental colonel. Wayne was the only brigadier general in his entire division; colonels led the two Pennsylvania brigades within his command.

General Stirling worried about unity within his division. Washington's order for Brigadier General William Maxwell to leave Stirling's division to lead the new brigade of picked marksmen left Colonel Elias Dayton in charge of four New Jersey regiments. Dayton, untested as a brigade commander, was not as much a concern to Stirling as was Conway, whose antics prompted Stirling to complain to Washington in writing. Brigadier General Thomas Conway had migrated all the way onto Stirling's wrong side. Reminding the General of a charge against Conway in June of "behavior unbecomeing a Gentleman and an Officer," Stirling now blasted Conway: "of late he has endeavoured to throw Contempt on every order I have Issued to the Division." Washington considered the matter too trifling to act upon.[34]

Maxwell's light infantry brigade turned out not to be the only independent command in the Continental army. A North Carolina-bred brigade of nine regiments, commanded by Brigadier General Francis Nash, had tarried in Trenton at midsummer before uniting with Washington in Delaware. Each of the nine North Carolina regiments was smaller than most and without a full complement of officers, but Nash's brigade still tallied upwards of 1,500 officers and men.

That brigade's size irritated Conway. The prickly brigadier sent a written complaint to George Washington—likely unaware that his division commander had just lodged a serious charge against him. Conway railed at Washington's order to strip his command of marksmen to fill Maxwell's specialized force, exaggerating that though Nash's brigade "is almost three times as strong as mine it Did not give more men than Mine toward the Light infantry." Conway derided Maxwell as the wrong choice to command. Maxwell "certainly never Commanded as many men as I Did before the enemy," Conway wrote. "It must injure my Character very much when it will be Known that though I am one of the More experienc'd officers on this continent of any one of my Rank i am entrusted with the smallest Command." Washington valued Conway's experience and coolness under fire, demonstrated against Cornwallis at the Battle of Short Hills on June 26. But while Washington had been willing to give him a stint of division command while Stirling was ill, Conway's ego, short fuse, and big mouth were destined to sink him.[35]

A cherished officer within arm's reach of George Washington was John Cadwalader, thirty-five, a major player as colonel of the Philadelphia Associators in Washington's nine-day turnaround victories at Trenton and Princeton in 1776–77. For his superlative efforts in command of the city militia, Congress awarded Cadwalader a brigadier general's rank in Washington's realigned Continental army in February. To Washington's chagrin, Cadwalader turned down that commission to take a reduced command of brigadier general of militia. Nevertheless, Cadwalader remained loyal to the General and agreed to organize Maryland militia exclusively from the Eastern Shore, independent of General William Smallwood's recruiting efforts. Cadwalader did more than recruit; he successfully wrangled cows and horses from the eastern side of the Elk River to deny them to the British. Cadwalader also posted sentries at intervals to force away Loyalists and minimize their ability to aid Howe.[36]

Talent had recently revealed itself within Washington's brigade of Light Dragoons. Within Theodorick Bland's Continental regiment shone a young captain; his Prince William County family was known to Washington before the war. Henry Lee III, twenty-one, would earn the nickname "Light Horse Harry." Lee celebrated an August 25 court martial acquittal (the charge of Disobedience of Orders was ruled "*groundless* and *vexatious*") by capturing twenty-four wayward British soldiers near Head of Elk four days later. Washington was more than pleased at Lee's accomplishments, insisting that any of his men detached to deliver prisoners swiftly return to Lee. "He is so enterprising and useful an officer," Washington raved to Colonel Bland, "that I wish him not to be [hampered] for the want of men."[37]

As pleased as Washington was with Lee, the five-hundred-man dragoon brigade still lacked an overall commander. Washington considered shifting an infantry brigadier general into that role, but he had none to spare. In fact, since Smallwood had not yet returned to the army, his absence within Sullivan's division had yet to be filled by a promotion from within the Maryland regiments of his former brigade command. By the end of August Washington had warmed to the idea of placing Count Casimir Pulaski—the Polish noble Washington had personally sent to Congress on August 21 with Benjamin Franklin's letter of introduction—in charge of all cavalry, since the Pole had ample experience as a horse soldier in his native land. Pulaski remained with Washington in early September, limited to service as a volunteer advisor and aide while he waited for his appointment to become official. Until that occurred, Washington seemed satisfied to approach a battle against Howe with a headless brigade of dragoons. "The nature of the horse-service with us being such, that they commonly act in detachment, a general officer with them is less necessary, than at the head of Brigades of infantry," he reasoned.[38]

Washington appeared unsettled regarding his artillery. The durability of his personal bond with Brigadier General Henry Knox was questionable. Knox had proved instrumental during the three victories in New Jersey nine months earlier, and his Herculean efforts the year before to haul fifty-nine cannons, mortars, and howitzers three hundred wintry miles from Fort Ticonderoga to Boston had obviously impressed the General enough to accept the autodidact artillerist without military experience before the war as artillery chief with a brigadier's rank at the close of 1776. But more recently, while Washington had shared with other subordinates, word of Howe's run up the Chesapeake—he apparently excluded Knox. The heavyset former bookseller seemed to know nothing of that August 21 dispatch. During encampments, Knox, twenty-seven, controlled several hundred artillerists organized as a brigade of three regiments as well as seven unattached companies operating independently of one another. Knox's jurisdiction had been limited through August, evidenced by most of his fifty cannons having been allocated to infantry divisions rather than existing as a separate wing of the army, particularly on marches. But Knox was fully in charge of his cannons during the defensive stand at Red Clay Creek. More than half of those guns were brass six-pounders; at least half a dozen others were four-pounders, the smallest weapons in Knox's armamentarium.[39]

Washington expected his 13,776 Continentals to receive adequate support from militias in Maryland, Pennsylvania, and Delaware, the states directly and indirectly threatened by Howe. Such had been the case earlier in the year in New Jersey, when militia there served effectively during scores of Forage War engagements. A week before John Adams had predicted that ten thousand roused-up Maryland, Pennsylvania, and Delaware militiamen—a number exceeding the figure of seven thousand called for in a resolution that Adams had helped pass—would be flocking to Washington's aid. Barely half of Adams's unrealistic expectation had materialized by September 1.

Washington anticipated much of General Smallwood's mission to recruit a significant force of Marylanders but was not expecting them anytime soon. Caesar Rodney had performed adequately with his Delaware minutemen in harassing Howe's soldiers around the Elk River, but Rodney's complement numbered in the hundreds at best. Nathanael Greene's sanguine prediction in late August that the militia would enlarge the total American military presence into "a formidable force" had by early September melted away to sheer disappointment. "The militia of this country are not like the Jersey militia," Greene observed, "fighting is a new thing with these, and many seem to have a poor stomach for the business."[40]

Pennsylvania's performance occasioned much of Greene's disappointment. Resolved by Congress to contribute four thousand militiamen, the state had mustered about three thousand by the first week of September. Most had had no experience in a war entering its twenty-ninth month. Delegate John Armstrong commanded the lot as their major general of militia, organizing a dozen regiments into two unequal brigades. The Pennsylvanians' lack of discipline and soldierly bearing—at least one brigade had no tents—deepened Washington's distrust of part-time soldiers; a stereotype of ineptitude to which he clung to, even though earlier in 1777 New Jersey militiamen had shone in battle.[41]

For the first time in a contested theater of the Revolutionary War, Washington and his available army, nearly nineteen thousand strong on September 3, outnumbered Howe and his nearly eighteen thousand troops. Resolved to force the British to go on the attack, Washington felt his numbers—suspect quality of regimental leadership and limited experience of his soldiery notwithstanding—offered decent odds for success in a head-to-head defensive fight. His strategy, no longer Fabian as in the spring months when he had conducted a war of posts, now emphasized fighting defensively but not breaking away before becoming fully engaged. He ordered his army to dig in behind Red Clay Creek with the intent to withstand Howe's full-on offensive thrusts. Given Howe's history of deft tactical maneuvering, Washington could only entertain faint hopes of drawing his opponent into costly frontal assaults. He knew that Howe's pyrrhic victory on June 17, 1775, at Bunker Hill—with ghastly numbers of killed and wounded in that nominally successful assault—was not to be repeated.

Washington established a solid, three-mile-long defense. Two-thirds of his force, including nearly all his artillery, aligned along the heights on the northeast bank of Red Clay Creek. With his front and right flank well protected by deep creeks, Washington effectively denied Howe any chance of pushing Crown infantry directly to Wilmington, five miles behind the Americans' left flank. Within two miles of the Red Clay Creek line, Washington posted advance pickets at White Clay Creek. Six miles southwest of those pickets Maxwell covered Cooch's Bridge over the Christiana River and Iron Hill to the west. Another five hundred militiamen held rearward posts at fords along Brandywine Creek, about seven miles northeast of the right flank of the Red Clay Creek line.[42]

It did not take long for Howe to contest Washington's most advanced position. On September 3, he sent two battalions of light infantry and one of jägers. Those troops struck Washington's advance guard near Iron Hill and drove those defenders back toward the Christiana River. These men constituted Maxwell's brigade—Washington's newest force under its newest independent commander. Maxwell's men fell back from Iron Hill and crossed Cooch's Bridge, defending the span's east end. Flanked on both sides, Maxwell withdrew after a fight of at least three hours. The outcome was inevitable as Howe had reinforcements close by. Between both forces in nearly equal measure, upwards of a hundred soldiers were killed and wounded in this first and only battle of the war fought in Delaware. Maxwell's solid performance did little to blunt criticism of him. Lafayette considered Maxwell the "most inept brigadier general" in Washington's army; a Virginian in the ranks likened his presence in battle to that of "an old-woman."[43]

After Maxwell's men were driven back eastward toward Washington's Red Clay Creek line, Howe planted his army along that newly gained real estate. By seizing the crossroads at Cooch's Bridge, Howe also controlled the shortest avenues north to Continental depots at Reading and Warwick furnaces (still forty miles north of Cooch's Bridge), as well as the town of Reading, fifteen miles northwest of those forges. Howe appears not to have expressed interest in those locales, and Washington's surviving correspondence makes no mention of this threat to his supply sources. The opposing armies held firm less than ten miles apart for two days, neither suggesting an inclination to fight. Both sides engaged in routine encampment activities, such as Washington's daily issuance of General Orders. In varying degree, the General dictated these to his secretary or penmen and reviewed and commented on drafts, likely providing more guidance to their creation than other reports or letters. Orders often detailed the next day's movements and other activities. Sometimes Washington announced impending courts martial; other times he announced sentences handed down. He relayed news from other departments and from Congress when it pertained to his men. General Orders also included encampment instructions and alerts in advance of mass movements.[44]

On Friday, September 5, Washington circulated a momentous set of General Orders. Appalled by British atrocities at the Maryland-Delaware border and responding to Howe's audacity, Washington employed language that reached beyond the usual instructions and declarations. In a rare instance during the Revolution, Washington threw down a gauntlet to his army and his countrymen—a challenge intended not only to be read aloud to his men but for publication in newspapers. He declared the enemy's target to be Philadelphia: "'Tis what they last year strove to effect; but they were happily disappointed." Washington stressed that all was at stake. "Now is the time for our most strenuous exertions," he pleaded:

> One bold stroke will free the land from rapine, devastations & burnings, and female innocence from brutal lust and violence. . . . Now is the time to reap the fruits of all our toils and dangers! If we behave like men, this third Campaign will be our last. Ours is the main army; to us our Country looks for protection. The eyes of all America and Europe are turned upon us, as on those by whom the event of the war is to be determined. And the General assures his countrymen and fellow soldiers, that he believes the critical, the important moment is at hand, which demands their most spirited exertions in the field. There glory waits to crown the brave—and peace—freedom and happiness will be the rewards of victory. Animated by motives like these, soldiers fighting in the cause of innocence, humanity and justice, will never give way, but, with undaunted resolution, press on to conquest. And this, the General assures himself, is the part the American forces now in arms will act; and thus acting, he will insure their success.[45]

Three years earlier to the day, John Adams and George Washington had met for the first time in Philadelphia as delegates to the First Continental Congress. Throughout much of 1777, Adams had accepted the strategy of a war of posts, but by early September he had changed his mind. Doubt was creeping into his letters home. "He is very prudent, you know," Adams, referring to the General, reminded his wife. "By my own inward feelings, I judge, I should put more to risk if I were in his shoes, but perhaps he is right." Adams, bearing in mind the supposed involvement of patriot militia from four states, mistakenly believed Washington's Continental army greatly outnumbered Howe, who, Adams assumed, commanded no more than ten thousand men. "I am sick of Fabian systems in all quarters," Adams wrote. Washington's September 5 orders starkly corrected Adams's misapprehension, greatly impressing the Massachusetts delegate. "The General has harangued his army, and published in general orders," he told his spouse, "in order to prepare their minds for something great."[46]

Henry Laurens considered the message "a very sensible animating public order."[47] Knowing Washington meant the document for widespread publication, Laurens sent a copy to South Carolina's Committee of Safety. That gesture or a similar move by another delegate assured that this would be a most public order. Washington's stirring words first reached Americans through the *Pennsylvania Packet,* which published a large excerpt four days later. "A gentleman has favored us with the General Orders of our great and illustrious commander," wrote the editors, "the prop and glory of this Western World, issued to his Army . . . which we publish on account of the virtuous and noble sentiments they contain." The *Pennsylvania Gazette* and the *Post* reproduced Washington's remarks the following day in Philadelphia in issues distributed around and beyond the city.[48]

The orders' contents circulated widely over the next four weeks. Marylanders read them on September 16; Massachusetts residents, two days later. The following week Connecticut and New Hampshire newspapers reprinted the declaration. The *Virginia Gazette* was later than most, publishing the orders on September 26 and October 3. South Carolina published the orders one week later.[49] The readership included Howe's men. Captain John André wrote to his mother about the General's statement of purpose. "He had in an involv'd Rhapsody spirited up his men to a belief they were to exterminate the British army," he told her. "I believe they never had been wound up to such a pitch of confidence."[50]

The General Orders of September 5 sought to inspire the Continental army and the American people to resist the British advance. Thanks to public officials and journalists, he lit fires of enthusiasm for The Cause. But no recipients of his message meant more than the eighteen thousand Continentals and militiamen concentrated within a few miles of his Quaker Hill headquarters. The army's rank and file heard Washington's orders the day he wrote them. As they stood in formation or perched within their works on the north and east banks of serpentine Red Clay Creek, selected officers shouted out their commanding general's challenge:

"If we behave like men, this third campaign will be our last."

CHAPTER FIVE

"Manuvring Appears to be Their Plan"

September 6 to September 11, 1777

Washington dismounted from Blueskin on Saturday afternoon, September 6, and walked with a retinue of aides into a two-story red brick residence. The house, built in two sections beginning in 1750, belonged to Quaker spiritual leader and miller Daniel Byrnes.[1] Located on the southwest bank of White Clay Creek, the home made a head-scratching choice for even a temporary headquarters, what with British troops on that side of the waterway and Continentals pickets across the creek from the dwelling, arrayed on the higher eastern banks.

Washington chose the house for a 5:00 P.M. council of war with his general officers.[2] No minutes from or details of this event survive. If the General chose to reiterate his general orders of the day, he may have skipped talk of burying offal from the camp slaughterhouses at proper distances from the men or remonstrated against letting dray horses loose to graze in the fields. He more likely would have remarked upon "suspicious characters" in camp in a bid to rid his armies of spies. The most draconian part of the latest General Orders most certainly would have fostered discussion before Washington arrived, if not after:

> [A]ny officers, or soldiers, so far lost to all shame as basely to quit their post without orders, or shall skulk from danger, or offer to retreat before order is given for so doing, from proper authority, of a superior officer; they are to be instantly shot down, as a just punishment to themselves, and for examples to others.[3]

The commander in chief was stressing duty in life and death terms as he placed his defensive position on heightened alert. Based on the record, Washington emphasized the inevitability, if not the imminence, of an attack by Howe. His Wilmington headquarters had stood four miles from the closest flank of the Red Clay Creek line. The distance had not been extreme, but it was greater than at most other sites at which Washington had headquartered relative to where his army was encamped. Likely for this reason, Washington had left his Quaker Hill headquarters and chosen a site toward the middle of his Red Clay Creek defense.

John Laurens and Peter Presley Thornton entered the council officially as Washington's newest aides de camp; their appointments had been approved by Congress and announced in General Orders that Saturday. This was also a special day for the Marquis de Lafayette. He departed Wilmington the day he departed his teens. The enthusiastic Frenchman—the youngest major general in American history—turned twenty.

Washington's concern materialized into direct threat thirty-six hours later. On the morning of September 8, pickets informed him that a large body of British troops was advancing directly on Christiana Bridge. He interpreted Howe's advance as a "seeming intention of attacking our post near New port." Alarm guns put the Continentals and militia on high alert. Within an hour the fourteen thousand American soldiers on the east side of Red Clay Creek had assumed the defensive, with artillerists at their guns. Some two thousand Pennsylvania militiamen were positioned to the rear of the Continentals, several miles northeast of Red Clay Creek. One brigade waited near Hockessin Meetinghouse, while a thousand or so more Continentals remained closer to White Clay Creek; most of Weedon's brigade from Greene's division crossed Red Clay Creek and advanced to a hill near a Presbyterian church. "We waited for them all day," the General noted.[4]

Hardly a gun was fired the entire day. Howe had never intended to assault Washington's strongest position. Deserters having provided him with some details of Washington's Red Clay Creek defenses, Howe demonstrated in front, feigning a direct assault as he simultaneously filed off to the north to flank the Americans on their right. His army formed into three divisions under Lieutenant Generals Charles Cornwallis and Wilhelm von Knyphausen and Major General James Grant. Howe had all three on the move for most of the morning. "A very disagreeable march," complained a Redcoat in his diary. The men on the march, he added, were "without anything to eat, and almost suffocated with dust, owing to the vast train of baggage wagons and cattle that were in front." An aide to Howe well understood his commander's orders. "We impatiently look forward to the end of these maneuvers," wrote Friedrich Münchhausen from Howe's headquarters on September 8, intuiting that Washington would be forced to retreat or to meet General Howe on ground of the Briton's choosing. "Either would mean the ruin of his army," Howe's aide added.[5]

Howe had stopped the movements by morning's end. By not pushing to turn Washington's flank, Howe was attempting to achieve what he had not been able to do in New Jersey months before. He sought to entice Washington to attack. Nearly half the daylight hours of September 8 were uneventful, primarily because the Americans had not detected the mass northward shift by British troops. Once Washington realized what Howe had just done, he was not going to remain on his Red Clay Creek line. As Howe's aide had discerned, Washington's options were to head northwest to battle Howe or retreat toward Philadelphia.

They all had underestimated Washington. The American commander would neither withdraw nor would he be drawn into Howe's trap. He had selected Red Clay Creek as his main line of defense, even though the southernmost portion of the Brandywine, four miles directly behind his defense, had steeper heights and a deeper channel. Washington chose not to post cavalry or small bodies of infantry upstream on Red Clay Creek, evidence that this was not to be his final defense. That afternoon Weedon's Virginians and one of Howe's columns had maneuvered within sight of each other very briefly, alerting Washington to Howe's flanking gambit. Washington anticipated that Howe merely "meant to amuse us in Front."

Headquarters notified Congress about the resurgent British threat. At 3:00 A.M. on Tuesday, September 9, John Laurens or another aide sped an alarm to Philadelphia that closed with "whether a dislike to our situation, or a desire to steal a march, I know not, but they have, and are still doing their utmost to file off to the right of us." Oddly, this particular "express" took over twelve hours to reach Congress, whereupon all present felt ill at ease. Their immediate solution to the communication gap was to inform Washington of a new resolution indicating that he was to send at least two messages to Congress each day, preferably expressed from headquarters. "Genl Howe has Stolen a march upon our great General," a delegate told a member of their state's safety committee. "He must be stopped this night or tomorrow morning [or] he will be on our Skirts. We are all now talking of adjourning to the Country. The question is, where?"[6]

Washington rendered that concern moot. After a late-night discussion among the generals (Lafayette dubbed it "a nocturnal council of war"), the commander in chief sent marching orders at about 2:00 A.M. on September 9; the Americans marched away well before sunrise. He ordered his entire army to reposition behind the Brandywine—not four miles directly behind but between ten and fourteen road miles northeast of their Red Clay Creek defense. (Initially defending the Brandywine near its confluence with the Delaware at Wilmington would have forced Washington to choose between attacking and retreating.) The Red Clay Creek defense had assured Washington that third option. He apparently knew all along about what he called "The Heights of Brandiwine," strong defensive ground of greater elevation on the great creek's east side than the opposite bank. Eight days earlier, he had ordered five hundred Pennsylvania militia to defend those Pennsylvania heights, specifically covering two of the many fords that traversed the Brandywine.[7]

Howe started out September 9 closer to the Pennsylvania mid-waters of the Brandywine than Washington but chose to idle until late in the afternoon when intelligence reached him about Washington's movements. Realizing Washington held the advantage to reach the heights of the Brandywine, Howe focused his army northwest of the Crown force's most advanced position near Hockessin Meetinghouse. Beginning at noon that Tuesday, Washington's army turned from north to east and splashed across the Brandywine at several points, including Chads's Ford, the primary passage over the river able to accommodate artillery.[8] With the British army seven miles west of the Brandywine at Kennett Square, and Philadelphia twenty-five road miles east of the creek, the American army occupation of the eastern heights and the terrain east and therefore behind it, assured Philadelphia's safety for at least two additional days due simply to distance. The Brandywine was the most significant watercourse west of the Schuylkill for sixty miles. Washington was out of fallback options. This is where he would make his stand.

Washington and most of his headquarters passed the Brandywine via Gibson's Ford (later known as Smith's Ford). Apparently assured that the British posed no imminent threat to the American redeployment, Washington and an unknown number of subordinate generals and staff briefly stopped on the east side of the ford at Jacob Smith's stone house, briefly enjoying the miller's hospitality before moving on. The headquarters moved northeast, entering Pennsylvania and picking up and following Ring Road northward until that artery T'ed into the east-west portion of the Nottingham Road.[9]

If standard procedure prevailed, Captain Gibbs and the Life Guard arranged the next headquarters stop. The September 9 choice was the home of Benjamin Ring, northwest of the T and nearly a mile east of the Brandywine at Chads's Ford. Benjamin Ring was unusual for a Quaker, having served in the Chester County militia. He owned 150 acres surrounding his modest two-story home where he resided with his pregnant wife and seven children ages two to eighteen, plus an indentured servant. Given the General's entourage of thirty, tents quickly clustered around the dwelling. Washington rewarded his men that Tuesday with a gill of rum for an efficient and swift relocation of fourteen thousand Continentals joining three thousand Pennsylvania militia, most of the latter already in position.[10]

The heights were the only advantage of this portion of the Brandywine. The large creek had several known fords above and below Chads's Ford. During the last ten days of summer, troops realistically could expect to be able to cross in many other places without resorting to a ford—although fords offered the benefit of roads leading to and from them, a necessity for wagons and artillery. Washington had a tall order to not only cover known fords, but also to pre-empt Howe's favored tactic of trying to outflank him. Washington yearned to do so by drawing Howe toward his strongest position where the Americans could inflict so disproportionate a number of casualties upon Howe's army as to force him to change course. Without admitting or perhaps even realizing it, Washington was seeking a battle like his January 2, 1777, victory at Trenton's Assunpink Creek, albeit on a scale that would devastate Howe.

Howe, on the other hand, was seeking to replay the tactics used at the Battle of Long Island. He had no intention or desire to conduct a major frontal assault. From Kennett Square few convenient roads led to the closest crossings south of Chads's Ford, where the waters were expected to be deeper. Howe spent Wednesday, September 10, studying roads and fords upstream from where he knew Washington had concentrated his army at Chads's Ford.

Not oblivious to the ingredients of Howe's success against him in New York, the General posted troops at fords above and below Chads's. Washington posted three thousand Pennsylvania militia across Harlan's, Chandler's, and Thomas Gibson's Fords, all traversing the twisting Brandywine for three miles south of Chads's Ferry.[11] The decision was double-edged. It made sense to place the least trained, least disciplined, and therefore least reliable division south of Chads's Ford, where those troops were least likely to be threatened. But, given that force's numerical strength and its ties to Pennsylvania, knowledge and talent in that vast body—even if among only a few men—was underutilized, as only one officer was known to have been tapped for detached service as a scout or guide.

At noon on September 10, with his army arrayed along an eight-mile middle segment of the Brandywine, Washington realized that well-known thoroughfares he could not possibly cover simultaneously from his current position crossed the creek. These included the Lancaster Road, seven miles off his right flank, and the King's Road through Delaware, six miles below his left flank. By noon that day, the General became aware that British patrols had appeared at both of those extreme locales, simultaneously sighted north and south. "Manuvring appears to be their plan," Washington's secretary, Robert H. Harrison, told Congress, channeling his superior's thoughts if not dictating his exact words. "I hope, notwithstanding, that we shall be able to find out their real—intended route & to defeat their purposes."[12]

North of the militia, 12,500 Continental infantrymen in a dozen brigades concentrated on the heights for five miles. All but Maxwell's brigade took positions east of the Brandywine. Nathanael Greene's division covered Chads's Ferry, a crossing three hundred yards south of Chads's Ford; this ferry not only offered opposing troops a chance to wade across but also an access road. The other Virginia division, under General Stephen, was protecting Chads's Ford by primarily being posted above the Nottingham Road, with General Wayne's division mirroring Stephen's position on the south side of the road. The Chads house stood off the right flank of Stephen's division; north of that dwelling extended General Sullivan's division of two Maryland brigades with General Stirling's Pennsylvania and New Jersey brigades directly east of and behind Sullivan's men. General Nash's North Carolina brigade also took a reserve position behind Greene's and Wayne's divisions. Most of the Light Dragoon brigade assumed a reserve role on the Nottingham Road east of headquarters, intermixed with artillery companies that could not reasonably be placed in battery on the heights above and below Chads's Ford.

Upstream of the militia, the massed force of Continentals covered six creek crossings, including Brinton's Ford, protected by the flanks of Sullivan's and Stirling's divisions. Washington decided to block the three fords along the next three and a half miles of heights of the Brandywine above Brinton's with individual regiments—all from Sullivan's division. Above this region, the upper waters of the Brandywine divided into branches flowing west and northeast. Washington was aware of these branches; he knew they each had their own sets of crossings, and that access roads ran between both branches. He determined that five miles of protection north of his position was the extent he could cover with any degree of strength. He chose not to place troops and artillery at either branch.

The first crossing of the western branch left undefended by the Americans was called Trimble's Ford, a little over two road miles from Washington's right flank at Buffington's Ford. Trimble's Ford was essentially indefensible from the northern—that is, the American—side due to a dominating ridge opposite the stream. From there British artillery could devastate any American detachment attempting to cover that crossing. And another viable crossing of the western branch existed a mile upstream. A decision to place troops at Trimble's Ford would necessitate thinning that force at least to overlook the next ford over from it.

The other branch of Brandywine Creek suggested a different scenario. The commonly named Jeffries's or Jeffrey's Ford—both labels a corruption of the name of the Jefferis family, owners of the surrounding land, which included Jefferis's Ford (that crossing's more appropriate name)—presented a low, flat stretch of ground west of the ford while on the eastern (American) side rose a formidable artillery position, a height with room for several cannons. This eastern branch of the Brandywine flowed southwest and three feet deep at this crossing—not a splashing passage by any means. The greatest impediment to covering this ford was distance; although merely one and a half miles above Sullivan's flank at Buffington's Ford, where the two branches met, forming the main course of the Brandywine, a deficient road network doubled that distance when it came to moving cannons and troops. As at the western branch, garrisoning Jefferis's Ford guaranteed no means of resisting a British flanking column because Taylor's Ford was less than two miles upstream. At the cost of an additional hour of marching, a British column could bypass a Jefferis's Ford defense.

Although no record of the event exists, a council of war at the Ring house on Wednesday, September 10—if one had not already transpired the day before—likely took place, as a battle appeared imminent. Topics discussed during the emergent Monday night council behind Red Clay Creek would naturally have carried over to the Brandywine. Howe's September 8 maneuver against the Red Clay Creek defensive line had to stand out in Washington's memory. His British counterpart had proven two days earlier that he preferred a feint and flank to a direct assault against a defensive line on higher ground fronted by a natural moat. What Washington did not do for the remainder of September 10 would be debated for centuries afterwards—he did not send a scouting party across the river and post those men at all northward and southward roads from Kennett Square and between there and Chads's Ford. Instead, he relied upon pickets from the forces stationed at each ford to penetrate westward to detect the presence and destination of any enemy troops north of the Nottingham Road. Regardless, it would not be possible to gainsay the destination of any Crown column detected on those roads thanks to the several fords defended by American troops for four miles north of Chads's Ford. Any of these fords could become Howe's object of attack with an overwhelming force, particularly the northernmost fords Sullivan was blocking with single regiments. These vulnerable positions were accessible from east-west roads intersecting with the north-south thoroughfare parallel to and west of the Brandywine, and compared to a broad sweeping flank march around all of them, Sullivan's fords would spare Howe half the time and marching distance to gain possession of any of them.

Just as important, if not more so, Washington never revealed, and perhaps had not seriously considered, a revised plan for what he expected to be inevitable: the need to thwart a Howe advance that penetrated deeply enough to seize an uncovered ford across the Brandywine from which to attempt to threaten the rear of the American defense. Several individual heights loomed along the Bradford-Birmingham Great Road—shortened locally to the "Birmingham Road"—a half-century-old major thoroughfare running north-south that roughly paralleled Brandywine Creek over a mile to the east.[13] Any of these heights from Jefferis's Ford to Dilworth were defensive positions whose suitability was limited by inadequate road networks connecting American positions along the Brandywine to those hills.

General Maxwell's picked corps was assigned the dangerous role of the lone force west of the Brandywine to engage Howe's advance. Maxwell had been maligned and outright mocked by parties who perceived him as having mishandled his men at Cooch's Bridge on September 3. Washington obviously did not share those sentiments, since he designated Maxwell's command the point of first contact for this long-building clash. Maxwell had not performed poorly in Washington's eyes. In fact, he may have bought the Continental army five days of big battle preparation. On September 3 Washington had seen a spirited and game commander with a new corps stand fast for hours against a vastly larger force. Had Maxwell been the pushover naysayers described, Howe might have threatened Washington's position immediately rather than five days later.

Headquarters personnel at the Ring house reached thirty, including the household staff that had been serving Washington for more than two years. (Washington ran up a bill for 180 individual meals served during his sojourn there: "30 person eating at 6 different times," stated the receipt.)[14] These individuals bustled through that Wednesday, September 10, in the dwelling and in the hamlet of headquarters tents dotting Benjamin Ring's yards. Anticipation was running high for the first great match against Crown forces in a year. Throwing in was Colonel Charles Pinckney, one of two South Carolinians sent to Quaker Hill a few weeks earlier as envoys of Continental Congress delegate Henry Laurens. Another participant was Major General Arthur St. Clair—two months removed from his inglorious July 5 abandonment of Fort Ticonderoga. St. Clair served as Washington's mediator, presenting letters and requests to Congress. Pinckney and St. Clair increased Washington's military family to at least eighteen volunteer and paid officers.

Washington's largest staff to date clearly was efficient administratively. But how would these officers perform in battle? Only Harrison and Tilghman had been a part of Washington's headquarters during Howe's victorious New York campaign, and only Fitzgerald had joined in time to serve the General with the other two during the smaller battles at Trenton and at Princeton. None of the other dozen officers at the Ring house had worked with Washington during the crash and commotion of a confusing, smoke-laden, and deafening battle fought by as many as thirty thousand opposing troops. The stark fact was that the Grand Army and its headquarters generally were shy of combat experience; only one man in eight of either entity had served in a major battle in the same roles they assumed along the Brandywine.

Washington welcomed what volunteer officers could bring to headquarters, though he was less inclined to accommodate politicians, toward whom he maintained a politely agreeable mien. This diffidence extended to the now requisite two reports per day to Congress. Defending heights with Philadelphia merely twenty-five miles distant invited the inevitable. Members of the Continental Congress personally roamed and meddled within his lines from the day after he arrived at the Heights of the Brandywine. Delegate Thomas Burke of North Carolina likely visited under the guise of inspecting the independent brigade from his state. Burke regaled a recipient in a September 10 letter penned from "Head Quarters near Shad's Ford" regarding the anticipation building for "a very important engagement" to occur at any time. "I have delayed my journey home for some time in expectation of this (now expected) event," Burke wrote, "and hope before many hours to have the satisfaction of seeing our enemies put to rout."[15]

Washington's pre-battle preparations included fixing or eradicating nuisances. General Orders now included warnings to end indiscriminate firing of weapons in camp so that alarm gun blasts could be heard and understood, to refrain from destroying farmers' fences for firewood, to keep two days' worth of cooked provisions on hand, to post pickets in front of every division, and to send all but the most necessary wagons to the rear. Washington's correspondence addressed complaints about ostensible inequities of distribution by the commissary department, efforts to hustle in reinforcements tarrying outside Pennsylvania, and enduring the problems presented by suspect militia.[16]

Delaware and Pennsylvania militia were a constant headache. The Delaware militia failed to nip at the heels of Howe's turning movement into Pennsylvania as the General had ordered. Washington vented to their overall commander, Brigadier General Caesar Rodney, about what he saw as "so irregular a spirit and temper" which "prevails among your Militia." The commander in chief chided Rodney about how "the public has suffered monstrous impositions" due to his unit's lack of a sense of duty even in defending their home state. Subordinate generals could not help but unfavorably compare the militia west of the Schuylkill to more impressive counterparts in New Jersey.[17]

The near-universal characterization of the Continentals portrayed a well-rested army in high spirits and yearning for action. General Nathanael Greene begged to differ. The division commander told his wife, Caty, on September 10 that he was physically spent: "I was on Horse back for upwards of thirty hours and never closed my Eyes for nearly forty." Greene lost sleep when a dusty bed triggered his asthma. He assured his wife he felt "finely refreshed" that Wednesday, which could not possibly have been true. Greene was shouldering more responsibility than other division commanders on September 10; he was tagged as "Major General of the Day" designated to process the General Orders from headquarters.[18]

The troops were less beleaguered than their officers. At noon, alarm guns were fired to summon soldiers at ease in camps near Birmingham Meetinghouse two to four road miles east of their Brandywine defenses. Units marched to designated fords and took assigned posts on the heights. They remained on guard all that quiet afternoon. As Wednesday waned, it became obvious there would be no battle that day. Leaving an evening and overnight observation post, the rest of the Continentals and militia pulled away eastward from the Brandywine and bedded down.[19]

Late Wednesday night or early on Thursday morning, September 11, Washington hedged his bet that Howe would repeat his Delaware maneuver and attempt to outflank the Americans to the north. This was a wise wager; the upper Brandywine would be easier to ford, even with two branches to cross. To ensure the safety of his right (northern) flank, Washington chose a Chester County militia officer, Major Joseph Spear, to position himself between the forks and to report to headquarters what he saw and did not see on Thursday morning.[20]

Washington was relying on an officer native to the region and its roads. Most important was positioning Major Spear between the forks. From Buffington's Ford at the junction of the two branches of the Brandywine down to Chads's Ford and below, American infantry patrols were expected to scout west of the fords from where they were stationed. Those scouts would be able to spot any flanking enemy columns marching northward on the Great Valley Road, but detection could not guarantee that the troops were attempting to flank Sullivan's defense until the head of that column passed the adjoining road to Wistar's and Buffington's Fords; that thirty-six-year-old county road bisected the Great Valley Road a mere two miles south of Trimble's Ford.[21] Major Spear's identification of Crown forces within two miles of the west branch of the Brandywine would confirm that those troops were attempting to outflank the American position. Any sighting south of that two-mile mark confirmed nothing.

Reaction time was paramount. With Washington's army spread along eight miles of fords, early detection was crucial to concentrating multiple divisions to oppose a numerically strong flanking column and thwart any attempt to gain Washington's side of the Brandywine. At minimum, troops would need upwards of three hours to pull a countering force from near Chads's Ford, align those men eastward toward the Birmingham Road, and quicktime that force eight miles to a threatened ford in the northern sector of the waterway. Deploying those men would take a minimum of thirty more minutes. Spear's instructions were not entirely revealed, but they may have included scouting from Trimble's Ford down the Great Valley Road that ran generally southward four miles to its junction with the east-west Street Road.[22]

A sunless dawn arrived a few minutes after 6:00 A.M. on Thursday, September 11, 1777. An ominous fog seeped into Chester County, heaviest around waterways, of which the Brandywine was the largest. The sounds of battle emanated from three miles east of Kennett Square at Welch's Tavern on the Nottingham Road. For two hours, the Battle of Brandywine appeared to be isolated along the Nottingham Road, closing on Chads's Ford as Maxwell's brigade slowly gave ground eastward to Howe's advance under Lieutenant General Wilhelm von Knyphausen. By 8:30 A.M. Crown forces had achieved a threatening position at the ford. Fifteen minutes later Knyphausen's artillery had unlimbered on the heights west of Brandywine and had begun an artillery duel with Knox's guns, which were ensconced on the ridge behind the Chads house, just north of the ford. Continental army headquarters secretary Robert H. Harrison informed Congress of the start of the fight with a brief letter signed, sealed, and on its way to Philadelphia by 9:00 A.M.[23]

Washington spent the mid-morning hours inspecting his defenses, largely on foot, according to Lafayette. Only Colonel Pickering remembered Washington on horseback that morning but offered no description of him or his horse. Likely he was on Blueskin, the dappled Arabian he had saddled and ridden at Princeton eight months earlier. British Major Patrick Ferguson later claimed that at Brandywine he had had Washington in his sights and well within killing range, but chose to spare the officer riding "a very good bay horse." But the general that Ferguson spared likely was not Washington atop his white mount—even if Ferguson were colorblind he could not have made that mistake.[24]

But death still stalked Washington at Brandywine. He spent considerable time near the main American artillery battery, positioned on high ground above the Chads house, six-hundred yards northeast of the ford bearing the householder's name. As he studied similarly elevated British guns on the heights opposite, the General, surrounded by aides, attracted the attention of the farm's superintendent and other civilians. Gawkers gravitated toward the knot of headquarters personnel. Noting the resulting crowd, enemy artillerists quickly spotted Washington. Cannon fire erupted. "Gentleman, you perceive that we are attracting the notice of the enemy," Washington told the onlookers. "I think you had better retire." He needed to say no more. A Loyalist in the Queen's Rangers, disappointed to see a

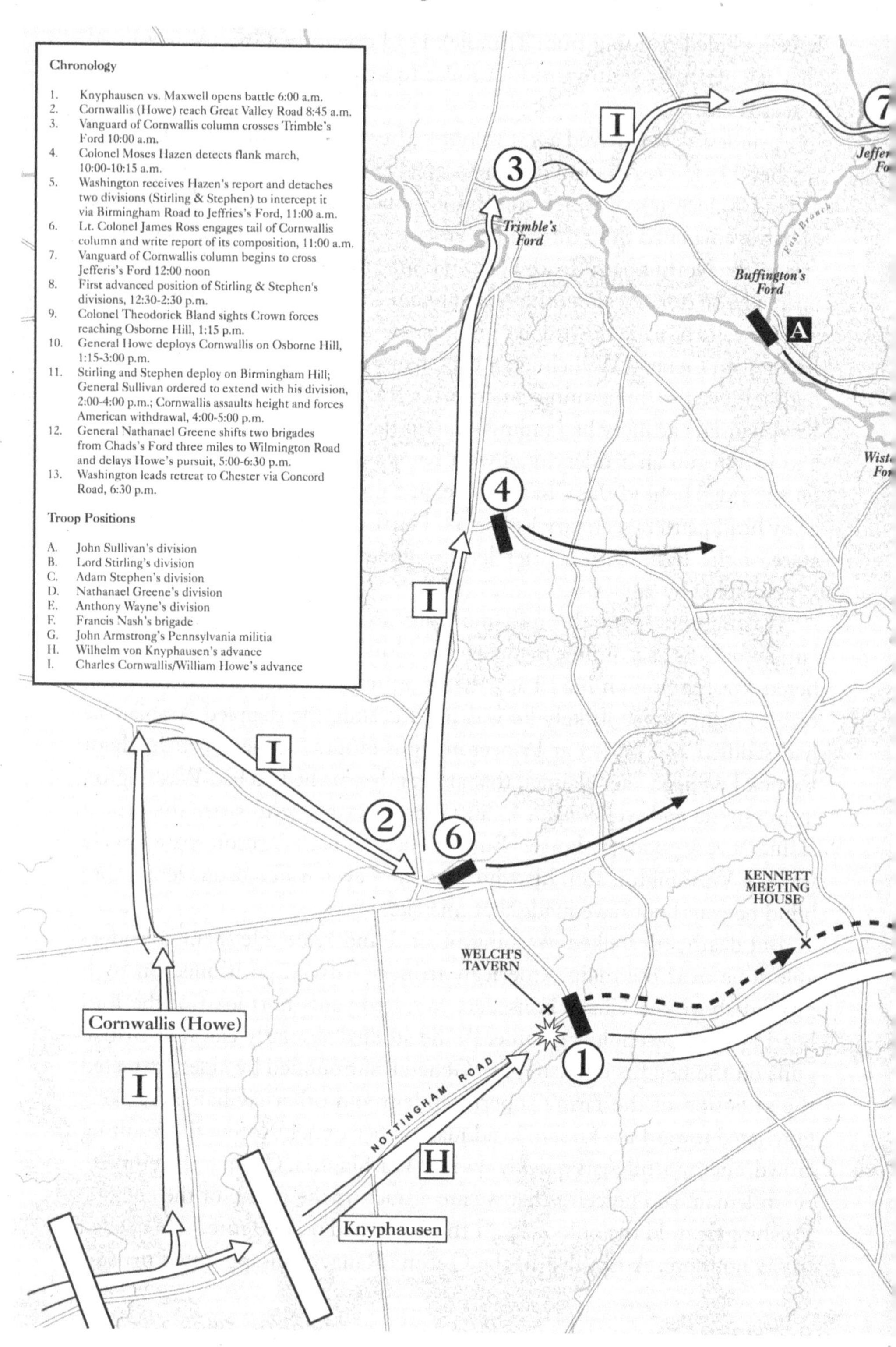
Chronology
1. Knyphausen vs. Maxwell opens battle 6:00 a.m.
2. Cornwallis (Howe) reach Great Valley Road 8:45 a.m.
3. Vanguard of Cornwallis column crosses Trimble's Ford 10:00 a.m.
4. Colonel Moses Hazen detects flank march, 10:00-10:15 a.m.
5. Washington receives Hazen's report and detaches two divisions (Stirling & Stephen) to intercept it via Birmingham Road to Jeffries's Ford, 11:00 a.m.
6. Lt. Colonel James Ross engages tail of Cornwallis column and write report of its composition, 11:00 a.m.
7. Vanguard of Cornwallis column begins to cross Jefferis's Ford 12:00 noon
8. First advanced position of Stirling & Stephen's divisions, 12:30-2:30 p.m.
9. Colonel Theodorick Bland sights Crown forces reaching Osborne Hill, 1:15 p.m.
10. General Howe deploys Cornwallis on Osborne Hill, 1:15-3:00 p.m.
11. Stirling and Stephen deploy on Birmingham Hill; General Sullivan ordered to extend with his division, 2:00-4:00 p.m.; Cornwallis assaults height and forces American withdrawal, 4:00-5:00 p.m.
12. General Nathanael Greene shifts two brigades from Chads's Ford three miles to Wilmington Road and delays Howe's pursuit, 5:00-6:30 p.m.
13. Washington leads retreat to Chester via Concord Road, 6:30 p.m.
Troop Positions
A. John Sullivan's division
B. Lord Stirling's division
C. Adam Stephen's division
D. Nathanael Greene's division
E. Anthony Wayne's division
F. Francis Nash's brigade
G. John Armstrong's Pennsylvania militia
H. Wilhelm von Knyphausen's advance
I. Charles Cornwallis/William Howe's advance
Trimble's Ford
East Branch
Buffington's Ford
KENNETT MEETING HOUSE
WELCH'S TAVERN
NOTTINGHAM ROAD
Cornwallis (Howe)
Knyphausen

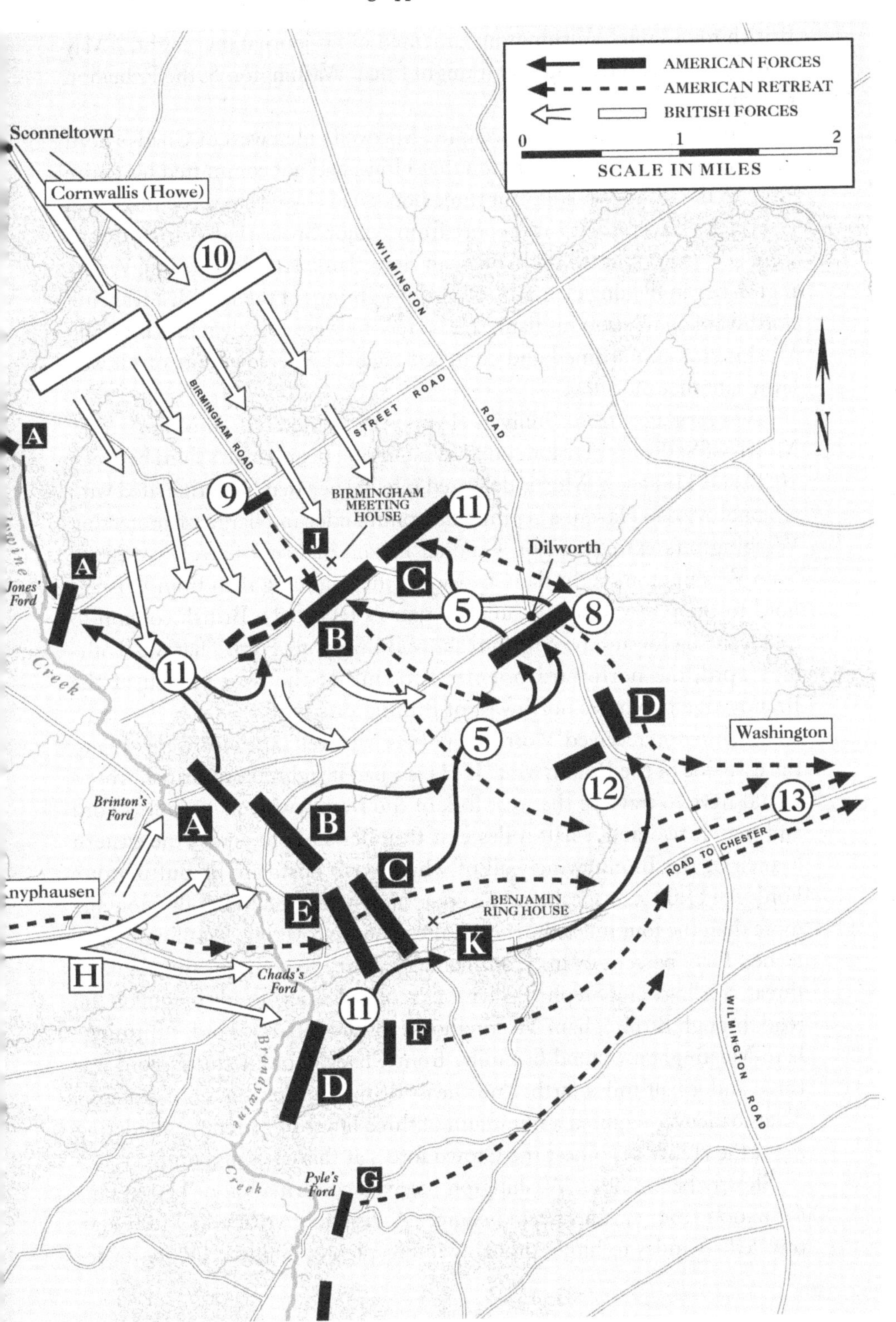
AMERICAN FORCES
AMERICAN RETREAT
BRITISH FORCES
0
1
2
SCALE IN MILES
Sconneltown
Cornwallis (Howe)
10
WILMINGTON
ROAD
STREET ROAD
BIRMINGHAM ROAD
N
A
9
BIRMINGHAM
MEETING
HOUSE
J
11
Dilworth
Jones' Ford
A
C
5
8
B
11
Creek
D
5
Washington
12
Brinton's Ford
A
B
13
ROAD TO CHESTER
C
nyphausen
E
BENJAMIN
RING HOUSE
K
H
Chads's Ford
11
F
WILMINGTON ROAD
D
Brandywine
Creek
Pyle's Ford
G

British round miss Washington, lamented in his journal that night, "[M]y prayers went with the ball that it might finish Washington & the Rebellion together."[25]

The protracted fight that occupied Maxwell's men west of Chads's Ford must have convinced Washington that Howe had not committed his entire army to the frontal assault. But three hours had passed since the first clash at Welch's Tavern, with no report from Major Spear that British troops were advancing toward the American right flank. At midmorning, Washington began fielding claims by others of sightings of the British advancing northward on roads to his flank. Those reports were quickly refuted, leaving Washington uninformed and confused regarding deployments of Howe's army late that morning.

Two messages from Sullivan cleared the General's fog. Major Lewis Morris of Sullivan's division found Washington near Chads's Ford between 10:30 and 11:00 A.M. Morris delivered intelligence that had originated with Colonel Moses Hazen, a regimental commander in charge of protecting Washington's extreme right. Colonel Hazen had sent patrols westward from Washington's right flank by way of the adjoining road from Wistar's Ford to the Great Valley Road. The patrols reported a British column to be advancing toward the next ford above Buffington's Ford. That was Trimble's Ford, the northward-oriented crossing of the west branch of the Brandywine two miles northwest of Buffington's Ford.[26]

Washington received Morris's report as Maxwell's men were crossing to the east side of the Brandywine. If Hazen had it right, those British troops would have to traverse the west fork of the Brandywine at Trimble's Ford and march two and a half miles east to Jefferis's Ford across the eastern branch of the Brandywine—all of which were upstream of Buffington's Ford. At 11:00 A.M., realizing he could not stretch Sullivan's division any more than the four miles those men already were covering, Washington detached forty percent of his Continental infantry to confront this flanking threat. Stirling's and Stephen's divisions received orders to advance upon the road through Birmingham Meetinghouse toward Jefferis's Ford.[27] Birmingham Meetinghouse stood five miles from Chads's Ford; Jefferis's Ford was three and a half miles farther northeast of the Quaker house of worship. That maneuver required a minimum of three hours of marching, rendering moot the ability to contest the Crown forces at this crossing point.

Shortly before noon Washington received confirmation of Hazen's information from an unexpected source. A dispatch written at 11:00 A.M. traveled six miles to him—probably intercepted by Sullivan before its delivery to Washington. The report was from Lieutenant Colonel James Ross, who that morning was leading one of at least three infantry scouting detachments from Maxwell's light infantry brigade. Ross's complement had moved westward on Street Road which crossed the Brandywine at Jones's Ford, running parallel and north of the Nottingham Road. From a knoll that served handily as an observation post, Ross spied a massive flanking column of British troops. He was not able to see the head of this column turn from southeast to due north on the Great Valley Road but, scrutinizing the column's remainder, he did count five thousand soldiers and at least sixteen cannons. Ross intuited from the column's change of direction that it was heading toward the fords crossing the branches of the Brandywine above Buffington's Ford. Declaring that he thought General Howe himself to be riding with that force, Ross noted that once across Jefferis's Ford, this column could move southward on the Birmingham Road behind Washington's infantry toward Chester via Dilworth Tavern.[28] The latter locale Washington well knew, as he had already ordered two divisions of four infantry brigades to access the same road heading northward.

Washington now lacked only confirmation from Spear to persuade him that Hazen and Ross were correct. Although Ross's sighting was valuable for assessing numerical strength and artillery power, he struck the enemy column two miles south of where Hazen sighted it, which limited Ross's ability to determine its true destination. Spear had yet to report to Washington regarding any enemy presence between the forks and on the Great Valley Road leading to them. At 12:20 P.M. the General ordered Colonel Theodorick Bland to head upstream from the east side of the creek toward the fords over the forks of the Brandywine; his assignment was to confirm what Hazen's and Ross's intelligence was implying. "It is said the fact is certain," Washington told Bland. "You will send up an intelligent—sensible Officer immediately with a party to find out the truth—What number It consists of, and the Road they are now on." Washington closed by stressing that Bland needed to "be particular in these matters."[29]

Washington did not know that Ross had underestimated the size of the British flanking column. Howe did personally lead this advance of Cornwallis's wing of the army, a column of some nine thousand officers and men stretching more than four miles along the Great Valley Road on the way to crossing the west branch of the Brandywine beyond the flank. Ross merely had observed the trailing half of that movement. By 11:00 A.M., as he was writing his report, Howe's vanguard had already crossed the west fork of the Brandywine at Trimble's Ford and was less than two miles from the bank of the eastern fork. Stephen and Stirling could never reach that area in time to impede the foe or even deploy competitive numbers of troops to contest the Crown forces that most assuredly would be on the American side of Jefferis's Ford before those four brigades of the Grand Army.

Confirmation that Howe had divided his army into two wings spurred an immediate change in Washington's tactics. The hours-long battle west of the Brandywine erroneously convinced Washington that the force directly opposing him lacked the numbers to dominate him in the field. With a detached wing of the British army heading away from Chads's Ford and committed for at least two more hours to a flanking march that Stirling's and Stephen's divisions would be opposing, Washington still had three infantry divisions and three thousand militia opposing Knyphausen's command—the wing of Howe's army deployed along and on each side of the Nottingham Road.

The General's boldness in battle during the Trenton-Princeton campaign imbued him again. At noon he ordered Greene's and Sullivan's divisions to cross the Brandywine and assault Knyphausen's troops. Washington audaciously decided he could dispel the undersized enemy in front of him in time to reverse direction and unite his troops against the other undersized enemy force (through Ross's intelligence, the General believed it to be five thousand enemy troops) attempting to flank him. Over the next hour American soldiers waded westward across the river from Brinton's Ford to below Chads's Ford. The plan called for five brigades from Greene, Sullivan, and Maxwell to reach the western side of the Brandywine, form two columns, and repel Knyphausen.

After a lull exceeding an hour, the battle west of the Brandywine appeared destined to recommence. Toward the last half of the noon hour, before Sullivan had sent any of the troops the General had ordered moved across the Brandywine, Major Spear—the militia officer Washington had assigned to scout the roads on each side of the branches of the Brandywine—finally rode into Sullivan's headquarters. Spear unexpectedly reported seeing no sign of the British above the American right flank. Sullivan later claimed to have been so suspicious of Spear's report that he sent another scout to the region.[30]

Sullivan summarized Spear's intelligence, handed the message to one of the few mounted soldiers at hand, and sent the man southward toward Chads's Ford, followed by Spear himself. Washington received that message shortly before 1:00 P.M. Sullivan's dispatch, which alarmed Washington, said that Spear "heard nothing of the Enemy about the Forks of the

Brandywine & is Confident they are not in that Quarter." Sullivan relayed that Spear had seen nothing all the way to Welch's Tavern, suggesting that no enemy troops had been on a flank march during the middle or late morning hours. Despite his doubts about Spear's accuracy, Sullivan instilled doubt into Washington regarding the earlier intelligence reports by writing, "So that Colo. Hazens Information must be wrong."[31]

Spear's route to Sullivan's headquarters cannot be divined with confidence, for had he accessed the roads west of the Brandywine he most certainly would have encountered an even larger column of British troops than Ross had observed. Spear's claim that he saw no enemy at the forks of the Brandywine is much easier to comprehend—he left the region by 9:30 that morning, before the British came in view marching toward Trimble's Ford. He did not take the Great Valley Road; he could not possibly have done so because he would have ridden headlong into a four-mile column of British and Hessian troops. Instead, Spear must have casually made his way east of the Brandywine, probably crossing Jefferis's Ford or one of the passages above it, and worked his way to Sullivan's headquarters, taking at least two hours to ride fewer than ten miles by the shortest route. He could have ridden to Welch's Tavern, as he claimed to Sullivan, but to do so without sighting British troops required a ride westward on Street Road beginning from Jones's Ford no earlier than 10:45 A.M.

Washington, who strongly trusted Spear, swiftly analyzed and acted upon this intelligence. "The Major's rank, reputation, and knowledge of the country gave him a full claim to credit and attention," the General said. If nearly the entire British army was in front of him, he had ordered a disaster by sending five brigades over the river to challenge an army outnumbering that force by more than three to one—with the Brandywine at the Americans' backs. Washington countermanded the order to attack Knyphausen; the brigades disengaged then retraced their steps to the Brandywine and crossed back to the safety of the east side. Few men were lost in this aborted attack. Washington sent a courier thundering eastward to Stirling and Stephen, likely with orders for them to hold their divisions in place. The messenger found the two near the Brinton farm, two miles southeast of Birmingham Meetinghouse, where their divisions stopped and waited along the road.[32]

Washington needed to sort out the mixed messages he had been receiving and consult with his staff about them. Between 1:00 and 2:00 P.M., headquarters personnel rode east to the Ring house for a meal and a council. No record was made of the discussion, but doubtless the table talk involved weighing conflicting evidence supplied by Hazen, Ross, and Spear as well as other scouting reports by locals. That tangle of competing information had brought about a divided deployment.[33] The Continental army existed as two idle pockets of troops—one consisting of three divisions and two additional brigades aligned along the eastern heights of the Brandywine, the other with divisions halted three and a half road miles behind the other three divisions. Uniting these two bodies of men would require at least an hour.

As Washington and companions were dining, the faultiness of Major Spear's intelligence came to light at 1:15 P.M., when Colonel Bland observed enemy troops advancing down the road from Jefferis's Ford toward Birmingham Meetinghouse. Washington received a dispatch to that effect shortly before 2:00 P.M., followed by a second message from Bland relayed through General Sullivan half an hour later. Bland's dispatches first characterized the British force as "a party of the Enemy," amended in Sullivan's relayed description to "about two Brigades of them." Washington equated that estimate to "Two or three thousand strong," but did not discount Lieutenant Colonel Ross's estimate of five thousand soldiers plus sixteen or more pieces of artillery. He hedged that Ross's estimate was the more accurate, particularly since a postscript to Sullivan's dispatch claimed that Bland "also Says he Saw a Dust Rise back in the Country for above an hour."[34] That road dust must have been kicked up by several thousand stomping feet extending for three miles (hence, "for above an hour") behind those two visible brigades.

Washington ordered what he believed was a numerically superior force to destroy the advancing enemy columns. He sent instructions for Stephen and Stirling to hustle their stationary soldiers north to seize the heights looming above Birmingham Meetinghouse. He told Sullivan to peel his men away from all four fords they had covered, head east toward Birmingham Meetinghouse, and take charge of all three divisions there as ranking major general. Washington fed verbal orders to some of his staff to deliver to the Brandywine defense; other staff personnel remained at headquarters while the General wheeled Blueskin east, intending to ride to the Birmingham force. The clock was passing 3:30 P.M.[35] At this time Stirling's and Stephen's four brigades and supporting artillery had marched up Birmingham Hill from south to north and, aided by the foe's fatigue and dispersion, deployed along the height.

Howe allowed nearly ninety minutes to rest his vanguard troops after an arduous seventeen-mile flank march; just as importantly, he needed to close his ranks. When he did, between 2:30 and 3:00 P.M., the deficiency and inaccuracy of Washington's intelligence network stood out clearly, as nearly nine thousand British officers and privates massed on and near Osborne's Hill, 2,500 yards north of the Americans on Birmingham Hill.

Howe took advantage of his numerical superiority, his men's greater combat experience, and good fortune to roll up half the American position on Birmingham Hill. The tide turned early in the action, as Sullivan was riding away from his division to confer with Stirling and Stephen. Sullivan's second in command, Brigadier General Prudhomme de Borre, proved unfit for the task of aligning the two Maryland brigades of Sullivan's force into a defensive battle line to extend the American left—west—flank under the command of Colonel Elias Dayton from Stirling's division. Hessian grenadiers and British guards descended Osborne Hill and advanced southward, crossed Street Road, and ascended Birmingham Hill at this exact point of American weakness and confusion. The enemy routed the Marylanders of Sullivan's division before those units could firmly form up on the height.[36]

Washington arrived behind Birmingham Hill at approximately 4:30 P.M., probably at the crossroads where Dilworth Tavern stood, as Stirling's and Stephen's men clung to the height north of him against relentless British assaults threatening to destroy this line. The sight of Americans retreating across the fields west of him and the clamor of fighting to his north made clear to the General that the battle was not working in his favor. Earlier, before Sullivan's division had advanced to Birmingham Hill, Washington had allowed Lafayette to lend a hand to Sullivan's men. Lafayette and his aides gained the height and attempted to spur on Stirling's command as that force began to buckle under the pressure of a British and Hessian onslaught. The Frenchman said later that "confusion became extreme." As he was trying to lead a rally, a British slug tore through Lafayette's left calf. The bullet missed bone, but the wound it left took Lafayette out of the battle. With his aides' help, he was lifted onto a horse and taken south to safety.[37]

At the Ring house, Colonel Robert H. Harrison, Washington's military secretary, drafted the second letter of the day to be delivered to the Continental Congress. That report summarized the day so far, underestimating Howe's flanking column as being a third of its actual size. Harrison noted that at 4:30 P.M. he had been able to hear "violent" action to the north of his location as well as a "very Severe Cannonade" west of the Ring house along the Brandywine. "I suppose we shall have a very hot Evening," concluded Harrison. "I hope it will be a happy One."[38]

That night was anything but happy for the Americans. The Birmingham Hill defense collapsed under Howe's attack. Washington personally back-tracked from Dilworth to the fields of the Brinton farm about half a mile down the Wilmington Road from the tavern and crossroads. Crossing the road, he met General Knox, who had positioned two cannons on a knoll to quell the British advance. As the Birmingham Hill defenders were with-drawing, reinforcements arrived in the form of Nathanael Greene's division, which had left the Brandywine defensive line and humped three miles in forty-five minutes to reposition themselves in a concave formation south of the Brinton house with the Wilmington Road running through the mid-dle. Though necessary, that redeployment severely weakened the Brandy-wine defense, allowing Knyphausen to force back the American line there and cross the creek.[39]

Shortly after sunset at 6:30 P.M., Greene's stellar defense held long enough for all American forces behind it to pull back southward to the area where the Nottingham and Wilmington Roads intersected. From there, Washington directed his army eastward on the Nottingham Road, but rather than have them continue due east toward Springfield, then turn southward to Derby, he redirected his men southeast onto the Concord Road, which led to Chester. Perhaps Washington was more certain of this route, a necessity given the blackening night. That choice would necessitate a very short respite at or near Chester, for if the Continental army and its attached Pennsylvania militia dared pause in the vicinity of Chester, Howe would be pressing them against the Delaware River, perhaps as early as Fri-day. But for now, the Continentals were safe as a combination of darkness and exhaustion kept the Crown forces closer to Dilworth overnight.

Defeat at Brandywine was costly but not catastrophic. Howe decimated Washington's infantry, who suffered 1,300 killed, wounded, and captured. The British took eleven pieces of artillery. Howe reported his total losses at 587 officers and men, likely an undercount. No known precedent exists in which an assaulting force on two separate sectors of a battlefield in a battle several hours in length had fewer than half the casualties of the de-fensive force. Most battles end with the assaulting force, victorious or not, losing more troops killed and wounded compared to the defenders. The true butcher's bill at Brandywine may never be known.

Without evidence of heavy pressure against the tail of his retreating army, Washington led his men in darkness toward Chester—not in a rout, but certainly at a quickened pace. The Battle of Brandywine engaged thirty thousand American, British, and German soldiers out of thirty-four thousand present; the fighting lasted twelve hours in the field and proceeded for another four hours of retreat.

Washington must have ridden into Thursday night regretting that Major Spear's wrong intelligence had persuaded him to call off his noon-time offensive against Knyphausen. Ironically, Spear's erroneous message spared Washington from what could have been one of his costliest decisions of the twenty-nine months of war. Washington had impetuously and flippantly thrown five brigades across the Brandywine in hopes of crushing Knyphausen's larger seven thousand-man force. That he expected to do this swiftly and before his flank was breached was nothing short of foolhardy. A bad Spear call led Washington to recall the assault and put the Brandywine between the opposing forces again, rather than at the backs of the outnumbered Americans. And under the influence of Spear's wrongheaded information Washington stalled Stephen and Stirling for an hour south of Birmingham Hill. Had those divisions kept marching, they would have confronted Howe's advance about three miles north of Birmingham Hill, between Osborne Hill and one of the next ridge lines north of that rise. This merely assured Howe the same numerical and experience advantage over two of Washington's divisions, with less assurance that Sullivan or any other American reinforcements would have reached the position in time.

Washington could blame poor intelligence for underestimating the force Howe deployed on Osborne Hill; that behemoth defeated his three-division defense on Birmingham Hill and sealed the British victory. Washington left that battlefield after sunset never appreciating that Howe had upwards of nine thousand men available. Had he known this, Washington certainly would have pulled at least an additional two brigades and more artillery to confront the foe. That would have weakened his Brandywine defensive line, leaving a maximum of two divisions, and still have provided no guarantee that his Birmingham Hill defense would hold.

Brandywine was the first true test of the new Continental army. The fields between Kennett Square and the Brandywine and the rolling landscape between Street Road and Dilworth Tavern revealed how battle-tested, experienced, and well-disciplined Redcoats and Hessians performed against very brave men who less than a year before September 11, 1777, had been toiling as farmers, day laborers, and tradesmen. George Washington lost the Battle of Brandywine due to the Grand Army's inferior performance against Crown forces on maneuvers and in battle, not to misinformation or mismanaged erroneous intelligence. Seventy-five percent of the men in Washington's army fired their guns in anger for the first time on September 11. The Americans proved game but were still no match in a drawn-out, stand-up fight against world-renowned soldiery.

Washington refused to accept that reality. In the wake of his defeat at Brandywine he made a crucial but personal decision. His days as a defensive tactician were over. Henceforth, Washington would attack, not defend. Future battlefields would resemble Trenton and Princeton, not Red Clay Creek and Brandywine.

He was to have an opportunity to test this tactical shift in four days.

GENERAL GEORGE WASHINGTON AND AIDES

Center, George Washington. (*Brooklyn Museum of Art*) Clockwise from top, Alexander Hamilton (*Museum of New York City*), John Laurens (*National Portrait Gallery*), Caleb Gibbs (*founderoftheday.com*), John Cadwalader (*National Portrait Gallery*), Tench Tilghman. (*New York Public Library*)

CONTINENTAL GENERALS

Center, Nathanael Greene. (*Metropolitan Museum of Art*) Clockwise from top, Anthony Wayne (*Philadelphia Museum of Art*), John Sullivan (*Anne S. K. Brown Military Collection, Brown University*), Marquis de Lafayette (*Independence National Historical Park*), William Alexander, Lord Stirling (*New York Public Library*), Henry Knox. (*Metropolitan Museum of Art*)

EUROPEAN VOLUNTEERS FOR AMERICA

Left, Casimir Pulaski (*New York Public Library*), right, Philippe Coudray. (*founderoftheday.com*)

CHALLENGERS TO WASHINGTON'S LEADERSHIP

Clockwise from top, Horatio Gates (*Independence National Historical Park*), Benjamin Rush (*National Portrait Gallery*), Thomas Conway (*Wikipedia Commons*), Thomas Mifflin (*Philadelphia Museum of Art*)

BRITISH AND HESSIAN COMMANDERS

Left to right, Charles Cornwallis, William Howe (*Anne S. K. Brown Military Collection, Brown University*), Wilhelm von Knyphausen. (*New York Public Library*)

BRITISH OCCUPIED PHILADELPHIA

"View of Philadelphia, 28 Nov. 1777," by Archibald Robertson, lieutenant in the Royal Engineers. (*New York Public Library*)

British draftsman William Faden's map of Philadelphia and the surrounding area published in 1778 showing the British defensive lines along the north side of Philadelphia between the Delaware and Schuylkill Rivers. The residence of John Penn, last colonial governor of Pennsylvania is shown along the Schuylkill just above the directional cross at the upper left. (*Library of Congress*)

WASHINGTON'S HEADQUARTERS

Top, left, City Tavern, Philadelphia (*New York Public Library*), right, Henry Antes House, Montgomery County, Pennsylvania. Middle, left, Benjamin Ring House, Brandywine, Pennsylvania, right, Peter Wentz Homestead, Montgomery County, Pennsylvania. (*National Park Service*) Bottom, George Emlen House, Montgomery County, Pennsylvania. (*Jerrye & Roy Klotz, MD/Wikimedia Creative Commons*)

THE BATTLE OF BRANDYWINE

Top, the Battle of Brandywine, September 11, 1777, by Johann Martin Will, published in Germany in 1777. American forces are to the upper center and left, while Cornwallis is shown on his charger at center, directing the British forces at right center. Will made a series of contemporary maps and illustrations of key battles in New York and Pennsylvania. (*Library of Congress*) Bottom, Frederick Yohn's stirring illustration, c. 1898, of the Continental Line challenging a British advance during the battle. (*New York Public Library*)

THE BATTLE OF PAOLI

The battle of Paoli, known to Americans as the "Paoli Massacre," September 20–21, 1777, painted by Xavier della Gatta in 1782 with consultation from a British officer present. (*Museum of the American Revolution*)

THE BATTLE OF GERMANTOWN

The attack on the Chew House during the Battle of Germantown, October 4, 1777, illustrated by Alonzo Chappel in the mid-nineteenth century. (*New York Public Library*)

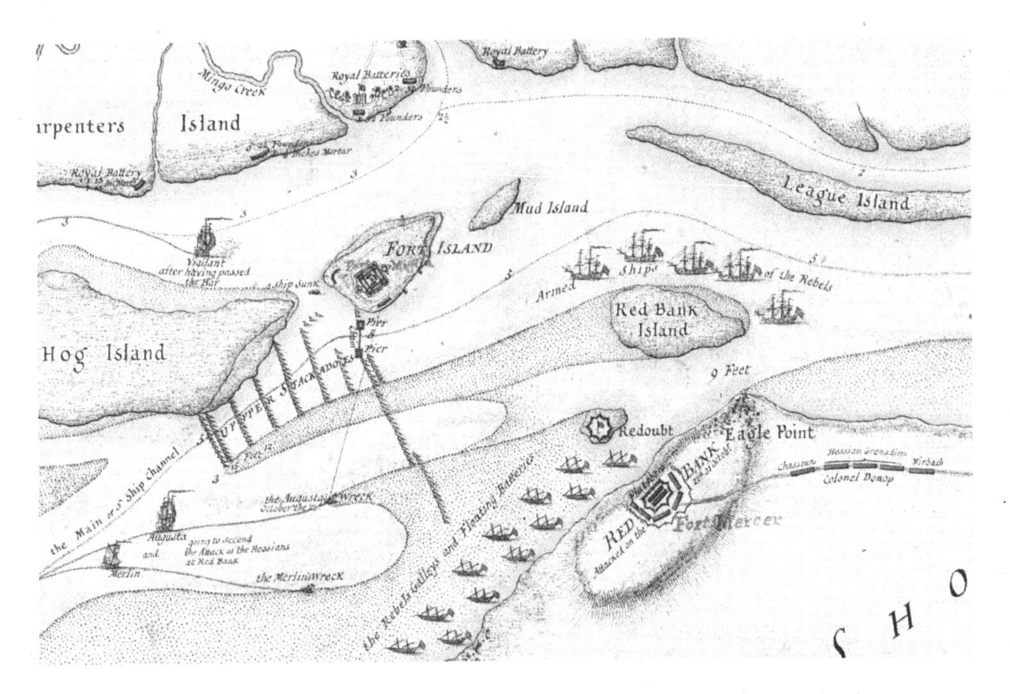

BATTLE FOR CONTROL OF THE DELAWARE RIVER

Top, detail from William Faden's 1778 map of British and Hessian operations around the Delaware River. Red Bank (labelled Fort Mercer in another hand) is at the lower right, along with Colonel Donop's troop movements. Fort Island, "Mud Island," is at center, labelled "Fort Mifflin" in another hand. HMS *Augusta* is shown at lower left, and the location of its explosion is immediately to its right. (*Library of Congress*). Bottom, "Destruction of HMS *Augusta* in the Delaware River, October 23, 1777," by an unidentified British naval officer, circa 1777. The explosion of the ship's magazine could be felt as far as Lancaster, Pennsylvania. (*Naval History and Heritage Command*)

FORT MIFFLIN, "MUD ISLAND"

A satirical print published in London in 1777 of the American defense of "Mud Island." (*Library of Congress*)

THE BATTLE OF WHITEMARSH

The Battle of Whitemarsh, or the "Battle of the Clouds," by Johann Martin Will. Edge Hill is at the right background (2), with Sandy Run at the top left (5); the British infantry and artillery are at right, as well as on Chestnut Hill at the bottom left (6). American forces (4) are shown between Edge Hill and the British at the upper left. The mounted figure at center is unidentified. (*Library of Congress*)

CHAPTER SIX

"A Prospect of Success"

September 12 to September 16, 1777

The Continental army distanced itself from the dangers of the Brandywine battlefield, putting fourteen miles between itself and Crown forces on the Concord Road as night enveloped eastern Pennsylvania. Sixteen thousand Continental and militia soldiers stopped in and near Chester, Pennsylvania's oldest incorporated city, named by William Penn nearly one hundred years before. This was Washington's second overnight stay there in six weeks. He and his staff established headquarters at Mary Withy's tavern on Third Street, seven-hundred yards from the Delaware River.[1] His most valuable wounded officer, General Lafayette, was conveyed by water to Philadelphia and thence to Bethlehem to convalesce.[2]

Washington remained active that night. Near midnight, he instructed his secretary, Lieutenant Colonel Harrison, to draft a letter to Congress summing up the battle, Harrison's first such communique since his 5:00 P.M. battlefield dispatch. Too spent to compose, Harrison recruited Timothy Pickering to write it. Pickering secluded himself in a side room and perhaps an hour later reappeared with a battle chronology, introduced with candor: "I am sorry to inform you that in this day's engagement we have been obliged to leave the enemy masters of the field." The rest of the report accurately recounted Howe's flanking movement, which divided the battle into two simultaneous afternoon engagements, and concluded by stating that the Americans were forced to retire, losing upwards of a dozen artillery pieces, but salvaging the baggage trains.

Washington studied the draft. Its casualty estimates were lower than what returns of losses would show in coming days—including a claim that as yet untallied battle casualties were likely lighter than Howe's—and he insisted encouraging phrases be incorporated. That Washington intended to face off against Howe again was implicit in the rewrite: "Notwithstanding the misfortune of the day, I am happy to find the troops in good spirits; and I hope another time we shall compensate for the losses now sustained."[3]

Both letters, sent by horse fifteen miles east to Philadelphia, reached John Hancock before 4:00 A.M. on September 12. Hancock replied immediately that he understood the circumstances and planned to assemble Congress before sunrise to read the reports to them. Hancock exhibited no panic in his response to the commander in chief, indicating that Washington's edit exerted the desired effect: "I am sorry for the unfortunate Issue of the Day, but from the Troops keeping up their Spirits, I flatter myself it will still be in our Power to retrieve the Loss of yesterday."[4]

Hancock was overoptimistic. No reclaiming of lost ground was in the offing. By pulling his army southeast to Chester, Washington had opened the most direct route for Howe to reach Philadelphia. Crown forces encamped a mere twenty miles from the United States seat of government, with the excellent Nottingham Road as their avenue—and with no significant body of American troops to oppose them. George Washington enjoyed very little, if any, sleep during his only night in his Chester headquarters on Thursday, September 11. Ten miles removed from the carnage and horrors of another loss to Howe and his elite army, the General appreciated what advantages his adversary enjoyed in terms of transit. The Nottingham Road from Chads's Ford led eastward to the Springfield Road, a fifteen-mile route that early war cartographers (and perhaps headquarters) failed to recognize. Springfield Road ran southeast and crossed the Chester Road to Philadelphia at Derby, the hamlet wedged between two forks of

Cobb's Creek. Derby lay ten miles northwest of the Continental army and fifteen miles from Howe's command. If Howe set out for Philadelphia two hours before Washington, the British would cut the Americans off from their capital, five miles east of Derby.

Washington issued General Orders after midnight for brigade officers to pick up stragglers along the Concord Road and on the routes to Wilmington. His parole—"Schuylkill"—and countersigns—"Derby" and "Germantown"—at the top of these General Orders left no doubt as to where the army was headed. (Paroles and countersigns were code words exchanged to distinguish friend from foe, particularly in contested theaters.) "At 4 A.M.," a soldier in Greene's division told his diary, "we proceeded thro' Chester, later to Derby . . ." Washington reached the town as early as ten that morning. He conspicuously wrote very little that day, apparently reflecting fatigue and a sleepless night in the aftermath of Brandywine. The army seems to have tarried in or near Derby for the remaining daylight hours that Friday. With no evidence that Howe had pursued him or made for Philadelphia, Washington directed his army to move the remaining five miles to the Schuylkill River, the natural barrier protecting Philadelphia from the west. Although the post-midnight General Orders directed the Grand Army to relocate to Germantown by day's end, most of the American forces had only touched the river's edge by 9:00 P.M.[5]

The river, crossed by ferries and fords throughout the 1700s, was by no means a perfect obstruction. No bridge existed across the Schuylkill prior to the Revolution. A moveable military bridge installed the previous year at Middle Ferry had allowed swifter and more dependable redeployment in both directions of fifteen thousand troops, approximately forty cannons, and several hundred supply wagons; an unknown number of American soldiers remained west of the river. This was the bridge the army had used after parading through Philadelphia weeks earlier. For reasons never explained, merely a small portion of the Continental army traversed the bridge that night. Most men, including the General, remained on the west side of the Schuylkill overnight. Washington either slept in his headquarters marquee between Derby and the river or overnighted in the same tavern in Derby where he had headquartered nearly three weeks earlier.[6]

Feeling better rested on Saturday morning, September 13, Washington advanced his army across the river just after sunrise. Part of the army crossed at Robin Hood Ford, which had been derided that very month as a "bad ford," while Washington, his wagons and cannons, and most of his foot and mounted soldiers used the Middle Ferry bridge emptying onto

Market Street at the midsection of the capital, albeit the less populous western side. To avoid Philadelphia's temptations, Washington turned his army left toward the north while he rode east to handle lingering business. The reason for the General's visit was never revealed, but a city resident noted that at 9:00 A.M., "General Washington this moment left this place, and is gone to Germantown." By 11:00 A.M., the army had trekked five miles from the Philadelphia side of the Schuylkill to the scene of its early August sojourn two miles south of Germantown and nearly due east of the Falls of the Schuylkill. Washington returned to the home of Henry Hill for headquarters.[7] After all the intended troops had crossed the moveable military bridge, Washington ordered its span to be removed from the moorings and drawn to the Philadelphia side.

While his fifteen thousand Continentals and Pennsylvania militia pitched tents and prepared for an afternoon and evening of rest, Washington dove into his characteristic heavy workload. By late afternoon a significant detachment of Howe's army had advanced to within four miles of Chester, fifteen miles from Gray's Ferry on the Schuylkill. Howe had sent a messenger under a flag of truce to deliver a request written on September 12. Washington reported receiving Howe's letter Saturday evening. The British courier's ultimate destination is unknown, but if he handed that message to Washington at Hill's house, Washington likely took care to reply by sending it with another man lest he reward Howe with an intelligence coup regarding Washington's exact location.

Howe requested that Washington send physicians to the Brandywine battlefield, a standard practice in eighteenth-century warfare. Howe assured Washington that "every possible Attention has been paid" to the American wounded, but he could no longer help those men "as I shall not be so situated as to give them the Necessary relief." Howe intended to drive home a painful reminder that Washington had been forced to leave unmanageable numbers of wounded Americans on the battlefield, but the General's subordinates warped that imputation. General Greene interpreted Howe's message as an admission by the British commander that the Continentals had inflicted "a terrible carnage among [Howe's] troops." Washington's reply was a curt acknowledgment of the situation; his remedy, sending six surgeons to the Brandywine battlefield, including Dr. Benjamin Rush, the renowned Philadelphia physician and signer of the Declaration of Independence.[8]

The first printed reports that Philadelphia and Germantown received about the Battle of Brandywine came from local newspapers. At least one such edition would have been procured by headquarters staff. The *Pennsylvania Evening Post* published its third and final issue of the week that Saturday. Washington's September 11 reports, issued at 5:00 P.M. and midnight, filled the first page of the four-page broadsheet. If this issue had reached Washington, he would have been drawn to page 2. There glowed "American Crisis No. 4," Thomas Paine's latest installment in his rousing series espousing the virtue of The Cause and the necessity for its success.

Writing at noon the previous day, Paine had, as with his original Crisis essay nine months earlier—"These are the times that try men's souls"—drawn inspiration from the defeat at Chads's Ford. "It is not a field of a few acres of ground, but a cause we are defending," Paine declared, "and whether we defeat the enemy in one battle, or by degrees, the consequence will be the same." Without naming the latest fight, Paine essentially equated Brandywine with Bunker Hill, another pyrrhic British victory that so weakened Crown forces that another such battle stood to "put them in a condition to be afterwards totally defeated." Assuring readers that Washington and his Continentals remained strong and resolute, Paine closed this installment with a message to Howe. Describing the Americans as continuing to shine with "the ardent glow of generous patriotism," he contrasted them with Howe and his men, "the hireling slaves of a beggarly tyrant." Paine's close of "American Crisis No. 4" ranks among the most powerful lines he ever created: "We fight not to enslave, but to set a country free, and to make room upon the earth for honest men to live in. In such a cause we are sure we are right; and we leave to you [General Howe] the despairing reflection of being a tool of a miserable tyrant."[9]

Notwithstanding the severe casualties of two days earlier, American officers and men in the ranks displayed confidence and eagerness about their next brush with combat. "Our army is now refreshed," a man wrote Saturday, "and if the enemy advance, [we] will meet them with that intrepid spirit which becomes men contending for liberty, and the great cause of their country." Another observed the same day, "Our troops, far from being discouraged, wish for nothing more ardently than another chance with the enemy."[10]

Washington and his generals voiced similar confidence. They gathered for a council at the Hill home on Saturday night. The minutes of this meeting have yet to come to light but based on a summary of it and subsequent events, the council decided to cut short the army's respite on the east side of the Schuylkill. Only fifty hours after the decimation of his Continental infantry, Washington and most generals present at Hill's house resolved to move immediately to battle Howe again—but not on the defensive. Washington's goal against Crown forces became "attacking them either in Front or on their Flank with a prospect of success." After the meeting, Washington issued orders for his army "to march tomorrow morning as soon as it is well light."[11]

Sunday, September 14, 1777, dawned with the sun rising into a cloudless cornflower-blue sky. Washington's headquarters was particularly active. His Excellency dictated in full or in theme at least eight letters that morning. He sent orders to General Heath in Boston to dispatch all Continental troops from his Eastern Department stationed in Massachusetts to join the General's army immediately: "The call for them is to the last degree, urgent." He reported the Brandywine battle to Heath as "a pretty general engagement with the enemy" and admitted that the outcome was a "disaster we have sustained."[12] Even if Heath complied the minute he read his commander's missive, the 250 miles between Boston and Philadelphia meant the Massachusetts complement would not be in the capital before October.

The commander in chief did expect one particular order that he had issued Saturday night to have been acted upon before daybreak on Sunday, only to learn that such was not the case. With the prospect of Crown forces inching closer to Philadelphia, Washington was dismayed to learn that the Middle Ferry bridge remained in place, despite his insistence that it be loosed from its moorings and drawn to the Philadelphia side of the Schuylkill and all boats removed from the west side of the river. At 7:00 A.M. on Sunday, Washington repeated the order to Major General John Armstrong, adding instructions to dispatch Pennsylvania militia to defend all the fords and ferry sites upriver from the Middle Ferry, advising him to construct light forts at his discretion to defend against these crossings but acknowledging that the militia was not expected "to stand a long defence."[13]

The Continental army's return to the Falls of the Schuylkill south of Germantown lasted less than twenty-four hours. At first light, officers and men struck their tents and packed their wagons. By 9:00 A.M. fifteen thousand soldiers were lurching northward toward Germantown. In perhaps his last letter from the Hill house Washington revealed his intent for the first time: "We brought the army to this place to refresh them with convenience and security and are just beginning our march to return toward the enemy."[14]

Washington and most of his generals were of a mind to attack Howe, whose army stood idle between Chester and the Brandywine. But why leave so soon? Thomas Wharton, head of Pennsylvania's state government, had worried to Washington in writing about the vulnerability of Swede's Ford, the likely route for Howe were he to cross the Schuylkill to assault Philadelphia. It lay sixteen miles northwest of the city. "Below this pass," Wharton noted, "there is no ford equally good or tolerably practicable." At a glance, the Continental army appeared to be taking Wharton's alert to heart; Swede's Ford could easily be a ten-mile, noon-hour destination. Orderly books named the ford as the object of the army's march.[15]

Wharton was mistaken—alarmingly so for a civilian official warning soldiers about river crossings. Swede's Ford, widely known and named for an early population of European settlers, was not the most obvious crossing point for Howe's army. Perhaps Wharton, not knowing the British army's condition after Brandywine, assumed the enemy to be closer than the thirty miles to Swede's Ford. From his occupation of Germantown six weeks earlier, Washington likely knew of other fords much closer to Philadelphia. Before 11:00 A.M., as the army was entering Germantown from the southeast, he turned the column southwest from Ridge Road onto a direct route to Levering's Ford. A week of summer remained, but temperatures were autumnal and the region's hardwoods already were winking the slightest hint to the most colorful season. About fifteen thousand soldiers—most shod but many barefoot—and at least one thousand headquarters, dragoon, artillery, and baggage animals splashed across Wissahickon Creek and tramped another mile to the east bank of the Schuylkill.[16]

Washington never attempted to explain why his troops were going to cross the river over and back in less than a day. Perhaps he realized that if Wharton—Pennsylvania's highest-ranking appointed official—felt confident enough to advise Washington about Schuylkill River fords yet was ignorant of Levering's Ford's utility, then Howe might have been equally unaware. This theory may have impelled Washington to cross the river and immediately distance himself from this ford to distract any British or Loyalist scout from paying attention to it.

Crossing Levering's Ford vexed Washington's staff. No urgency had marked the waist-deep crossing. This irritated the Adjutant General, Colonel Pickering. "We lost here much time," he complained to his journal that night, noting that soldiers stripped off shoes, stockings, and even breeches before entering the river instead of wading fully clothed and allowing their garments to dry naturally on such a fine day. Officers failed to speed the crossing. Several left the ranks to find horses and even canoes to stay dry. By the time the Continentals picked up the march on the west side of the Schuylkill, the day was nearly gone. The vanguard advanced only six more miles along the Lancaster Road before stopping for the night.[17]

Washington did not appear to share the collective irritation; perhaps he understood that Howe was not going anywhere on Sunday. By nightfall the General had accomplished two goals. He had entered and evacuated Philadelphia rapidly in less than thirty hours to draw Howe's attention away from the capital and to the rebel army. And by taking the east-west Lancaster Road, Washington had interposed an armed force of men in numbers equivalent to the entire population of Boston between Howe and the upper fords of the Schuylkill. If his plan worked, it would distract Howe from discovering Levering's Ford, the shortest route into Philadelphia. Washington yearned to avenge his Brandywine defeat as soon as possible. As he explained a week later: "When I last recrossed the Schuylkill it was with a firm intent of giving the Enemy Battle wherever I should meet them."[18]

The army grew slightly as stragglers from the Brandywine battle returned to the ranks, as well as troops who had been stationed west of the Schuylkill when Washington encamped his men near Germantown. The Americans resumed their march westward on the Lancaster Road at 6:00 A.M. on Monday, September 15. By day's end the vanguard had passed White Horse Tavern and the rear had stopped five miles from there at Paoli Tavern. A Pennsylvanian exuded a combination of nervous excitement and confidence, raving, "The men are all in fine spirits and panting to have at the Enemy again, Confident of their Abilities, in giving them a total defeat." His division commander was less ebullient. At the start of the advance, General Anthony Wayne realized the gamble Washington was making by distancing himself from Philadelphia. "May [Howe] not steal a March and pass the fords in the Vicinity of the Falls [of the Schuylkill] unless we immediately March down and Give them Battle?" Wayne wondered.[19]

Washington's actions Monday suggested he harbored the same concern. While the Continental army advanced westward on the Lancaster Road, their commanding general remained rearward for most of the day. Near dawn he departed his headquarters at the Sign of the Buck, a tavern eleven miles from Philadelphia run by the widow Miller. He mounted Blueskin and rode in the opposite direction of his army. He and his aides and their servants split up and ate breakfast at taverns two to four miles from Miller's tavern.

At 3:00 P.M. Washington returned to the Sign of the Buck, from which he dictated a letter to Congress. "We are moving up this Road," he told John Hancock, "to get between the Enemy and Swedes Ford & to prevent them from turning our right flank, which they seem to have a violent inclination to effect by all their Movements." Washington also attempted to extinguish a smoldering fire regarding Major General John Sullivan, who had been investigated by a Court of Enquiry for his allegedly suspect performance on the Staten Island expedition in August. Washington received an order from Congress to recall Sullivan from his army until that inquiry had been completed. The commander in chief would have none of it. "How can the Army be possibly conducted with a prospect of Success, if the Genl Officers are taken off in the Moment of Battle?" he wrote. Reminding Hancock of the deficiencies of leadership in his army, Washington argued successfully for temporarily delaying Sullivan's recall. The collapse of his division on Birmingham Hill rendered Sullivan's leadership more suspect with Congress, and he was not alone in being scrutinized. "As to the affair at Brandywine," delegate James Lovell of Massachusetts wrote, "I doubt whether we will even accurately know whether fortune alone is to be blamed, or whether Sullivan and the Chief should not share with her in the slanderous murmurs."[20]

Leaving widow Miller's place, Washington and his staff stopped for dinner at the Sorrel Horse Tavern two miles west. After the General and his thirty personnel and servants dined, he purchased meals for the next day as well as wine, toddy, spirits, and rum. For the rest of Washington's Monday headquarters traversed twelve miles of Lancaster Road to Malin Hall, the home of Randall Malin. The house stood somewhat toward the center of his encamped army, but before midnight it was more easterly after that flank shifted from Paoli Tavern to Warren Tavern.[21]

For wisely choosing against defending within the trapped environs of Philadelphia and rolling the dice that his movement away from the city would lure his opponent toward him, Washington was gratified with affirmation by nightfall. He received an intelligence report from a lieutenant who sent him three spies who had infiltrated British lines and claimed to have learned that Howe believed part of Washington's army to be in Philadelphia and part at Swede's Ford.[22] That the intelligence did not mention Levering's Ford or the Lancaster Road and that Howe had barely budged since the Battle of Brandywine together may have persuaded Washington that Howe was likelier to be drawn toward Washington by the roads to Swede's Ford than more directly to Philadelphia by way of Levering's

Ford. As far as Washington knew from having loitered along five miles of the west bank of the Schuylkill for several daylight hours on September 15 without seeing enemy troops, Howe may have never known that the Continental army had ever been on the Philadelphia side of the river. The British commander was more likely not to know that the usable and virtually undefended Levering's Ford was there for his taking.

Washington undervalued the quality and extent of his foe's intelligence gathering. That Tuesday afternoon Howe, visiting General Cornwallis near Chester, learned of Washington's whereabouts. Captain Montresor told his journal, "At 4 o'clock P.M. learnt that the rebel army which had crossed the Schuylkill at Philadelphia had repassed it to this side of Levering's Ford and were pursuing the road to Lancaster."[23] Washington personally remained within five miles of Levering's Ford for most of the day, but he had been committing his army westward on the Lancaster Road since dawn's early light, putting more miles between them and their capital. Howe could easily ignore Washington's presence north of him and do exactly what General Wayne feared: march his advance guard under Cornwallis unopposed for eighteen miles to Levering's Ford, cross there, and capture Philadelphia—and perhaps officials of the Pennsylvania and U.S. governments—all by September 16. Howe stood to have accomplished this grand achievement in just three weeks after landing near Head of Elk, and without suffering a crippling number of losses that required three-thousand ocean miles plus three-hundred road miles to replace, since September 11. Washington and his Continentals were encamped along a five-mile segment of the Lancaster Road, forming the point of a triangle twelve miles north of Crown forces and seventeen miles west of Levering's Ford, clearly no longer a threat to Howe if he chose the path of least resistance to take Philadelphia.

Subsequent orders from Howe's headquarters were astounding. He ordered Cornwallis to start moving from Chester at 8:00 P.M.—ninety minutes after sunset—but not eastward toward Levering's Ford. Instead, Howe directed Cornwallis to head northwest with his force toward the Lancaster Road. Howe would take the rest of the army and do the same on a more northerly course starting the next morning.[24] He was not moving north to cross at Swede's Ford, which would have carried his army several more miles away from Philadelphia than the unopposed easterly route and crossing at Levering's Ford. Howe decided late in the afternoon of September 15 that he would destroy Washington's army, then capture Philadelphia. This would not be the turning point of the American Revolution; it would be the ending point.

The Lancaster Road lined the center of the Great Valley, bordered by the North Valley Hills and the South Valley Hills. This road was absolutely the worst place for an army to linger, with any enemy blocked from his southward view. Washington woke well before sunrise on Tuesday, September 16, an ominously overcast day. He had his entire army continue to line the road but to concentrate in positions that blocked the paths to Swede's Ford Road. They had held the area since sunset on Monday. Dawn broke shortly after 5:30 A.M. Washington exhibited no sense of urgency to get a significant portion of his army onto the hills. Five hours were absolutely wasted as the Americans held the least defensible position an army could hold—the valley.

The lone American force sent over the South Valley hills was a party of dragoons led by Casimir Pulaski, named brigadier general a day earlier by the Continental Congress but several days from officially being placed in that role. At mid-morning on Tuesday, September 16, with the Americans disorganized on the Lancaster Road and strung out for nearly five miles between Warren Tavern and White Horse Tavern to the west, Washington conferred with his staff at Malin Hall, south of the Lancaster Road at the fork of Swede's Ford Road, near the center of the resting army.

Howe targeted George Washington as his chief campaign objective over seizing the rebel capital. The British, Hessians, and Loyalists had injured Washington's army on September 11; they had decimated Continental manpower and dramatically weakened its firepower. But they had not killed it. Howe's orders to shun the bloodless route into Philadelphia in favor of another slugfest made clear that he meant to finish this game once and for all. With detachments left in his rear, the British commander was still able to advance more than fifteen thousand in two wings converging toward the Lancaster Road.

Washington still had some sixteen thousand Continentals and militia under arms. His infantry carried five-hundred thousand bullets. They had lost eleven cannons at Chads's Ford and Birmingham Hill, but the Americans still pulled thirty-nine artillery pieces—four more were sent to Swede's Ford—with enough three- and six-pound ammunition to tear gaping holes in Howe's ranks.

The Battle of Brandywine had transformed George Washington in a contest reminiscent of the nightmare summer of 1776. Howe had exposed Washington's flaws as a defensive tactician at Brooklyn, on Manhattan, at Red Clay Creek, and most recently along the Brandywine. No longer would Washington battle on the defensive. John Hancock and the Continental

Congress were the first witnesses to his abandonment of defensive tactics the third week of September. Washington informed them that he sought to attack Howe on September 16 rather than be attacked by him.[25]

Except for Howe's discovery of Levering's Ford, Washington's great gamble to draw Crown forces away from Philadelphia and face him in battle twenty-five miles northwest of the capital appeared to have succeeded. Washington's mid-morning position on the Lancaster Road was no accident. His army's western flank—Wayne and his Pennsylvanians with Sullivan's Marylanders just east of them—rested near White Horse Tavern, a popular inn since its construction on the old Allegheny Trail. The venerable public house was the hub of six roads spoking in all directions. Greene and his Virginians covered the army's eastern flank near Warren Tavern. This division covered roads that eventually led to Swede's Ford on the Schuylkill. Washington and the American army stood firmly in Howe's path, believing he meant to cross the river and take Philadelphia. Not realizing Howe intended to destroy the rebel army and its wily commander, Washington was unintentionally providing him with a second opportunity in five days to wipe out the Continentals and capture the American seat of government, all on the same route of march.

Washington yearned to meet Howe in battle again, and on ground of Washington's choosing. The obvious place to reposition his army was on the southern height paralleling the Lancaster Road. Uncertain about the best option, Washington huddled with his staff in Malin Hall. General Casimir Pulaski, unofficially "Commander of the Horse," had made a crucial discovery while patrolling the southern heights of the Great Valley: Redcoats were at the base of those hills and climbing. Pulaski's patrols had seen Cornwallis's detached column advancing northeast on the Chester Road toward Goshen Meetinghouse at the junction of that road with Boot Road, less than five miles south of Malin Hall.

Barely familiar with the English language, Pulaski relayed this intelligence through Alexander Hamilton, John Laurens, or another interpreter. His news startled Washington. Hamilton protested, suggesting Pulaski had "made a mistake, and had only seen some of our own people." Hamilton's remark, once translated, infuriated Pulaski, who "flew into a violent passion." Washington calmly defused the ruckus, sent surplus baggage wagons east to the wagon park at Warren Tavern, and ordered his Continentals to climb the South Valley Hills by way of the roads that led from his army's east flank. Portions of his army crossed the Lancaster Road and waited at the base of the South Valley Hills. Although he had not committed his force to that locale, all indications pointed to Washington planning to occupy the heights in front of him.[26] The unexpected appearance of British troops had not vanquished Washington's desire to attack Howe, or to prepare to accept Howe's offensive. Before Washington could solidify his battle line, he had to commit the bulk of his force to the South Valley Hills in front of him or the North Valley Hills behind.

Washington had carelessly declined to post men on the South Valley Hills at dawn, or he would have been able to pounce on Cornwallis's anemic, disconnected force. This column was vulnerable while isolated from Howe's main body at Goshen Meetinghouse, a condition not possible to remedy before noon. As the British ascended the South Valley Hills from the south, Washington sent troops from the north to occupy the crest. They aligned near or on Caln Road, a generally east-west thoroughfare along the crest of the height. Only part of his army was atop that position. The rest of his soldiers were advancing to this location or had no orders to march at all. The 4th Maryland Regiment, for example, was encamped by the Lancaster Road, and—according to its colonel— "there was no idea of an attack by the enemy." Major John Eager Howard of the same regiment recalled that the regiment had formed a right angle with the Lancaster Road at the White Horse Tavern and not on the heights south of the inn. Chances are that the entire one thousand-man brigade to which this regiment belonged was with the men on the Lancaster Road, and perhaps their entire division under Sullivan. The dispositions of the other regiments in the army are unknown, but Washington's chief of staff spoke volumes by informing his general, "The order of battle is not completed."[27]

Making matters much worse were the terrain and, to a lesser extent, a blanket of dark clouds hanging as far as the eye could see and threatening rain. Rain disabled flintlock weapons, forcing riflemen to rely more on the bayonet, a British specialty but a skill generally alien to Americans. As Howe's army neared, signaled by scattered fire from skirmishers, Washington must have realized that the ground he had chosen not only sapped his ability to attack Howe, but did not offer the strong defense a force expected to enjoy on a hill. Across Caln Road to the south, toward the approach being taken by the Crown force, was not the downslope of a hill but a plateau. This landscape neutralized Washington's expected advantage as his opponent would not be fighting uphill.[28] Washington and his army had survived at Brandywine by engaging in the art of escape; the available avenues from South Valley Hills limited this capability. Three roads led from Caln Road on the southern height to the Great Valley, the eastern and westernmost ones 2,500 yards apart. Washington's partial army occupied the ground on which the two western roads, both unnamed county byways, terminated at the Caln Road; the right flank of the force likely extended westward beyond the westernmost road. Those two roads converged at White Horse Tavern, assuring a bottleneck if a rapid retreat proved necessary. The southeast-northwest Chester Road, the third and easternmost of these roads, did not converge with the other two behind Washington's advanced position. It could have offered a route out of trouble but most of Howe's army was advancing up this artery while Washington's left flank stood too far west of it for the Americans to file out using that route without danger to the soldiers' flank. Washington was near the point of no return. He would lose artillery and men if he attempted to funnel them all onto the Chester Road, and a logjam would form at White Horse Tavern if he chose to retreat from his western—right—flank.

The American situation was dire. An unformed partial army faced one of the most successful forces on Earth—a foe which thrice in thirteen months had routed and whipped the Continental army. Never in America had Howe been presented with such a potential prize: several thousand soldiers ill-trained at hand-to-hand combat; opposing him with multiple field pieces on open, level ground with no defensive barrier save for meager fencing; poor escape routes; and a history of repeatedly caving under the weight of Howe's attacks, particularly on their flanks. On the South Valley Heights two thousand yards off the Lancaster Road near noon on September 16, 1777, both converging wings of Crown forces glided to within a mile of contact, honed and skilled at deployment from column to line, and closing in on a most assured kill—perhaps the biggest one of the century.

George Washington's army was facing annihilation.

CHAPTER SEVEN

"Pray, Sir, Decide"

September 16 to September 20, 1777

Pompous. Arrogant. Abrasive. General Philip Charles Jean Baptiste Tronson du Coudray embodied all three pejoratives when he had arrived at Congress's doorstep back in June with a military staff of twenty-eight and an oversize ego. "He arrived here with the airs of a lord," a fellow French officer said, voicing concern that Coudray risked ruining French influence on the American military because he "has disgusted the whole Congress" and in doing so "has done us the most damage."[1]

The concerns were overstated. Coudray had atoned for his poor first impression with steady, strong, and dedicated work through the summer of 1777. He diplomatically allowed many of Silas Deane's lofty promises to fade away for the sake of harmony, accepting Congress's August 11 compromise appointment to a staff position without disruptions to the chain and hierarchy of command among appointed generals in the field.

Coudray had come to the United States in quest of military power and authority, but The Cause captured his attention, devotion, and spirit. After the Battle of Brandywine, Coudray came to Congress looking to fight, not pose. On September 15, Congress received his written request to serve directly in the Continental army, asking for a new and relegated appointment of captain for himself, lieutenancies for his subordinates, and the title of ensign for members of his non-commissioned staff. He reasoned that if he or his aides were captured, the equal-rank prisoner exchange would be less costly to America. Even James Lovell—Coudray's chief critic and foil in Congress—was impressed by the magnanimous request. Congress granted the commissions and advanced "Captain" Coudray money to conduct his mission to join Washington and his army.[2]

Captain Coudray's mission started on September 16 in Philadelphia. Shortly after 11:00 A.M., he led nine of his lieutenants onto a boat at Gray's Ferry to cross the Schuylkill. Although these flat boats were designed to load cattle and horses without unharnessing them, when Coudray hopped onto a craft atop an overly spirited mare, the horse galloped to the other side of the ferry boat and went overboard, plunging into the Schuylkill with the Frenchman still on her back. Coudray managed to disentangle himself from his horse, but he could not swim. Nicholas Rogers, his aide de camp and a strong swimmer, leaped into the river. He got a firm hold of his commander, but the panicked Coudray thrashed so much that Rogers released him to save his own life. Coudray sank and drowned in seconds. The Schuylkill's powerful currents swept the dead man under; his corpse was not located and pulled from the river until evening.[3]

"No newspapers this morning," began John Adams's diary entry for that Tuesday. Unaware of Coudray's fate, Adams had grim forebodings in mind, nonetheless. "Is there a Possibility that Washington should defeat How[e]?" he wrote. "From whence is our Deliverance to come? Or is it not to come? Is Philadelphia lost? If lost is the Cause lost? No–the Cause is not lost–but it may be hurt."[4]

Adams had not asked himself if General Washington could misstep so severely as to lose his army. That became a very real possibility at noon. Washington had placed an undersized and disorganized force along Caln Road from east to west, lining the crest of South Valley Hills of the Great Valley. Between a third and a half of Washington's army was up there at noon. Before any more Continentals departed the Lancaster Road, the General realized time was not on his side. He could not get the bulk of his force deployed quickly enough on high to take the battle to Howe. Nor could he be assured that he could mount an adequate defense on the South Valley Hills in time to repel a most assuredly unrelenting assault by Crown forces.

After inspecting and attempting to organize the right side of the Continental line arrayed on the north side of the Caln Road, Colonel Pickering trotted to the center of the haphazard formation. He found the commanding general in a knot of staff officers. Pickering joined his colleagues in pressing the issue. Dismayed at Washington's poorly set table of troop positions, Pickering attempted to stir him to action, later admitting his discomfort at having had "to accost the General with ease." He laid out the ominous situation and options of quickly reinforcing and organizing on the forward heights or to falling back immediately to the rearward heights before the enemy could assault the troops while they were unorganized and divided.

"Pray, Sir, decide," pleaded Pickering.[5]

"Let us move," answered Washington instantly. Washington ordered a withdrawal from his potential offensive on the South Valley Hills to a purely defensive position on the opposite heights. As he did, a secondary threat arose. The morning had been dark, foretelling rain. But what blew in was a full-on "nor'easter," a wicked storm, perhaps the remnant of a hurricane, that six days earlier had sunk British ships in the Caribbean Sea.[6] Around noon a moderate shower pattered upon Chester County as Washington's troops, including men on the Lancaster Road and all but the militia on the South Valley Hills, marched back to the Lancaster Road and up the elevations of North Valley Hills. Over the next forty-five minutes Washington's men moved to this height. They congregated between the northeastward Swede's Ford Road and the northwestward road leading to Yellow Springs.

Washington's most prudent decision had been to pull his entire army back to the North Valley Hills. A British witness subsequently admitted that his adversary had chosen the "strong ground." Seeing the height afterwards, John Montresor, Howe's chief engineer, deemed it "a most favourable position being a prevailing gradual height in the valley."[7] If swept from this position, Washington would need to find advantageous ground between Warren Tavern and Swede's Ford, but he did not think that a necessity. Based on Brandywine, confronting Washington's thirteen thousand Continentals and upwards of two thousand militiamen would require a force of numbers Howe did not possess. The American position was more than twice the size of what Howe had been able to knock off Birmingham

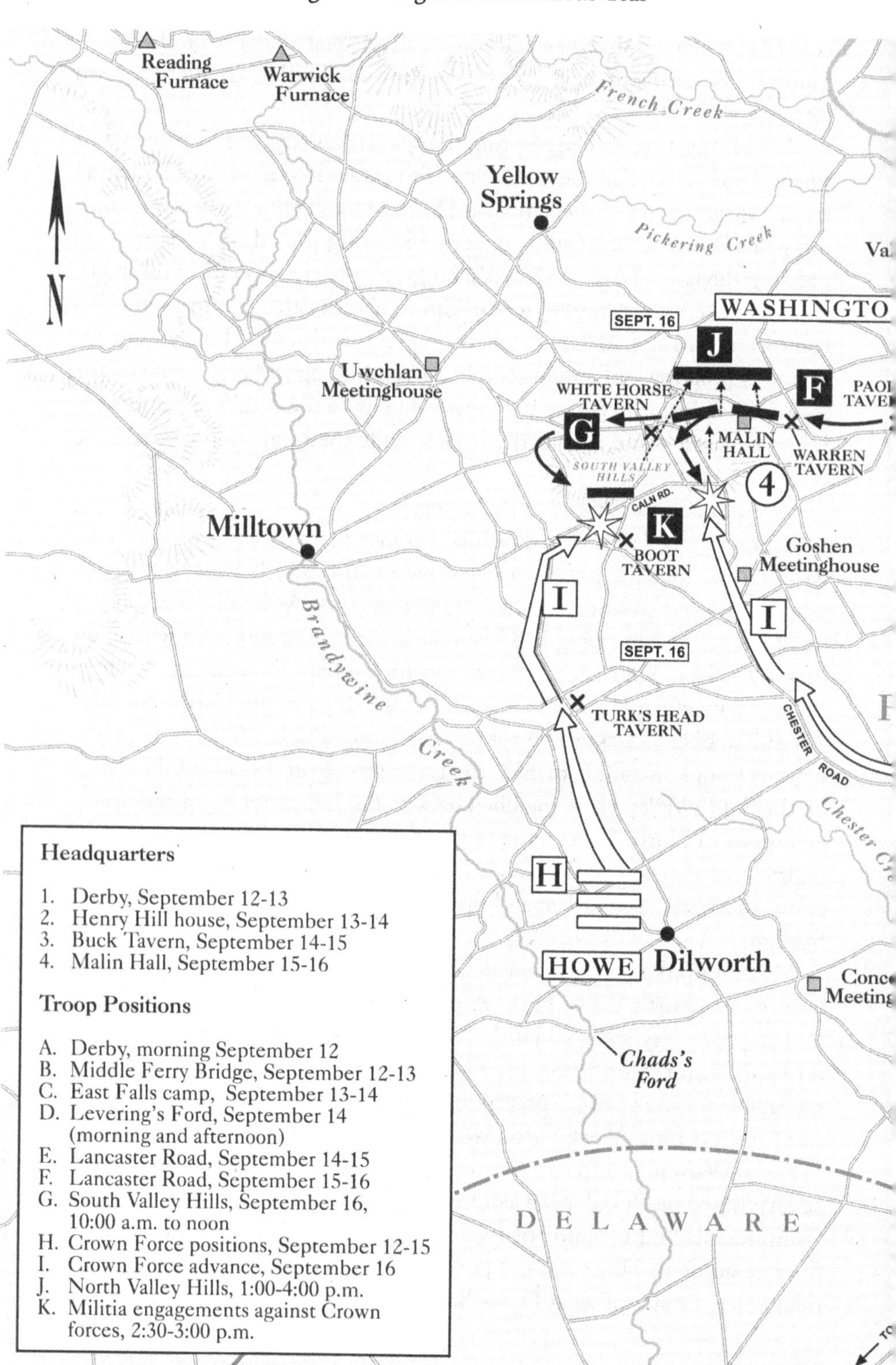

Reading Furnace
Warwick Furnace
French Creek
Yellow Springs
Pickering Creek
N
WASHINGTO
SEPT. 16
J
F
PAOI TAVE
Uwchlan Meetinghouse
WHITE HORSE TAVERN
G
MALIN HALL
WARREN TAVERN
SOUTH VALLEY HILLS
CALN RD.
4
K
BOOT TAVERN
Milltown
Goshen Meetinghouse
I
Brandywine Creek
SEPT. 16
TURK'S HEAD TAVERN
CHESTER ROAD
Chester Cr
H
HOWE
Dilworth
Chads's Ford
DELAWARE
Headquarters
1. Derby, September 12-13
2. Henry Hill house, September 13-14
3. Buck Tavern, September 14-15
4. Malin Hall, September 15-16
Troop Positions
A. Derby, morning September 12
B. Middle Ferry Bridge, September 12-13
C. East Falls camp, September 13-14
D. Levering's Ford, September 14 (morning and afternoon)
E. Lancaster Road, September 14-15
F. Lancaster Road, September 15-16
G. South Valley Hills, September 16, 10:00 a.m. to noon
H. Crown Force positions, September 12-15
I. Crown Force advance, September 16
J. North Valley Hills, 1:00-4:00 p.m.
K. Militia engagements against Crown forces, 2:30-3:00 p.m.

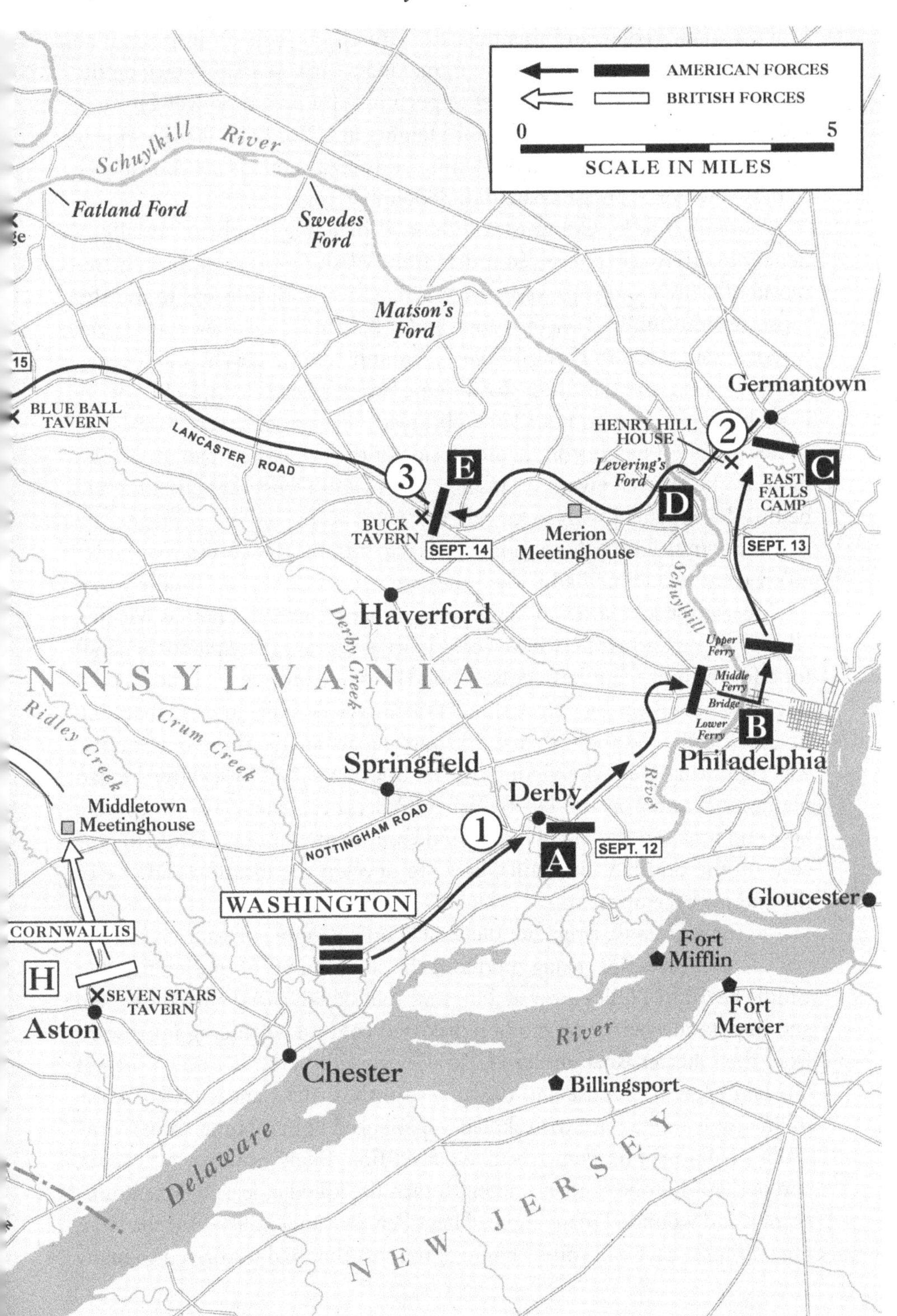
AMERICAN FORCES
BRITISH FORCES
0
5
SCALE IN MILES
Schuylkill River
Fatland Ford
Swedes Ford
Matson's Ford
15
BLUE BALL TAVERN
LANCASTER ROAD
3
E
BUCK TAVERN
SEPT. 14
Merion Meetinghouse
HENRY HILL HOUSE
Levering's Ford
D
2
Germantown
C
EAST FALLS CAMP
SEPT. 13
Haverford
Derby Creek
Schuylkill
Upper Ferry
Middle Ferry
Bridge
Lower Ferry
B
Philadelphia
River
NNSYLVANIA
Ridley Creek
Crum Creek
Springfield
Derby
1
A
SEPT. 12
NOTTINGHAM ROAD
Middletown Meetinghouse
WASHINGTON
CORNWALLIS
H
SEVEN STARS TAVERN
Aston
Chester
Gloucester
Fort Mifflin
Fort Mercer
River
Billingsport
Delaware
NEW JERSEY

Hill five days earlier, and this time the Americans were all in place. The open territory prevented Howe from making a surprise flank attack on the heights. It was Washington's best opportunity for a victory over Howe—indeed his only one—since Harlem Heights in 1776. Even if the memory of that battle crossed Washington's mind, it is doubtful that the coincidence of the New York contest's date did: September 16.

Clement Biddle, Commissary General of Forage and (informally) a deputy quartermaster, received orders from Washington to oversee the removal of army wagons parked near Warren Tavern. Biddle was to transfer those several hundred wagons four and a half miles northeast along the Swede's Ford Road to Howell Tavern. Around 1:00 P.M., as he was looping clockwise from the Lancaster Road to the Swede's Ford Road, Biddle, writing a bit more than an hour later, observed, "Our troops were formed on some very good heights on the north side of the Lancaster road, two miles up from the Warren tavern . . . in high spirits, and I trust that our arms will be this day crowned with success."[8]

Biddle transferred those thoughts to paper in the dry confines of Howell's Tavern, where he had parked the wagons. At 2:30 P.M., Biddle wrote in a postscript to a letter to his superior, Major General Thomas Mifflin, "Both cannon and artillery have been smart and heavy (though not general) for a few minutes, but have ceased, and the rain continues."[9] Biddle could not have been hearing Howe's and Washington's main lines exchanging fire, for they stood more than 2,500 yards apart at this time. Battle noise was clamoring from the vicinity of the South Valley Hills. After he had planted his army on the North Valley Hills, the General had directed a bookend force, consisting of militia and Continentals on each flank, to proceed up the South Valley Hills, likely to develop the location and size of the enemy force up there.

On the east flank, Brigadier General Scott's Virginia brigade and Pennsylvania militia 1,500 strong produced the sharp bursts of musket fire that Biddle heard five miles away at 2:30 P.M. Pulaski advanced with these men and impetuously charged into a red-coated column advancing northward from the Chester Road under General Cornwallis. About a mile north of Goshen Meeting House and two miles south of the Lancaster Road, the militia came face to face with skilled, experienced light infantry from Cornwallis's column. The Pennsylvanians fired first, likely from seventy yards, and perhaps hit one British soldier. Return fire killed at least a dozen militiamen and wounded many more. These Pennsylvania militia fled the field, not willing to face a bayonet charge of the sort that had terrorized so many

Americans in previous battles. The militiamen's rapid withdrawal—Pickering later scoffed that they "shamefully fled at the first fire"—must have been convincing enough to discourage Scott's Virginians from offering battle. They withdrew without firing a shot or losing a man.[10]

Near Boot Tavern, two and a half miles south of White Horse Tavern, Potter's Pennsylvania militia clashed with Colonel Carl von Donop's Hessian detachment of jägers, grenadiers, and the Lieb Regiment. Von Donop had carelessly advanced beyond the support of Knyphausen's column and found his force nearly surrounded at Boot Tavern, where the Pennsylvania militiamen acquitted themselves more favorably than their counterparts to the east had, dropping a dozen jägers with musket balls. Hessian horse soldiers broke through to free von Donop from his self-inflicted predicament.

The action at Boot Tavern cost the Americans approximately ten more casualties, but Crown forces wanted at least ten thousand more. Several miles northeast of this encounter, in Howell Tavern, Clement Biddle wrote at 2:30 P.M., "The rain continues, and renders a general action for to-night impracticable."[11] The storm that shocked the region shortly after 2:00 P.M. was nothing like what had started around noon. Rain now fell hard enough to hurt. This nor'easter was never recorded or recalled as having been particularly cold that day, but it nonetheless completely froze nearly thirty thousand British, German, and American soldiers, interrupting the business of war. The Continental army stood in line upon the North Valley Hills; Crown forces occupied ground near the crest of South Valley Hills. No one fired a shot. As the American army stood on those hills, Washington and some of his staff returned to Malin Hall to gain shelter and to dissect dispatches.[12]

The storm won the Battle of the Clouds, but for practical purposes victory went to the British, since the weather made the ground untenable for Washington to stay upon it safely, turning his force into a toothless, clawless tiger. Nearly all the tents were in Biddle's baggage train four miles east at Howell's Tavern. With his left flank at Swede's Ford Road, Washington, lacking shelter, had no choice but to stand his men in line for hours in a devastating downpour. He could not abandon his position by moving toward safer ground at the heights near Yellow Springs, to the northwest, because doing so would cede to Howe his campaign objective. The British could set forth on an unchallenged march from the heights south of White Horse Tavern seventeen miles to Swede's Ford, then advance sixteen more uncontested miles into America's largest, most important city. Howe could reasonably conquer a defenseless Philadelphia by Friday, September 19.

Not only would this eventuality open Washington to endless criticism for seeming to turn tail, it would also invalidate the offensive that Washington had been planning to undertake from the moment he crossed Levering's Ford two days earlier. More immediately disturbing to Washington was the fact that his right flank was not anchored on the road network spoking from White Horse Tavern, leaving that flank vulnerable to be turned by Howe's army. Washington sensed this, as Howe was managing to operate well enough in the rain to appear to be threatening that flank.

The commander in chief received a message from Swede's Ford that sealed the decision. The dispatch, likely written by 2:00 P.M., had been authored by his former adjutant general, Joseph Reed, who knew the region well; his home was nearby. Reed reported that General Armstrong personally was protecting the ford with artillery and the bulk of his detached militia. The next largest portion of militia was at the Middle Ferry assuring the bridge and boats were removed. A much smaller force had been partitioned to cover the other eight known crossings of the Schuylkill between those two locales. Reed's most important revelation was that the river was rising rapidly, rendering Swede's Ford scarcely passable. Washington well realized that more than ninety minutes had elapsed since Reed wrote the dispatch; during that hour and a half the downpour must have erased any trace of Swede's Ford and every other ford within a few miles.

With the storm giving no indication of letting up within the next several hours, Washington reasonably determined that Philadelphia was safe from Howe for at least a couple of more days. If he led his army toward Swede's Ford, he risked marching into his own trap with Howe's army in his front and an impassable river behind him. The action at Boot Tavern suggested to Washington that Howe was attempting to turn his right flank. This induced the General to move to heights better protecting the road leading to his supply depot at Reading, across the Schuylkill, as well as his more vulnerable ammunition production centers at Warwick and Reading Furnaces on his—and Howe's—side of the river.[13] Washington was so confident about Howe's inevitable delay that he did not send a courier to alert Philadelphia to imminent danger; he believed that no such danger existed.

Between 3:30 and 4:00 P.M. on September 16, Washington led his men off the battlefield with no threat visible in front—although the horrid weather did limit visibility. The artillery and wagon train left a few hours later using roads farther east. All American forces—except Maxwell's brigade and Potter's militia, who were left behind, worked their way via converging roads to Yellow Springs, a path churned to slick mud as the sun set behind a curtain of storm clouds.[14]

Creeks swelled to dangerous breadths and depths, making unwanted adventures of usually easy crossings. "All the small Branches that we were obliged to Cross on this march were so rais'd by the Hard rain that they took us to the waists and under the Arms when we Waded them," a Maryland captain wrote. Any gunpowder within the ammunition cartridges soldiers carried would not remain dry. The trek became arduous, slowing the army's pace at times to no more than one agonizing mile every two hours. "We marched all night through as heavy a rain as ever fell," recalled Major Samuel Shaw to his father two weeks later. "Never was seen a more horrid time for troops to march," General Knox wrote in his diary, describing rain that fell "with as much violence as [ever] it did since the flood of Noah."[15]

What felt to the men like a ten- or twelve-mile march was little over half that distance. They required nearly eleven hours to cover those six miles. During the march, Washington received a second dispatch from Reed at Swede's Ford. Writing at 6:00 P.M., Reed pronounced the ford impassable and predicted that no artillery or baggage would be able to cross even twenty-four hours later. With the rain still unrelenting past midnight, Washington realized he still had time to oppose Howe should he attempt to cross the Schuylkill.[16]

Washington took his quarters at Yellow Springs Tavern during Wednesday's earliest hours. His troops had no tents. Ten miles north of Yellow Springs was Parker's Ford, which crossed the Schuylkill upstream of Swede's Ford twenty-two serpentine river miles, but only fifteen miles by road. Not only would this upper river ford be passable much earlier than Swede's, but Washington feasibly could march to Parker's Ford in the morning, cross there, and plant his army opposite Swede's Ford well before that downriver passage was in a condition that allowed Howe any attempt to cross it.

If Washington organized any semblance of this plan, his idea immediately changed Wednesday morning. His drenched staff's appearance gave him pause. His newest aide de camp, Lieutenant Colonel John Laurens, wore a hat whose unstable dye had splotched Laurens's white waistcoat and breeches; his sash soggily showed the effects of the unrelenting rains.[17] Washington received an alarming report indicating that nature had wiped out his army's firepower. Rainwater leaked into defective cartridge boxes, which were then submerged into armpit-high creeks on the overnight march. Each man now carried forty ruined rounds. The roughest of estimates was four-hundred thousand rounds lost; the tally was likely closer to half a million. Entries in orderly books stressed that men were to "spare no pains to preserve such Ammunition that is not already damaged."[18] The closest depots at which Washington could replenish his army were Warwick and Reading Furnaces, a few miles down French Creek of each other, a day's march west from the Continental encampment and half a day's march to Parker's Ford.

A congressional letter Washington dictated at Yellow Springs for delivery to John Hancock purposely omitted any reference to concern about Philadelphia's safety. He described his waterlogged ammunition and added another woe—Biddle's wagons had been unable to travel the previous night. Biddle had stopped at a tavern eight miles east of Washington's encampment, unable to cross rain-swollen Pickering Creek. He listed for Washington available commissary and quartermaster supplies. These included twenty thousand or more tomahawks, two thousand barrels of flour, three thousand bushels of wheat, an army-sized twenty-five-barrel allotment of horseshoes, and perhaps seven hundred camp kettles. These supplies were stored in a depot within a cluster of mills, homes, and an iron forge two and a half miles east of Pickering Creek known as Valley Forge, near the junction of Valley Creek and the Schuylkill.[19]

With a British detachment of dragoons and light infantry a mere eight unopposed miles from those supplies, and water-logged Americans five miles farther west of them, it was imperative for Washington to act. He needed to send a responsible team to spirit those critical resources out of danger and to get the baggage train—including the soldiers' tents—safely to their next encampment. Before Washington marched off to the furnaces with the bulk of his army, he ordered Greene's and Wayne's divisions to escort the train through Yellow Springs to Warwick Furnace, where Washington expected to unite the supplies with the army. Maxwell's brigade and Potter's militia lagged behind with a special mission to assist the wagons closer to Valley Forge in removing the supplies stored there. Vexed by the Quartermaster Department vacillating, Washington sent orders for Major General Thomas Mifflin or an assistant to get the wagons under way to Warwick Furnace, if need be shifting loads to better navigate soupy roads.[20]

The leading brigades of Washington's army encamped between Reading Furnace and Warwick Furnace late on Wednesday; most of the rest had joined them by the afternoon of Thursday, September 18. The trip required a detour by a lone bridge due to high water on French Creek, extending the intended nine-mile march to nineteen. Washington chose a locale west of Reading Furnace for his headquarters. He learned in the early afternoon from his horse soldiers that Howe was not heading his way but instead had pushed forward to the Swede's Ford Road just north of his previous headquarters at Malin Hall. Washington realized his necessary diversion had made it more difficult to place his army on the bank of the Schuylkill opposite from Howe's advance if water levels returned to normal. To delay Howe's progress, Washington ordered Brigadier General Anthony Wayne in a series of three dispatches to peel off from his rearward position at Yellow Springs and double back to the contested ground of Tuesday. From there Wayne was to work his way to the rear of the plodding British army. Washington assured Wayne that he was "fully satisfied that you will do everything in your power to Harrass & Distress them on their March, without suffering yourself to be reduc'd to any disagreeable situation."[21]

Inexplicably, General Maxwell never followed Washington's orders to assist in the removal of the Valley Forge supplies, a pressing problem that now caromed back to Washington. Apparently convinced it was too late to prevent the stores at Valley Forge from ending up in Howe's hands, Washington decided to destroy the flour at the depot there. To that end, he sent a small party of Colonel Theodorick Bland's regiment of Virginia Continental dragoons. In command the General placed the intrepid Captain "Light Horse" Harry Lee. Reflecting Washington's wish to have someone from his inner circle manage the mission, Lieutenant Colonel Alexander Hamilton sped eastward from Yellow Springs on Thursday, September 18, to oversee the Valley Forge operation. The twenty-three-year-old aide de camp had been taking on responsibilities beyond serving as a penman. The sortie to Valley Forge by far was his most important mission yet. But when he and the Virginians reached the riverbank due north of Valley Forge, they were set upon by British dragoons and light infantry before the work could even start. Lee and Hamilton escaped the casualty list but barely; Hamilton's horse was shot before his flatboat reached the opposite side of the Schuylkill, north of the contested region, while Lee wheeled westward and galloped away.[22]

Hamilton's inexperience and excitability now impelled him to send a series of dispatches to John Hancock warning the Continental Congress that the British had access to boats enabling them to convey men fifty at a time to the Philadelphia side of the river, where they would be within two days' march of the seat of U.S. government. He advised Congress to leave Philadelphia immediately. The messages reached the city in the first hours of Friday, creating a ruckus as Congress departed the city for the second time in ten months. This time delegates crossed the Delaware River into New Jersey, making their way northward before crossing back to Pennsylvania, but safely north of the capital. Sixteen settled temporarily in Bethlehem during the next four days. One of the newer delegates, James Lovell of Massachusetts, stayed in Philadelphia. He soon realized that Hamilton's warning had been a false alarm. Lovell distilled his reaction to a single word: "Scandalous!"[23]

Back at the furnaces, a dispatch sent by Captain Lee sank Washington's heart. Lee told the General he had heard gunshots directed at Hamilton's boat and feared the worst. But late on Thursday evening Hamilton rode up to headquarters two miles west of Reading Furnace. Hamilton filled in the General on the failed mission, saying he feared Lee had been cut off and perhaps captured. Likely amused, Washington handed Hamilton Lee's letter and watched his relieved reaction. Hamilton admitted warning Congress about Howe, but not that his alert included the line, "If Congress have not yet left Philadelphia, they ought to do it immediately without fail." No punishment befell Hamilton, partly because Hancock, with most of the legislature on the move, did not write to Washington for a week.[24] The delay softened the animus.

Washington's intelligence network had informed him of Howe's September 18 advance toward Swede's Ford. For the first time in the campaign Howe was separating Philadelphia from Washington as his primary target. Washington's headquarters west of Reading Furnace stood thirty-three road miles from the Philadelphia side of Swede's Ford. Getting his army there meant hours of marching and more hours to cross twelve thousand men—three Continental infantry brigades were detached and thus absent from the main body—as well as coping with a bottleneck at Parker's Ford near the halfway point. The most optimistic timetable for reaching Swede's Ford from the north and east side of the Schuylkill was a two-day venture. The American defense there consisted of four or possibly six cannons, as well as an undetermined number of Pennsylvania militia.

Washington marched his men out at dawn, hoping to reach the Philadelphia side of Swede's Ford before Howe's army overpowered the defenders there. Anthony Wayne shared that hope. "[F]or God's sake, push on as fast as possible," he urged his commander. Wayne had led his two brigades toward Paoli Tavern, two miles from the rear of Howe's encampment on the Swede's Ford Road. Washington had told Wayne that Smallwood and his division of newly raised militia of Marylanders, as well as General Maxwell's light infantry corps, would be supporting him. Smallwood was advancing down Caln Road from the west, but Washington apparently had either withdrawn Maxwell and his brigade without updating Wayne, or Maxwell had utterly failed to push his light force and Potter's militia close to the British rear. "I expect General Maxwell on [Howe's] left flank every Moment," Wayne declared Friday morning.[25]

Parker's Ford over the Schuylkill became the Grand Army's next destination. The vanguard was there by 2:00 P.M. Friday, September 19, after a sixteen-mile trek from the furnaces. The Continentals and militia needed more than four hours to cross. The baggage train never reached Warwick Furnace and would cross at Buckwater's Ford five miles downriver from Parker's. The upper waters of the river at Parker's Ford unexpectedly were running chest high—fifty dry hours after an eighteen-hour storm—and the current was strong enough to force the soldiers to interlock arms as they crossed.[26]

Given the coming of night and high water twenty-two miles upstream from Swede's Ford, Washington had expected Howe not to try to cross before Sunday at least. That being so, the General might be able to rest his men on the north side of this east-west segment of the Schuylkill. Intelligence altered his calculus. According to General Knox's Friday entry in his diary, "By the time the army had crossed night came on, but his Excellency having information of the enemy being at Flatland Ford on [the] Schuylkill and appeared as if intending to cross, thought it necessary for the army to march all night." The ford Knox called "Flatland" was Fatland Ford, a crossing four miles upstream of Swede's Ford. If the report proved accurate, Washington's destination was several miles closer to Swede's Ford than expected. He hoped "that I shall be down in time to give them a meeting, and if unfortunately they should gain Philadelphia, that it will not be without loss."[27]

No one could fault George Washington if he felt pangs of angst throughout the four-hour ordeal of crossing twelve thousand soldiers and nearly two score of cannons through a rapid river running over three feet high at this ford. During this fraught passage at Parker's, Washington took the time to study the daily drumbeat of letters and dispatches, particularly messages from Congress. Enclosed within the envelope containing John Hancock's letter was a resolution from Congress similar to one granted him during the desperate close to 1776.

Desperation returned ten months later. Congress, on September 17, vested Washington with sixty days of special war powers, authorizing him to act without legislators' approval to suspend misbehaving officers, single-handedly fill army vacancies with company and regimental officers, and confiscate property as needed from citizens for his army, provided he pay or provide certificates to dispossessed owners. Washington learned his authority extended to "the circumference of 70 miles of the headquarters of the American army."[28] This equated to authority generated from a headquarters location in Philadelphia to Perth Amboy on the New Jersey coastline, a mere half mile from Staten Island.

Although reminiscent of similar powers granted him before, Washington was no less honored and humbled by the responsibilities of this authority. "I am much obliged to Congress for the late instance of their Confidence, expressed in their Resolution of the 17th," replied the General at a moment where he truly was recognized by Congress as His Excellency, "and shall be happy if my conduct in discharging the Objects, they had in view should be such as to meet their approbation."[29]

The Grand Army reached the Philadelphia-Reading Road after dark and turned right. Washington continued to advance them southeastward down the pike. The night turned cold and foggy as wet, hungry soldiers cursed in the mist. At 2:00 A.M., the vanguard negotiated Perkiomen Creek. The army camped along a three-mile stretch of the road on both sides of the tributary.[30]

Washington had hustled much of his army forty-six miles in two days, a trek interrupted by pauses for ammunition at the furnaces and a difficult river crossing, both stops consuming several hours. He continued to press for reinforcements, particularly urging Brigadier General Alexander McDougall to rush his brigade of Connecticut Continentals from the Highlands Department to the Middle Department. The Continental army that bedded down on each side of Perkiomen Creek was drained and noticeably smaller than the force that had left Yellow Springs, probably numbering fewer than ten thousand. Subordinates told Washington that straggling was the chief reason for a strung-out command, along with orders sending unusually large detachments rearward to guard two immense trains. Some seven hundred ammunition wagons had crossed the Schuylkill on September 15, a day before the nor'easter. and stayed above the upper fords, and several hundred wagons of Washington's main baggage train crossed on Friday, September 19. Upwards of 1,500 wagons waited somewhere west of Washington's army, though even His Excellency knew not where. He issued orders to limit the baggage guards and to corral stragglers. Now was the time to concentrate his command.[31]

Washington likely did not sleep that night. He had stopped the head of his command about seven miles short of Fatland Ford based on wrong information that Crown forces had already reached his side of the Schuylkill. Relieved to learn that Howe and his army had barely moved along the Swede's Ford Road on September 19, the General roused his men to complete the mission. He pushed his troops forward beginning two hours before sunrise on Saturday, September 20. Celerity paid off. By Saturday afternoon the Americans could view British picket encampments across the river from Pawling's Ferry; these were some of Cornwallis's troops positioned north of Howe's Swede's Ford Road vanguard. Washington's Life Guard chose as headquarters Thompson's Tavern, less than three miles west of Swede's Ford and four miles northeast of Fatland Ford.[32]

Washington sent reinforcements to the militia fort at Swede's Ford and now had the next six crossings for ten miles above that location covered. Howe could not conduct an unopposed crossing. Washington had him nearly in complete check. Crown forces could not cross a river for several hours without immediate, continuous challenge by the Continentals facing them. Still, Washington worried. The fording of the Brandywine on the right of the army on September 11 must have played in the General's mind. But this time, he was ready, having assigned Sullivan's division to break up and obstruct six fords along a ten-mile stretch of river: three fords leading to French Creek (Richardson's, Long, and Gordon's) and three westward up the river (Buckwater's, North, and Parker's).

John Sullivan had, for the time being, successfully recovered from his summertime bout with the bottle to battle the British on Birmingham Hill and afterwards congressional delegates, facing charges for his performance in the failed American efforts on Staten Island and at Brandywine. Thanks to Washington's influence and insistence, Sullivan continued to serve The Cause in the field while awaiting a court martial. Sullivan, a pre-war militia major and lawyer, began the Revolutionary War as a thirty-five-year-old New Hampshire delegate to the Continental Congress, first appointed in the summer of 1774 and reappointed six months later. He departed Congress as a freshly minted brigadier general in June 1775, joining Washington's army at Boston. A brief stint in Canada followed in the spring of 1776. By August of that year, Sullivan was a major general, endorsed by Washington as "active, spirited and zealously attached to the cause."[33]

He joined the General in New York, where on August 27 he and General Stirling were both captured in the Battle of Long Island. Officially exchanged two months later, Sullivan returned to the army as a subordinate general under the irascible Charles Lee. Sullivan took over Lee's command after the latter's capture on December 13, 1776, at Basking Ridge, New

Jersey, and ably led those men through the Battles of Trenton, Assunpink Creek, and Princeton. By the summer of 1777, due to Lee's prolonged captivity and the departure of General Gates to the Northern Department, Sullivan, after uniting his independently operating division with the Grand Army on September 3, had become Washington's highest-ranking subordinate. His newest orders—to disperse his Marylanders to all crossing points along the Schuylkill—must have been uncomfortably reminiscent of his responsibilities along the Brandywine ten days earlier.

Washington painstakingly instructed Sullivan to block all these fords, specifying areas the region's inhabitants insisted the foe would not attempt. After the crossing points were adequately broken up and obstructed, Sullivan was ordered to post exactly thirteen soldiers at each crossing with additional parties directly across from the western wing of Howe's army. Each post was to alert Washington the instant that position was challenged, or movements discovered.[34] The commander in chief assured that Brooklyn and Brandywine would not be repeated on the Schuylkill.

But he assured much more than that. General Howe's great gamble—foregoing the short, bloodless march into Philadelphia via Levering's Ford on September 16 and opting instead to attempt to win the war by destroying Washington's army at White Horse Tavern—appeared to be a British catastrophe by noon on September 20. As close as he had come to destroying Washington four days earlier, Howe was now separated from his much more agile adversary by several miles with a river in between. Howe must have realized by noontime on Saturday that Washington was too wary to be surprised again and too elusive to be chased down.

It was much worse for Crown forces on the opposite side of the river. Thirty road miles separated the troops from their depot at Wilmington and they were seventy miles from their remaining stores at Head of Elk. Howe was short on foraging opportunities. Washington had two brigades of Continentals and two brigades of militia operating southwest of him. Any foraging party heading away from his army risked being swept away by the force Washington had planted near the junction of Swede's Ford Road and Lancaster Pike. That force also kept any supply line from reaching Howe's army from the Delaware or Chesapeake.

A day earlier, Howe had enjoyed the advantage of time and distance over Washington to cross the Schuylkill and head toward Philadelphia and its provisions and forage. Washington's superlative marching effort gained thirty miles and crossed the river. Howe needed several hours to cross his army and supply train over an upper Schuylkill ford, but Washington had skillfully prevented him from even attempting that, as well as placing American dragoons on Howe's side of the river to alert Washington of any such bid. General Wayne had told Washington his presence behind Howe's rearguard had not been detected. Once Smallwood's Marylanders, who were less than half a day away from Wayne, reached his position south of Warren Tavern, their combined force of three thousand would present a major obstacle to Howe if he attempted to shift rearward.

Three sides of a box formed by American soldiers and the Schuylkill River restricted Howe's freedom of maneuver. By all appearances, Washington should have effectively kept Howe on the west side of the Schuylkill and well away from Philadelphia indefinitely. His Excellency also could starve Howe's force stuck on Swede's Ford Road. "I think we have no reason to be Cast Down," wrote Joseph Reed, "for I have not the least Doubt (with the permission of Heaven) but we shall ruin their Army before the end of the Campaign."[35]

Washington held Howe in check at noon on September 20. Provided his troops and his will held, check could advance to checkmate before the close of the month.

CHAPTER EIGHT

"He Does Not Know How to Improve Upon the Grossest Blunders of the Enemy"

September 21 to September 26, 1777

With sunrise near on Sunday morning, September 21, a British trumpeter signaled for and was granted permission from American troops to pass across the Schuylkill River near Gordon's Ford. The man held a message from General Howe for General Washington. In the message, vague but ominous, Howe informed Washington that he had "some" wounded American prisoners, officers and men, at Howell's Tavern and neighboring dwellings, asking that Washington send a surgeon to tend to them. As prisoners of war, Howe noted, once healed the men would need to be exchanged before they could return to the Continental army. Inexplicably, the message miscarried. Washington spent the daylight hours of September 21 oblivious to a midnight disaster involving one of his divisions that came to be known as the "Paoli Massacre."[1]

September 21 was the nadir of the campaign for the Americans. Washington departed headquarters that morning to inspect his ford and ferry defenses. Following the eighteen-hour storm that ended Wednesday morning, dry, windy weather had reigned regionally for four days and nights. The Schuylkill "has fallen and is fordable at almost any place, the enemy can have no reason to delay passing much longer," Tench Tilghman wrote Saturday morning. As Washington was approaching the Schuylkill crossings from the north, Howe was redeploying his army from Swede's Ford Road north to the banks of the Schuylkill. By early afternoon, much of Howe's army covered the five miles of east-west road between Fatland Ford and Gordon's Ford. By moving forward en masse, Howe appeared to be challenging one or more of the six crossing points (four fords and two ferry sites) in that five-mile stretch opposed by Washington's army.[2]

Incredibly, Washington ensured that that would happen. At 3:00 P.M. he ordered all infantry guarding the fords downriver from Richardson's Ford to pull back five miles northwest to the Philadelphia-Reading Road, there to await further orders. Washington was planning to shift them toward Reading. Five miles in that direction, civilians living near Trappe had been advised that a battle might be fought there and that the return of the American army was expected.[3]

Washington now chose to act upon the sixty-day war powers recently granted him by the Continental Congress and received by him the morning he led his army from the furnaces to Parker's Ford. His focus this day was on one of those extensive powers: "to take . . . all such provisions and other articles as may be necessary for the comfortable subsistence of the army," And to remove and secure, for the benefit of the owners, all goods and effects which may be serviceable to the enemy."[4] Should Howe verge on occupying Philadelphia, Washington planned to impress property in Philadelphia not only for his army's needs, but also to deny his foe those luxuries.

Hamilton, Washington's operative for this mission, was to ride twenty miles from Thompson's Tavern to Philadelphia to procure blankets and clothes from the city's inhabitants. Hamilton also was to herd the city's horses out of town to deny them to Howe, whose supply of horseflesh was inadequate, which had become apparent at Head of Elk four weeks earlier. Instructing his aide to give certificates of payment for the property and to procure whatever he felt necessary, Washington sent him, presumably with dragoons and most definitely with an impressive degree of faith and trust in Hamilton's talent and ability.[5]

Hamilton departed for Philadelphia that Sunday. Later that day, most of Washington's army began to move farther from the capital. Without Wayne and Smallwood challenging Howe's shift of direction, Washington relied on his cavalry across the river and on intelligence from residents along the river. He believed Howe was strengthening and extending westward, perhaps seeking a surprise crossing, maybe one even farther up the Schuylkill from Parker's Ford, the extent of the American defensive line. Reading stood on Washington's side of the river, thirty-five road miles from Swede's Ford. Besides holding prisoners, Reading—not to be confused with Reading Furnace—was home to the Americans' largest depot of military supplies. As the General later explained, the loss of Reading "must have proved our Ruin."[6]

He refused to be ruined. At 8:00 P.M., Washington sent orders to General Sullivan through Lieutenant Colonel John Fitzgerald: "By order of his Excellency I have to inform you that this Army is about to March up the Road by which we came down & is not to Halt untill we get beyond that Road which leads from Parker's Ford into the Reading Road, beyond the Trapp." Instead of protecting the fords that had checked Howe, Washington abandoned them. Sullivan was to parallel the army's westward advance, keeping between them and the river, and merely leave a few soldiers at each of the six fords he had been guarding as observational posts rather than serious forces capable of offering resistance.[7]

About this time the General learned for the first time that Howe had removed the threat to the rear of his army. Washington perceived a vague hint of trouble in Howe's request for a surgeon—a message that reached him half a day late.[8] At about the same time, Washington opened a dispatch from General Wayne delivered by a courier who had carried it thirty miles. The noon heading stated Wayne was at Red Lion Tavern, eight miles west of his original position near Paoli Tavern, alerting Washington to a problem that had arisen over the previous night. Wayne described a surprise bayonet attack near midnight which dislodged Wayne from his position, along with Smallwood, who was just arriving, and drove both commands completely away from Howe's rear. Wayne's wording lacked the urgency the action and outcome deserved, failing even to allude to the lopsided nature of the contest or its viciousness.[9] Washington did not learn that at the cost of only eleven Crown casualties, British troops had killed, wounded, and captured 272 Americans—bayoneting fifty-three of those men to death.

The manner of Wayne's defeat, particularly the brutal British tactics, was to resonate far beyond Sunday evening. Washington told Wayne, in perhaps his last message from Thompson's Tavern, to march with Smallwood and his force to join him near Pottsgrove, a town on the Schuylkill halfway between Washington's army and Reading. Washington and nearly three dozen headquarters personnel departed Thompson's Tavern as the army was marching away from the region at 9:00 P.M.[10] At midnight the vanguard had passed Trappe, ensuring that Washington would not be flanked at Parker's Ford or upstream.

Washington was overreacting. Howe had no intention of flanking the Grand Army farther up the Schuylkill. The British general had made clear by complete omission since September 3, the day he drove the Americans from Cooch's Bridge, of any references to having designs on Reading, even though for the next two weeks, until the action at the White Horse Tavern, he had the option of interposing his army between Washington and that supply depot. Likewise, Washington made no mention in conversation or writing of any concern during those two weeks that Howe's inside track to Reading stood to threaten that prized depot. Through Sunday, September 21, Howe anchored his left (western) flank on French Creek, a meandering tributary which emptied into the Schuylkill at Gordon's Ford. There the Hessians and British stood, ten miles as the crow flew below the easternmost segment of Washington's force.[11] Washington's exaggerated response to a perceived threat placed Howe between the Continental army and Philadelphia and opened wide all six crossings to Crown forces.

General Greene and Colonel Pickering stayed in the rear as part of that portion of the army that night. Together they watered their horses at Perkiomen Creek. Dismayed by what he saw as Washington behaving like a "passive spectator" at Brandywine and his "dangerous indecision" on September 16, Pickering had something to get off his chest. "General Greene, I had once conceived an exalted opinion of General Washington's military talents," Pickering said, "but, since I have been with the army, I have seen nothing to increase it." Pickering held back from voicing his conviction that he saw nothing to support his once-awestruck opinion of the General, let alone anything to "increase" his regard now.

Rather than remind Pickering of Washington's successes at Trenton, Assunpink Creek, and Princeton, Greene joined Pickering in carping about Washington's shortcomings, particularly his indecisiveness. "[F]or my part," Greene then said, "I decide in a moment."[12] Washington's excessive rashness—flippancy, some might say—had propelled this retrograde movement. Had he taken the opportunity to pause, or to consult with his most trusted confidants within his headquarters staff and his division commanders, the

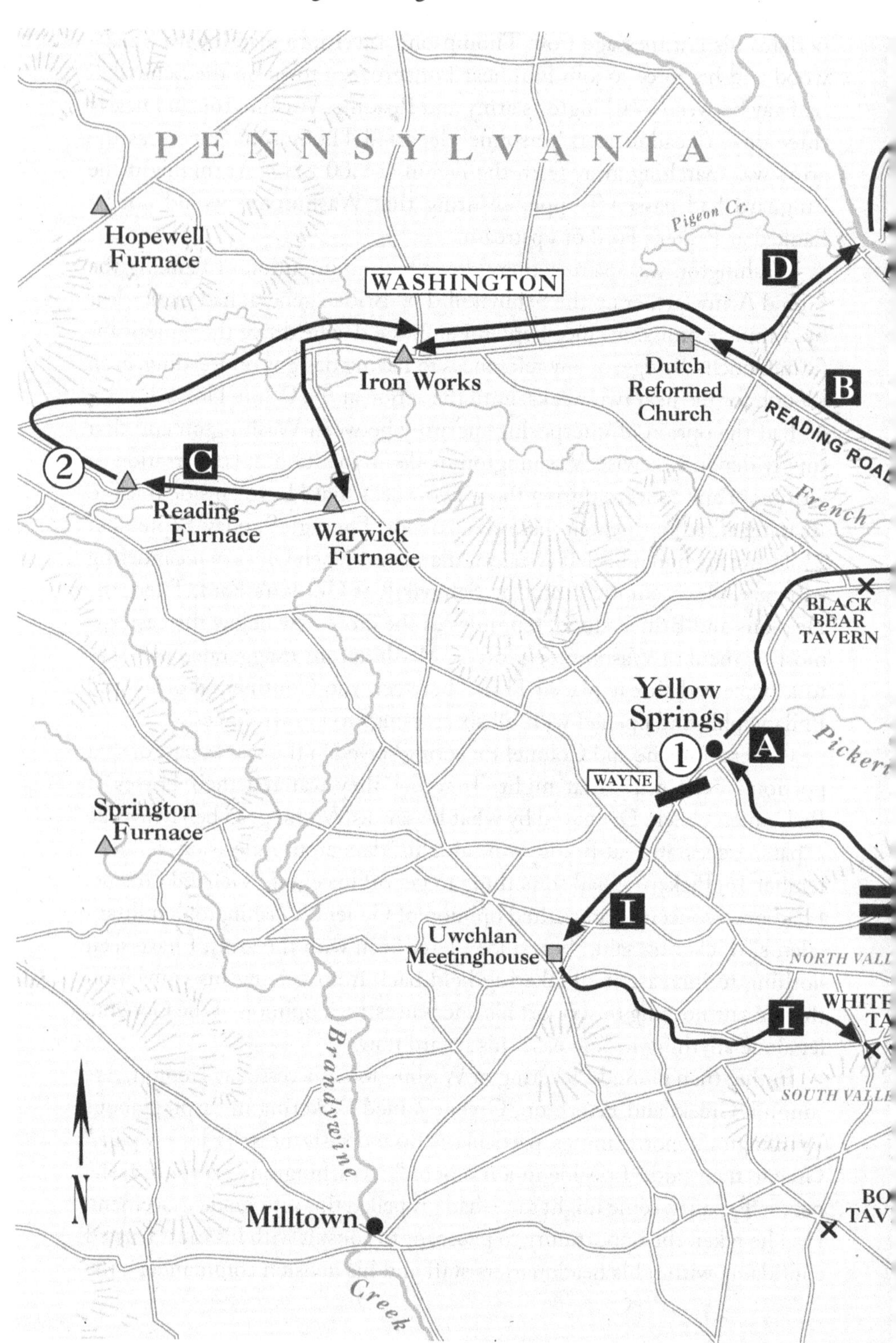
PENNSYLVANIA
Hopewell Furnace
WASHINGTON
Pigeon Cr.
D
Iron Works
Dutch Reformed Church
B
READING ROAD
C
2
Reading Furnace
Warwick Furnace
French
BLACK BEAR TAVERN
Yellow Springs
1
A
Pickeri
WAYNE
Springton Furnace
I
Uwchlan Meetinghouse
NORTH VALL
WHITE TA
I
SOUTH VALLE
Brandywine
N
Milltown
BO TAV
Creek

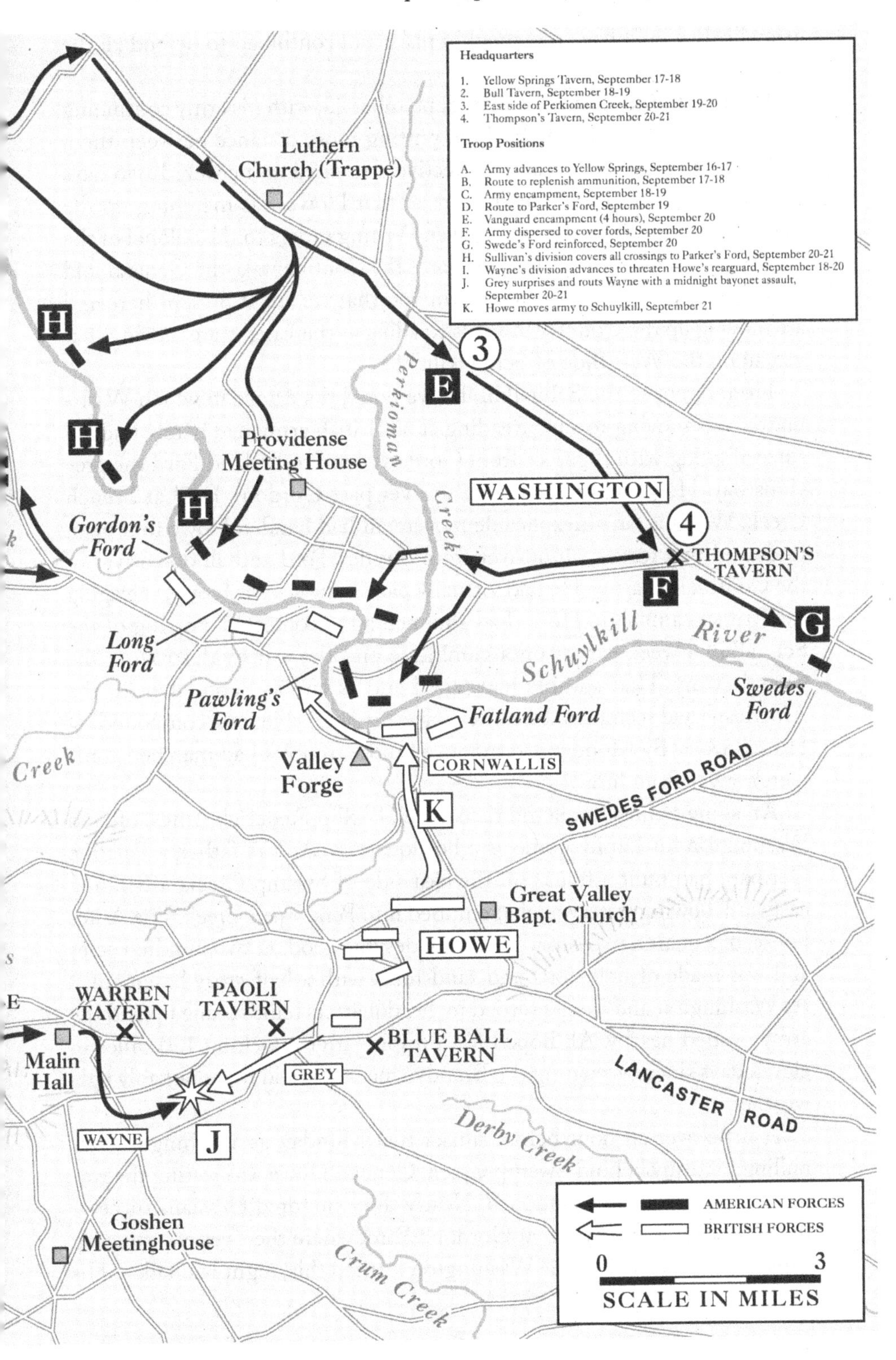
Headquarters
1. Yellow Springs Tavern, September 17-18
2. Bull Tavern, September 18-19
3. East side of Perkiomen Creek, September 19-20
4. Thompson's Tavern, September 20-21
Troop Positions
A. Army advances to Yellow Springs, September 16-17
B. Route to replenish ammunition, September 17-18
C. Army encampment, September 18-19
D. Route to Parker's Ford, September 19
E. Vanguard encampment (4 hours), September 20
F. Army dispersed to cover fords, September 20
G. Swede's Ford reinforced, September 20
H. Sullivan's division covers all crossings to Parker's Ford, September 20-21
I. Wayne's division advances to threaten Howe's rearguard, September 18-20
J. Grey surprises and routs Wayne with a midnight bayonet assault, September 20-21
K. Howe moves army to Schuylkill, September 21
Luthern Church (Trappe)
Providense Meeting House
Perkioman Creek
WASHINGTON
THOMPSON'S TAVERN
Gordon's Ford
Long Ford
Pawling's Ford
Fatland Ford
Schuylkill River
Swedes Ford
Valley Forge
CORNWALLIS
SWEDES FORD ROAD
Creek
Great Valley Bapt. Church
HOWE
WARREN TAVERN
PAOLI TAVERN
BLUE BALL TAVERN
Malin Hall
GREY
WAYNE
LANCASTER ROAD
Derby Creek
Goshen Meetinghouse
Crum Creek
AMERICAN FORCES
BRITISH FORCES
0 3
SCALE IN MILES

army likely would have remained in place and continued to defend all the fords.

Washington woke on Monday, September 22, with his army continuing to shift westward toward Reading, putting more distance between them and fords that the men had so effectively reached and covered two days earlier. Washington continued to insist that Howe was marching up the roads on the opposite side of the river. Writing orders to the colonel of the 1st Virginia State Regiment to reinforce the Continentals, the General told him, "I think it [is] proper to inform you that we are at present here and are moving up the Country towards Reading as the Enemy are moving that way upon the West Side of Schuylkill."[13]

From opposite the Schuylkill, Howe noted the extent to which Washington was moving toward Reading. The British army had barely budged since aligning with the river from Gordon's Ford to Fatland Ford the previous day. Howe was not moving upriver past Gordon's Ford at French Creek. Washington's inexplicable movement had handed Howe four open fords and two ferries, all upriver from Swede's Ford and all downriver of the Continental army. He had virtually parted the sea for Howe, salvaging the British campaign. Howe had shunned an uncontested crossing of the Schuylkill a week earlier on a gamble to end the war by destroying the Grand Army. That gamble had failed and as late as September 20 the Americans had seemed to be contesting every accessible ford, compounding Howe's woes. By Monday afternoon, all those troubles had marched completely away from him.[14]

An aging Pennsylvania militia colonel, Phillip Frederick Antes, offered Washington his family home as a headquarters. Antes's father, a Palatine German, had built a house on the east side of Swamp Creek, a winding eastward-flowing waterway that emptied into Perkiomen Creek. The Antes house, of a quaint, two-story Moravian design, stood on two hundred acres and was made of fieldstone and sandstone, with a half-story basement.[15] As Washington and troupe settled in, headquarters tents sprang up and the army nestled nearby. All hoped for a respite after marching 120 miles in eleven days since evacuating the Brandywine battlefield in remarkably ugly weather.

A little over an hour before sunset that Monday, as Washington was pulling his army behind Swamp Creek, General Howe was testing the waters Washington had abandoned. Nearly three hundred Hessians successfully crossed the Schuylkill at Gordon's Ford, where the river was running three feet deep. By the time Washington learned this, night had fallen. His army rested eighteen miles by roads to Fatland Ford, and fifteen miles from Gordon's Ford. By acting immediately, he could have had troops at Gordon's Ford in five hours to disrupt part of Howe's crossing or at least harried his several hundred baggage wagons. But Washington never pulled that trigger, convinced by what proved to be faulty intelligence claiming Howe was not crossing the river. Washington dispatched hand-picked troops to gather more intelligence, but he did nothing else.[16]

Washington's vacillation cost him the nation's most important city. Unopposed, Howe crossed his entire army beginning at midnight at the two fords, but primarily using Fatland Ford. Howe's baggage did not even begin to ford until the forenoon of Tuesday, September 23, and was not rolling onto dry roads on the Philadelphia side of the river until after 1:00 P.M., while Washington and his army remained in place northwest of the Crown force, offering no resistance. By allowing Howe more than thirteen hours unmolested, during which he glided past what two days before had clearly been an impenetrable barrier, Washington committed an error far greater than any on the Brandywine battlefield a dozen days earlier. A few hours later, Howe rubbed salt into Washington's freshest campaign wound by driving Armstrong's militia away from Swede's Ford, the Americans reportedly leaving several cannons behind.[17]

Howe and his army encamped below Stony Creek, ten miles southeast of the Continental army and sixteen uncontested miles northwest of Philadelphia. Howe remained there for another entire day, appearing to invite Washington to attempt an attack before he commenced his march down to Germantown and eight miles farther to the great city. Washington reassessed. As much as he wanted to attack, he was rightly concerned about his troops' condition. Nearly ten percent of his soldiers were barefoot. He had sent Hamilton to Philadelphia for shoes, among other necessities, but Howe's approach likely aborted that mission.[18]

Shortly after receiving confirmation of Howe's escape, Washington called a council of war in the Antes house. Except for Anthony Wayne, who was still detached, all of Washington's division commanders and a few brigadiers participated. The newest face at headquarters and a Washington favorite, John Cadwalader, was also present, standing very near Brigadier General Thomas Conway. The two hardly knew each other but were destined to engage in an ultimate display of acrimony in the not-too-distant future.

Washington said he was expecting his visibly smaller army to be reinforced by four bodies of troops: Wayne's division, Smallwood's newly recruited Marylanders, New Jersey militia under Dickinson, and a Continental brigade approaching from Peekskill, New York, led by Brigadier General Alexander McDougall. Washington queried the generals as to whether they should "attack the Enemy" with the force at hand or wait for reinforcements. Implicit in the question was the understanding that Howe had crossed his army over the Schuylkill and would be attacked on the Americans' side of the river. The answer was unanimous: wait until reinforced. That they would attack was assumed. Washington would not consider defensive tactics for the rest of the campaign.

Unlike the General's previous three councils at Derby, Wilmington, and Germantown, the meeting in the Antes house was recorded on paper, and unlike most councils the previous two years this one was documented by three participants. Tench Tilghman, a veteran of many councils, took notes and completed the army headquarters draft. Stirling and Greene each personally created a record. Stirling's is likely the most complete and unvarnished narrative of the meeting, differing only by summarizing events since leaving Germantown on September 14, a sidebar that Washington provided at the start of the conclave.[19]

Why did Washington summarize the events? He claimed during the meeting to have done so for the benefit of participants who had been detached from the army during the movements. There may be much more to this. Washington apparently was attempting to rewrite history, replacing actual events and decisions with a more convenient explanation. He claimed that after crossing the Schuylkill nine days earlier, the army was impeded on September 15, a day that the commanding general had "intended to go on towards the Enemy," but could not due to neglect and confusion in the commissary department. This neglect resulted in a lack of provisions for the troops. Washington's attempt to remedy this was effective but costly: "this Greatest part of that day was lost, by which means the Enemy had time to gain Intelligence of our motions, and were preparing to Attack us the next day."

This was General Stirling's version, an account not repeated in the surviving headquarters draft. The seemingly accurate note-taking likely was by Stirling's aide but the claim he captured on pen and paper was entirely fictitious. Not only does no evidence exist to document a catastrophe in the commissary department grinding the army to a halt for "this Greatest part" of September 15, but the soldiery completed a successful day of advance that Monday, with the vanguard marching fifteen miles before stopping west of White Horse Tavern in the afternoon. Had Washington's men moved considerably farther that day, they would have inadvertently opened all the roads from Howe's position to the Schuylkill rather than blocking the most widely used one to Swede's Ford. The Continentals had marched so efficiently as to worry Washington, who uncharacteristically had stayed back with most of his staff that day, most likely to assure himself that Howe had no intention of slipping in behind his westward advancing force to cross Levering's Ford and head to Philadelphia. Washington's complaint that Howe "had time to gain Intelligence of our motions," is exactly what Washington desired, in hopes of diverting Howe from a quick and bloodless entry into Philadelphia and instead drawing him toward the Continentals.

Washington's headquarters version of the meeting did not include the fictitious account. But the fabricated story is what he told subordinates, as confirmed by Stirling's version. Confecting a scenario to explain why a confrontation with Howe failed to materialize indicates Washington was becoming sensitive regarding his errors and the impression they may have been leaving on those he was leading into battle.

Washington's chagrin at Howe's getaway so fixated him that Tuesday as to reveal more puzzling thoughts and decisions beyond the council. He blamed regional impediments for the exaggerated twelve-mile shift that took his men four marching hours away from fords by which they had planted themselves two days earlier. He complained that a strong "disaffected" Loyalist element was impairing his intelligence gathering and keeping Howe several steps ahead of him. He briefly entertained the notion that he was the victim of a feint: "After various maneuvers and extending his army high up the Schuylkill . . . General Howe made a sudden countermarch on Monday night." Not only did this countermarch never occur, but the point from where Washington claimed it started—Gordon's Ford—would have gone unchallenged by the Americans had Howe chosen to cross all his troops there rather than just his Hessian posts.[20]

As Washington was telling Congress what happened on the upper Schuylkill, he was deceiving John Hancock regarding Wayne's defeat near Paoli. Two days before, on Sunday, September 21, the commander in chief had known very little about that debacle's extent. Howe's request for surgeons to tend to "some wounded Officers & Men of your Army" barely hinted at a major defeat of Wayne—those casualties could just have easily derived from a surprised American dragoon patrol. Wayne then reported that his division had been surprised and driven from the field by a bayonet attack, and that he planned to return soon to collect and bury the dead.

That report, now coupled with Howe's dispatch, more ominously suggested a costly, casualty-laden contest. Knox in his September 22 diary entry wrote that Wayne's defeat was catastrophic, a characterization deduced that Monday from additional intelligence.

Yet more than twenty hours after receiving this news, Washington disingenuously informed Hancock, "I am obliged to wait for Genl Wayne and Genl Smallwood who were left upon the other Side of the Schuylkill in hopes of falling upon the Enemy's Rear, but they have eluded them as well as us."[21] However Hancock interpreted the pronouns in that statement's final phrase, Washington had misled the head of the Continental Congress by using the phrase "eluded them" to describe a reported catastrophic battle defeat, even in preliminary form.

Whether the General was purposely withholding this information from Congress pending receipt of a full report or coyly hiding another setback, momentum had turned sharply in Great Britain's favor. This shift was unmistakable and had begun to damage Washington's reputation. As General Greene and Colonel Pickering demonstrated, this first surfaced in the military. A disappointed and perhaps disillusioned General Smallwood informed Maryland's governor about Howe's embarrassingly easy crossing of the Schuylkill: "they seem to have nothing to do but push forward and of course we run away," Smallwood said. "It is to be lamented that human Nature is subject to so much Degeneracy, but I will drop the subject; I can't think of it with patience."[22] Major General Johann de Kalb, appointed to the Continental army in the same September congressional resolution that tapped Pulaski, was stewing in Lancaster while he awaited a command post. Although frustrated from inactivity and apparently a little biased against Washington for harboring "old prejudices against the French," Kalb had earlier considered the General "the most amiable, kind-hearted, and upright of men." But Kalb had nothing else positive to write about Washington in a September 24 letter to the Comte de Broglie in France:

> [A]s a General he is too slow, too indolent, and far too weak; besides, he has a tinge of vanity in his composition, and overestimates himself. In my opinion any success he may have will be owing to good luck and to the blunders of his adversaries, rather than to his abilities. I may even say that he does not know how to improve upon the grossest blunders of the enemy.[23]

Most damaging to Washington was the effect the campaign was having on his most trusted subordinates, as seen in Greene's and Pickering's griping at Perkiomen Creek, but also among the rank and file. One soldier, describing the incidents that led to Howe's army slipping between Washington and Philadelphia, nonetheless refused to criticize his commanding general over the blunder. This commentator described a critic as "some blustering hero, in fighting his battles over a glass of madeira, may take upon him to arraign the conduct of our general, and stigmatize the army as cowards." Another officer addressed the public through his hometown newspaper. "I hope . . . no one will suspect our General of neglect, or want of military skill," he said in a letter to the editor.[24]

On Thursday, September 25, Howe's army marched into Germantown. The next day he took control of Philadelphia. Friday, September 26, 1777, starkly embodied the failure of Washington's campaign, rife with miscues of maneuver and machinations. Long-gestating seeds of failure had sprouted. Washington's response would determine whether those sprouts would yield fruit or thorns.

CHAPTER NINE

"This Happy Opportunity"

September 27 to October 10, 1777

Charles Willson Peale entered Continental army headquarters, just inside the west bank of Perkiomen Creek. Peale, twenty-six, had an appointment with General George Washington. A Pennsylvania militia captain, Peale, in prewar days a Son of Liberty, had failed as a saddle maker, clock fixer, and metalsmith but had honed another talent for which he was renowned—painting portraits and miniatures.[1]

George and Martha Washington had met Captain Peale several years earlier, even before the Maryland native had moved to Philadelphia from Annapolis. General Washington first sat for Peale at Mount Vernon in 1772 when, at 40, he posed for his earliest known portrait, which his wife had commissioned. Peale rendered her spouse as a three-quarters length image clad in the uniform he had worn as colonel of the Virginia Regiment fourteen years before. Early in the Revolutionary War several paintings followed, at least two by Peale.[2] Copies of those images, somewhat altered, circulated as miniatures—personal keepsakes housed in lockets and bracelets. In the summer of 1776 Martha Washington commissioned Peale to fashion a miniature to be derived from a large portrait commissioned by John Hancock earlier that year. Mrs. Washington's dissatisfaction with that portrait had prompted her to hire Peale again in 1777, insisting that her husband sit again for the artist.

The General rebuffed several attempts by the artist to arrange a sitting that summer when he was monitoring activity along the Raritan River. Peale's only "success" was an inexact June 26 sketch of two men on the riverbank watching action taking place across the water. One of the figures was Washington; the other, Peale.[3] The summer otherwise passed without the desired sitting; the General alleged that he could not spare the time.

Washington now surprised Peale by offering his full attention to sitting for a sketch "from life" that the artist would convert to a miniature. Given the General's circumstances, this was a most unusual change of heart. His days were ever more harried as he sought to edge closer to Philadelphia to attack. He had been planning this action in broad strokes since September 13; in the next ten days his thinking had gained purpose and definition. Arriving at Perkiomen Creek on September 26, Washington a day later summarized the campaign to a confidant. Seeking what he called "a Second Action" after the defeat on the Brandywine, he insisted that "a General Attack would have been made on their Front" on the heights south of White Horse Tavern, a battle sought by both sides but obliterated by the storm of September 16.[4] The quest for that "Second Action" only intensified in the wake of that storm, bringing the Continentals to the creek and within two days' march of Howe's army.

With the war gaining intensity, why sit for a painting? Washington understood that when launching a mass assault against a world-renowned military force, defeat was not the worst outcome. Washington's last tactical offensive, at Princeton, almost killed him. That January assault involved but a few British regiments. His next offensive could happen within the week and pit him against an army at least ten times larger. He might not survive that clash. Perhaps he was sitting for mortal posterity—or maybe a letter from Martha either sweetly importuning him or sternly remonstrating with him to sit had in one way or the other struck home.

No doubt Washington's agreeability thrilled Charles Peale, whose enthusiasm perhaps was tempered by his cramped working conditions. Washington's quarters could hardly accommodate a table, a chair, and the general's borrowed bed. Peale positioned himself near the room's low window while the General sat at the edge of the bed, stilling his head so the artist could capture his visage for a detailed sketch.

Washington so dedicated himself to the endeavor that even an incredibly important interruption did not end the early evening sitting. Tench Tilghman entered to hand Washington a dispatch from an unidentified source whom Washington called "a pretty direct Channel" to the Northern Department. Washington opened the dispatch and glanced at its contents long enough to absorb the gist. Eight days earlier, at Saratoga, New York, Major General John Burgoyne had launched multiple attacks on Gates's position but each time was repulsed. Washington hailed the news with an uncharacteristic and uncontrolled exclamation. He handed the dispatch back to Tilghman, then snatched it for further study after the sitting.[5] Perhaps owing to the encouraging words he had just read, Washington seemed to Peale to soften his expression compared to his mien in 1776, when he sat for the portrait commissioned by Hancock. Confident that Mrs. Washington would approve of what he had just captured and created, Peale next would convert his sketch into the miniature she had commissioned.[6]

Afterwards Washington scrutinized the dispatch from Saratoga. On September 19, Burgoyne's army assaulted Gates's left flank at John Freeman's farm. Four British assaults were repulsed with mounting bloodshed against an American line commanded by Major General Benedict Arnold and supported by Colonel Daniel Morgan's riflemen. Both commanders and Morgan's troops had been handpicked by Washington to aid the Northern Department, choices vital to success. Tactically, at Freeman's farm the British outlasted the Americans; Arnold withdrew his men eastward one and a half miles to the chief American defense at Bemis Heights on the west bank of the Hudson River, twenty-five river miles north of Albany. But Burgoyne's victory was pyrrhic. He suffered six hundred casualties, compared to slightly less than half that on the American side.[7]

Washington briefly summarized the intelligence from Saratoga at the end of a letter he had Caleb Gibbs draft for him. In it he acknowledged that his source was "yet not so authentic, as I could wish." Authenticity would have meant Gates communicating directly and in a timely manner to him. No one could fault Washington if the unofficial news caused some frustration. Gates's headquarters near Bemis Heights stood 270 road miles north of Washington's encampment. Eight days was not an unreasonable timeline for covering that distance on horseback, but Washington did expect Gates or an acceptable surrogate to be his source. Regardless, the account was fairly accurate, save for an incorrect aside about General Burgoyne suffering a shoulder wound during the battle. Washington trusted the dispatch enough to have it included in General Orders the following morning: "To celebrate this success, the General orders that at four o'clock this afternoon all of the troops be paraded and served with a gill of rum a man—and that at the same time there be a discharge of *Thirteen* pieces of artillery at the park.[8]

That celebration was memorable for the troops and local residents, but the generals had a more important matter to address. Washington's fifth council of war in five weeks commenced on the west side of Perkiomen Creek. His headquarters was now the spacious two-story stone house in which he had posed the day before for Peale. Owner Henry Keeley happily hosted the General in his home, located about 1,200 yards southwest of a grist mill built by John Pawling, to which Peter Pennypacker had added a fulling mill eastward on the opposite bank. Those surnames came to be interchangeable identifiers for the surrounding Continental encampment. Staff tents sprouted among the walnut and pear trees that surrounded the house, outside which that Sunday nineteen additional horses were hitched while the generals who had ridden them gathered inside.[9]

This council was a carryover from one five days earlier at the Antes house. Washington had moved only five road miles southeast, but much had transpired, indicated by the crowded council. In addition to all five Continental division commanders, artillery chief Knox and the head of his militia, Armstrong, attended, along with nine brigade generals. These included two commanders reporting to Armstrong. James Irvine, a former Philadelphia hatter with Seven Years' War experience, had been stationed near Wilmington. James Potter, a Scots-Irish immigrant, had marched with Washington from Delaware. That Washington had finally received reinforcements was evident from the presence of Brigadier General Alexander McDougall, whose brigade of Connecticut Continentals had reached Washington's army two days before. So had Brigadier General William Smallwood with his newly recruited Maryland militiamen. John Cadwalader—a brigadier general of militia and a Washington favorite—was present as a headquarters guest, as was Joseph Reed, Washington's former adjutant general.[10]

The carry-over topic from the previous council was a plan to attack Howe's army, which had captured Philadelphia two days earlier. Washington began by saying that the enemy was essentially split into two, one force in Germantown and one in Philadelphia. Most participants knew the environs well enough to calculate that the two wings were about five miles from each other. Washington quickly followed with an estimate of the British numbers at Germantown—eight thousand. He inadvertently undercounted by more than one thousand officers and men.

Washington reviewed the status of much needed reinforcements. McDougall's Continentals and Smallwood's militia soldiers brought the infantry count to eleven thousand officers and men. He did not mention artillery or Continental dragoons, whose presence added another 1,500. The remaining militia, primarily Pennsylvanian, came in at three thousand, similar to what he had had at the Battle of Brandywine. Although McDougall had reinforced the Continental army with nine hundred soldiers, Washington still had five thousand fewer Continental infantry with him near Pennypacker's Mill on September 28 than he had had on the eve of battle along the Brandywine on September 10. There had been two thousand Continental casualties, mostly at Brandywine and Paoli. This left three thousand other soldiers absent from his ranks. Hundreds were sick in makeshift hospitals near Yellow Springs and scores of others were on detached service, for example as guards in Bethlehem minding nine hundred baggage wagons. Still unaccounted for were upwards of two thousand men.[11]

As at the previous council, Washington said he was expecting more reinforcements, specifically about two thousand Virginia militia. These men were poorly armed, he admitted. He indicated that he had sent an express to General Putnam to dispatch over one thousand men from the Highlands Department on McDougall's route to reinforce him. Unlike the Virginia militia, these men would be well-armed Continentals, but they could not be expected soon even if Putnam moved immediately. What Washington did not reveal to his gathering is that two days earlier he had sent a request to Gates asking him to return Daniel Morgan and his riflemen to Washington's army, "if his services can be dispensed with now."[12]

The generals voted against an immediate attack but resolved that Washington's assault would be inevitable. To that end, they agreed to move closer to Philadelphia. The Pennypacker's Mill encampment on the Perkiomen was twenty-five miles from Howe's most advanced location in Germantown. The generals recommended halving that distance by seeking and securing "Grounds proper for an Encampment within about twelve miles of the Enemy, or to wait further Reinforcements."[13]

On Monday, September 29, Washington—through Tench Tilghman's quill—notified John Hancock of the army's plan to advance toward

Philadelphia to "enable us to make an attack should we see a proper opening." The letter was read into the congressional record on October 1, a delay caused by the relocation of the Continental Congress from Philadelphia to Lancaster and then to York. The eighty road miles between Congress and Washington was not unwelcome to the General, even if important news to and from his current encampment now spent three days in transit. As September gave way to October, twice-daily messages from the army commander to the Continental Congress had become a distant memory. "Have heard nothing directly from Genl Washington these 2 or 3 Days, but hear he has approached nearer to Howe," reported a newly seated Connecticut delegate, "probably a most important Action will soon insue."[14]

Members of Congress, new and seasoned, had to acclimate to their new capital of York, Pennsylvania. They were dumbfounded that Howe had taken Philadelphia without a fight. A chagrined John Hancock told his wife, "If you Ask me how he [General Howe] came to pass our Army without a Battle, & get into the City, my Answer must be suspended till I receive a full Accott. of the Transactions, & then you shall know." Nathaniel Folsom already knew. The New Hampshire delegate, noting the Schuylkill's many fords, explained, "Genl. Washington was obliged to string his Army for twenty miles on said River, which weakened him to such a Degree, together with the frequent Marches and counter Marches of the Enemy, that when they crossed over Genl. Washington was fifteen Miles above them, without a possibility of overtaking them."[15] The General's performance in the field was beginning to get more intense scrutiny.

Washington, ever sensitive to criticism, never revealed at the time his awareness of complaints accumulating against him, but he must have expected them. Probably more upsetting to him was another unremarked upon development from the first days of October: that dispatch regarding events at Saratoga. But that information had not come from Major General Horatio Gates, commander of the Northern Department. On October 3, Washington opened a short letter from John Hancock, who enclosed ten written exchanges he had had with Gates; Hancock summarized the intelligence by declaring that "it appears that our affairs in the northern department wear a favourable aspect."[16] The enclosures validated Hancock's optimism.

Washington doubtless bristled to think that Gates had conveyed this intelligence to Congress and not to him. Gates flagrantly short-circuited the chain of command while grandstanding in a most unseemly way, in effect assuring that the commanding general of all the American forces would receive important news from a subordinate or from Congress only after a days-long delay. Gates's headquarters stood two days farther from Congress than from Washington. A message would be diverted nearly 130 more miles by its triangular route of delivery to York and to the encampment at the Perkiomen. The delay would naturally lengthen as Washington got closer to Germantown.

Washington did not hesitate. The Continental army broke camp at Pennypacker's Mill and crept nine miles closer to Philadelphia, marching on the Skippack Road. By late afternoon, October 2, troops blanketed the landscape surrounding the branches of Zacharias Creek, while headquarters tents dotted the Peter Wentz homestead. The Crown force's outpost at Germantown was fifteen miles from the Americans, well within a day's march of contact and conflict.[17]

All through the campaign, headquarters personnel performed extra duties. Joseph Reed and John Cadwalader were no exceptions. The two had worked together in the Trenton Campaign, Reed as Washington's Adjutant General and General Cadwalader as the head of the Pennsylvania Associators. Both turned down congressional appointments as Continental brigadier generals in 1777, refusals that in no way indicate any diminishment in their dedication to The Cause. They were considered and called "Generals." Cadwalader was a brigadier general of militia; Reed officially had no rank in the fall of 1777.

Within two days of the late September council of war at Keeley's house, Cadwalader and Reed rode out to scout enemy deployments around Germantown. Word of their presence spread among the Quakers and Loyalists who remained in the region. Thomas Livezy, a Wissahickon Creek miller, lived and worked barely a mile from the most advanced British deployment on the Germantown Road. A Quaker, Livezy seemed to lean Loyalist, for when two men in crimson coats and riding jaded horses called at his home, he determined them to be from that nearby outpost and welcomed them, sharing local scuttlebutt that had Cadwalader and Reed skulking in the region. He also offered the visitors a fine horse that might help them capture "those two Generals" who Livezy reasoned must be close by and perhaps easily nabbed. The pair accepted gratefully, immediately riding off with the miller's gift.

Livezy soon learned he had been duped. Those "Redcoats" were not British soldiers. Nor were they taking his fine horse to ride down Cadwalader and Reed, because they *were* Cadwalader and Reed! Disguised as British Light Horsemen to conduct their reconnaissance, they safely approached Livezy's house, easily winkled intelligence from him, and completed the ruse by wangling away a prize mount.[18]

Cadwalader and Reed found the new headquarters in an ideal locale. Methacton Hill loomed a mile south of the Wentz farm and the entire army encampment, nicely hiding the Americans from British and Hessian pickets. This let Washington to craft a plan for attack requiring a nighttime march. The American army on October 3 proved to be considerably stronger than Washington had estimated at the September 28 council. He had 11,678 Continental infantry officers and men, five hundred Continental dragoons, and six hundred artillerists, as well as 3,574 Pennsylvania and New Jersey militia. In all, Washington could field 16,372 soldiers.[19] Not only was this force nearly equal in size to his Brandywine defense, but it would be the largest American offensive to date in the two-and-a-half-year-old war.

Numerical strength did not necessarily confer confidence. Washington rarely revealed a flair for inspiring words, spoken or written. Usually, his physical presence—mounted, standing or walking—more than sufficed to infuse his troops with *esprit de corps*. But during the summer and early fall campaign, Washington had sensed the need to rouse his soldiers with a rallying cry. A month earlier, at Wilmington, he had crafted General Orders meant not only to steel his men, but to incite the American public regarding Howe's bold invasion into Delaware. That uncharacteristic essay had found its way into newspapers throughout the states. Those September 5 General Orders appeared on October 3, 1777, in the *Virginia Gazette*.

For the assault on Germantown, he wanted to focus his rhetoric solely on his fighting men. How could he imbue those troops with the will to win? In Wilmington, he had used the British threat to Philadelphia and reports of atrocities against Marylanders to rouse his soldiers and countrymen. Howe had provided him the impetus. In late September the British general had issued a proclamation canceling all blandishments previously offered Americans in his late-August Head of Elk proclamation. One of Howe's subordinates explained that the latest decree signified "no further indulgences to Rebels, all former proclamations now being void."[20] News of this new Draconian measure had already spread through the Continental and militia camps.

The commander in chief crafted a second patriotic proposal. Recognizing on October 3 that "Genl Burgoine seems to be in a fair way of being utterly ruined,"[21] Washington threw down the gauntlet for a second time in exactly four weeks after his well-known Quaker Hill General Orders.

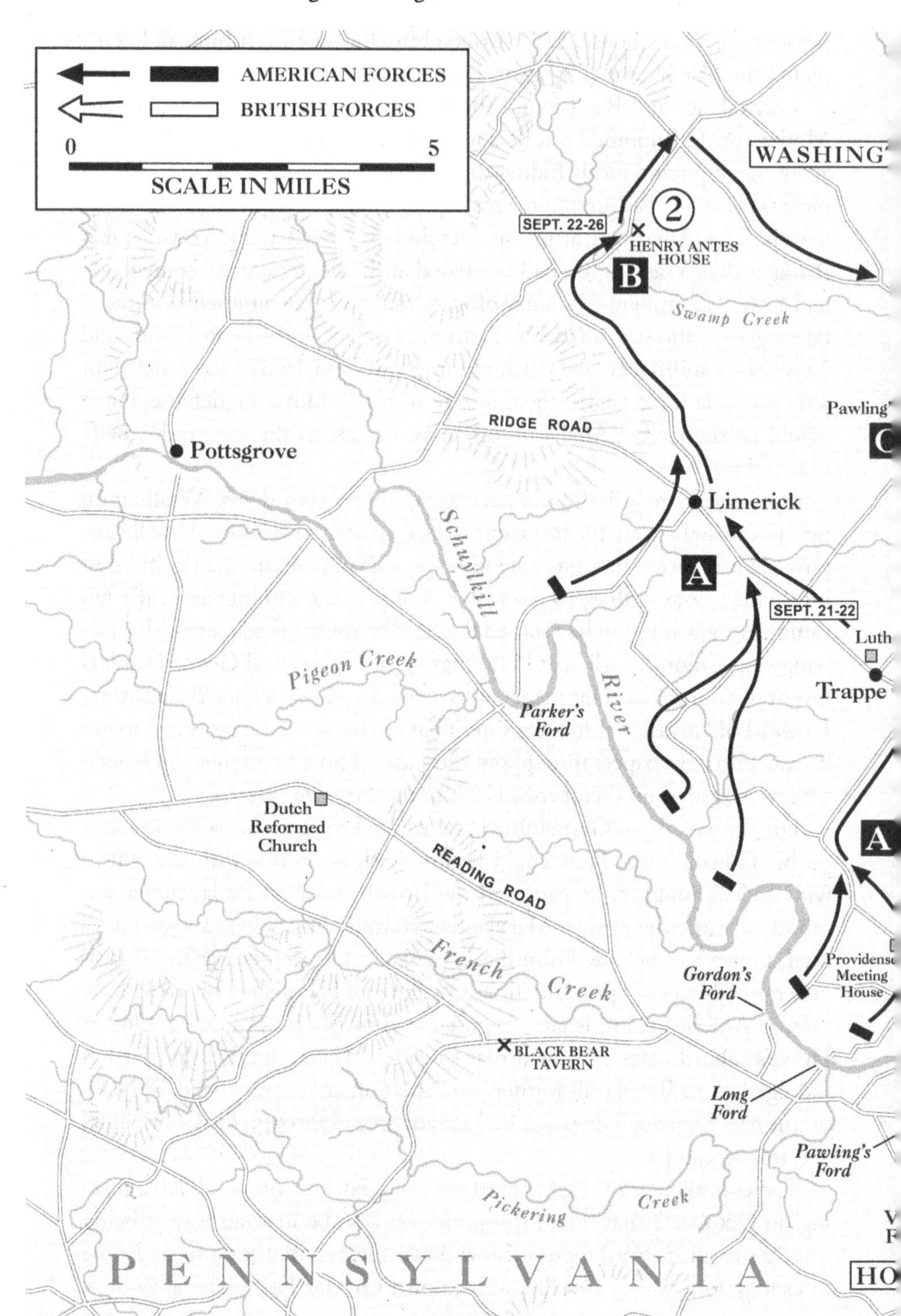
AMERICAN FORCES
BRITISH FORCES
0
5
SCALE IN MILES
WASHING
SEPT. 22-26
2
HENRY ANTES HOUSE
B
Swamp Creek
Pawling'
RIDGE ROAD
Pottsgrove
Limerick
Schuylkill
A
SEPT. 21-22
Luth
Trappe
Pigeon Creek
River
Parker's Ford
Dutch Reformed Church
A
READING ROAD
French
Creek
Gordon's Ford
Providense Meeting House
BLACK BEAR TAVERN
Long Ford
Pawling's Ford
Pickering
Creek
PENNSYLVANIA
HO

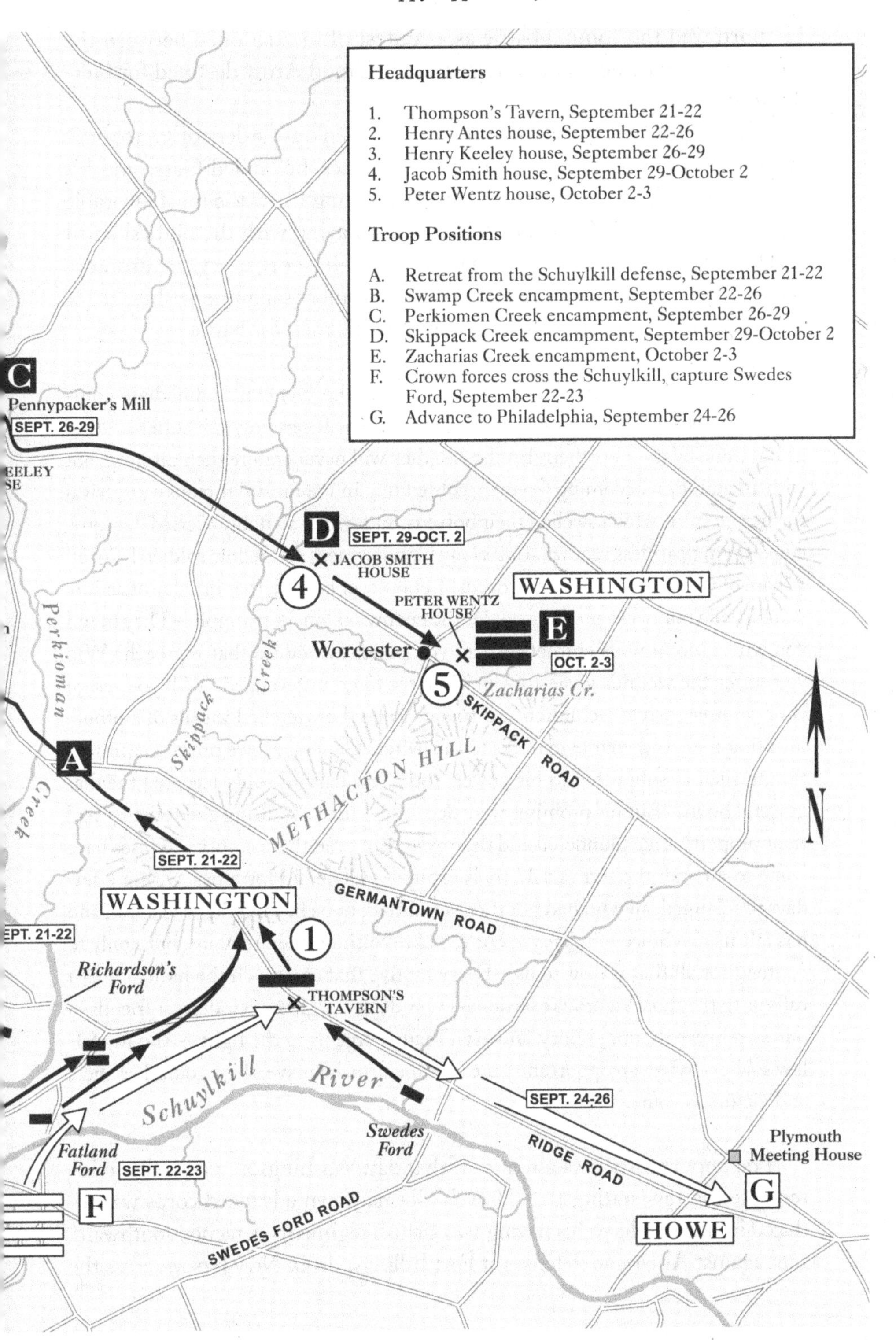
Headquarters
1. Thompson's Tavern, September 21-22
2. Henry Antes house, September 22-26
3. Henry Keeley house, September 26-29
4. Jacob Smith house, September 29-October 2
5. Peter Wentz house, October 2-3
Troop Positions
A. Retreat from the Schuylkill defense, September 21-22
B. Swamp Creek encampment, September 22-26
C. Perkiomen Creek encampment, September 26-29
D. Skippack Creek encampment, September 29-October 2
E. Zacharias Creek encampment, October 2-3
F. Crown forces cross the Schuylkill, capture Swedes Ford, September 22-23
G. Advance to Philadelphia, September 24-26
C
Pennypacker's Mill
SEPT. 26-29
EELEY
SE
D
SEPT. 29-OCT. 2
JACOB SMITH HOUSE
4
WASHINGTON
PETER WENTZ HOUSE
E
Worcester
OCT. 2-3
5
Zacharias Cr.
Perkioman
Creek
Skippack
Creek
SKIPPACK ROAD
METHACTON HILL
A
SEPT. 21-22
WASHINGTON
GERMANTOWN ROAD
N
EPT. 21-22
1
Richardson's Ford
THOMPSON'S TAVERN
Schuylkill
River
SEPT. 24-26
Swedes Ford
Fatland Ford
SEPT. 22-23
RIDGE ROAD
Plymouth Meeting House
G
F
SWEDES FORD ROAD
HOWE

He portrayed the coming battle as a contest of martial mien between the Northern Department at Saratoga and his Grand Army destined for Germantown.

Washington put this all together in his General Orders of October 3. After running through courts martial outcomes, he lauded Gates and his men for their valor. "At the northward, everything wears the most favorable aspect" declared the General, "our troops behaving with the highest spirit and bravery, during the whole engagement; . . . In short, every circumstance promises success in that quarter, equal to our most sanguine wishes." Like Henry V at Agincourt, Washington girded his men for battle:

> This surely must animate every man, under the General's immediate command—This army—the main American Army—will certainly not suffer itself to be out done by their northern Brethren—they will never endure such disgrace; but with an ambition becoming freemen, contending in the most righteous cause, rival the heroic spirit which swelled their bosoms, and which so nobly exerted, has procured them deathless renown. *Covet!* my Countrymen, and fellow soldiers! Covet! a share of the glory due to heroic deeds! Let it never be said, that in a day of action, you turned your backs on the foe—let the enemy no longer triumph—They brand you with ignominious epithets—Will you patiently endure that reproach? Will you suffer the wounds given to your Country to go unrevenged? Will you resign your parents—wives—children and friends to be the wretched vassals of a proud, insulting foe? And your own necks to the halter? General Howe promised protection to such as submitted to his power; and a few dastard souls accepted the disgraceful boon—But his promises were deceitful—the submitting and resisting had their property alike plundered and destroyed: But even these empty promises have come to an end; the term of *Mercy* is expired—General Howe has, within a few days proclaimed, all who had not then submitted, to be beyond the reach of it; and has left us no choice but *Conquest* or *Death*—Nothing then remains, but nobly to contend for all that is dear to us—Every motive that can touch the human breast calls us to the most vigorous exertions—Our dearest rights—our dearest friends—our own lives—honor—glory, and even shame, urge us to the fight—And my fellow soldiers! when an opportunity presents, be firm, be brave, shew yourselves men, and victory is yours.[22]

The opportunity presented itself that day. Washington received two intercepted letters stating that Howe's Germantown advanced corps was reduced in size thanks to his having two British regiments detached southward, sent against American defenses at Fort Billingsport in New Jersey, across the

Delaware River from Chester. This diminution by several hundred troops handed Washington an opening—one he would later call "this happy Opportunity." He considered the development so advantageous to him that he decided to act upon that intelligence within hours of receiving it. A written plan of attack immediately followed, mostly dictated to Lieutenant Colonel Hamilton.[23]

Washington chose a field off the Skippack Pike to convene a council. According to a local boy who witnessed the event, Washington and Greene had conferred in the same meadow the previous day, but this time all the general officers convened in the field, forming a semicircle facing their commander in chief. There was no evidence of a colloquy. Instead, his generals and guests listened to Washington describe his plan for assaulting the isolated force of British and Hessian troops at Germantown.[24]

The advance to action would kick off within a few hours, at 6:00 P.M. that day. Five roads to Germantown would carry American troops on overnight marches averaging roughly fifteen miles. On the west flank, General Armstrong's militia would take Ridge Road near the Schuylkill River to surprise and engage Hessian troops near Vanderlin's Mill. On the far eastern flank, General Smallwood's two brigades of Maryland militia would sweep along the American left, picking up Church Road at Whitemarsh and then the old York Road, which would carry them southwest into Germantown. General Greene's division, joined by Stephen's two Virginia brigades, would pick up Church Road after Smallwood and company had cleared that artery, then proceed to Germantown on a parallel route to Smallwood's, but inside—north—of him. The largest column, consisting of Sullivan's division, Wayne's division, and Conway's brigade from Stirling's division, would take the direct centered route via the Germantown Road. Maxwell's brigade from Stirling's division and Nash's independent brigade would follow this column as Washington's reserve. A diversionary column of Pennsylvania militia, led by General James Irvine, would advance on the western side of the Schuylkill to feint toward Middle Ferry, simply to hold the Philadelphia detachment in place and slow their deployment to reinforce the Germantown troops once they came under attack. Spearheading the attack from the east would be McDougall's brigade in front of Greene's division and Conway's brigade in front of Sullivan's division. The plan called for simultaneous attacks at the break of dawn on Saturday, October 4.[25]

Washington had engineered the plan to isolate and assault the Germantown force with the entire weight of his available infantry and artillery. This onslaught would satisfy the unfinished business rankling Washington and his more bellicose subordinates, as well as the ranks of an army yearning for victory. The lost opportunities for an offensive at Head of Elk on August 28, at White Horse Tavern on September 16, and at Fatland Ford on September 23 could be purged from the annals with a successful strike at Germantown.

An important aspect of Washington's plan is what it omitted—Philadelphia. Knowing that Howe's force was divided with a substantial portion near the latticed streets of the city, Washington wisely determined that true success hinged on a powerful assault against Germantown, but one designed not to proceed southward from the town. He decided to keep his wagons rearward with no orders to roll behind the attacking force. Nor did he establish an end-point objective. He did not tailor a contingency to carry the momentum of a Germantown victory five to eight miles southward to battle the Philadelphia portion of Howe's army, because the diversion with Pennsylvania militia across the Schuylkill was designed to prevent Howe's Philadelphia force from marching north to reinforce or assist the Germantown wing once it was assaulted.

This introduced a Trenton-like component. After the Germantown assault was completed, all available evidence, as well as lack of evidence, indicated that Washington would pull his army back from the battlefield to avoid a confrontation with British troops fresh from Philadelphia. Germantown would certainly be an American offensive, but with limited expectations. Germantown would be Washington's test of what he had desired and planned to achieve since the wake of the Battle of Brandywine: a full-scale surprise assault upon a significant portion of Howe's army. He meant to communicate to the British commander, his subordinate officers, and rank and file Crown forces that the Continental army would be a continuous and imminent threat as long as Howe intended to occupy Philadelphia.

Washington underestimated Howe's Germantown defense at the late-September council which he further reduced when he learned of detachments sent to Fort Billingsport. His preference for tallying his own army's numerical strength only in terms of rank-and-file infantry could easily comport with how he estimated an opponent's numbers. No evidence exists to confirm the extent of Washington's awareness regarding Howe's deployment of his British, Hessian, and Loyalist soldiers. The Crown forces in and around Germantown were organized as three unequal sized entities. Germantown Road ran through the center of town and divided two wings of the army. General Knyphausen commanded 4,500 soldiers on the left side of the road; that force extended all the way to the Schuylkill. Major

General James Grant held the right side of the road with three thousand officers and men. An additional 1,600 British and Loyalists occupied positions north of those wings as a separate outpost force.[26]

In all, Howe had nine thousand soldiers at and near Germantown, a command that seemingly stood to be overwhelmed by a force approaching twice the Crown complement's size. But if prepared for the assault, aligned on a height, and with artillery well situated, Howe still would be expected to win a battle against Washington who would be attacking with just under a two-to-one numerical advantage. The key for Washington was the element of surprise. His numbers would be telling—and early—only if he hit that Germantown army hard, with most of his attackers, and while the enemy was unprepared to meet the American onslaught.

From the top ranks to the bottom, Crown forces underestimated Washington's will. A captain of the British Guards echoed the sentiments of thousands when he declared, "We imagined that the defeat of Brandywine had dispirited the enemy to such a degree that it would be utterly impossible for Washington to give us any further trouble, for some time, at least." Perhaps due to this mindset, early reports of the American attack plan were gleaned from British intelligence and sent to Howe, who dismissed their veracity. He was headquartered less than a mile south of his Germantown force at Stenton, the home of the late jurist James Logan. Washington had used the dwelling for a day as his headquarters six weeks earlier, on the eve of his August 24 march through Philadelphia.[27] Howe took the reports more seriously in the early morning hours and had his troops in town alerted to the same. That warning failed to reach his northernmost pickets.

The Americans broke camp and initiated the movements on Friday evening without complications or impediments. If Washington intended to recreate the weather and conditions that had greeted his great victory at Trenton forty weeks earlier, he could not have picked a better day. His army approached the point of attack in stealthy darkness. The Continentals and militia numerically dominated their intended targets. And as pre-dawn light attempted to illuminate Germantown, morning fog hovered across the landscape to subdue the gleam. A New Jersey colonel rated the murky mist "perhaps the thickest fog known in the memory of man."[28] This was problematic for both sides, but before the first shot was fired, the fog served purely to benefit the Americans.

First contact occurred two miles north of Germantown's upper border. At Mount Airy, the name given to the residence of William Allen, around which the red-coated men of General Howe's northernmost force, the elite

2nd Light Infantry Battalion, had positioned themselves. Shortly after 5:30 A.M., General Sullivan detached two regiments in front of Conway's brigade to launch with orders to attack the unsuspecting outpost. A brief exchange of musketry and a few booming rounds of cannon fire tore at the still, cloudy air. Some Americans claimed afterwards that these volleys were all that was required to send the British force reeling, but Sullivan described a stubborn, spirited, and protracted fight that required him to unfold several columns of troops from the road and deploy them to overwhelm the skilled and stubborn Redcoats.[29]

Advancing with Sullivan's force, Washington would naturally have ridden Blueskin, his dappled Arabian as he had at Princeton and Brandywine, though during the latter battle the General had spent much of the time dismounted. When he did ride Blueskin at Brandywine, it was in the rear of the action—a location welcome to subordinates and staff who had witnessed his near-death exploit at Princeton in January when he charged his horse past the vanguard. Washington's blood was up at Mount Airy. He dashed forward toward the front to inspire his men. Whether the sight of their larger-than-life commander, immaculately dressed in blue and buff and atop that beautiful horse, accomplished the commander in chief's objective is unknown. But most certainly, he horrified his headquarters personnel. Sullivan also caught sight of "our brave Commander Expos[ing] himself to the hottest fire of the Enemy." Later describing how this startled and terrified him, Sullivan recounted that "regard to my Country obliged me to ride up to him & beg him to retire." To Sullivan's relief, Washington wheeled Blueskin northward, resuming a more reserved role.[30]

The attackers forced the 2nd Light Infantry Battalion back but as they withdrew this elite British force contested every fence line in the two miles that Sullivan pursued them. Sullivan's two Maryland brigades received support on their right from Conway's brigade and on their left by Wayne's division of Pennsylvanians, who aligned on the east side of the Germantown Road. Those five thousand officers and men proceeded on each side of the Germantown Road.

The Americans pushed past Cliveden, the stately stone home of Benjamin Chew. Washington did not. Mindful of Sullivan's plea at Mount Airy, Washington reined himself in, remaining with several members of his military family on the Germantown Road north of town, before Knyphausen's regiments, now on the alert, stopped the Americans a few blocks above the center of Germantown. Washington planted himself and much of his staff in front of the John "George" Bensell home, a forty-seven-year-old stone house in northern Germantown. Sullivan had gone out of view, but the General could hear his infantry firing, likely at enemy troops they could not see.

Washington sent Colonel Pickering forward to tell Sullivan to conserve his ammunition; each infantryman would have to make do with the forty rounds he was carrying.[31] Greene's Continentals and Smallwood's militia had entered the action, as intended, swinging in from the east. By 7:00 A.M., upwards of fourteen thousand American officers and men in thirteen infantry brigades had joined the assault, the largest attack on American soil to date and a record that would stand for eighty-four years. They had outnumbered Howe's Germantown force by nearly five thousand soldiers.

Preventing an unalloyed rout was the fog that enabled the surprise attack. Colonel Elias Dayton remarked that soupy fog and gunpowder smoke "brought on almost midnight darkness," rendering friend and foe undistinguishable from one another at a mere five yards. "The fog together with the smoke Occasioned by our Cannon and Musketry made it almost as dark as night," Wayne said, "our people mistaking one Another for the Enemy frequently exchanged several shots before they discovered their error."[32]

Howe's 2nd Light Infantry Battalion, his prized vanguard, was rocked and knocked backwards for two miles. Most of the red-coated regiments began the battle from the southwest, behind Indian Queen Lane, an east-west street perpendicular to the Germantown Road. Except for a few regiments from Major General James Grant's wing that marched northeast to unsuccessfully challenge Greene's assault, most of these infantrymen were able to maintain their positions between School House and Indian Queen Lanes. On the far west, along the bank of the Schuylkill, Pennsylvania militia led by General Potter failed to uproot Hessian jägers Howe had planted at Vanderlin's Mill, thanks mainly to Wissahickon Creek's deceptively high banks. Because those jägers were in place and intact on Howe's left, General Knyphausen was able to hold his position west of that town.[33]

The 40th Regiment of Foot, commanded by Lieutenant Colonel Thomas Musgrave, was stationed near Cliveden when Sullivan's men drove the 2nd Light Infantry Battalion from Mount Airy and through Germantown. Most British occupiers cleared out of the northern Germantown sector upon Sullivan's surprise advance, but not Musgrave. He gathered between one hundred and 120 members of his regiment and had them barricade themselves inside the Chew house as the battle literally passed them by, with American troops rushing southward on both sides of the house.[34]

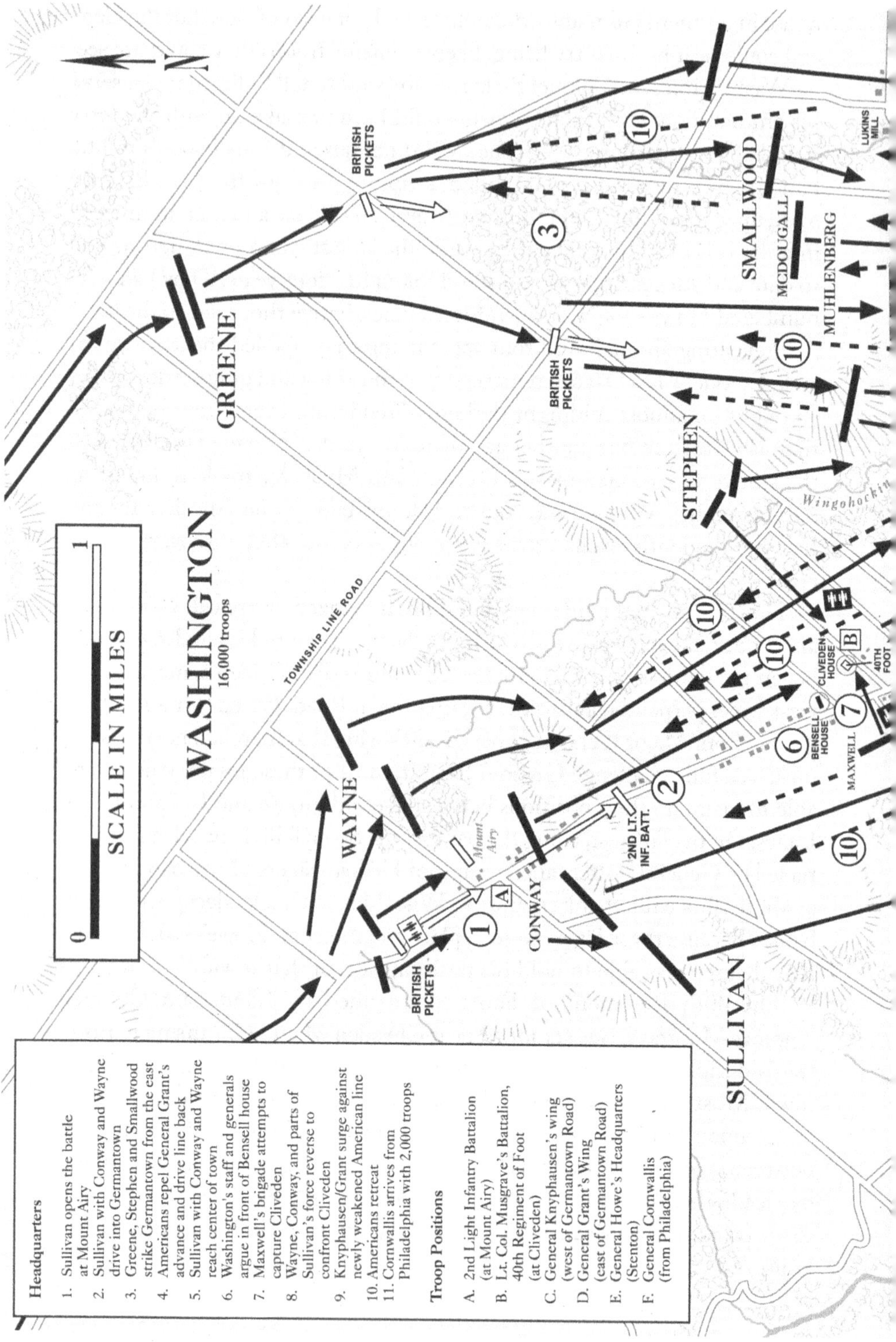

Headquarters

1. Sullivan opens the battle at Mount Airy
2. Sullivan with Conway and Wayne drive into Germantown
3. Greene, Stephen and Smallwood strike Germantown from the east
4. Americans repel General Grant's advance and drive line back
5. Sullivan with Conway and Wayne reach center of town
6. Washington's staff and generals argue in front of Bensell house
7. Maxwell's brigade attempts to capture Cliveden
8. Wayne, Conway, and parts of Sullivan's force reverse to confront Cliveden
9. Knyphausen/Grant surge against newly weakened American line
10. Americans retreat
11. Cornwallis arrives from Philadelphia with 2,000 troops

Troop Positions

A. 2nd Light Infantry Battalion (at Mount Airy)
B. Lt. Col. Musgrave's Battalion, 40th Regiment of Foot (at Cliveden)
C. General Knyphausen's wing (west of Germantown Road)
D. General Grant's Wing (east of Germantown Road)
E. General Howe's Headquarters (Stenton)
F. General Cornwallis (from Philadelphia)

0 1
SCALE IN MILES

N

WASHINGTON
16,000 troops

GREENE

WAYNE

CONWAY

SULLIVAN

STEPHEN

SMALLWOOD

MCDOUGALL

MUHLENBERG

MAXWELL

BRITISH PICKETS

BRITISH PICKETS

BRITISH PICKETS

TOWNSHIP LINE ROAD

Mount Airy

2ND LT. INF. BATT.

BENSELL HOUSE

CLIVEDEN HOUSE

40TH FOOT

Wingohocking

LUKINS MILL

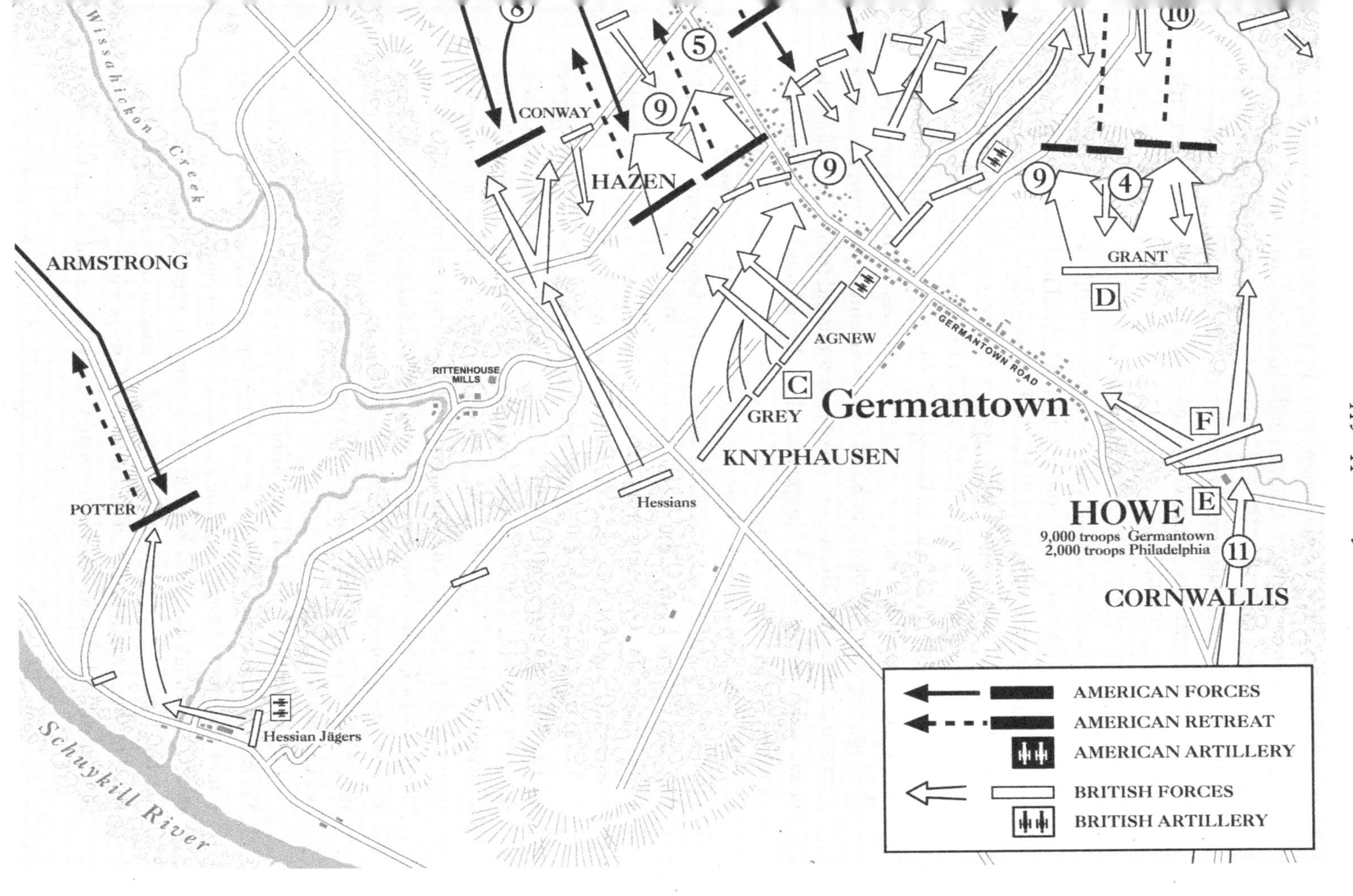
CONWAY
5
9
HAZEN
9
9
4
10
8
GRANT
D
ARMSTRONG
AGNEW
RITTENHOUSE MILLS
C
GERMANTOWN ROAD
Germantown
GREY
KNYPHAUSEN
F
POTTER
Hessians
HOWE
E
9,000 troops Germantown
2,000 troops Philadelphia
11
CORNWALLIS
Wissahickon Creek
Hessian Jägers
Schuykill River
AMERICAN FORCES
AMERICAN RETREAT
AMERICAN ARTILLERY
BRITISH FORCES
BRITISH ARTILLERY

Ignoring these few enemy troops and allowing them to remain behind the American line while the Continentals pressed Howe's troops posed no peril to Washington's plan. The attacking Americans quickly outran the Redcoats' sporadic small arms fire, which was unlikely to inflict severe casualties on the reinforcements Washington continued to order into battle, beginning north of Cliveden.

Washington still had two fresh brigades to feed into the fray: General Nash's North Carolina brigade and General Maxwell's New Jersey brigade, the latter from Stirling's division, to which Maxwell had returned after his month-old light infantry force disbanded. With at least two thousand officers and men in those two units, at least one brigade seemed poised to extend the American right just north of School House Lane, currently anchored by Conway's brigade. In doing so, Sullivan's wing stood to comprise seven Continental brigades of at least seven thousand officers and men. Adding firepower by rolling in Knox's reserve cannons here would solidify a force outnumbering the maximum of four thousand troops, excluding the jägers near the river, which Knyphausen had aligned south of Sullivan's advanced position within Germantown's western sector. With Greene's wing of seven more brigades—five Continental and two militia—inching in from the northeast and east, its ranks of eight to nine thousand men not only prevented Howe from reinforcing his left (west) flank, but also placed the British general's remaining three thousand men directly in the path of a numerically superior force east of Germantown Road.

Washington must have realized that his advantage was fading. Howe swiftly called forward half his remaining troops from Philadelphia, a wing of nearly two thousand officers and men under Lieutenant General Charles Cornwallis. Alerted by 7:30 A.M., Cornwallis wasted no time in getting his men marching the six miles north out of the city that would deliver his vanguard to Germantown two hours later. Washington could not have known this timeline, but as 7:00 A.M. passed he would have known he needed to deploy either Nash's or Maxwell's brigade or even both to the west of Sullivan's line.

The General likely paid no mind to the possibility that Sullivan's, Wayne's, and Conway's troops, even if reinforced by Nash and Maxwell, might not immediately overwhelm and rout Knyphausen's wing. In that event, Washington would be risking wasting his reinforcing brigades on the far American right because Cornwallis's march up the Germantown Road to the battlefield directed him toward Greene's wing of attackers east of the road. A leftward bend in the road Cornwallis would face at the south end of Germantown would enhance this scenario, allowing Cornwallis to continue straight, then deploy from column to line by fanning out northeastward before the bend. If all that came to pass, the General would have uselessly deployed Nash's and Maxwell's brigades more than one and a half miles from Cornwallis's likely flank. To maintain his edge in momentum in this context Washington would have to make quick work of Knyphausen.

As it turned out, the seemingly ineffectual defense of Cliveden by men from the 40th Regiment of Foot did have an impact on the larger battle. It started with a spirited quarrel among members of Washington's military family in front of the Bensell house. Rather than continue to pass the British-occupied Chew house as Sullivan's and Wayne's men had, General Knox argued, the Americans should force Musgrave's men to yield. Ignoring Cliveden, he said, was like leaving a "castle in our rear." No one else in on the debate agreed, especially Alexander Hamilton and Timothy Pickering. The Adjutant General, fresh from delivering Washington's instructions to Sullivan, had en route come under fire from windows at Cliveden. Even so, Pickering pressed to keep ignoring the Cliveden riflemen. Instead of besieging the Chew house, Pickering urged simply posting one "small regiment" from the two reserve brigades to monitor the house "to guard against the danger from the enemy's sallying, and falling on the rear of our troops."[35]

Washington essentially agreed to both arguments. He told a headquarters officer he planned to detach only the 1st New Jersey Regiment under Colonel Matthias Ogden to monitor the house.[36] Earlier, however, the General had acceded to Knox's demands to issue a summons to surrender. The officer selected to take that message to the occupants of the house was Lieutenant Colonel William Smith, a Virginian who served as Deputy Adjutant General directly under Pickering, who, certain that Smith would die in the process, protested. Minutes later, Lieutenant Colonel Smith was borne from the field on a litter, mortally wounded with a shattered leg.[37]

The clock ticked past 7:15 A.M. Perceiving the Cliveden occupiers as more of a threat but opposed to posting a regiment around the house, Washington ordered Maxwell's New Jersey brigade and Knox's artillery to subdue the nuisance. Maxwell deployed his regiments west of the house, facing Cliveden eastward in line of battle. Supported by four cannons, New Jersey men crept close to the house, but could not overrun it. Several men were shot in the west yard of the house, whose thick wooden doors and stone walls were withstanding cannonballs and musket balls. Two New Jersey regiments counted forty-six officers and men wounded and dead from this failed venture, probably falling in less than twenty minutes. Staff officers also took part and paid dearly; two of Sullivan's aides lost their lives. A spent ball struck Lieutenant Colonel John Laurens in the right shoulder but damaged no bones.[38] The troops in the house showed no sign of giving up.

The British occupation of Cliveden and the subsequent effort by Washington to rid the house of its inhabitants did not initially weaken the front-line attackers at Germantown. Nash's North Carolina brigade was the lone uncommitted body of American troops in the Battle of Germantown. Although deployed along a stone wall a few hundred yards north of the Chew house, this brigade was not solely detained by "the castle in our rear" but also by Washington's intent to have a reserve force for an emergency. The same intent likely did not hold for Maxwell's men. Had they not been diverted to Cliveden they would have reasonably been fed into Sullivan's sector to add one thousand more gun-carrying men into the stalling offensive. No one will ever know whether the deployment of this brigade would have made a difference, no matter when they were sent to extend Sullivan's line.

The firing confused American ears at a time when fog was still shrouding the field. General Wayne could hear the booming of at least four cannons directed by Knox toward Cliveden, as well as the echo of small arms volleys from Maxwell's New Jersey troops being countered by sporadic gunshots from the British infantry positioned at the windows. Wayne mistook this exchange behind him for British troops who had slipped around one of the American flanks and now were deployed behind them and firing in their rear. Convinced his brigades had become wedged between British forces, Wayne wheeled his men 180 degrees. Now facing north, the Pennsylvanians headed toward the cacophony near Cliveden, stripping Sullivan of his left flank support. Wayne described the new objective as a "windmill attack . . . made upon a house."[39]

Sullivan complained that Wayne's reverse "Totally uncovered the Left Flank of my Division." Minutes later, Sullivan lost his right flank when Conway's brigade pulled away from the advance and mimicked Wayne's intent to neutralize the enemy north of them. Without orders, significant bodies of troops within Sullivan's own division mirrored what the flanks had done. By 8:00 A.M. what had been five infantry brigades in Sullivan's advanced line were reduced almost seventy-five percent to no more than 1,500 officers and men. General Wayne later admitted that this mass retrograde movement to the Chew house was a critical mistake, for they were "deceived by this attack, taking it for something formidable."[40]

As at least three-thousand Americans were about-facing north toward Cliveden, Knyphausen's and Grant's men counterattacked. The assault focused on Washington's utterly depleted line west of the Germantown Road; Americans east of the road were scattered in an arc nearly 180 degrees from the roadbed. The attackers overwhelmed the defenders, many of whom lacked adequate training and military discipline—most had been under arms for six months or less. That morning's thick, persistent fog exacerbated the situation; friendly fire deepened the confusion. A chaotic retreat began, magnified to brigades and whole divisions as men reversed field on most of the thoroughfares that brought them to the battlefield.

Washington made a token effort to remedy the disaster. As Continentals who had coalesced around Cliveden buckled under the weight of Knyphausen's advancing troops, particularly from around the flanks, the General's instincts overtook him, impelling him to react to what Sullivan called "his anxiety for the fate of the Day." For the second time on the morning of October 4, Washington wheeled his horse to the point of conflict. There, with visibility still diminished to fifty yards, he attempted to rally his retreating men. It was to no avail. By 10:00 A.M. his army was in full flight.[41]

Three grenadier battalions of Cornwallis's force arrived at the southern outskirts of Germantown at around 9:30 A.M. Knyphausen's and Grant's troops already had near-complete control of the town. Outnumbered more than two to one, the British and Hessians magnificently turned the tables on the American commander, slagged by British officers as "Major Washington." Cornwallis's men assisted in the pursuit of Washington's retreating columns, chasing them five miles north to Whitemarsh, where an effective rearguard alignment on the heights around an Episcopal church directed by General Wayne squelched the threat.[42]

Washington ordered the men back to the site of their late-September encampment at Pawling's Mill on the west side of Perkiomen Creek. He returned to Henry Keeley's home for a headquarters. October 4 ended with the General and his army not only having engaged in an unrelenting four-hour contest at Germantown but also forty miles of marching and riding to and from the battlefield. No single day of Revolutionary War action before or after could possibly have been more physically taxing to his foot soldiers.

General Howe achieved a tactical victory at the Battle of Germantown—adding to his wins at Cooch's Bridge, Brandywine, White Horse Tavern, and Paoli. He retained and controlled Germantown. In responding to a surprise assault, he inflicted 1,100 American casualties while incurring 535 losses of his own. The swift response to the surprise assault earned Howe and his veterans the battlefield honors on October 4, 1777. The professionalism of Knyphausen's and Grant's men shone brightly. Those British, Loyalist, and Hessian troops recovered handily from an initial rout, coolly refusing to evacuate Germantown. Although Howe's right wing of the Germantown line under General Grant was forced back well beyond its initial position, Crown soldiers stood fast in a horizontal and inverted "L" long enough to prevent Washington's men from capitalizing on their successful surprise. Conversely, General Greene indicated that his division's problem lay not in pulling back from the most advanced point of their assault, for "a Partial Retreat to change a position is often necessary." What mortified Greene was that instead of rallying, American troops fled the battlefield.[43]

Washington left no impression that he intended to hold advantageous ground around Germantown or push toward Philadelphia even if he had succeeded in uprooting and routing his adversary. No wagon train rolled behind his advancing army, and he identified no advance point beyond Germantown in his written attack orders, so Washington's definition of victory on October 4 required all four of his advancing lines of attack to strike at about the same time, to surprise his opponent, to drive them from Germantown, and to safely pull all his men from the battlefield before Howe's army could counterattack.

The Americans succeeded on two of those counts. "Fortune smiled on us for full three hours," Anthony Wayne declared, "the enemy were broke, dispersed, and flying in all quarters." For that reason, the Americans did not view the Battle of Germantown as a soul-sapping loss. Almost to a man they saw a contest they initially won, a victory they were forced to relinquish, partly by circumstances outside their control. "Though we gave away a complete victory," noted an infantry captain, "we have learnt this valuable truth, that we are able to beat them by vigorous exertion, and that we are far superior in point of swiftness."[44]

That initial rout of Crown forces scintillated and inspired the troops. "Our army is in higher spirits than ever, being convinced from the first officer to the soldier, that our quitting the field must be ascribed to other causes than the force of the enemy," insisted an infantry major after the battle. Noting that Crown forces occupied the same ground they had at the start of the day and captured no American baggage or artillery, another participant surmised that "the Enemy have gained no advantage of any consequence over us." He added, "On the other hand our men are now convinced they can drive the chosen Troops of the Enemy, their Light Infantry & Grenadiers whenever they attack them with ardour. . . . They are now in high Spirits & appear to wish ardently for another Engagement."[45]

This was no collective attempt to put an optimistic gloss on a dispiriting loss. On the contrary, the mood in camp was upbeat. General Stirling could hardly control himself when he raved that "this affair will Convince the World that we Can out General our Enemy, that we dare Attack them, that we can Surprise them, that we can drive them before us Several Miles together and that we know how to Retreat in good Order and dare them to defy us." Equally optimistic, although less exultant, General Weedon admitted disappointment at the outcome of the battle but believed he spoke for the entire army when he said there were "no Objections to another tryal which must take place soon." General Wayne declared, "Upon the whole it was a glorious day. Our men are in high spirits, and I am confident we shall give them a total defeat the next action, which is at no great distance."[46]

Field officers and the rank and file echoed their generals. "It was a grand enterprise; an inimitable plan, which nothing but its Godlike author could equal," a private proclaimed. "All our men are in good spirits and I think grow fonder of fighting the more they have of it," noted another soldier. "Tho' we gave away a complete victory, we have learned this valuable truth," reasoned Lieutenant Colonel William Heath, "that we are able to beat them by vigorous exertion, and that we are far superior in point of swiftness." Colonel Richard Parker called Brandywine a "loss" but characterized Germantown as "an unsuccessful attempt" in his letter to Richard Henry Lee. Together, he asserted, both contests "have not depressed the spirits of our men in the least; but they are much more confident of success than ever, and wish for nothing more than to be led to action." Another officer declared, "The foginess of the morning was very much against us. I believe in my soul had it not been for that we should have totally routed their army. We drove them near three hours."[47]

George Washington felt the same. Back in the comfort of the Keeley homestead, he was convincingly sanguine about the battle. Noting that his men "are not in the least dispirited," Washington termed it "rather unfortunate than injurious," a statement more understandable given Washington's misguided belief at that moment that he had suffered only a third of his true losses and inflicted two hundred more casualties upon the enemy than was so. He heaped praise on his troops "for the spirit and bravery they manifested in driving the enemy from field to field. . . . This they will remember, and assure themselves that on the next occasions, by a proper exertion of the powers which God has given them, and inspired by the cause of freedom in which they are engaged, they will be victorious."[48]

Washington wrote frequently about the battle of Germantown for four days after the contest. He was precise in his description of what he called "this happy Opportunity," at least from the western side of the attack that he had observed. He noted that the battle lasted two hours and forty minutes, and that Greene's attack on the left began forty-five minutes after Sullivan's on the right. Except for individual acts of less-than-heroic behavior, he hailed his army's showing and its positive effect on The Cause, for "it has serv'd to convince our people that when they make an Attack, they can confuse and Rout even the Flower of the British Army with the greatest ease and that they are not the Invincible Body of Men which many suppose them to be." The commander in chief had reviewed enough post-battle intelligence, much of it unconfirmed, to conclude that his surprise attack caused Howe to consider reforming across the Schuylkill at Derby or Chester. Regardless of these reports' accuracy, Washington was convinced that under the right circumstances he could wrest a battlefield from the best troops in Europe.[49]

That post-Germantown confidence and re-dedication to The Cause spilled to the home front in a way uncharacteristic of reactions to a lost battle since Bunker Hill. "For my own part, I am so fully convinced of the justice of the cause in which we are contending," a man wrote, " . . . that were I to see twelve of the United States overrun by our cruel invaders, I should still believe the thirteenth would not only save itself, but also work out the deliverance of the others." That dedication spoke of sacred martyrdom. "My eldest son fell in the battle of Germantown," penned a mother in 1779. "His death served only to increase my affection for my country, and after paying the tribute of maternal grief, I consoled myself with reflecting that I had been honoured in giving birth to a youth who had fallen gallantly in defence of the liberties of America."[50]

Congress was ebullient as well. On October 8 delegates ordered a special medal struck and presented to George Washington. Unanimously, they resolved:

That the thanks of Congress be given to General Washington, for his wise and well concerted attack upon the enemy's army near Germantown on the 4th instant, and to the officers and soldiers of the army, for their brave exertions on that occasion; Congress being well satisfied that the best designs and boldest efforts may sometimes fail by unforeseen incidents, trusting that, on future occasions, the valour and virtue of the army will, by the blessing of Heaven, be crowned with complete and deserved success.[51]

William Howe appears to have come to that same conclusion. He had witnessed first-hand from Stenton and in the area surrounding those headquarters how George Washington had overwhelmed elite Crown soldiers by a combination of surprise and force. As satisfied as he must have been by his forces' rally, Howe did not enjoy the sense of victory perhaps to be expected from a commander who had conquered the same foe for the fifth consecutive time. Howe was unsettled by his opponent's vigor and tenacity. Rather than retreat to a safe locale and defend it as Howe expected Washington to do after the Battle of Brandywine, Washington seemed hell-bent on seeking Howe and attacking him ever since. Even after outmaneuvering Washington along the Schuylkill and watching his opponent overreact and head forty miles away from Philadelphia to start the final week of September, Howe found himself stunned by Washington at the northern gate to Philadelphia on the first Saturday of October.

Washington had even communicated with Howe twice within two calendar days of the Battle of Germantown. One letter answered a complaint of Howe's about American soldiers destroying mills near Philadelphia. "I can hardly believe you to be serious," Washington scoffed, sarcastically remarking on Howe's supposed concern about "the sufferings of inhabitants, as it gives room to hope" that Howe would end an extant policy of destruction of citizen property by his soldiers so frequent and commonplace as to "not need be enumerated." Washington's second communique directly to Howe was a post-battle oddity. "General Washington compliments to General Howe," wrote Alexander Hamilton to the British commander on Monday, October 6; "He does him the pleasure to return him a dog, which accidently fell into his hands, and by the inscription on the Collar appears to belong to General Howe." Those two disparate messages served notice to Howe that Washington loomed within striking distance. He refused to go away.[52]

Clearly Washington would never shy away from Howe. Equally convincing to the British commander was that the best opportunity to destroy Washington's army had passed somewhere between Red Clay Creek and White Horse Tavern. Howe might continue to force Washington from battlefields but would never completely conquer him. There was little likelihood of another Brandywine in Washington's future, realized Howe, but another Germantown in Howe's future seemed inevitable.

Less than a week after the battle, Howe wrote a campaign report to George Germain, describing the marches and battles of the British army from their landing at Head of Elk to their present occupation of the city of Philadelphia and Germantown.[53] Although reveling in writing this summary, Sir William Howe hardly fit the mold of the conquering hero basking in the glory of having achieved the martial goal he had set at the start of the year.

That goal had changed. From mid-September on, Howe had prioritized conquering or destroying George Washington over all else, and as he wrote his report to Germain, William Howe kept hidden his realization that he would never achieve that objective. George Washington led an army as large as his, an army that gained valuable experience with every battle, and an army that somehow was gaining confidence even in defeat. Most of all, that army was led by a general who would never concede, would never relent, would never quit.

Less than two weeks after he sent his report across the ocean, General Howe wrote again to George Germain.[54] This time he composed a letter of resignation.

CHAPTER TEN

"We Have a Force Sufficient, by the Favor of Heaven, to Crush our Foes"

October 10 to November 1, 1777

On October 10, Benjamin Rush was beyond unimpressed—he was disgusted. Dr. Rush, Surgeon General of the Middle Department and signer of the Declaration of Independence, had been a rare eyewitness to the natures of the opposing armies during this campaign. After the Battle of Brandywine, he was one of six surgeons sent by Washington to care for wounded Americans in British custody.[1] That while toiling behind British lines Rush was not detained, arrested, or harassed while in the enemy camp—in contrast to a New Jersey Declaration signer who, upon being captured, was forced to recant and swear fealty to the Crown—testified to the esteem in which Howe must have held him. Dr. Rush departed the British camp in the third week of September, grudgingly acknowledging the professional bearing of both officers and men of the enemy army.

The reality of what he perceived as American amateurism struck Philadelphia's famous physician three weeks later and twenty-five miles north of the British-occupied capital, when Rush was inside American lines as a guest of the commanding general. The differences between the two armies immediately stood out to him. Howe, Rush recalled, replaced his pickets at least once a day and usually twice; Continental army pickets, he observed, typically spent up to five days at their posts. British sentries rotated in and out every two hours while their American counterparts stood guard for up to twenty-four hours. "The troops dirty, undisciplined, & ragged," Rush meticulously jotted into his journal, under the heading "State and Disorders in the American army."[2]

Conditions at that American headquarters fed Rush's pessimism. Headquarters now was the home of Friedrick Wamboldt (whose name was rendered as "Frederick Wampole" in the household accounts). Dr. Rush noted that Wampole's kitchen lacked tableware to accommodate Washington's entire staff at one time, requiring two seatings, one after the other at the same table. Few family homesteads would have had table space and dining ware to feed nearly thirty diners at once, even previous houses chosen for the General, but this never used to matter because Mount Vernon tableware had always been available to compensate for the deficiencies.

This elegant yet festive dining experience as a guest of George Washington at his headquarters abruptly ceased two weeks before Rush's visit when the General packed off much of his personal but nonessential baggage among several hundred surplus supply wagons that rolled in a vast train to Bethlehem. Gone were the finely woven tablecloth and the ornate flatware and dishware. Even Washington's favorite Madeira, once a routine touch, had disappeared, replaced by rustic alternatives. Rush complained that no wine was available that day—"only grog." Most striking to him was Washington's absence from the head of the table. By tradition, an aide occupied that seat, serving those dining their food and drink. Washington usually sat one chair over from the head, but the day of Rush's visit the General chose to sit a few places to the left of the head chair. Rush did not view this unpretentious gesture as admirable. The extremely rare experience of observing both opposing encampments from the inside left a lingering impression. "I was much struck in observing the difference between the discipline and order of the British and Americans," noted Rush in his memoir. "I lamented this upon my return."[3]

The preceding day, October 9, Brigadier General Francis Nash, the North Carolina commander who had died October 7 of a wound suffered at Germantown, was laid to rest in Godshall's burial yard half a mile south of the Wampole house.[4] The army encamped nearby, within Towamencin Township. Although saddened by the loss of his brigadier general, Washington was also laboring to retain his highest ranking major general. John Sullivan had requested to resign over charges relating to his performance at Brandywine. Also at issue were charges against him arising from an August 24 engagement at Staten Island. A court martial began on October 10. Two days later, the court acquitted him "of any unsoldier like Conduct in the expedition to Staten Island."[5] (Later that month Sullivan was acquitted of any wrongdoing at Brandywine.)

All summer and for four weeks of autumn, Washington had been striving to secure three theaters of operation in the United States: the Philadelphia vicinity and the upper Hudson River region, divided between his Northern Department and his Highlands Department. Washington's Philadelphia Campaign had taken an ugly turn with the loss of the city to the British. Washington learned in mid-October that the attention he had devoted to the two departments had been sufficient and worthwhile. Horatio Gates led those combined troops to a hard-fought defeat at Freeman's Farm near Saratoga on September 19. Three days after the Battle of Germantown, Gates won a decisive victory at Bemis Heights near Saratoga, and in doing so, sent a devastated force under General John Burgoyne into retreat.

As he habitually had done with previous positive news from the Northern Department, Washington used the Saratoga victory to inspire his troops. He trumpeted the news in General Orders on October 15. "They behaved with great bravery and intrepidity," the General declared, "and have thus a second time triumphed over the valor of veteran troops." At 5:00 P.M. of their last full day at the Towamencin encampment, the men paraded by brigade to have the news read to them by a designee for each brigade. Besides word of the stupendous victory and a thirteen-gun salute by booming cannons, a *feu de joie* discernible in Philadelphia[6], they heard a challenge from their commanding general:

> The General congratulates the troops upon this signal victory, the third capital advantage, which under divine providence, we have gained in that quarter; and hopes it will prove a powerful stimulus to the army under his immediate command; at least to equal their northern brethren in brave and intrepid exertions when called thereto—The General wishes them to consider that this is the Grand American Army; and that of course great things are expected from it—'Tis the army of whose

superior prowess some have boasted—What shame then and dishonour will attend us, if we suffer ourselves in every instance to be outdone? We have a force sufficient, by the favor of Heaven, to crush our foes; and nothing is wanting but a spirited, persevering exertion of it, to which, besides the motives before mentioned, duty and the love of our Country irresistably impel us. The effect of such powerful motives, no man, who possesses the spirit of a soldier can withstand, and spurred on by them, the General assures himself, that on the next occasion his troops will be completely successful.[7]

Three days later, Washington got preliminary news that he found startling and elating in equal measure. To accompany a letter to family that he had just finished writing on Saturday, October 18, he added an enclosure he labeled in a postscript "Important and glorious News." The enclosure was a forwarded note from Governor George Clinton of New York to Major General Israel Putnam that described a signed capitulation by General John Burgoyne. This agreement indicated that Burgoyne surrendered his entire army to Major General Horatio Gates on October 14. Washington scheduled another *feu de joie* in General Orders issued the day he received the news. Washington awaited an official surrender report from Gates. That wait was longer than expected.[8]

Starting from behind Perkiomen Creek after the Battle of Germantown, Washington had marched his army sixteen road miles back toward Philadelphia in two weeks. He changed headquarters from Henry Keeley's house to Fred Wampole's home, then returned to the Peter Wentz farm. On October 20, the Life Guard established army operations in Whitpain Township. Washington settled in at Dawesfield, the 1736 home of James Morris, east of the Skippack Road.[9] Morris's unassuming career had not called particular attention to him before, but with the newest Grand Army encampment surrounding Dawesfield and dubbed "Camp Morris," in soldiers' letters to loved ones, "Morris" literally became a household name throughout the country. That Washington is known to have named Morris only once in the headings of the dispatches generated from Dawesfield did not signify any lack of appreciation he held for the owner's hospitality. With temperatures dropping, the General was using houses more and tents less.

Fourteen miles south of where Washington and his army had settled in, Howe toiled in his Philadelphia headquarters, having relocated nearly three weeks after his close call at Stenton near Germantown on October 4. (He and the Germantown victors held that vulnerable region until a line of defenses built across the entire northern sector of Philadelphia, spanning river to river, met Howe's satisfaction.) Howe had controlled Philadelphia only partially for four weeks; the Americans still controlled the Delaware River above the line between Chester and Fort Billingsport. The fort, a bastion on the New Jersey side of the river, fell to the British without a fight two days before the Battle of Germantown. But Admiral Richard Howe's fleet could advance little farther upriver owing to the presence underwater in the otherwise navigable channel of a series of marine *chevaux de frise*. One lurked just upstream from Fort Billingsport; others stretched between the northern tip of Hog Island to a sand bar, three miles up the river from the Billingsport chain. By mid-October the British had been able to remove only a segment of the southernmost rack of American river spikes. Those closer to the city were untouchable, protected as they were by the forts nearby.

Fort Mifflin and Fort Mercer were the most formidable—though not invulnerable—obstacles facing the Howe brothers. The forts stood on opposite sides of the river, a mile from each other, half a mile below the mouth of the Schuylkill River, and seven meandering river miles from the captured city. Fort Mifflin protruded from Mud Island and was garrisoned by Lieutenant Colonel Samuel Smith with three hundred Continentals manning over thirty cannons behind its walls.

Fort Mercer loomed over the river from a portion of New Jersey shoreline called Red Bank. Named for Brigadier General Hugh Mercer, a Virginian martyred in battle ten months earlier at Princeton, the bastion was mischaracterized as "Fort Mercy" by at least one defender. Essentially defenseless in the first days of October, Washington was fortunate that the British force that took over Fort Billingsport on October 2 chose not to advance; instead, the victors receded back to the Pennsylvania side of the river. By the close of the third week of October, Fort Mercer had welcomed reasonable numbers to defend it: close to five hundred Continental infantry in two Rhode Island regiments, sixty-plus artillerymen, and enough New Jersey militia to raise the total to over six hundred American defenders, supported by fourteen cannons, including a couple of eighteen-pounders. The senior commander at the fort was Colonel Christopher Greene, a distant cousin of Nathanael Greene.[10]

According to a mid-October return, Howe had 11,740 rank and file infantry soldiers present for duty; this equated to an entire soldiery of fifteen thousand in Philadelphia when all military personnel were included.[11] With all the obstacles in the river and artillery-laden forts and the Pennsylvania navy plying the waters of the Delaware, Howe approved an attempt to neu-

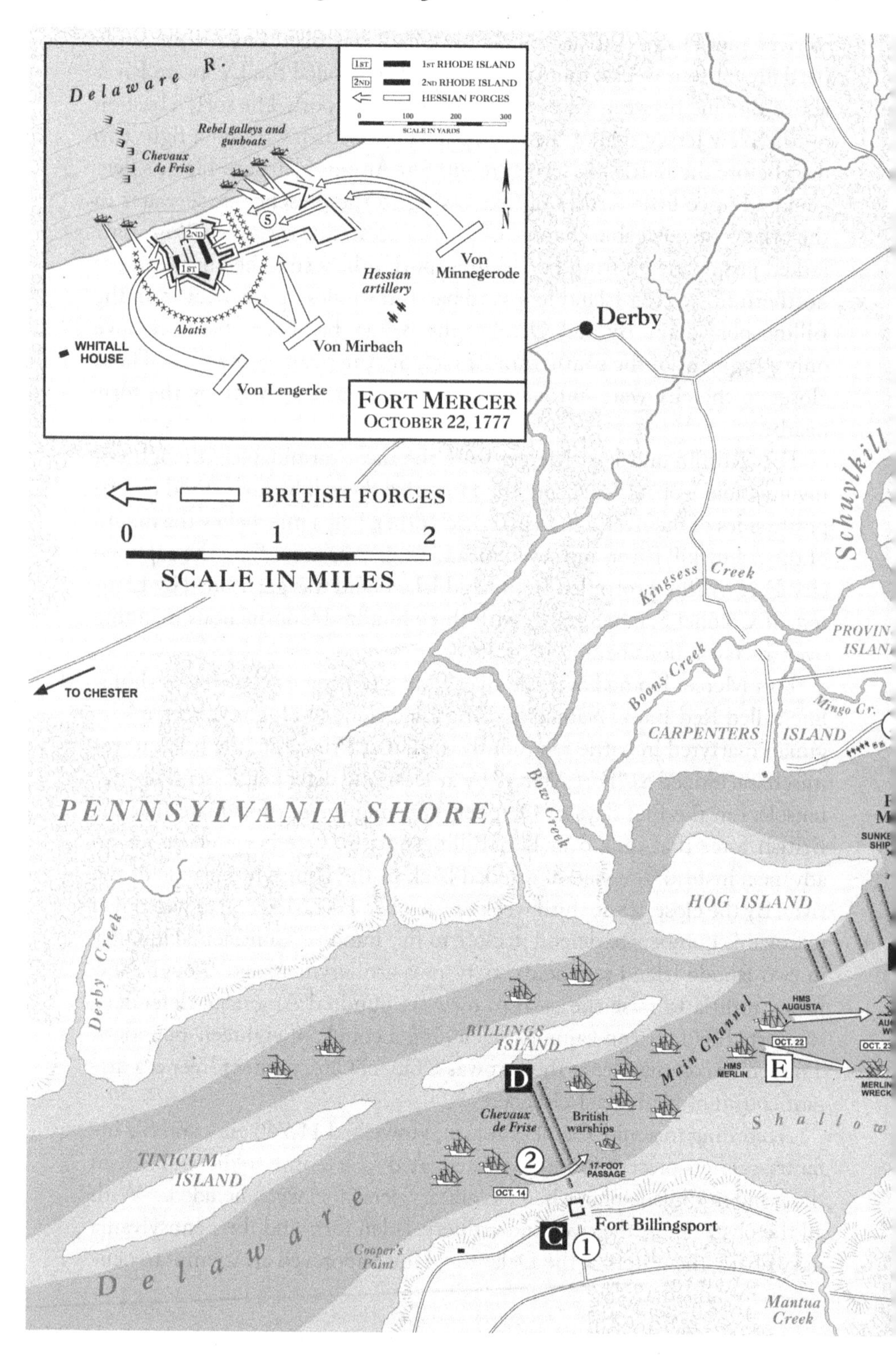

Delaware R.
1st RHODE ISLAND
2nd RHODE ISLAND
HESSIAN FORCES
0 100 200 300
SCALE IN YARDS
Rebel galleys and gunboats
Chevaux de Frise
N
5
2ND
1ST
Von Minnegerode
Hessian artillery
Abatis
WHITALL HOUSE
Von Mirbach
Von Lengerke
FORT MERCER
OCTOBER 22, 1777
Derby
BRITISH FORCES
0 1 2
SCALE IN MILES
Schuylkill
Kingsess Creek
TO CHESTER
Boons Creek
Mingo Cr.
CARPENTERS ISLAND
PENNSYLVANIA SHORE
Bow Creek
HOG ISLAND
Derby Creek
HMS AUGUSTA
BILLINGS ISLAND
Main Channel
OCT. 22
OCT. 23
HMS MERLIN
E
MERLIN WRECK
D
Chevaux de Frise
British warships
2
17-FOOT PASSAGE
OCT. 14
TINICUM ISLAND
Fort Billingsport
C
1
Cooper's Point
Delaware
Mantua Creek

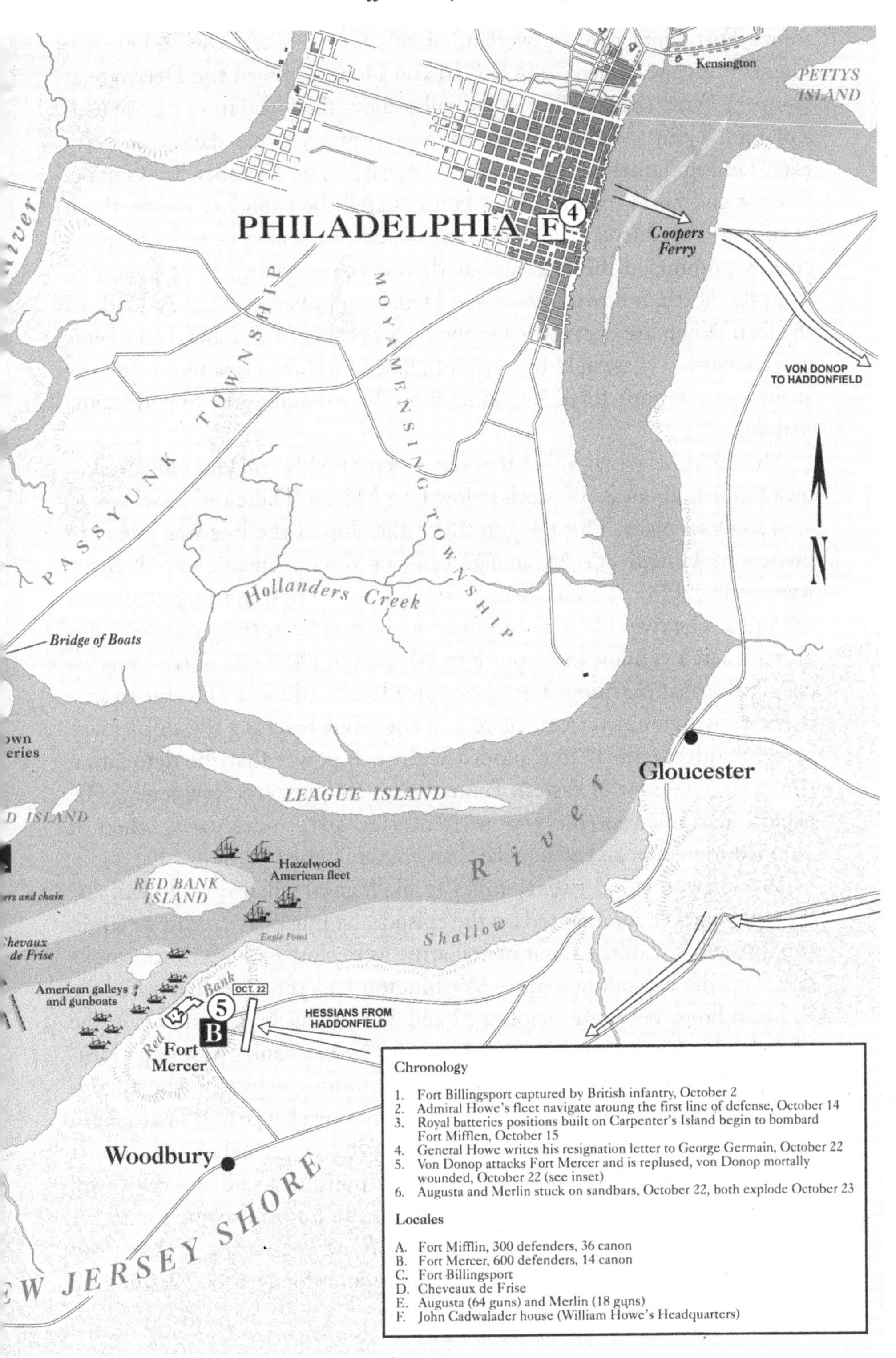
Kensington
PETTYS ISLAND
PHILADELPHIA
F
4
Coopers Ferry
VON DONOP TO HADDONFIELD
N
MOYAMENSING TOWNSHIP
PASSYUNK TOWNSHIP
Hollanders Creek
Bridge of Boats
Gloucester
LEAGUE ISLAND
River
Hazelwood American fleet
RED BANK ISLAND
Eagle Point
Shallow
Chevaux de Frise
American galleys and gunboats
Red Bank
OCT. 22
5
B
HESSIANS FROM HADDONFIELD
Fort Mercer
Woodbury
NEW JERSEY SHORE
Chronology
1. Fort Billingsport captured by British infantry, October 2
2. Admiral Howe's fleet navigate aroung the first line of defense, October 14
3. Royal batteries positions built on Carpenter's Island begin to bombard Fort Mifflen, October 15
4. General Howe writes his resignation letter to George Germain, October 22
5. Von Donop attacks Fort Mercer and is replused, von Donop mortally wounded, October 22 (see inset)
6. Augusta and Merlin stuck on sandbars, October 22, both explode October 23
Locales
A. Fort Mifflin, 300 defenders, 36 canon
B. Fort Mercer, 600 defenders, 14 canon
C. Fort Billingsport
D. Cheveaux de Frise
E. Augusta (64 guns) and Merlin (18 guns)
F. John Cadwalader house (William Howe's Headquarters)

tralize Fort Mercer by an overland attack. On October 21, a 2,400-man Hessian brigade under Colonel Carl von Donop crossed the Delaware at Cooper's Ferry, about a dozen land miles above the fort. Howe had devised a plan for a joint assault by land and sea to commence two days later; however, Donop launched his assault a day earlier, on October 22. Colonel Greene and his Rhode Islanders consolidated their force at the southern portion of Fort Mercer and—aided by Pennsylvania navy boat guns—mercilessly pummeled the Hessians as the Germans attempted to penetrate from the north, followed by a second failed assault against the east side of the fort. When the dust settled in the early evening of October 22, Greene, despite battle losses, held his position, having inflicted a punitive 382 casualties on Donop's force, including mortally wounding the brigade commander.[12]

Howe's misery magnified that day when H.M.S. *Augusta* ran aground on a sandbar about 2,500 yards below Fort Mercer. There the vessel would stay, stuck in place. This 64-gun third-rate ship of the line was joined in distress by H.M.S. *Merlin*, an eighteen-gun frigate. Unable to pull either warship free, Howe's men worked fervidly into the next morning to protect the ships. The river filled with boats from both sides as the grounded ships also attracted cannon fire from Fort Mifflin, 1,500 yards north. *Augusta* caught fire that morning. The blaze spread across the ship. Unable to save it, the crew scrambled to evacuate as flames were reaching the ship's magazine. Suddenly, the ship exploded with such power that the detonation shook large regions of eastern Pennsylvania and western New Jersey. The explosion rippled all the way to Lancaster, sixty miles away, where it "seemed more like an earthquake than anything else."[13]

Washington stood twenty miles from *Augusta* when it exploded. Although he never commented on the episode, he must have heard or felt it. (Some members of the Continental army were close enough to see smoke rise from the exploding ship.[14]) Washington had yet to realize it but the eighteen hours between October 22 and 23 were his best moments of the Philadelphia Campaign. The failed late afternoon assault by Donop's Hessians on Fort Mercer, followed by the late morning explosion aboard *Augusta*, meant that Washington's men had removed nearly four hundred troops from Howe's command as well as an artillery arsenal on the *Augusta* that exceeded Washington's retinue of cannons attached to the Grand Army. (Another eighteen cannons sank to the bottom of the Delaware when the British torched the stranded *Merlin* to keep it out of American hands.) October 22-23 marked a British low point for a reason Washington had yet to learn. October 22 was also the day William Howe wrote out his request to resign as commander in chief of Crown forces in North America. The letter would require half a year to travel overseas, be debated and discussed by British authorities, and come to fruition in the form of an acceptance sent to Howe. For the next several months of his tenure as commander in chief, Lord William Howe worked on borrowed time.

Drafting a letter of resignation did not overtly diminish Howe's quest to open the Delaware River to his brother's fleet. Fort Mercer's defenders had gained a respite from direct threat, a luxury Fort Mifflin never enjoyed. Howe subjected that fort to repeated bombardment from naval guns and field artillery west of the back channel to the fort.

Washington was not certain the Americans had prevailed at Fort Mercer until Friday, October 24, two days after the fact. He announced the victory in General Orders the following morning, noting the demises of *Augusta* and *Merlin* and the British fleet's failure to conquer Fort Mifflin. These achievements stood in contrast to the fact that the commander in chief of all American forces in North America had not received official confirmation from General Gates of Burgoyne's surrender at Saratoga. Washington chafed at the snub, writing to John Hancock, "If Congress have had authentic advices about it, I wish to be favor'd with them."[15]

Washington finally received a copy of Burgoyne's surrender agreement on October 26—nine days post facto. He called it "the first authentic intelligence I recd of the Affair." Significantly, that intelligence had come second-hand through Israel Putnam, not directly from Gates. Gates's behavior prevented his commander from levying an appropriate and timely recognition of his achievement—and fueled Washington's suspicions regarding a subordinate who felt no compulsion to go through the chain of command with important news. A courier could have traversed the three hundred road miles between Gates and Washington from the time of the surrender in six days, not nine, but when Gates's rider reached Bethlehem, Pennsylvania—a day's ride from Washington's headquarters—he instead rode ninety miles southwest to York, where another ninety miles separated York from headquarters. This veer turned what should have been a fifty-mile trip from Bethlehem to Washington's hands into a 180-mile, four-day journey.

Rather than read Gates the Riot Act, Washington chided him more gently than the subordinate deserved. "By this Opportunity, I do myself the pleasure to congratulate you on the signal success of the Army under your command," he wrote to Gates. "At the same time, I cannot but regret, that a matter of such magnitude and so interesting to our General Operations, should have reached me by report only, or through the channel of letters not bearing that authenticity, which the importance of it required, and which [that authenticity] would have received by a line under your signature, stating the simple fact."[16]

Fifteen generals of the Continental army entered Dawesfield on October 29 for the first council of war in four weeks. The General and select staff members greeted them. Washington opened by summarizing the opposing armies' numerical strengths and current dispersals. He reported on the American victory at Fort Mercer, Continental and militia defenders' stubborn defense at Fort Mifflin, and that lone British success, opening "communication with their ships by way of Tinicum Island." Washington explained that their numerical advantage over Howe was about to evaporate when nearly two thousand militiamen's enlistments expired. He stressed that he used "the strongest terms" to acquire more militia from Pennsylvania and New Jersey.

Washington then described the tremendous victory of the Northern Department over Burgoyne's army and his capitulation to Gates, which may have struck the generals as odd given that they had commemorated that surrender ten days earlier. Washington noted that General Clinton had abandoned any attempt toward Albany and had returned to New York.

Washington posed questions to his generals, beginning with a query as to whether it would be prudent "to attempt by a general attack to dislodge the enemy from Philadelphia." His council bluntly responded in the negative, causing the General to drop his follow-up—where should they retreat if the attack failed? Washington asked instead where to relocate temporarily before they set out for a winter encampment. The answer vaguely referred to an area to the left of the army which engineers had studied; the subordinates also agreed on the need to reinforce Forts Mercer and Mifflin. The next questions concerned location and activities for the coming winter. All agreed to defer discussions of those topics. And what specific forces should be pulled from the Northern Department to reinforce Washington's army? The answer was twenty regiments, mostly from Massachusetts and New Hampshire.

Discussion shifted to military protocol and management. Topics included the possible need to create an office of Inspector General "for the purpose principally of establishing and seeing practiced one uniform system of manual and manoevres." Washington did not originate the idea, but he had devoted considerable time and thought to it. He originally had hoped that the Adjutant General would handle those duties, but the demands placed upon Colonel Pickering rendered that delegation unrealistic. The subordinate generals agreed with the importance of an inspector general. Most importantly, the generals said they believed that the regulations established through that office should undergo review by and the concurrence of the commander in chief or his appointed board of officers.[17]

Lieutenant Colonel Alexander Hamilton took minutes. The following day, Washington assigned Hamilton an independent mission, his third in five weeks. Unlike the Valley Forge and Philadelphia assignments in September, this undertaking required five hundred miles of round-trip travel. Washington said he was sending Hamilton to Albany "to point out in the Clearest and fullest manner, to Genl Gates, the absolute necessity that there is for his detaching a very considerable part of the Army at present under his Command to the reinforcement of this [army]." The general commanding all American forces had been reduced to this bizarre step because he felt unable to simply order a large shift of troops from an inactive theater of operations to his still-active command without proffering an explanation to his subordinate general. Hamilton would also carry and deliver to Gates Washington's letter of congratulations and rebuke.[18]

Angst permeated Hamilton's mission. After meeting with General Putnam near Fishkill to direct him to forward some of his Highlands Department Continentals and militia toward Philadelphia, the aide rode to Albany and delivered Washington's order to Gates. He was disappointed to find Gates unwilling to do as ordered. "I used every argument in my power to convince him of the propriety of the measure," wrote Hamilton to the General. Gates insisted on retaining two Continental brigades to protect what he considered "the finest arsenal in America" should Clinton make another run up the Hudson from New York. Hamilton did persuade Gates to send one more brigade to Washington, only to learn afterwards that Gates had intended that to be General John Paterson's brigade—"by far the weakest of the three now here," according to Hamilton. That unit included two hundred militia whose enlistment were within weeks of expiring.[19] "I found myself infinitely embarrassed, and was at a loss how to act," Hamilton said, unburdening himself to Washington regarding the ominous reason for his discomfort:

I found insuperable inconveniences in acting diametrically opposite to the opinion of a gentleman whose successes have raised him to the highest importance. General Gates has won the entire confidence of the Eastern States; if disposed to do it, by addressing himself to the prejudices of the people he would find no difficulty to render a measure odious which it might be said, with plausibility enough to be believed, was calculated to expose them to unnecessary danger, notwithstanding their exertions during the campaign had given them the fullest title to repose and security. General Gates has influence and interest elsewhere; he might use it if he pleased to discredit the measure there also. On the whole, it appears to me dangerous to insist on sending more troops from hence while General Gates appears so warmly to oppose it. Should any accident or inconvenience happen in consequence of it, there would be too fair a pretext for censure, and many people are too well disposed to lay hold of it. At any rate it might be considered as using him ill to take a step so contrary to his judgment in a case of this nature.[20]

The friction Washington suspected of being generated by Horatio Gates's freshly found fame presaged the rise of a monster lurking behind the General. The Americans' abject failure to prevent Howe from capturing Philadelphia came to light in the worst way when compared to the success Gates had achieved in the Saratoga campaign. Never mentioned in the weeks after Saratoga was the extent to which Washington contributed to Gates's success well before Gates replaced Schuyler in command of the Northern Department army by sending him Benedict Arnold and Daniel Morgan, among other talented commanders and hundreds of valuable troops. Superlative performances by American subordinate commanders and their troops figured at least as much in Burgoyne's defeat as Gates's generalship did. But, two weeks after Saratoga, Gates was the cynosure of the eyes of American patriots while Washington appeared ineffective and overmatched. Months of joyous appreciation for his stunning achievements at Trenton and Princeton had waned to whispers. The year 1777 started with His Excellency on top, but with two months remaining in the year he was nearly as low in the public's estimation as he had been after the New York debacle of 1776.

Criticisms of Washington's generalship extended far and wide. Inside information from the Continental Congress in York had reached army headquarters in the form of letters from South Carolina delegate Henry Laurens to his son. Lieutenant Colonel John Laurens, receiving his father's October 16, 1777, missive, learned that informal chatter among delegates—which the elder Laurens defined as "not regular Congress"—had become critical of Washington's habit of bemoaning his army's deficiencies; delegates also were noting what they perceived as a lack of regulation and discipline in the ranks. This gossip dismayed Henry Laurens, who regarded

Washington as "the Man whom I think, all in all, the first of the Age," but, he admitted to his son, "I am afraid there may be some ground for some of these remarks."[21] The younger Laurens likely did not speak of his father's confidential information to General Washington, but he probably did discuss it in some form with others at headquarters.

Washington's army was the source of the most compelling complaints about his leadership. Smallwood, Pickering, Kalb, and Greene had written or voiced disapproval of Washington's command decisions prior to Burgoyne's surrender. Dr. Benjamin Rush—previously an enthusiastic Washington man—clearly soured on his idol in the wake of Philadelphia's fall and the outcome at Saratoga. Writing to John Adams a few days after Gates's victory, Rush was blunt. "I have heard several Officers who have served under General Gates compare his Army to a well regulated family," Rush wrote. "The same Gentlemen have compared Genl. Washington's imitation of an Army to an unformed mob. Look at the Characters of both! The one on the pinnacle of military glory—exulting in the Success of Schemes planned with wisdom, and executed with vigor and bravery—and above all see a country saved by their exertions. See the Other outgenerald and twice beated—obliged to witness the march of a body of men only half their number thro' 140 miles of a thick setled country—forced to give up a city the capital of a state and After all outwitted by the same Army in a retreat."[22]

John Adams certainly required no prodding by Rush (or anyone else) to vent his spleen. Never comfortable with the monarchical treatment accorded the general informally dubbed "His Excellency," Adams appeared as relieved as he was exultant regarding Gates and Saratoga. "Congress will appoint a Thanksgiving," he wrote to his wife, "and one Cause of it ought to be that the Glory of turning the Tide of Arms, is not immediately due to the commander in chief, nor to southern Troops. If it had been, Idolatry, and Adulation would have been unbounded, so excessive as to endanger our Liberties for what I know." The close of Adams's late-October letter required no parsing: "Now We can allow a certain Citizen to be wise, virtuous, and good, without thinking him a Deity or a saviour."[23]

Washington was not privy to such private correspondence. But soon his ears would burn upon hearing a line that could also be found in a written exchange between Rush and Adams—hearsay attributed to a Continental brigadier general. The replacement of "Washington" with a dash in one sentence of Rush's letter (a decision originating either from Rush or the officer he identified and quoted) intentionally fooled no one: "A great and good God (says Genl. Conway in a letter to a friend) has decreed that

America shall be free, or — and weak counsellors would have ruined her long ago."[24]

Thomas Conway had endeared himself to Rush and also impressed General Sullivan, displaying leadership skills seemingly absent in other brigade commanders. "I have been in two battles with General Conway," Sullivan wrote, "and am confident no man could behave better in action.... His regulations in his Brigade are much better than in any in the Army, and his knowledge of military matters in general far exceeds any officer we have."

But Conway's self-confidence, which exceeded his talent in battle, got in his way. He wrote to the Continental Congress requesting promotion to major general. Using Major General Baron de Kalb—"my inferior in France"—as an example, Conway reasoned, "It is with infinite concern that I find myself slighted and forgot when you have offered rank to officers who cost you a great deal of money and have never rendered you the least service." Arguing on his own behalf, Conway belittled his immediate superior, Lord Stirling. Conway complained to Congress that he was languishing in charge of five hundred men "under the orders of a major general who is not able to command one hundred."[25]

Sullivan turned out to be the only general in the Grand Army in awe of Conway. General Greene, for example, assessed Conway as "a most worthless officer as ever served in our army."[26] The brigadier's rampant ambition stirred up fellow generals in a manner reminiscent of Major General Coudray's controversial appointment by Silas Deane, a summertime imbroglio that Congress and Coudray ironed out without the need for Washington's intervention. But Conway's quest for promotion upset fivefold more officers than did the Coudray controversy—every single one of the Continental army's twenty-three brigadier generals outranked him—which required Washington to react. "I must speak plain," he insisted, primarily because he had been misinformed that Congress had already promoted Conway. Jumping the Frenchman over nearly two dozen brigadier generals who were senior to him, Washington said, would deliver "a fatal blow to the existence of this army." He reasoned that if he forced Conway upon a given division no brigadier general therein would serve and mass resignations would destroy affected brigades throughout the army.[27]

Conway's ambition drew General John Cadwalader to make a sensational accusation. Cadwalader and Joseph Reed had assisted Washington in the week before Germantown and during the battle of October 4. That morning, as that conflict raged, engaging all thirteen front-line brigades,

General Conway could not be found. Cadwalader and Reed located him in a farmhouse north of the American battle line. He appeared unusually agitated. Cadwalader asked why he wasn't with his men. Conway said his horse had been wounded in the neck. Cadwalader and Reed, emphasizing that Conway's men needed him to return, urged that he replace his mount, saddle up, and rejoin his brigade. Conway refused, repeating that his horse was wounded in the neck.[28] It was likely at this time that Conway's leaderless brigade pulled away from Sullivan's right flank and drifted back toward the fight north of the battle line at Cliveden.

Cadwalader personally appeared at Dawesfield, where he revealed his story and adamantly accused Conway of cowardice under fire. He also "desired to be called upon as an evidence" against Conway in a court martial. Washington credited Cadwalader's claim enough to repeat it in conversation with aides, but not enough to carry through the request for a trial. Telling aides if he investigated the charge he might render himself vulnerable to assumptions that his inquiry was motivated by personal resentment at Conway's relentless bid for promotion, the General sidelined the matter.[29] Once Congress assured him that Conway would remain a brigadier general for the near future, the Frenchman's ambition, while persistently unsettling, no longer was catastrophic.

A potential solution to the Conway affair brewing at York may have been even more unnerving for Washington. The last week of October 1777 Congress, angling to reinvigorate the Board of War, had listed three men being considered for Board service in 1778: Joseph Reed, Timothy Pickering, and Robert H. Harrison. Unaware that Pickering had privately expressed doubts about the General's abilities, Washington believed all three would be sympathetic to him. They intimately understood machinations at headquarters. But pulling them out of the roles they had been playing in the field would be devastating to Washington. Reed was expendable; his presence at headquarters had not been a year-long routine. But the sudden departure from Washington's inner circle of military secretary Harrison and Adjutant General Pickering promised to wreak havoc with headquarters efficiency, particularly since the death October 26 of Deputy Adjutant General Lieutenant Colonel William Smith from a wound inflicted at Germantown. "I do not imagine Congress would appoint Colo. Harrison without first knowing you could spare him," explained Virginia delegate Richard Henry Lee in a letter to Washington, "nor do I think that so important an office as that of A.G. should be touched without maturest consideration."[30]

The Virginia delegation recommended replacing Pickering with Conway, hoping that stowing the Frenchman in a staff position may placate the field generals. Washington disagreed. "He is a bad scribe," he declared while acknowledging that handy assistants could help remedy that shortcoming. Washington had in mind substituting for Pickering an experienced adjutant general from the Northern Department, but that officer was in bad health. To Washington's relief, Colonel Pickering promised to stay on the job until a replacement was set to take over.[31]

Pickering himself had a candidate: Lieutenant Colonel Alexander Hamilton. Hamilton had so impressed him starting in early summer that he asked "Ham" why Washington had not appointed him Adjutant General in June rather than sending for Pickering. According to Pickering, at the time Hamilton had surmised that "his youth was a material objection." (Hamilton posed as being three years younger than his true age of twenty-three years.) "He is young, 'tis true," Pickering said of Hamilton, "but he possesses all the stability of mature age, genius rarely to be equalled, and a most excellent heart. In a word, he is a great character."[32] Hamilton, however, was less than physically robust. After his October meeting with Gates in Albany, he was laid up there with an undisclosed but debilitating illness, needing three weeks to recuperate before returning to headquarters. No indications exist to suggest that Washington ever considered Alexander Hamilton for Adjutant General.

His worries eased by Pickering's offer to stay on pending his replacement's arrival, Washington warmed to the Virginia delegation's proposal, provided that Harrison remain at headquarters with an appropriate substitute to take his place. He expected the trio that Congress agreed upon to make up the small but influential Board of War and to be sympathetic to the wants and needs expressed by headquarters throughout these arduous autumn months, as well as allies to the commander in chief's present and future plans for the appropriate conduct of the war.

He was wrong.

CHAPTER ELEVEN

"One Heap of Ruin"

November 2 to November 21, 1777

George Washington had headquartered at or in thirty homes and taverns from July through October 1777, rarely staying more than a few days and never more than a couple of weeks. On November 2, Washington departed Dawesfield. He moved his army five miles closer to Howe and Philadelphia, encamping at Whitemarsh, a range of hills watered by creeks—ideal defensive ground a dozen direct miles north of Philadelphia. Washington's army had overnighted there in August. His headquarters this stop was an elegant two-and-a-half-story stone house built thirty years earlier by George Emlen, a scion of a Quaker family prominent in Philadelphia and environs since the 1600s. Emlen had died at fifty-eight of apoplexy in 1776. He was survived by his wife and their eight children, some of whom still resided at Whitemarsh with their widowed mother, Anne, fifty-seven.

Washington, a dozen aides, advisors, and other penmen, as well as twelve servants, stayed a month, during which this quiet setting functioned as the brain of the Grand Army of the American Revolution.[1]

Tents sheltered many personnel day and night but given the encroaching winter the snug Emlen house tended to be where Washington and staff convened, whether to work or to relax. Writing to his father of his first week there, John Laurens closed, "[I]t begins to be time for me to join in the concert of my snoring companions, who are extended before the fire."[2]

Henry Laurens was now President of the Continental Congress, replacing John Hancock, whose term had ended October 31. Washington began November with an expansive letter to the senior Laurens—in drafting it Richard Kidder Meade wrote nearly three thousand words—summarizing the campaign to date and enumerating challenges he was expecting to encounter. He sought confirmation from Henry Laurens of information he had been receiving from the army's other departments, a tacit admission that he needed Congress at times to update him about his own subordinates' activities and whereabouts. This was evidenced by Washington relaying a rumor to Laurens of a nebulous but apparently successful American expedition in Rhode Island, as well as acknowledging receipt of Gates's October 18 signed report of Burgoyne's surrender—a letter Gates addressed to Congress and not Washington, which the General finally received more than two weeks after the fact on November 2. Henry Laurens's ascent must have pleased Washington; it elevated the importance of his son, John, as a fixture at army headquarters and a direct conduit to his father.[3]

During his second night at Whitemarsh, the whispering campaign regarding his generalship reached Washington's eyes. General Stirling had been sent up the Schuylkill River, apparently to assess crossings at Pottsgrove and Reading. On November 3, Stirling sent a report by courier to the Emlen house; the rider arrived the following night. Washington weeded through Stirling's assessment of ferries and crossings and an update on the major general's health (he had been recovering from an earlier fall from a horse), standard contents for such a message. But Washington's eyes must have popped at Stirling's attached note, a single-sentence nugget: "In a letter from General Conway to General Gates he says, 'Heaven has been determined to Save your Country; or a weak General and bad Counsellors would have ruined it.'"[4]

In his cover letter Stirling characterized the attached statement he attributed to Conway as being of "such wicked duplicity of Conduct, I shall alway's think my duty to detect."[5] As Washington eventually learned, Stirling was relaying a snippet of a second-hand conversation recounted to him from one of his aides, Major William McWilliams. McWilliams had heard it from Colonel James Wilkinson, an aide to General Gates assigned to deliver Gates's report about the Battle of Saratoga to Congress. Stirling had quartered at Reading, a town on the 250-mile route between Albany and York; Wilkinson had stopped there as a respite on a rainy night from his journey to York, resulting in an invitation to dinner with General Stirling and his staff. After Stirling retired for the night subsequent chatter between Wilkinson and Stirling's aides continued, primed by alcohol and rumor passing.[6]

Washington did not know that Conway's criticism was circulating among other parties, and he had no idea whether Wilkinson had seen the line while reading Conway's letter to Gates, or if Wilkinson overheard, memorized, and regurgitated the comment to McWilliams before he in turn conveyed it to Stirling. Regardless, Wilkinson had good recall; the phrasing was nearly identical to what Dr. Rush had written to John Adams a week earlier:

> Rush to Adams: "A great and good God (says Genl. Conway in a letter to a friend) has decreed that America shall be free, or —— and weak counsellors would have ruined her long ago."[7]
>
> Wilkinson to McWilliams: "Heaven has been determined to Save our Country; or a Weak General and bad Counsellors would have ruined it."

George Washington was not privy to Rush's correspondence with Adams, but the fact that Rush had relayed to Gates his version of the same line from General Conway's post-Saratoga letter meant that Rush had read the line in a copy of the letter or in the original before it was sent, or that Rush had been fed the line by its author, General Conway. Washington eventually learned that Conway denounced him further in the same letter to Gates, or another one written shortly before or after: "What a pity there is but one Gates! But the more I see of this army, the less I think it fit for general action under its actual chiefs and actual discipline. I speak to you sincerely and freely, and wish I could serve under you."[8]

Conway's criticisms of Washington had been circulating deep into Pennsylvania before Wilkinson's loose and inebriated lips hastened the General's discovery on November 4 of what he was bound to learn shortly thereafter. According to Wilkinson, on a stopover ten miles northeast of Bethlehem, two days before the aide reached Reading, "I was asked whether I had seen Gen. Conway's letter to Gen. Gates, in which he assigned thirteen reasons for the loss of the battle of Brandywine." Even at Reading, hours before his powder keg remarks to McWilliams, Wilkinson said, "General Conway's criticisms were again mentioned" in a meeting between Wilkinson and "two eastern members of Congress" at General Mifflin's house on October 27.[9] Indeed, Conway's remarks would inevitably reach Washington's eyes or ears.

Stirling's note sufficed to convince Washington that Conway considered him a "Weak General" guided by "bad Counsellors" whose collective decisions and actions had set America on a path to ruin. But that demise had been blessedly interrupted by Horatio Gates. As if heaven-sent, Gates had saved the country, according to one Thomas Conway, currently in charge of Stirling's division at Whitemarsh while his ailing superior was on detached service; Thomas Conway who propped himself up at the expense of all others in disrupting army cohesion with his application to become a major general; Thomas Conway, whom Congress—or at least the Virginia delegation thereto—was proposing to install as Timothy Pickering's replacement in Washington's military family as Adjutant General of the Continental army.

Whether by the General's actual name, obscurantist dashes, or the transparent sobriquet "Weak General," Thomas Conway declared that George Washington would "ruin" the country. Washington slept on it and perhaps stewed a little over it but come morning he knew exactly how to address the matter. He sent a laconic dispatch to Conway. "A letter I received last Night contained the following paragraph," Washington wrote. But it wasn't a paragraph; it was that single sentence in Conway's letter to Gates that Washington flung right back at him. No question followed; nor any comment. Washington simply closed with "I am Sir Yr Hble Servt." and his signature. As Washington later explained, he returned Conway's remarks to him "to shew that Gentn that I was not unapprised of his intrigueing disposition."[10]

If Washington intended his message to wreck Conway's Wednesday, he succeeded. Once Conway read his superior's two sentences and closing, he immediately became defensive and confused, wondering how his words had re-entered his brigade quarters and slapped him in the face. Eventually that day Conway crafted a 550-word response (a comparatively short letter, based on his history of correspondence). In a moment of unabashed contradiction and doublespeak, Conway explained, "I Believe i can attest that the expression *Weak General* has not slipped from my penn - however if it has, this Weakness by my Very Letter can not be explain'd otherwise even by the most Malicious people than an excess of Modesty on your side and a confidence in Men who are Much inferior to you in point of judgment and Knowledge." Conway waxed paranoiac over "several unfavourable hints" that Washington's aides had attributed to Conway "as the author of some Discourses Which I never uttered." He painstakingly and pointedly rattled off Washington's admirable traits, oblivious to the fact that he used the exact terms in another portion of the letter: bravery, honesty, patriotism, honor, and judgment.[11] John Laurens mocked Conway's "most shameless manner to explain away the word weakness."[12] Washington's earlier assessment of Conway bears repeating: "He is a bad scribe."

As Conway fretted away time writing his response, his commanding general could not be found at Whitemarsh. Washington customarily departed headquarters for a ride at forenoon or early afternoon. Most days he headed to where he could take in his army's position and the surrounding landscape. Waking from his third night at the Emlen house, he changed things up. Howe's occupation of Philadelphia was keeping Continental officers from observing the brewing Delaware River campaign, though some had ventured as far south as Germantown. The village stood more than ten miles from the contested portion of the river, but that was as close as any American soldiers were going to get; Germantown sat barely five miles north of Howe's defensive line and redoubts. Adjacent high ground and rooftops within the town let observers monitor events along the river. Clement Biddle, for example, had written to his wife in late October that he heard the *Augusta* explode from Germantown and watched smoke rise from the burning ship.[13]

On November 5, cannon fire at and from Fort Mifflin reverberated in the still morning air sixteen miles north at Whitemarsh. General Washington decided to investigate. His Excellency rode seven miles south to Germantown with John Laurens and perhaps others. Finding a battered stone house with a roof walk, he climbed to that vantage point, extended the tubes of his brass Dolland spyglass, and scanned the southern horizon. "We could discover nothing more than thick clouds of smoak," Laurens wrote later, "and the masts of two vessels, the weather being hazy."[14]

Except for his return to Trenton within days of his surprise assault in 1776, this sally into Germantown was the only other known time to date in the war that saw Washington revisit a place at which he had directed men in life-or-death decisions. Inevitably making this trip a dual mission was the house they chose for a viewing station. The sturdy if battered dwelling atop which Washington stood was Cliveden.

Stopping in front of Benjamin Chew's house—where British infantry had gone to ground and helped turned the tide of the October 4 battle in favor of Crown forces—Washington, Laurens, and the unidentified members of the headquarters party dismounted. The men traversed ground contested in blood thirty-two days earlier to the battle-scarred front door. They entered Cliveden, not long ago temporarily transmogrified by the 40th Regiment of Foot into "A Castle in Our Rear," and wormed single file through an upper story hatch opening to the roof.[15] Afterwards, perhaps, Washington and companions rode around the village. As veterans of battles always have when returning to the settings where they fought, they must have talked, but no one discussed those conversations in any known letter, diary, or memoir.

Two weeks earlier, Washington had written to a relative about the battle, describing it as too foggy to see more than thirty yards. Since the view eleven miles out to the Delaware was too limited from that rooftop, Washington must have eyed the surrounding battlefield he couldn't see on the day that it had mattered most. On October 18, he had insisted that, but for fog, "we should, I believe, have made a decisive & glorious day of it. But Providence—or some unaccountable something, designed it otherwise." Two weeks later, Washington was on the roof of the "some unaccountable something" that had changed the momentum of the battle.

Washington's return from Germantown took him from the past to the present, which he sought to make more comfortable for himself and everyone at headquarters. Ever since he'd sent his personal baggage train away seven weeks earlier, Washington had forsworn the lavishness that had come to be associated with his headquarters, including the Mount Vernonesque dinners arranged in his tent or a requisitioned residence. At the Emlen house, Washington pursued normalcy. Although his fine tablecloths and silverware were still stowed away, the Emlen family seems to have been able to accommodate grander dinners than could Frederick Wampole at the Towamencin encampment. With that in mind, General Orders emphasized a return to tradition:

> Since the General left Germantown in the middle of September last he has been without his baggage, and on that account is unable to receive company in the manner he could wish—he never-the-less desires, the Generals, Field Officers, and Brigade Major of the day, to dine with him in future, at three o'clock in the afternoon.[16]

Washington had been toiling seven days a week for thirty months. He had taken no furloughs and enjoyed very few daytime respites—and those he did take lasted but a few hours. "I have been a Slave to the service; I have undergone more than most men are aware of," he declared in a moment of pique. He treasured simple pleasures as a tonic for the stress and the tedium of simultaneously commanding an army in the field and overseeing all military endeavors throughout America. He cherished a pair of fine stockings sent by his sister-in-law and appreciated a wagonload of fresh oysters sent by the head of New Jersey's militia, Brigadier General Philemon Dickinson.[17] Letters from his civilian friends and acquaintances, particularly from Virginia, lightened his mood, although he often failed in his striving to answer them in a timely fashion.

While he enjoyed fine food and clothing, he kept up on his troops' condition, particularly as November banished temperate weather, also reminding him that those sparsely supplied soldiers he was sending into combat soon would be sequestered in winter encampments. "[I]f we can get our ragged and half naked soldiers clothed," Washington postulated, ". . . I think General Howe may be forced out of Philadelphia, or greatly distressed in his Quarters there, if we can draw a large body of Troops round the City." At a November 8 council of war he told his generals that a force coming from New England included 1,600 Massachusetts militiamen whose enlistments were up at month's end. He added that "the Enemy mean a formidable attack upon Fort Mifflin very soon," and sought consensus on a proposal to attack the British "with our present Force" should Howe attack the fort. The response was a unanimous "No" vote.[18]

Four days later, Washington summoned his generals for an afternoon session featuring an alarming report from Brigadier General James M. Varnum. Varnum, stationed in Woodbury, New Jersey, and whose Rhode Islanders and Connecticut regiments were manning the Delaware River bastions, told the group that Fort Mifflin could hold no longer. Plans were under way to evacuate.[19] With all hands watching, Washington dictated to Tench Tilghman a response to Varnum: "I hope it is not carried into execution. If it is not, it is the unanimous opinion of a Council of General Officers now sitting, that the Fort be held to the last extremity."[20]

How to save the fort? At meeting's end Washington recruited Major General Nathanael Greene. Only two days removed from a wrenching injury incurred when he was brutally bucked from a horse, the aching Greene nonetheless saddled up and rode toward Philadelphia with a small party to reconnoiter British positions at Fort Mifflin's siege points and to study the

Schuylkill River crossings from the western side of the river. Despite his generals' unanimous refusal on November 8 to endorse an attack on Howe's defenses at Philadelphia and their similar reluctance to move to ease British pressure on Fort Mifflin, George Washington clandestinely undertook to attack.

General Greene had sat and voted as a member of that unanimous council on November 8, and just a day before accepting his latest mission he had told a confidant his injury was serious enough to keep him from the field. In August, while the upper Hudson River theater was being hotly contested, Greene flatly scorned the Continental army's emphasis on Philadelphia over the Hudson region. But Greene showed himself ready to sacrifice his health—even risk his life—to rescue a city he now called "the Rome of America."[21] With his unidentified escorts and officers, Greene dodged British patrols while spending two days studying the assigned region.

Headquarters received Greene's report late on Friday, November 14. Writing from a locale about ten miles west of Philadelphia, Greene indicated he would return to Whitemarsh on Saturday after they "examin the ground a little more about Darby." Greene assured Washington that as he was starting to draft his report the flag was still flying at Fort Mifflin. He described the numbers and types of British vessels threatening the American forts. In general terms he characterized Howe's "chain of redoubts with Abatis between them" stretching between both rivers bordering Philadelphia. In greater detail, Greene explained approaches to the Schuylkill. Based on his personal reconnaissance of that river's southernmost dozen miles, he determined that the Schuylkill was running too high and too fast to cross anywhere, including Levering's Ford. This left the Middle Ferry bridge as the prime crossing point into the city. Greene also reviewed what he saw as the ideal upper crossing for Washington to use in leading a large force from Whitemarsh twenty-five miles to Derby. This was Matson's Ford, eight miles west of the Emlen house. Greene estimated that two days of preparation were necessary there to create a sturdy pontoon bridge to funnel most of his army across.[22]

Most noteworthy about Greene's report was its tone. No longer the curmudgeon, he had turned around to become an enthusiastic advocate of Washington's plan to save the fort by military might:

> [F]rom the present view Darby appears the only eligible position for the Army for the purpose of their crossing the river—It is the opinion of several of the gen-

tlemen that the enemy may be best dislodged from the Islands by detachment, others are of opinion that it would be dangerous unless the party was coverd, by the Army, but all are of opinion, it is practicable either the one way or the other and considering the good consequences that will result from it, it ought to be attempted—Darby is not the most eligible post I ever saw, but it is not so dangerous as to discourage the attempt to relieve fort Mifflin.[23]

Greene and his party returned to Whitemarsh on Saturday. Later that day Washington called him and the rest of his generals to headquarters for the third council in a week. No headquarters record of this meeting survived but, according to a private letter written three days afterwards by participant Anthony Wayne, "the practicability as well as the Immediate Necessity of raising the Siege was urged in the most clear and pointed terms." Treading the same topical ground as on November 8, the November 15 meeting delved into details such as how to relieve the siege and the destruction of Fort Mifflin by planned assault. The other major difference between these two councils was General Greene. Although present at both, Greene was an active advocate of the plan on November 15, and very likely assisted Washington in explaining the details to other Continental commanders. Two wings of the army would operate almost simultaneously, separated by five miles at their respective points of contact with the British. While Washington was to lead the bulk of the army on a circuitous route beginning westward over Matson's Ford, then south to Derby, Wayne and his two Pennsylvania brigades and Morgan's riflemen were to move directly south toward Fort Mifflin. Morgan's endpoint was Province Island, just east of where the Schuylkill emptied into the Delaware. There, on the portion of the island between the mouths of the Schuylkill and Mingo Creek, British infantry buttressed the Royal batteries that were hammering Fort Mifflin's northern and western walls. While Washington was opening the battle with an assault at the Middle Ferry bridge, General Wayne, on Province Island, was to "Storm the Enemies lines, spike their Cannon, and Ruin their works."[24]

This plan's audacity must have surprised the council, but even more so Greene's promotion of it. The room jittered with desperation. Wayne, who was to be carrying the heaviest responsibility and risk, was absolutely sold on the plan's prospects. He acknowledged the difficulties involved in reaching the point of contact and the peril implicit in leading no more than two thousand men against an enemy certainly stronger. Regardless, he reasoned, "the success depended more on the fortitude of the Troops, and the Vigor with which the attack was made—than upon the Numbers—His Excellency had charged me with the Conduct and execution of this business—I knew my Troops & gladly Embraced the Command."[25]

Most, if not all, of the others rejected the plan. Wayne was not surprised; caution had been the watchword at councils considering attack plans, including the October 29 and November 8 meetings. The generals appeared to favor no-risk operations or undertakings in which the numbers were so lopsided as to render an attack inevitable. Since neither characteristic applied in this instance, objections rang loudly in the meeting room. Wayne, who earlier had been a naysayer, vented frustration at seeing that unified response; although he and General Greene understood the moment's urgency, the other generals declined to risk their commands in operations where casualties were certain to be excessive. Wayne concluded that councils of war are "the surest way to do nothing"—at times necessary but "the doubts raised, and the Delays Occasion'd by these Councils, Often prevent a General from taking advantage of the Most favourable Circumstances, and from Striking the most Capital Strokes." Hearing the generals' near-unanimous rejection, Wayne concluded that the forts and the American fleet on the Delaware stood doomed by what he aptly defined as "this Supineness—an over stretched caution."[26]

Washington overrode the council; he refused to let the forts go without a fight. According to Wayne, "His Excellency had Determined to act the General" and so overruled the overruling and ordered the offensive to commence the next day.[27] Washington shared Wayne's mindset regarding councils. The Continental Congress had urged him to hold these meetings frequently, but Washington had come to understand that as winter neared his generals were less likely to agree to risky offensive operations and campaigns. He strove to change that protective mindset. Thomas Paine's mesmerizing opening sentence to *The American Crisis*, written eleven months earlier, summed up mid-November 1777: "These are the times that try men's souls." Once the decision was made, subordinate generals indicated the import and registered support. General Scott declared that same Saturday that "we are in High spirits and full of hope of Bringing This most Horrid War to a Conclusion by Defeating Genl. How in a few days."[28] Washington worked out details for preparing his army for the assault, convinced he was not too late to save Fort Mifflin.

But he was. Barely withstanding over one thousand rounds of solid shot per day fired by several British batteries on land and on water—all within a few hundred yards—Fort Mifflin was hardly recognizable as the redoubt that had been intact in October. On November 15, Lieutenant Colonel Samuel Smith notified Washington that "it is now one Heap of Ruin."[29] Unable to garrison the wreckage without being killed or captured, its last stalwart defenders were ordered to evacuate overnight on November 16, traversing the icy Delaware to the protection of Fort Mercer. Fort Mifflin now belonged to the British.

Fort Mifflin's demise may have been inevitable, and the fact that it had deprived Howe of a direct riverside access to Philadelphia for nearly two months after he captured and occupied the city could be viewed as a limited victory for the Americans. But those in the know did not see it that way. Silently approving of Washington's decisiveness, Wayne in a private conversation indicted Washington for being far too late in "acting the General," saying, "[T]hat Garrison has done its duty—would to God that it had been equally done in an Other Quarter!"[30]

Brazen as always, the egregious Conway communicated with Washington at mid-month. Anticipating French entry into the war against England, Conway wished to serve France directly, he wrote to Washington, "I hope your Excellency will permit me to Depart the army, in order to return to France as soon as possible." He wished America success and oozed praise for Washington, thanking him "for the civilitys you have shew'd me while I had the honour of being under your orders."[31]

Washington yearned to be rid of Conway, less for his carping about the General's leadership than for his disruptive egomania. But the rules took precedence, so Washington replied that only Congress held the authority to accept his resignation; he could not permit Conway to leave the army until the delegates approved. Washington cordially thanked Conway for his encouraging words, closing by saying that "in case you are permitted to return by Congress, you will have my hopes for a favourable passage and a happy meeting with your Family & Friends." Conway followed up that evening by requesting a leave of absence for up to twelve days to collect his effects from storage in Easton, Reading, and Bethlehem. Washington granted the request, likely to begin after Conway was done serving on a court martial. Washington pointedly allowed his secretary to send the leave approval without signing it himself.[32]

The ugly mechanics of war came to the fore at Whitemarsh on Thursday, November 20, 1777. Washington announced in General Orders the outcome of a court martial whose officers coincidentally had included Conway. After two weeks of proceedings, the court of generals rendered a verdict on Major General Adam Stephen, primarily up on charges relating to his conduct at the Battle of Germantown, but also to his leadership on the march from the Clove in New York State in July and his conduct at Brandywine. He was recommended for acquittal on all charges leading to and including the Battle of Germantown but was found guilty of two after-battle charges: "unofficer-like behaviour, in the retreat from Germantown" and having "been frequently intoxicated since in the service." Because those charges violated Congress's 1776 Articles of War, Stephen's sentence was immediate dismissal. Washington approved the cashiering.[33]

Stephen's departure removed the sixth major general since summer who had been with Washington as a field or staff officer in the Philadelphia theater. He was the latest division commander to be lost to Washington since Benjamin Lincoln was detached to the Northern Department (Lincoln later was wounded in the Saratoga campaign). Major Generals Horatio Gates and Benedict Arnold were also pulled north; Arnold had been severely wounded and Gates had remained in command in the Northern Department. Major General Coudray's drowning took away another valuable officer, but one whose duties had generally been assumed by other French engineers, particularly Brigadier General Louis Duportail.

The sixth major general to depart the Philadelphia arena did so quietly—and rather clandestinely, given that he wished to escape the commanding general's notice. Major General Thomas Mifflin resigned as chief quartermaster. He submitted his resignation to Congress on October 8 without informing Washington, who three weeks later acknowledged Mifflin's rumored departure without clear confirmation. Congress approved the resignation on November 7, informing Washington in a postscript to a letter announcing that Mifflin would retain his major general's rank but without pay.[34]

Besides half a dozen major generals, six brigadier generals who had been expected to be active with their commands since the summer of 1777 or who expected to join the campaign afterwards, were also gone. Though appointed, Brigadier General John Phillip de Haas never officially took command, but the result was no different than with Woodford, Nash, Conway, and de Borre who had led their men and had since departed. Alexander McDougall, promoted to major general, departed brigade command. Regimental officers assumed brigadier duties for more than half of Washington's Continental infantry brigades. To this point in the campaign, only McDougall's brigade had received a replacement general; the Connecticut troops were now led by Brigadier General Jedediah Huntington. Other units were commanded by regimental officers. Brigadier General Anthony

Wayne continued to lead Lincoln's former division, while colonels led both of his brigades.

As well aware as Washington was of growing leadership problems, he remained oblivious to a cacophony of dissent. The whispering campaign against the commander in chief gained volume. Jonathan Dickinson Sergeant had vacated his seat as a New Jersey delegate to Congress to commence his newest duties as the attorney general for his newly adopted home state of Pennsylvania. Meeting with the state's Commission of Safety in Lancaster, a despairing Sergeant penned his opinion of George Washington:

> Things look gloomy enough below. We want a General; thousands of Lives & Millions of Property are yearly sacrificed to the Insufficiency of our Commander in Chief. Two Battles he has lost for us by two such Blunders as might have disgraced a Soldier of three Months Standing; and yet we are so attached to this Man that I fear we shall rather sink with him than throw him off our Shoulders. And sink we must under his Management. Such Feebleness & Want of Authority, such Confusion & Want of Discipline, such Waste, such Destruction will exhaust the Wealth of both the Indies & annihilate the Armies of all Europe & Asia. Twenty Thousand Recruits annually would be absolutely necessary to maintain an Army of forty thousand. I believe this is the most moderate Calculation. In the mean Time People are so disaffected to the Service that no more Recruits can be got . . . we may talk of the Enemy's Cruelty as we will, but we have no greater Cruelty to complain of than the Management of our Army.[35]

Only hours after Sergeant signed that letter, matters looked even gloomier for The Cause. A bulletin from Nathanael Greene alerted headquarters that overnight on November 20, beset by mounting enemy pressure from the west and south (the latter from a detachment led by Cornwallis), Fort Mercer's defenders had evacuated.[36] The Delaware River from its bay to Philadelphia was now completely open to Crown forces.

General Mifflin had anticipated this turn, regarding it as inevitable. Loss of the forts, particularly the one bearing his name, left him furious for weeks. But Mifflin had a plan he thought would right America's wayward and sinking ship. He accused Washington of arrogantly fostering an environment in which officers disinclined to "pay an undeserved Tribute of Praise & Flattery to the great & powerful" were eased or driven out of the army. Mifflin vented his ire in a letter to Horatio Gates meant to sweep away that state of affairs, for which he blamed the commander in chief.

Gates read Mifflin's rant in Albany a few days after Admiral Richard Howe opened the Delaware to his brother, General William Howe. In his communique, Mifflin denigrated Washington as "the Image" and "a gone Character," importuning Gates to join forces with him and like-minded officers. "In short the Army will be totally lost unless you come down & collect the virtuous Band, who wish to fight under your Banner. . . . Prepare yourself for a Jaunt to this Place. Congress must send for you."[37]

Ever since his triumph at Saratoga, Gates had been basking in accolades. But Mifflin's praiseful rhetoric soared above and beyond those huzzahs. Mifflin's closing sentences were not empty promises, as Gates was to learn. Soon after he read the letter, the 1777 Board of War, about to dissolve, undertook its final tasks. One was getting congressional approval to enlarge the incoming three-member 1778 board per a belated special request by Mifflin:

> General Mifflin has expressed a warm Solicitude that Major General Gates should be appointed President of this Board, from a Conviction that his Military Skill would suggest Reformations in the different Departments of the Army essential to good Discipline, Order and Economy, and that his Character and Popularity in the Army would facilitate the execution of such Reformations when adopted by Congress; a Task in the opinion of this Committee more arduous and important, than the formation of any new Establishment, however wise it may be in Theory![38]

Formidable opponents now assailed Washington on every imaginable front. He was accustomed to parrying Crown forces' blows coming from all angles on battlefields and contested theaters. But now he was in a shadow fight with foes at his back, ostensibly allies but in reality dangerous adversaries determined to usurp his power, if not eject him from command.

CHAPTER TWELVE

"It is in Our Power to Produce a Conviction to the World"

November 22 to December 1, 1777

The woeful Commissary Department's deficiencies revealed themselves at the Emlen house. On Saturday, November 22, General Washington dictated General Orders to a penman, not identified. Announcing the next day's courts martial, to occur at General Huntington's quarters, the orders informed field officers in Pulaski's dragoons that they were to call at General Stirling's quarters to sort out their ranks. A new division under Major General Baron De Kalb consisted of two brigades freshly arrived from the Northern Department and commanded by Brigadier Generals John Paterson and Ebenezer Learned. Then came the day's After Orders, a stunning bolt from the blue:

> The commander in chief offers a reward of Ten dollars, to any person who shall, by nine o'clock on Monday morning, produce the best substitute for shoes, made

of raw hides—The Commissary of hides is to furnish the hides, and the Major General of the day is to judge of the essays, and to assign the reward to the best artist.[1]

That Saturday morning saw an uncharacteristic earthquake shake the region, but that shifting of the very ground beneath the army's feet more than had its match for shock value in the shoe affair. Besides revealing the existence of a Commissary of Hides, the announcement dripped with the desperation afflicting the Continental army. Alas, no one ever identified the footwear contest winner or recorded the winning substitute for shoes.

Besieged as he was by the loss of the Delaware River forts, a lengthening roster of vacancies on his general staff, and metastasizing lapses riddling the Commissary and Quartermaster Departments, the Grand Army became more formidable during the third week of November. Its numerical strength ballooned by 5,400 infantry officers and privates, thanks to the arrival of four Continental brigades along with a few independent battalions from Massachusetts, New Hampshire, and New York. The ranks at Whitemarsh also stood to grow by an additional 1,360 infantry soldiers once General Varnum's Connecticut and Rhode Island troops departed New Jersey for Whitemarsh.

Washington finally had accepted that Fort Mercer was lost. As a consequence, he decided that Greene should continue to operate in New Jersey so long as Cornwallis was maneuvering on that side of the Delaware. "As you have crossed the River," the General instructed Greene, "an attack upon the Enemy's Detachment if it can be made with success, would be a most desirable object." Washington wished Greene to "advance to meet it as much in force as possible," while appropriately delegating authority to him: "But I must leave the propriety of it entirely to your own judgment."[2]

Greene, save for a tender wrist recovered from his fall of the month before and eager to lock horns with Cornwallis, wrote to his wife, "I am in hopes to have the pleasure to meet his Lordship." His independent operation was massive. He had four Continental brigades, Morgan's riflemen plus detached battalions from other Continental commands, dragoons, artillery, and militia, amounting to nearly seven thousand officers and men in New Jersey. Outnumbering Cornwallis, this detachment's implicit puissance moved Greene to plan an assault. Headquartering at Mount Holly, he awaited the last Northern Department brigade, an all-Massachusetts force under Brigadier General John Glover. Once Glover reinforced Greene, his corps in New Jersey would exceed eight thousand soldiers.[3]

As November was ending, the Grand Army exceeded twenty-two thousand Continental and militia soldiers encamped on the heights and in the swales at Whitemarsh or detached with General Greene in New Jersey. With winter impending, Washington did not collect an army of this size to park it like a wagon for the season. Although his best opportunity had passed to attack a divided Crown force in Philadelphia while defending the Delaware forts, his numerical advantage over Howe expanded further, thanks to the influx of those five brigades.

Unexpectedly, Washington enjoyed the services of a superlative intelligence operation. His chief spymaster was Major John Clark, twenty-six, a most impressive officer from York, Pennsylvania. Clark had begun the war in Hugh Mercer's command but graduated to running independent operations in New Jersey between the battles of Trenton and Princeton. There, leading a band of two hundred members of the Flying Camp, he first caught Washington's eye. The commander in chief personally rewarded Clark with a British officer's sword. Clark had served as an aide de camp to General Greene for much of 1777, at Brandywine suffering a nagging shoulder wound and at Germantown capturing a British captain. Immediately after that battle, Clark took it upon himself to head an operation of locals collecting intelligence on Howe's casualties at Germantown.[4]

Clark's energy and initiative impressed Washington so much, according to Clark, that the General "gave me unlimited command and power to act as I pleased." Clark personally studied British troop and ship movements west of the Schuylkill and during October and November established a network of agents in Philadelphia to keep Washington apprised of British and Hessian operations. From Major Clark, Washington learned on Saturday, November 22, exactly where Howe's army was. Just so, Clark pinpointed the enemy's protective abatis—created by felling apple orchards—which bristled for two miles between the Schuylkill and Delaware. He also calculated the strength of Howe's army behind those works—"not above 4 or 5,000"—and noted the Redcoats' generally paranoid and defeatist demeanor.[5]

John Cadwalader matched Washington when it came to maintaining an aggressive mindset; sometimes Cadwalader's passion for the offensive exceeded his commander's. Cadwalader, a fixture at headquarters since late September, attended councils and took to the field to observe the foe. He had seen personally the week previous near Derby a force of at least five thousand "chiefly British" soldiers cross from Chester to Billingsport, obviously on their way to assault Fort Mercer, already abandoned. That detached unit, under Cornwallis, remained in New Jersey several days while other Crown detachments were occupying the newly won islands on the Delaware. Studying British defensive works that ran from river to river as best he could, and determining that no detachments were stationed any closer than seven miles to that line, Cadwalader realized over the weekend of November 22-23 that the time was ripe to overwhelm that British line and wrest Philadelphia from Howe.

Cadwalader crafted a finely detailed plan of attack—"offered for Consideration"—to be conducted simultaneously by Washington from Whitemarsh and by Greene from New Jersey. Eight American brigades fielding 4,750 privates would attack at dawn, while an additional 2,400 men in three brigades crossed into New Jersey at a ferry a few miles above Trenton. Those troops would follow the east bank of the Delaware, cross back to Philadelphia between two specified streets, "march through the Streets in Columns as wide as the Streets will admit," and strike Howe's weakened defense from the rear. Pennsylvania militia were to feint toward the enemy's right along specified streets and "penetrate when an Opportunity offers," supported by a two thousand-man corps de reserve of Maryland militia added to the North Carolina brigade and three independent Continental battalions.

The grand proposal identified and specifically positioned every brigade of Washington's Whitemarsh army. He was less specific regarding Greene's force at Mount Holly: "If two thousand men could be drawn from the Detachments of Gen. Greene to make the Attack by water the main attack upon the Lines might be more strengthened & the plan rendered more compleat." Apparently, Cadwalader hesitated to rely on a force that Cornwallis's detachment could block. Greene's force was at least as massive as Cornwallis's. The day Cadwalader finalized his attack plan, Greene's adjutant, having collected troop-strength returns for the entire detachment, tallied 5,500 Continental infantry privates, of whom no more than eight hundred were unavailable due to illness or on detached duty away from their regiments. Working with reduced figures, Cadwalader produced a conservative calculus calling for less than half of Greene's complement present and fit for duty, a count diminished further given that the last arriving brigade was within seventy-two hours of reinforcing Greene's detachment.[6]

Cadwalader's plan totaled 8,200 Continental infantry rank and file from Whitemarsh plus two thousand from Greene's detachment, supported by three thousand Pennsylvania and Maryland militia. Cadwalader's breakdown did not include field and line officers for the participating regiments,

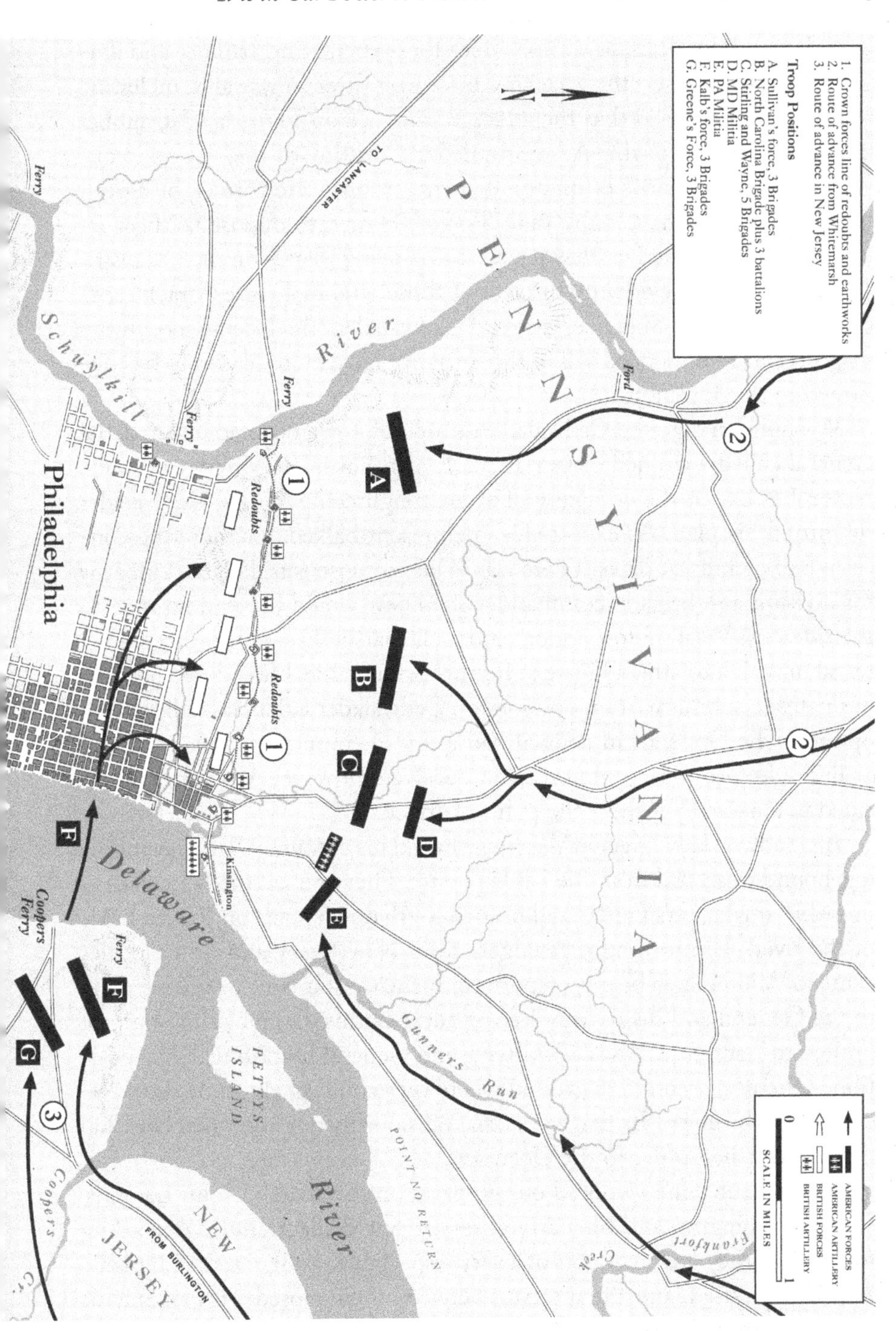
1. Crown forces line of redoubts and earthworks
2. Route of advance from Whitemarsh
3. Route of advance in New Jersey
Troop Positions
A. Sullivan's force, 3 Brigades
B. North Carolina Brigade plus 3 battalions
C. Stirling and Wayne, 5 Brigades
D. MD Militia
E. PA Militia
F. Kalb's force, 3 Brigades
G. Greene's Force, 3 Brigades
AMERICAN FORCES
AMERICAN ARTILLERY
BRITISH FORCES
BRITISH ARTILLERY
0
1
SCALE IN MILES
N
PENNSYLVANIA
TO LANCASTER
Schuylkill River
Ferry
Ford
Redoubts
Philadelphia
Kinsington
Delaware River
Coopers Ferry
PETTYS ISLAND
Gunners Run
POINT NO RETURN
Frankfort Creek
NEW JERSEY
FROM BURLINGTON

brigades, and divisions, as well as tallies for participating artillery and dragoons, but they raised the attacking force past fifteen thousand, including reserves. He proposed that the attack commence on Thursday, November 27, "a little before daybreak." Cadwalader's scrutiny of the city had convinced him that Clark's estimates of enemy troops were correct; he agreed that "they cannot have more than 5 or 6,000 men to oppose us" because the rest were detached in New Jersey or occupying islands on the Delaware. "The advantage is evidently in favor of those who make the Attack especially if you effect a Surprize," stressed Cadwalader, "the Enemy too, always magnify our Numbers & will in this Instance have more reason to be confirmed in this Opinion."[7]

Washington digested Cadwalader's proposal. Intrigued and inspired, the General called a council of war at the Emlen house on Monday evening, November 24. In the company of at least eighteen generals, Cadwalader submitted his plan. As expected, some present balked, enumerating concerns and picking at flaws. There was to be no consensus. Feeling empathy for division and brigade commanders he knew would be sending men to their deaths, Washington understood well that he had only a limited interval in which to attack Howe at his most vulnerable. He ordered his subordinates to submit written opinions on Cadwalader's plan, including fresh options. The Generals in council had a day to compose and deliver their analyses; before those opinions were received, however, Washington decided to personally inspect the point of attack.

A cloudless dawn greeted Washington and his entourage Tuesday morning, bound westward from the Emlen house. They crossed the Schuylkill—probably at Matson's Ford—and headed south down roads on the west side of the river. All morning messengers from New Jersey and other locales came to Whitemarsh bearing reports; only the most urgent were sent along to the General and his reconnoitering advisors this day, including but not limited to Laurens, Cadwalader, Reed, and General Duportail. They positioned themselves on high ground where they could safely study the western side of the line of British works that presumably ran from the Schuylkill three-and-a-half miles to the Delaware.

"A clear sunshine favoured our observations," remarked John Laurens. What Washington and his party observed was disheartening. According to Laurens, they "saw redoubts of a very respectable profit, faced with plank, formidably raised, and the intervals between them closed with an abbatis unusually strong." Joseph Reed assessed the works as "so exceedingly strong as to damp the ardour of the most enterprising." Not only had Howe's engineers chosen "the most commanding" ground on which to construct the works, Reed said, but a chain of accompanying redoubts, even seen from afar, appeared to have been "framed, planked, and of great thickness, surrounded with a deep ditch enclosed and freized. The intervals are filled with an abbatis composed of all the apple trees in the neighborhood, and many large trees from the Pennsbury woods." The Americans chafed to see that the enemy had commandeered the homes of Philadelphians adjoining those works, stripping dwellings of windows, roofs, floorboards, and doors to make huts for Crown forces, leaving to stand only pathetic, bare walls. No residential fencing could be seen. Where apple and pear trees had dotted the neighborhood not a single fruit tree remained.

General Duportail proved the reconnaissance's most valuable participant. Gazing at the British position and deducing what probably existed out of view, the army's chief engineer deemed the position so strong that Howe needed only five thousand men behind those works to counter any force that dared assault them. It would be far less advantageous than they had been expecting to attack the position while large enemy forces were detached from Philadelphia. Reed, who had been for "some vigorous measure," now declared an assault "too hazardous," adding, "If there was an opportunity of forcing them out of the city, I fear it is gone, and that we must lay our account with their wintering there."

Washington reluctantly sided with Reed that it was "too hazardous" to carry out Cadwalader's plan only two days hence. Washington had departed Whitemarsh that Tuesday morning making final preparations to attack a vulnerable portion of Howe's divided army; he returned to headquarters having concluded the opposite. "I had a full view of their left," he reported, "and found their works much stronger than I had reason to expect from the Accounts I had received." Gloom had deepened as couriers found Washington on the road and delivered their messages. These dispatches convinced Washington that British detachments, including Cornwallis's several thousand troops, were expected back in Philadelphia within twenty-four hours.

Pondering what he had seen on that staff ride and studying intelligence reports, Washington deduced, "All those movements make me suspicious that they mean to collect their whole force while ours is divided, and make an Attack on this side." This perception changed everything. Greene's eight thousand-man force in New Jersey, including Glover's still-inbound brigade, had been an asset but now was his prime vulnerability, given distance and the fact that the Delaware separated them. Washington ordered all available boats at Coryell's Ferry floated down to Burlington. He sent a courier to Greene's headquarters; that urgent message, written by Lieutenant Colonel Harrison at 8:00 P.M., told Greene that unless he was already attacking Cornwallis he was to cross his men into Pennsylvania at or near Burlington and "rejoin me with your whole force as quick as possible."[8]

That Tuesday, November 25, Greene had moved fifteen miles from Mount Holly to Haddonfield, where Washington's letter reached him. Finally reinforced by Glover's brigade, Greene's eight thousand soldiers had begun the day pursuing Cornwallis toward the Delaware, but the increasingly swampy route forced a halt with five miles separating the combatants. Greene learned that Cornwallis had perched his six thousand men at Gloucester, well supported with Royal Navy ships now able to ascend the Delaware River. "I should not have halted the troops," admitted Greene in hindsight, "but all the Genl officers were against making the attack" based on the protection Cornwallis had arranged for his troops. This circumstance reduced Greene to planning a skirmish with enemy pickets in hopes of drawing Cornwallis out from his protection, but Cornwallis refused to budge from Gloucester.[9]

Working to concentrate his army and awaiting Howe's assault, Washington ignored the matter of generals' analyses of Cadwalader's plan. Even if Howe did not advance toward him, he said, "the Enemy had fortified themselves so strongly that it is now impossible to attack them with the least hopes of success."[10] As it turned out, Howe chose not to advance toward Whitemarsh at this time. The last days of November were spent with opposing forces in essentially the same positions they occupied since the second day of the month.

Had Washington studied his subordinates' opinions of the Cadwalader plan he would have learned much about his generals. Of fourteen opinions that Washington retained, four supported the attack plan with minimal alterations, five rejected engaging Howe in battle, and five outlined alternative plans primarily based on drawing Howe away from Philadelphia and battling him north or northwest of the city.

General Sullivan went on at length attacking the plan, declaring that Cadwalader and other proponents "Deceive themselves & you: for if you are unsuccessful the Credit of the Army will be Destroyed & the Confidence of the people Lost beyond recovery & your own Character must Suffer." Citing the difficulties of reducing even one structure, he reminded Washington "at German Town one Stone House Snatched from us a victory which was almost Completed."[11]

General Wayne persuasively endorsed Cadwalader's plan. He wrote, "however hazardous the Attempt and Altho' some loss is Certain—yet it is my Opinion—that you will not be in a worse Situation—nor your Arms in less Credit—if you should even meet with a misfortune—than if you were to Remain Inactive. . . . It's not in our power to Command success but it is in our Power to produce a Conviction to the World that we Deserve it."[12]

Washington's newest brigade commanders, Generals Paterson and Poor, each succinctly turned thumbs down. In similar fashion, Generals Scott and Woodford supported the attack, as did Generals Armstrong, Irvine, Maxwell, and Smallwood. But none of them wanted to attack Philadelphia, instead endorsing drawing Howe's army away from the city and operating against it in more open territory. Maxwell wrote, "I am for attacting and Harrassing them by every means in our power; by any other Method than that of attacting them in their works."[13]

General Greene and his entire detachment crossed from New Jersey and settled into Whitemarsh to end the month of November. The concentration of the entire army in that locale established Whitemarsh as having the second largest population on the continent. On November 30 at least 24,647 Continental and militia soldiers were encamped on the heights and in the swales at Whitemarsh.[14] (This tally would be logged into the monthly return in two days.) Seventeen Continental infantry brigades, militia, dragoons, and artillerists manning forty-three cannons comprised this force. Regiments from every state except South Carolina and Georgia shouldered firelocks in Washington's large army.

Washington had lost nine generals from Continental ranks since the Fourth of July. Major Generals Coudray, Gates, Lincoln, Mifflin, and Stephen, along with Brigadier Generals Conway, De Borre, Nash, and Woodford, were permanently or temporarily gone. To compensate, Washington labored to incorporate available generals—especially major generals—into field commands. He had been able to bypass congressional approval and directly place Major General Kalb in charge of two newly arrived Northern Department brigades a month earlier, primarily because he was not replacing a departed commander. Newly minted Major General McDougall rose from brigade command earlier in the campaign. Washington slyly dodged a problem by never seeking to name an official replacement to lead Major General Lincoln's division. Anthony Wayne remained in command of this division, a nice fit that put a Pennsylvanian in charge of two Pennsylvania brigades. But what did not fit was Wayne's rank. Congressional law froze his status as brigadier general, even though Major Generals St. Clair and Mifflin had no active role during the final weeks of autumn. By officially holding Wayne's status as a division commander with a brigadier's rank, Washington could keep an experienced general content with his elevated responsibilities.

The first week of December, Washington sought a swift means of replacing Adam Stephen, fired two weeks earlier. Washington had an available major general eager to take over the Virginia brigades. Marquis de Lafayette had returned to service nearly a month before, recovered from his wound at Bethlehem. The twenty-year-old Frenchman increasingly endeared himself to his commanding general after a turbulent start in mid-August.

Lafayette's blend of energy and ambition had vexed Washington during the heat of summer but in the chill of descending autumn he was charmed by the young man. Lafayette proved a tonic for the Continental army. His vivacity was balanced by an inherent ability to lead men in life-or-death events. On November 1, Washington expressed concern that Lafayette's desire for assignment did not match what Congress had intended for him, but Washington trumpeted Lafayette's attributes: "in all his letters has placed our affairs in the best situation he could. Besides, he is sensible—discreet in his manners—has made great proficiency in our Language, and from the disposition he discovered at the Battle of Brandy Wine, possesses a large share of bravery and Military ardor."[15]

Lafayette's instinctive ability to keep his head and bravely lead men in the midst of battle chaos, as he demonstrated by his wounding while rallying troops on Birmingham Hill in September, had not been an aberration. Lafayette joined Greene's detachment as a volunteer and on November 25 led four hundred militia and Morgan's riflemen out of Haddonfield. This small detachment located and engaged three hundred Hessians from Cornwallis's force in a running fight westward toward Gloucester on the bank of the Delaware, four miles upriver from Fort Mercer. At a minimal cost, Lafayette inflicted thirty casualties among the jägers. General Greene encouraged the young general to write a report of the battle; Lafayette complied. "The Marquis is determined to be in the way of danger," remarked Greene, with obvious admiration, to Washington.[16]

The dustup east of Gloucester did not alter the campaign, but it certainly benefited Lafayette and Washington. Washington used Greene's letter to him as evidence of Lafayette's abilities. "I am convinced he possesses a large share of that Military ardor which generally characterizes the Nobility of his Country," Washington told Henry Laurens. The commander in chief also assured Congress that Lafayette's desire for field command had not slackened. "I fear," warned Washington, "a refusal will not only induce him to return [to France] in disgust—but may involve some unfavorable consequences." The hint that Lafayette's assignment could sway French recognition may have persuaded Congress to act. Early in December, Washington announced in General Orders: "Major General The Marquis La Fayette is to take command of the division lately commanded by General Stephen."[17]

Naming Kalb and Lafayette division commanders partially resolved a dire deficiency. The French generals (including Duportail) could help The Cause by generating support at home. Washington's seventeen Continental brigades at Whitemarsh had six appointed major generals (Sullivan, Greene, Stirling, McDougall, Kalb, and Lafayette) heading divisions of two brigades each, with a capable brigadier general to lead a seventh. This left three brigades loosely organized and lacking division chiefs—evidence that Washington's army had simply grown too fast to be led properly by available subordinates. This would induce Washington to consider restructuring his force based on wing commands with independent brigades attached to those wings.[18]

The quality of the men serving under the revised wing structure did not concern him. An outside observer marveled at the Continentals and militia of the Grand Army and uniquely contrasted it against Crown forces:

> I believe there are not finer materials for an irresistible army in the whole world than the troops now under the command of General Washington. Howe's soldiers are actuated by nothing but rage—and a lust for plunder. Washington's are actuated only by courage and a superlative love of their country. They have been defeated it is true, but they have never been conquered. I have been often astonished not only at their patience, but at their chearfulness under cold, fatigue—and all the common hardships of a soldiers life. Had Howe's army suffered only half as much as these brave fellows have done, I am sure, from the common character of European armies, their spirits would have been broken long ago, and Howe would have been left before this time with scarcely a regiment to cover his flight from this country.[19]

Four weeks into the Whitemarsh encampment, with the Americans looming within striking distance of Philadelphia, many in the ranks expected Howe to strike soon against Washington; to a man, anyone mentioning that expectation was looking forward to it. "We are now in full force, and in perfect readiness for them, and wish nothing more than to see them out," declared General Cadwalader. A Continental infantry major said Crown forces "have got their shipping up to the town and talk much of their coming out to drive Genl. Washington into the mountains which I hope they may attempt." A chaplain remarked, "Our troops in general expect action soon and many of them I [believe] sincearly wish it—I never saw so much of a spirit of fight among the troops."[20]

Power lies in numbers, but true strength lies in efficient and organized use of those numbers to maximize combat effectiveness to attack and crush an opponent, and to withstand an opponent's offensive thrust. As Washington was seeking to demonstrate his power, William Howe was about to test Washington's strength.

CHAPTER THIRTEEN

"They are Determind to Attack You Where You Now Are"

December 1 to December 8, 1777

Washington's army, whose numbers exceeded twenty-four thousand at Whitemarsh, may have carried the distinction on December 1, 1777, as the largest single-location field army on the face of the Earth. The American force certainly exceeded Howe's garrison in Philadelphia numerically by several thousand. Winter was coming. Washington polled his generals regarding a winter encampment site. He did not relish having to convert an actively campaigning force into a stagnant mass of under-employed fighting men. Seventeen Continental infantry brigades, militia, dragoons, and artillerists shepherding forty-three cannons comprised this force. Even encamped, the army was voracious; it required a million pounds of breadstuffs and a million pounds of meat each month to feed this monstrous force.[1] Washington needed a setting large enough to accommodate those tens of thousands—now larger than the civilian population of America's second largest city, New York—as well as near enough to sources of provisions for them. The site had to be somewhat proximate to Philadelphia, the better to monitor the foe and disrupt some of his operations, but far enough from Philadelphia to discourage surprise attacks on the encampment.

His subordinates' responses began to stream his way on December 1 and within a day he was regretting ever asking their opinions. He complained of having "so many" options offered to him and "such capitol objections to each mode proposed, that I am exceedingly embarrassed, not only in the advice given me, but in my own judgment." Lieutenant Colonel Harrison compiled the recommendations. Seven favored Wilmington; nine plumped for "Lancaster—Reading &c.;" one was categorized as "hutting in a strong position." General Stirling alone favored "the Great Valley or Trydruffin," the latter being closest to the plateau east and south of the iron forge and the collection of mills and dwellings on Valley Creek known as Valley Forge.

General Pulaski urged a winter campaign. His opinion likely was not one that "exceedingly embarrassed" Washington, because even if it was out of season, he was holding out for assaulting enemy defenses at Philadelphia's outskirts and retaking the city. He had not amassed so large an army only to have it loll shivering for months. Time had run out for the Cadwalader plan, but was there not a viable alternative? Consensus among the generals was about evenly split on taking the war to Howe prior to winter encampment, but of those inclined to engage him, more preferred to draw him away from Philadelphia than to assault him at the edge of town.

Washington queried his generals for the third time in nine days. On December 3, prodded by Henry Laurens to react to Congress, which had voted for a winter campaign, he invited his generals' written sentiments regarding "the Advisieability of a Winters Campaign, & practicability of an attempt upon Philada with the Aid of a considerable body of Militia to be assembled at an appointed time & place."

Washington also learned from Laurens that a three-member congressional delegation was en route to confer with him about a winter campaign and a winter encampment. The trio arrived at Whitemarsh that noon. After dinner, they met formally with Washington, who summarized the responses from November 25 regarding Cadwalader's plan and the winter cantonment poll results.[2]

The renewed topic of a winter campaign consumed the rest of that night's meeting at the Emlen house—the reason the delegates had ridden ninety miles from York. They, too, had an attack plan in mind that emphasized militiamen over Continentals. Washington probably was not surprised at his guests' inflated opinion of militia, which spurred him to explain that the season was too late to expect enough militia to be raised to power the assault. He stressed that enhancing recruitment for his professional army was the most reliable improvement. An officer's rank was to be "preserved from degradation & contempt," he said. And he gave his visitors an earful about introducing inducements to enlistment and preserving the force under arms, including half-pay for the soldiers, updated regulations for rank, pensions for officers' widows, and reimbursement for back rations.[3]

The latest round of opinions from the generals arrived, indicating multiple changes of heart and a consolidation of sentiment. They wanted no winter campaign at all. General Wayne was representative. He had endorsed the Cadwalader plan as a single-day attempt to catch Howe off guard. Militia mostly held a reserve role in that plan, which Wayne endorsed. But a protracted winter campaign failed to stir Wayne's passion. He questioned reliance on militia and cited deficiencies in the supply departments as his reason for predicting failure if the Continentals remained active. "I am not for a Winter Campaign in the Open field," he told Washington, because "the Distressed and naked State of your Troops will not admit of it."[4]

Wayne and most other dissenters were succinct in their obduracy. Generals Greene and Sullivan presented their customary multifaceted monographs, each a well-argued "No!" though Greene said he was open to a winter attack on Philadelphia under the right conditions—which conditions, he pointedly declared, did not presently exist. Joseph Reed listed ways of converting a winter encampment into a limited campaign. Washington and Reed were quite close; they conversed personally about encampment sites. Washington must have been bemused by Reed's closing statement of his two thousand-word essay on choosing a winter site: "The Shortness of Time & a sore Finger has obliged me to throw together these Sentiments with very little Accuracy—they may serve as Hints perhaps for better Heads to improve."[5]

Other than Pulaski and his enthusiasm for a winter campaign with or without added militia, Washington also had Cadwalader's backing for a winter war. Cadwalader scorned winter encampments as old-school ritualism, noting how the previous winter Washington's rule-breaking unorthodoxy at Trenton "set America again on her Legs. . . . By having the river as a Barrier you kept the field till an opportunity offered, and by a well [timed], well executed blow, you gave hopes again to all the States." Acknowledging that a winter campaign would be a "great distress" to the soldiers compared to lodging in a cantonment, Cadwalader confidently called for the sacrifice: "I am obliged from the necessity of the case to declare, that I think, if our army was reduced by action & sickness, to one half its present number, the consequences would not be so fatal, as if we were to take winter quarters."[6]

More than twenty responses advised against a winter campaign. More were coming but intelligence from Philadelphia altered the dynamic. For two days Washington had been sifting rumors that Howe intended to attack him at Whitemarsh. By the morning of December 4, those rumors became fact. Multiple sources alerted Washington that "Beyound all Doubt they are Determined to Attack at all Events." Howe was biding his time, expecting the Americans to uproot from Whitemarsh. When that movement commenced Howe planned to vault north and strike Washington at his most vulnerable position, likely the flank or rear.

Washington drafted an order of battle. He created a command structure that compensated for excess brigades and a shortfall of major generals—especially experienced ones. His solution was to divide his force into wings, General Greene commanding the left wing of five brigades and General Sullivan with five brigades on the right, both with cavalry support on the flanks and with General Stirling leading a reserve wing reminiscent of his Germantown role although at Whitemarsh he commanded seven reserve brigades. Within the wings and reserves, the remaining major generals subdivided commands of divisions, each of two or three brigades. According to a December 4 report Washington received that day, once Howe had been corrected about Washington's plans to remain at Whitemarsh, "it is Expected they are Determind to attack you where you Now Are."[7]

And they did. The wee-hour stillness of Friday, December 5, exploded into controlled frenzy when the alarm gun fired at 3:00 A.M. Howe approached Whitemarsh with most of his Philadelphia force of over fifteen thousand officers and men. Washington's pickets monitored Howe's progress but did not seriously resist through the morning. Howe's advance halted on Chestnut Hill, four miles south of the American position. Counting all the soldiers at Whitemarsh, nearly thirty-nine thousand men prepared to make war on the outskirts of Philadelphia, the conflict's largest contested theater.

Washington had chosen his defense very well, configuring it to hold Howe's force in front. Transferring from Camp Morris a month earlier to Whitemarsh was deemed necessary by the army engineers. The ground within Howe's view from Chestnut Hill on December 5 indicated exactly why. Three miles northeast of Chestnut Hill stood the highest terrain, a ridge known hence as Camp Hill. Maryland militia anchored the American eastern flank, with most of Greene's wing of brigades populating the height, protected by a redoubt. West of Camp Hill loomed Fort Hill, a smaller ridge line, but still with a two hundred-foot escarpment, at which most of Sullivan's wing was positioned. Fort Hill protruded north of Sandy Run and more directly in front of Howe's gaze with a redoubt as well. Both hills added abatis protection on the downslopes, above their marshy bases.

Farther west and a little south of these hills loomed a height called Militia Hill, on which two brigades of Pennsylvania militia perched around six American guns. This hill stood across the Wissahickon Creek from Chestnut Hill and was three miles mostly north and slightly east of that rise. Due north of Chestnut Hill on the east side of the creek stood Church Hill with four hundred American advanced troops and guns on each side of the church atop it, between Chestnut Hill and the five miles of heights held by the Americans.[8] Another wooded ridge rose northeast of Chestnut Hill, a continuation of the same ridge line. This was known as Edge Hill; American patrols occupied the height. It stood two miles south of Washington's east flank. Several roads ran through the valleys between the heights.[9] Washington held a strong reserve force under Stirling behind his front-line troops and out of Howe's view.

With five miles of Americans and their artillery crowning those heights, Howe would dare not advance from Chestnut Ridge. His vanguard halted while the rear closed in from Germantown. "Having now so respectable a force in the field," remembered Connecticut Major Benjamin Tallmadge of this moment, "and especially the Northern army being flushed with recent victory, and hoping that the other troops would vie with them in the contest, a battle was rather desired than avoided."[10] Taking in this moment of viewing the British atop Chestnut Hill, a Virginia gentleman reported the sight to his home paper. The *Virginia Gazette* highlighted his inevitable-battle news with an emphasized and capitalized battle cry: "Success to General WASHINGTON!——The RISING STATES!"[11]

Washington blinked first. He ordered the militia to advance off their protective height and work their way to the British left flank "to annoy them on the march." Rather than follow General James Potter on the road toward Barren Hill, General James Irvine took six hundred Pennsylvania militiamen on a more direct road to Germantown that joined the Bethlehem Pike directly in front of Chestnut Hill. That was a mistake, and a costly one. British lead blew three fingers off one of Irvine's hands and unhorsed him. Many of his men were skirmishing at a distance from where he was when he was hit, but those immediately around Irvine disappeared, leaving the wounded commander to easy capture, along with dozens of other militia. Potter's men did strike more on the British flank and inflicted several casualties upon Howe before disengaging and returning to their position on the ridge.[12]

Washington felt safe enough to maintain his headquarters at the Emlen house, despite its vulnerable location a mile southeast of the bulk of his army aligned on Fort Hill. His army, larger than it had ever been for a battle with Howe, was supplied with filled wagons. Six days of rations had been issued by the Commissary General to the division and brigade commissaries by Friday. But not enough subordinate commissaries were up to the task of dispersing rations. And axes were scarce. The army teemed with stocks of that essential tool, but the supply wagons hastily rolled north when the alarm gun fired Friday, depriving foot soldiers of a simple means of cutting firewood. Stocks of blankets and clothing had also rolled too far away from the heights to be retrieved. Regardless, enough campfires blazed along the hills near Whitemarsh Church to impress and perhaps surprise General Howe and his staff with the size of Washington's force.

Washington did not expect to have to intervene in an encampment issue on a day he was waiting to be assaulted; nevertheless, he issued General Orders on such a matter Saturday morning, December 6. He chided his commissaries for dereliction and promised that a "severe example will be made of" persistent laggards. Washington had recalled a lesson from September, when scores of healthy soldiers suddenly were pulled away to guard wagons or retrieve supplies from them. Now he assured men that their baggage would be returned, directing officers to take charge of retrieving clothes and shoes, "And to prevent the strolling and loss of men," while "the commanding officer . . . is to see, that the rolls are called every two hours, and to know where every man is."[13]

"We expected their approach hourly," Joseph Reed, recalling the wait in pre-dawn darkness and daylight, wrote of December 6. Washington stood fast, to the chagrin of Howe, who spent much of the day poking at Washington's flanks. Washington allowed his men to ground their arms at their alarm posts, cook two days' rations, and use their freshly delivered axes to cut wood for huts and fires on a freezing night.[14]

From the British perspective, Washington appeared to be reinforcing western heights from which the Pennsylvania militia had attempted to pounce on them the previous day. Howe's scouts continued to probe the American position for weaknesses. American alarm guns fired twice that Saturday. Each time the soldiers "Recd. Intiligence that the enemy was advancing," a Rhode Island officer wrote in his diary, "but did not Come to attack us." They saw no sign of Howe or any Crown forces. Unknown to Washington and the Americans was that at 9:00 P.M. Howe began marching his force south from Chestnut Hill. "Everybody supposed that we were marching back to Philadelphia," Howe's aide de camp said. Instead, they turned left at Germantown and made for Whitemarsh to fall upon Washington's left flank. Shielded by Edge Hill, at 5:00 A.M. Howe skillfully shifted several thousand infantry and artillery soldiers to his right. By the time Washington's scouts detected that move, Howe's troops had formed a half circle around the eastern flank of Washington's army and extended the British vanguard northeast toward the Abingdon Presbyterian Meetinghouse. An aide to General Stirling was posted at the building; he alerted Washington to the flanking maneuver as it crossed the York Road.[15]

Washington delegated battle duties to two trusted figures not directly assigned within the army. He sent General Cadwalader and Joseph Reed south to monitor for enemy troops attempting to flank on the western side of this British second position. The men trotted two miles south of the Emlen house. Joined by General Potter, they fell in with the 2nd Connecticut Infantry and Potter's militia, who had marched west to east to confront the British advance after not finding them retreating from Chestnut Hill.

The Americans came under fire before noon from General Charles Grey, the victor at Paoli eleven weeks earlier, who tormented the American left flank by pushing his column of light infantry, Queen's Rangers, and jägers up both sides of the Limekiln Pike. Overwhelmed by the vast numbers of British, Loyalists, and Hessians, the militia absconded, while the Continentals clung on. Reed's horse collapsed under him, a bullet through its head. Soldiers whisked Reed rearward to safety as Grey's men pushed the Connecticut men off the western end of Edge Hill and took over the position, not advancing until support materialized on their right. Captain John André, Grey's aide, estimated thirty-five American casualties and ten British, Loyalist, and German losses in this noon-hour fight.[16]

The American position on Edge Hill comprised 1,500 officers and men, but the Pennsylvania militia and Connecticut regulars at the southwestern end of the height were clustered and separated from the eastern defense by more than a mile. Here, Washington had sent arguably his best fighting troops to take control. Colonel Daniel Morgan and his Virginia and Penn-

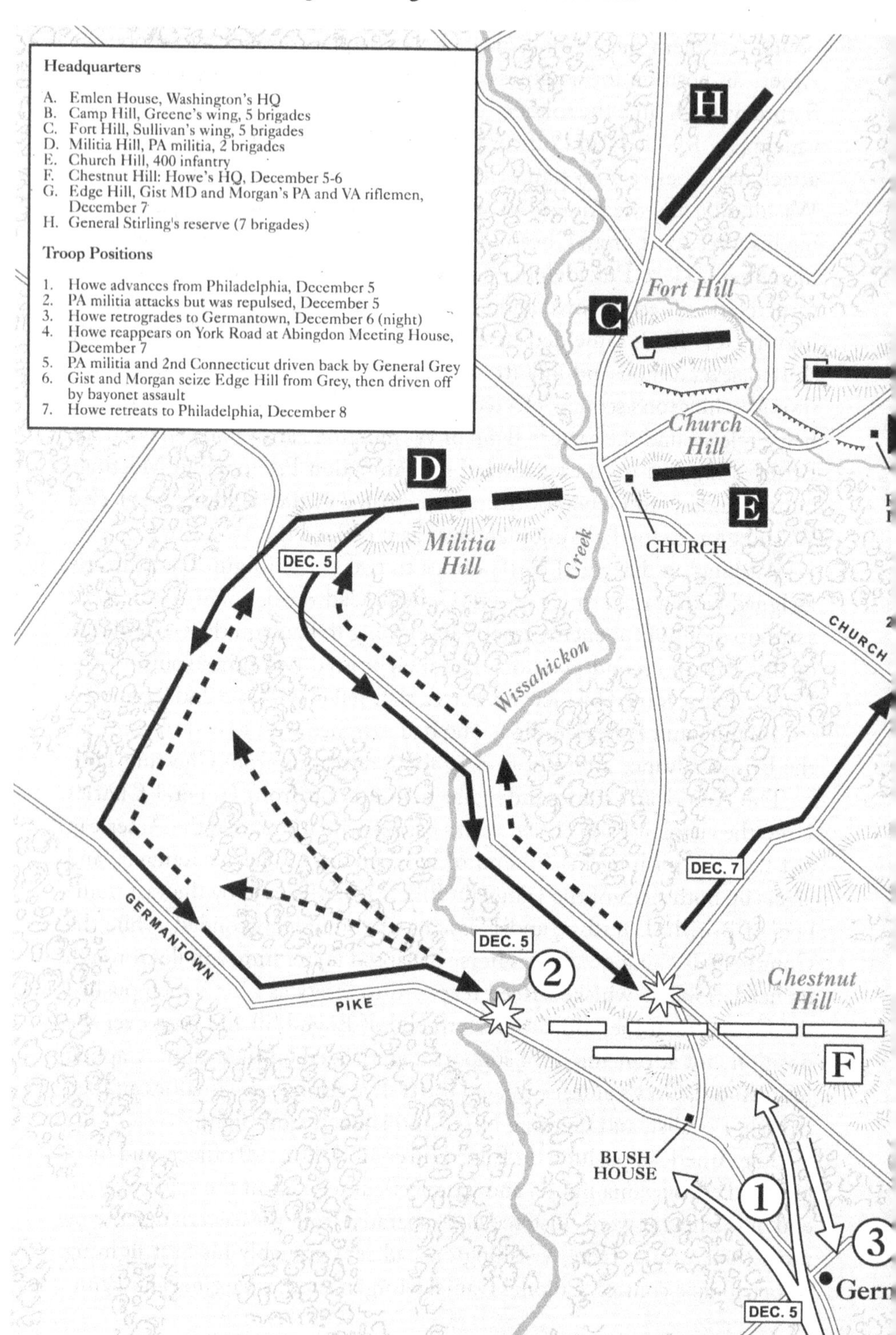

Headquarters
A. Emlen House, Washington's HQ
B. Camp Hill, Greene's wing, 5 brigades
C. Fort Hill, Sullivan's wing, 5 brigades
D. Militia Hill, PA militia, 2 brigades
E. Church Hill, 400 infantry
F. Chestnut Hill: Howe's HQ, December 5-6
G. Edge Hill, Gist MD and Morgan's PA and VA riflemen, December 7
H. General Stirling's reserve (7 brigades)
Troop Positions
1. Howe advances from Philadelphia, December 5
2. PA militia attacks but was repulsed, December 5
3. Howe retrogrades to Germantown, December 6 (night)
4. Howe reappears on York Road at Abingdon Meeting House, December 7
5. PA militia and 2nd Connecticut driven back by General Grey
6. Gist and Morgan seize Edge Hill from Grey, then driven off by bayonet assault
7. Howe retreats to Philadelphia, December 8
H
Fort Hill
C
Church Hill
D
E
CHURCH
Militia Hill
DEC. 5
Wissahickon Creek
CHURCH
GERMANTOWN PIKE
DEC. 7
DEC. 5
2
Chestnut Hill
F
BUSH HOUSE
1
3
DEC. 5

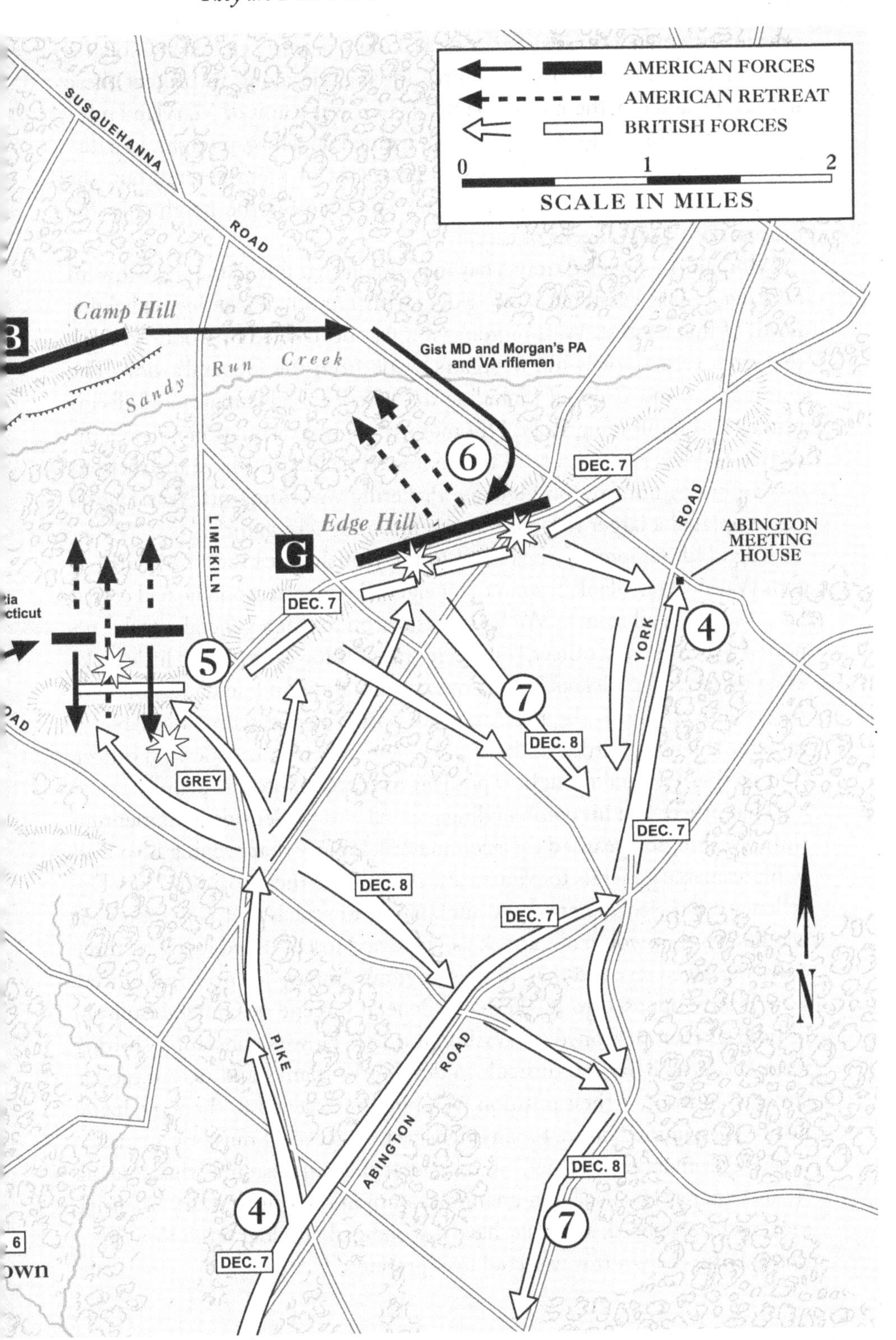

AMERICAN FORCES
AMERICAN RETREAT
BRITISH FORCES
0
1
2
SCALE IN MILES
SUSQUEHANNA
ROAD
Camp Hill
Gist MD and Morgan's PA
and VA riflemen
Sandy Run Creek
6
DEC. 7
ROAD
ABINGTON
MEETING
HOUSE
Edge Hill
G
LIMEKILN
DEC. 7
4
YORK
5
7
DEC. 8
GREY
DEC. 7
DEC. 8
DEC. 7
N
PIKE
ROAD
ABINGTON
DEC. 8
4
7
DEC. 7

sylvania riflemen, heroes at Saratoga and more recently victors at Gloucester, arrived. Only one small infantry force came along to protect these marksmen and buy them time to reload. This was a unit of Maryland militia, led by Colonel Mordecai Gist, that formed on Morgan's right. In a disjointed battle waged after Grey's contest west of them petered out, the Virginians and Marylanders drove Howe's men off the heights, in the process absorbing dozens of casualties.[17]

Morgan's men reeled from a bayonet assault that forced them northward off Edge Hill as Washington was riding with Timothy Pickering on heights north of that contest. Washington's view was obstructed by woods so thick that even leafless trees hid Morgan's battle from the General's view. The commander and Colonel Pickering discussed the advantages and disadvantages of reinforcing Edge Hill more strongly. Washington issued a directive to Pickering to ride to the contested height and have instructions carried out to not fire too high. As Pickering was riding off, Washington contemplated a larger response than reinforcing Morgan.[18]

Edge Hill temporarily belonged to the British, but Howe had failed to turn Washington's flank beyond that height. By midafternoon he had ceased his advance on all fronts. "We had great reason to fear a general attack," reported a Continental officer, "but there was nothing more than a little bickering between our pickets." With over twenty thousand defenders on high ridges with strong flanks, the American position appeared unassailable. "I thought a general battle was inevitable," remembered an American officer, "but neither General thought it prudent to descend into the plain."[19]

That officer had his commanding general wrong. Sensing a momentum shift, Washington yearned for a counterstrike. Early that evening he pulled in his available generals to plan an attack opposite their position. "His Excellency expressed the strongest inclination to attack them, as soon as it was known they would not attack us," reported Joseph Reed less than three days later. Reed revealed that, to Washington's dismay, "his principal officers were utterly opposed to it." Perhaps General Greene or General Sullivan or both of them reasoned to Washington that Howe's constantly shifting force rendered it far too difficult to develop his flanks and determine his strength in front of their position. Washington acceded to them, realizing he needed a unified desire for an offensive to succeed. "I must say, in justice to the Commander-in-chief," Reed said at the conclusion of this council, "that there has been such an unanimity of opinion against every offensive movement proposed, as would have discouraged an older and more experienced officer than this war could yet produce."[20]

Reed was acknowledging Washington's patience with subordinates who did not share his outlook because lower-ranking generals lacked the years and the experience to know that counterstrikes on battlefields came when momentum favored the assault. At the same time Reed understood the risk inherent in hasty tactics undertaken to accomplish a sudden offensive. Regardless of how many enemy troops were in Washington's preferred attack zone, the Americans outnumbered them and could deploy several brigades of Continentals who for three days had observed the Battle of Whitemarsh without ever raising their weapons.

Washington was trying to capitalize on the sudden change in momentum. His decision to consult his subordinates was a curious one. At the Battle of Brandywine, he had not hesitated or first queried his generals before ordering Sullivan, Greene, and Maxwell to cross the creek and attack Knyphausen's detachment minutes after learning that General Cornwallis had separated from him. That September 11 counterstrike took place in extreme haste and had Washington not received erroneous intelligence that Cornwallis was close to Knyphausen, it could have become catastrophic. Alternatively, at Germantown, Washington encouraged a battlefield debate with subordinates and allowed the influence of Henry Knox to ultimately decide to invest infantry and artillery against the British bastion at Cliveden. Neither of those two battles likely entered Washington's mind at Whitemarsh, but Whitemarsh would be the last time he would consult his generals on a battlefield.[21]

Howe convened his generals, probably within hours of Washington's meeting with his. The British had observed the American line for two days and were not pleased with what they saw. Washington's position seemed impenetrable. The council unanimously determined that "from the advantageous situation of Mr. Washington, and the extraordinary strength of his intrenchments, it would be unadvisable, and in the highest degree dangerous to attempt to force them." Howe did not object. He had reconnoitered the position until night had fallen. "He found everywhere strong natural and man-made obstacles, which prevented any hope of success."[22]

Whitemarsh vexed Howe. His resignation submitted and likely to be accepted, he sought a glorious conclusion to his tenure as commander in chief in North America. That desire suffused his army before it headed to Whitemarsh. "Sir William Howe is determined to bring Washington to a general Engagement," noted one of his officers shortly before the army headed out of Philadelphia to Whitemarsh; "if that can be accomplished, I have not a Doubt but an End will be put to the Independency of the High and Mighty States of America."[23]

Crown forces remained in position overnight and through the early afternoon of Monday, December 8. Concealed by a line of troops in front, they began withdrawing. When darkness fell, Howe ordered fires lit across his lines as he decamped, marching south. The pace was too rapid for pursuing American infantry to seriously engage the enemy's rear, but not fast enough to prevent a brief engagement with a squadron of dragoons led by General Pulaski. Dozens of Redcoats and jäger deserters and stragglers—"for the most part drunk," an officer noted—surrendered to the Americans.[24]

As Howe retreated and led his fifteen thousand men back toward Philadelphia, he relinquished the field to Washington. Howe had led essentially his entire force to Whitemarsh not to make a demonstration, but to drive the Americans away from the region where their position had been a direct threat to his army in and around Philadelphia. In this he failed. The result defined the December 5-8 Battle of Whitemarsh as a tactical victory for the Americans. Like the limited engagement at White Horse Tavern, this battle, considering the number of troops involved, produced a paucity of casualties—fewer than three hundred total, with the Americans losing twice as many men as the British.[25]

Crown forces had been set to greet the winter after an impressive string of accomplishments. The British occupied Philadelphia, defeated Washington directly at Brandywine and Germantown, and scored a crushing victory against his detachment at Paoli. They conquered all the forts on the Delaware. The cost in casualties was dear. The loss of upwards of two thousand killed, wounded, captured, and missing soldiers stripped Howe's ranks and weakened his infantry. But Washington's omnipresence and his relentlessness—even after a series of defeats—had taxed the British, the Hessians, and the Loyalists to a level they struggled to pay. Army insiders penned their observations and perceptions and shipped those thoughts to Great Britain on boats emptied of their provisions. "Letters from Philadelphia, brought by the . . . transports, mention, that the Kings Troops there are very sickly," reported London's *St. James Chronicle*, adding that the collective poor health was "occasioned by the great Fatigues they have undergone in the Operations against Washington's Army." The newspaper informed readers that the soldiers in Philadelphia "are in great Want of Provisions and Clothing, having received no fresh Supplies from England since the Middle of December."[26]

The supply pipeline had begun to dry up earlier. So desperate was Howe to supply his army that, within less than thirty-six hours of returning to Philadelphia, he ordered a pontoon bridge to span the Schuylkill River at

Gray's Ferry; the morning after that was accomplished Cornwallis crossed the span with five thousand Redcoats ordered to round up cattle and garner other necessary supplies.[27] That decision, and the movement that followed, assured one more military contest before winter officially arrived.

By outward appearances, the Philadelphia campaign through the first week of December was a failure for the Americans. Howe's army had bested Washington's men in six contests, driving Americans away from Cooch's Bridge, Brandywine, White Horse Tavern, Paoli, Germantown, and Fort Mifflin. Howe had occupied Philadelphia a month after anchoring his armada within sixty miles of the city near Head of Elk. Taking complete control of the Delaware River from Philadelphia to the Capes seven weeks later secured the city for Crown forces as a base of operations, seemingly safe for the winter.

Washington's campaign failure was not a catastrophe. Three and a half months had passed since the General decided on August 22 at the Moland house to forego the Hudson River and entirely commit his force to directly opposing Howe. During those eleven weeks Howe's army received enough reinforcements from New York to offset its losses, but Washington's army grew fifty percent. None of Howe's battle successes of late summer and autumn had demoralized the Americans. Even cold, sharp steel at midnight on September 20 failed to terrorize Wayne's Pennsylvanians, who made "Remember Paoli!" their battle cry two weeks later at Germantown, a contest "more unfortunate than injurious" according to Washington, his subordinates, and his men.

Permanent desertions in the Continental army were surprisingly low, and the spirit to continue to serve in that army remained surprisingly high. Routing Redcoats at Germantown and forcing them to turn their backs to their foe and retreat from Whitemarsh not only instilled the first multi-year, professional army in American history with valuable experience, it imbued those soldiers with invaluable confidence. With proper training, they could stand toe-to-toe against what had been considered one of the world's most successful armies.

The Continental Congress did not view the professional army as the soldiers did. Although Congress commissioned a gold medal honoring General Washington for his performance in defeat at Germantown, two months later delegates were grousing ever louder and more often about Washington's surrender to inertia. Rather than regard Whitemarsh as a successful repulse, politicians saw another lost opportunity. James Lovell of Massachusetts complained, "our Army was not inclined to fight Howe when he gave them 4 days opportunity."[28] Lovell was echoing what North Carolina delegate Cornelius Hartnett predicted before the conclusion of the battle: "I fear . . . we shall suffer ourselves to be attacked, instead of attacking. This conduct I believe has often proved disadvantageous."[29] The committee of three delegates that had witnessed the opening of the Whitemarsh battle soured Lovell's mood further when they returned to York speaking of "a general discontent in the Army and especially among the Officers." They concluded:

> That an attempt on Philadelphia with the present Force under General Washington, either by storming the Lines and Redoubts, crossing the Schuylkill, or by regular approaches to the City is an enterprise, under the circumstances of the Army attended with such a variety of difficulties as to render it ineligible.[30]

That was not how Washington saw things. He must have considered Whitemarsh a disappointment, as Massachusetts delegate Lovell did. The commanding general had defeated Howe on the defensive, though his troops were bested in front of Chestnut Hill and on Edge Hill, with additional troop losses incurred skirmishing against the British on December 8. In fact, Whitemarsh marked Washington's fifth tactical victory in the tenth battle of the war in which he commanded personally on the battlefield.[31] But any satisfaction Washington obtained from forcing Howe to retreat to Philadelphia doubtless was tempered by what he must have considered a lost opportunity to inflict significant casualties upon Crown forces with a timely counter assault on the evening of December 7.

No evidence exists that Washington resolved to spend the waning weeks of 1777 preparing for, traveling to, and settling into a winter cantonment—at a location yet to be determined. He continued to seek an opportunity for his massive army to wrest Philadelphia from Howe's Crown forces. Washington understood that his Grand Army's achievements would continue to be compared to the amazing success of General Gates's army in the Northern Department. Washington himself had challenged his men in General Orders to match the Saratoga victors' accomplishments. At an intellectual distance, it seems odd that the commander in chief's performance would have been pitted against that of one of his subordinate commanders, particularly one who had previously worked at Washington's headquarters as adjutant general. The backlash over Washington's inability to keep the British army from Philadelphia was taking root with the potential makeup and rumored agenda of a new Board of War.

Ten years after the fact, George Washington, civilian, visited the region surrounding his Emlen house headquarters, escorted by the mayor of Philadelphia. He jotted in his diary on August 19, 1787, that he "rode up to the White Marsh, traversed my old Incampment, and contemplated on the dangers which threatened the American Army at that place."[32]

Washington's tour of Whitemarsh a decade after the battle took him back to the end of the first week of the last month of 1777, five months removed from the first Fourth of July celebration in American history. That he chose not to formally recognize American Independence in 1777, when every state in the country engaged in festive celebrations, suggested the dangers he was contemplating in Morristown that first Friday in July. Then and there, the nascent threat posed by Crown forces, as yet without concrete form, had consumed the American commander in chief. But the dangers George Washington reflected upon at Whitemarsh extended well beyond the enemy soldiers wearing red coats. His enormous, voracious army could not be fed and supplied indefinitely east of the Schuylkill River—or perhaps even west of it. His brigade and division commanders had no stomach or little heart to campaign, at least until spring. And in July 1777 Washington could not have known that the reverence accruing to his abilities and accomplishments through the first half of 1777 was to evaporate in the latter six months of the year. His personal leadership of the Grand Army since July met with rancor in his military family, among his subordinate commanders, and across a spectrum of politicians and civilians.

The dangers he contemplated at Whitemarsh were so considerable—though rooted more in politics and logistics rather than in enemy threats—as to stir some doubt that Washington would be in command of an American army by the following summer, or that a functioning American army would even exist at that time. But, unknown to George Washington, his allies, his critics, and the American populace, during the first week of December, the Philadelphia Campaign—particularly the Battle of Germantown—was being analyzed and debated by influential decision makers through fresh, unbiased eyes.

The status of the American War for Independence was reported early in December to Britons, who for the first time received and read news from the United States. A six-to-eight-week delay to carry news 3,500 miles, mostly by sail, placed the Philadelphia Campaign through the Battle of Germantown before the British public in the form of letters and reports. "After the Public has been kept in anxious Expectations for upwards twelve weeks," a London paper declared in its first December issue, "the long looked for Dispatches are come at last."[33]

The London *Public Advertiser* on December 2 reported on news from the newly arrived aide de camp of General Howe. "The News he brings, it is said, is neither so great nor so decisive as we were made to believe," the paper stated. The aide acknowledged Washington's "several obstinate and bloody Engagements with the British Army," noting that "The Loss on the Side of Great Britain, as well as America, is considerable; . . ." Three days later the same paper portended doom for General John Burgoyne by discussing private letters from Philadelphia provided to the editors and describing the faint but distinctive sounds of the *feu de joie* emanating from Washington's camp north of the city. "The Provincials were so much elated with the News, that they demanded to be led on immediately to attack Howe's Army," the paper wrote. "General Washington commended their Ardour, and assured them, that in the Course of a few Days he would find an Opportunity of signalizing their Courage, and of emulating the heroic Exploits of their Brethren in New England."[34]

Not only were Londoners informed that Washington and his army remained an imposing threat to Howe and Crown forces, but the citizens were also warned by the free press not to accept as accurate published reports from Howe to George Germain. On December 2, Londoners reading the *Evening Post* would not have missed the droll mockery of Howe's upbeat claims by a critic impressed by Washington's display of aggression at the Battle of Germantown:

> On the 4th of October, General Washington *attacked* General Howe, when a very bloody action commenced. General Howe had the worst of it for a considerable time. . . . The public are to be told, the Americans have lost above 4000 men; How does General Howe know this? That the British and Germans have not lost above 800. This is not true . . . it would appear that our army have lost (sickness, desertion, made prisoners, killed, &c &c. included) at least 2400 men; but these are *facts* not proper to be told. Only the *favourable* side, with a good deal of *colouring, adding, omitting*, &c. will be given by the Ministry, yet upon the whole, the news is far, very far from giving satisfaction at St. James's. General Washington having *attacked* Gen. Howe, *after* the taking of Philadelphia, and retreating in *full force*, and Gen. Howe *fortifying* Philadelphia, (thereby confessedly reduced to stand upon the *defensive* in that quarter) are circumstances so *unpleasant* and *unfortunate*, that nothing can counterbalance them.[35]

Emmanuel Marie Louis de Noailles, Marquis of Noailles, the French ambassador to Great Britain, certainly took in those news reports, letter excerpts, and statements of opinion. Noailles also used his inside channels to confirm and reinforce those sources. In October, he had assured King Louis XVI's foreign minister, Charles Gravier Comte de Vergennes, that he would provide detailed, ongoing intelligence on the war in America, particularly related to the outcome of the two-pronged advance by Generals Burgoyne and William Howe. "I will neglect nothing, Monsieur le Comte," the ambassador declared.[36]

French officials discussed and analyzed Washington's campaign as well as General Gates's campaign against Burgoyne throughout the autumn. Vergennes was the key intermediary of discussions with American diplomats Benjamin Franklin, Silas Deane, and Arthur Lee, who were in Paris seeking an alliance with France in the war against Great Britain. Only evidence of American military success in 1777 would bring about formal negotiations for the alliance.

Vergennes relied on several information sources. By the first week of December, Burgoyne's surrender of 5,900 officers and men to General Gates had been reported with confidence. As momentous as this news was, by itself it was not enough. The French yearned for news from the American Grand Army under Washington. The American loss at Brandywine and subsequent British capture of Philadelphia had been known in Europe since November. By early December, Washington's attack at Germantown was being presented to Vergennes in brilliant light via reports from the secretary of the Board of War of Massachusetts. This included one of Washington's sanguine after-action letters. Not only was Washington's army in "high spirits" following the battle, but it was also positioned to bottle up Howe in Philadelphia with strong prospects for forcing his surrender—accompanied by more than twice the number of men who capitulated with Burgoyne.[37]

Ambassador Noailles also proved a most valuable source for Vergennes, and not one whose information was tainted by American propaganda. The first week of December, Noailles wrote to Vergennes about the Battle of Germantown with nearly the same pro-American interpretation as in Massachusetts Board of War reports. Noting no loss of cannons when Washington withdrew from the field, the ambassador concluded that "the American army intact, experienced, no longer fearing to attack, or defend itself, is camped sixteen miles from the English Army, and able to receive all sorts of aid in provisions and men, while General Howe has not yet been able to establish communications with his Navy which is, nevertheless, his only resource for subsisting in a position where he will soon be encircled on all sides."[38]

The news thrilled Vergennes. His apprehensions about two formidable British advances were vanquished by the intelligence of one advance destroyed, the other in jeopardy. Events of the two months since the Battle of Germantown rendered the ambassador's letter stale; nevertheless, newer information could be interpreted as even more uplifting. True, Howe was not encircled, and the Delaware River had finally been opened to him, yet he still was so desperate for provisions that he was mounting huge foraging missions. And Howe was a lame-duck commander awaiting official acceptance of his late October resignation. The ambassador had described Washington's army as "powerful" at a correct strength of fifteen thousand soon after the battle of Germantown and looming sixteen miles from Philadelphia. By early December, Washington had advanced four miles closer to the city with more than twenty-four thousand officers and men, his force nearly ten thousand soldiers stronger than the one the ambassador characterized as "powerful." Regardless of intelligence deficiencies caused by the mails, the ambassador and the foreign minister shared a notion that the French king was near to making strong decisions concerning the American war. On December 6, King Louis XVI approved their recommendations, allowing the French government to publicly receive the American commissioners so as to jointly arrange "a closer understanding between the Crown and the United Provinces of North America."[39]

No doubt the surrender at Saratoga strongly influenced King Louis's approval, but George Washington's anti-Fabian mindset in the wake of the Battle of Brandywine, evident four weeks later at Germantown, and continuing thereafter as a constant threat to Crown forces, also swayed King Louis to approve the negotiations for "a closer understanding" between France and the United States of America. The seeming failure of the Philadelphia Campaign in American officials' eyes was viewed conversely by those who now mattered in London and Paris. Moreover, in those distant eyes George Washington had not been diminished from the conquering hero at Trenton and Princeton. Instead, they viewed him as evolving into the survivor and aggressor against the best army the British Empire could mount against him.

As far as the French diplomats and hierarchy were concerned, two men named "George" commanded nations at war. One ruled Great Britain and the other commanded the armies of the United States of America. The result of the pending arrangement between France and America was destined to influence which "George" would prevail.

Notes

ABBREVIATIONS

AH	Alexander Hamilton
GW	George Washington
JCC	*Journals of the Continental Congress*, 1774–1789 34 volumes. Edited by Worthington C. Ford et al. Washington D.C.: U.S. Government Printing Office, 1904–1937.
JH	John Hancock
JS	John Sullivan
LDC	*Letters of Delegates to Congress*, 1774–1789. 26 volumes. Edited by Paul H. Smith and Ronald M. Gephart. Washington, D.C.: Library of Congress, 1976–2000.
LOC	Library of Congress, Washington D.C.
LPJS	Letters and Papers of Major-General John Sullivan, Continental Army. 3 volumes. Edited by Otis. G. Hammond. Concord, New Hampshire: New Hampshire Historical Society, 1930–1939.
NG	Nathanael Greene
PGW	*The Papers of George Washington*. Edited by W. W. Abbot, et al. Charlottesville: University Press of Virginia, 1987–.
PHL	The Papers of Henry Laurens. Edited by Chesnutt, David R. and Taylor, C. James. 16 vols. Columbia: University of South Carolina Press, 1968–2002.
PMHB	*Pennsylvania Magazine of History and Biography*.
PNG	*The Papers of Nathanael Greene*. 13 volumes. Edited by Richard K. Showman et al. Chapel Hill: University of North Carolina Press, for the Rhode Island Historical Society, 1976–2005.

CHAPTER ONE: USA

1. Quote from an eyewitness observing Washington October 2-3, 1777. Samuel K. Brecht, ed., *The Genealogical Record of the Schwenkfelder Families* (New York, NY: Rand McNally & Company, 1923), 1441; Eric Olson, "Weight of a War, or The 'Big Men' of the Continental Army," https://www.nps.gov/fost/blogs/weight-of-a-war-or-the-big-men-of-the-continental-army.htm.

2. Controversy exists regarding Washington's true height. His body was measured in his coffin at six feet, three-and-a-half inches, surely influenced by post-mortem elongation or pointed toes. He was specifically described while alive as "six feet two inches in his stockings" by a Virginia contemporary in 1760. See Eugene Parsons, *George Washington: A Character Sketch* (Dansville, NY: Instructor Publishing Co., 1898), 36. A recent biographer suggests he was no taller than six feet, citing his 1761 orders for clothes from an overseas tailor. See Ron Chernow, *Washington: A Life* (New York, NY: Penguin Books, 2010), 29-30. The same haberdashery order convinced another biographer to note that Washington was considerably taller than six feet because he often complained that "my Cloaths have never fitted me well." See Joseph J. Ellis, *His Excellency: George Washington* (New York, NY: Alfred A. Knopf, 2004), 44-45. Taking known descriptions into consideration, and factoring in the life-sized statue by Jean-Antoine Houdon (begun late in 1785 when the aging general's spine likely had compressed half an inch from its peak length), this author surmises that in 1777 Washington stood at least six feet, one-and-a-half inches tall in stockings, and approached six feet, three inches in shoes or boots, which is how he was exclusively viewed in public—"the tallest man in the room."

3. Another party's account recalled Martha Washington's critique of an artist's image of her husband produced the following winter: "The defects of this Portrait I think are that the visage is too long, and old age is too strongly marked in it." See HL to JL, March 3, 1778, *PHL* (12), 505.

4. Ellis, *His Excellency*, 10; Carol Eaton Soltis, *The Art of the Peales in the Philadelphia Museum of Art: Adaptions and Innovations* (New Haven, CT: Yale University Press, 2017), 102-103. One of the only documented acknowledgments of Washington's smallpox scars was provided by Hance Supplee who closely observed Washington on October 2-3, 1777, as a nine-year-old. Supplee conveyed this observation to his grandson in 1844, who wrote it down as a second-hand account. See Brecht, ed., *The Genealogical Record of the Schwenkfelder Families*, 1441.

5. HL to JL, March 3, 1778, *PHL* (12), 505; JL to HL, March 9, 1778, *PHL* (12), 533.

6. "Return of the American Forces in New Jersey, 15 March 1777," *PGW* (8), 576.

7. Hasselgren, Per-Olof, "The Smallpox Epidemics in America in the 1700s and the Role of the Surgeons: Lessons to be Learned During the Global Outbreak of COVID-19." *World Journal of Surgery* 2020, 44(9): 2837-2841.

8. May 20 strength is derived from "Arrangement and Present Strength of the Army in Jersey, May 20, 1777," George Washington Papers. Series 4, MSS 44693 (Reel 041), Manuscript Division, LOC. This report tallies men in thirty-eight out of forty-three infantry regiments at 8,188. This does not include infantry officers, artillery, and cavalry.

9. "Masquerade," *Ipswich Journal*, July 12, 1777; *Newcastle Weekly Courant*, May 10, 1777; *London Public Advertiser*, August 27, 1777. Estimates of 40,000 in Washington's army published in *Leeds Intelligencer and Yorkshire General Advertiser*, July 8, 1777.

10. Robert Morris to Captain La Roche, June 18, 1777; Robert Morris to Silas Deane, June 29, 1777; Thomas Burke to Richard Caswell, July 22, 1777; New York Delegates to the New York Delegation, June 19, 1777; Charles Carroll to Charles Carroll, Sr., June 13, 1777; James Lovell to Joseph Trumbull, June 24, 1777; *LDC* (7), 189, 219, 233, 247, 268, 362.

11. "A Jersusalem Blade" to editors, n.d., *Boston Independent Chronicle*, July 10, 1777.

12. GW to John Augustine Washington, June 29, 1777, PGW (10), 149; Receipt Plunkett Fleeson to Joseph Read [Reed], May 11, 1776, George Washington Papers, Manuscript Division, LOC; "George Washington's Marquee Tent," https://www.mountvernon.org/library/digitalhistory/digital-encyclopedia/article/george-washingtons-marquee-tent/; "His-

torical Timeline," Museum of the American Revolution. For evidence that Washington lived in his tent on the return to Morristown rather than the house, see Alexander Graydon, *Memoirs of His Own Time with Reminiscences of the Men and Events of the Revolution* (Philadelphia, PA: Lindsay & Blakiston, 1846), 275. Historian Jennifer Bolton is acknowledged for identifying the red/white striped exterior appearance of the marquee.

13. "1777 July 10 . . . to cash paid Mr. Hathaway," Series 5, Financial Papers, Caleb Gibbs and Mary Smith, 1776-1780, Revolutionary War Household Expenses, George Washington Papers, Manuscript Division, LOC. Hathaway's home specifically located in Julia K. Colles, *Authors and Writers Associated with Morristown, with a Chapter on Historic Morristown* (Morristown, NJ: Vogt Bros, 1895), 189.

14. "Military Departments in the Continental Army," https://revolutionarywar.us/continental-army/military-departments/.

15. Arthur S. Lefkowitz, *George Washington's Indispensable Men: The 32 Aides-de-Camp Who Helped Win American Independence* (Mechanicsburg, PA: Stackpole Books, 2003), 3, 6, 8, 55.

16. Ibid., 14.

17. Ibid., 46, 323 (#8).

18. Ibid., 81-82, 114; "George Johnston," https://www.mountvernon.org/library/digitalhistory/digital-encyclopedia/article/george-johnston/; "John Fitzgerald," https://www.mountvernon.org/library/digitalhistory/digital-encyclopedia/article/john-fitzgerald/; "Richard Kidder Meade," https://www.mountvernon.org/library/digitalhistory/digital-encyclopedia/article/richard-kidder-meade/.

19. Michael E. Newton, *Discovering Hamilton* (Phoenix, AZ: Eleftheria Publishing, 2019), 7-12; Michael E. Newton, *Alexander Hamilton: The Formative Years* (Phoenix, AZ: Eleftheria Publishing, 2015), 189-91.

20. Lefkowitz, *George Washington's Indispensable Men*, 47; Francis B. Heitman, *Historical Register of Officers of the Continental Army During the War of the Revolution, April 1775, to December 1783* (Washington, DC: n.p., 1898), 189.

21. Ibid., 46-47; Bob Ruppert, "His Excellency's Guards," *JAR*, August 18, 2014, https://allthingsliberty.com/2014/08/his-excellencys-guards/; "Life Guards," https://www.mountvernon.org/library/digitalhistory/digital-encyclopedia/article/life-guards/; GW to Caleb Gibbs, April 22, 1777, *PGW* (9): 236.

22. Mark M. Boatner, *Encyclopedia of the American Revolution* (Mechanicsburg, PA: Stackpole Books, 1994), 12, 867; Timothy Pickering to his wife, June 23, 1777, in Octavius Pickering, *The Life of Timothy Pickering*, Vol. 1 (Boston, MA: Little, Brown, and Company, 1867), 143.

23. See *PGW* (10), 189-93 for these July 4, 1777, headquarters letters.

24. General Orders, July 4, 1777, *PGW* (10), 177-182.

25. John W. Wright, *Some Notes on the Continental Army* (Vails Gate, NY: Temple Hill Association, 1963), 10; Lefkowitz, *George Washington's Indispensable Men*, 72; General Stirling to GW, July 3, 1777, *PGW* (10), 176.

26. Chernow, *Washington: A Life*, 290; Lindsay M. Chervinsky, *The Cabinet: George Washington and the Creation of an American Institution* (Cambridge, MA: The Belknap Press of Harvard University Press, 2020), 46-47.

27. Martha Daingerfield Bland to Frances Bland Randolph, May 12, 1777, *N.J. Hist. Soc. Proceedings*, n.s., 51 [1933], 250–53.

28. Lefkowitz, *George Washington's Indispensable Men*, 70-71, 332; GW to Thomas Wharton, April 17, 1778, *PGW* (14), 543.

29. "Philadelphia, July 8, 1777," *Boston Gazette*, July 28, 1777; "Philadelphia, July 10, 1777," [Baltimore] *Maryland Journal*, July 15, 1777. A detailed description of the celebration in Philadelphia is provided in Thomas J. McGuire, *The Philadelphia Campaign*, Volume 1: *Brandywine and the Fall of Philadelphia* (Mechanicsburg, PA: Stackpole Books, 2006), 63-68. John Adams revealed to his daughter that "the thought of taking any notice of this day, was not conceived until the second of this month, and it was not mentioned until the third." See John Adams to Abigail Adams 2d, July 5, 1777, *LDC* (7), 293.

30. "Portsmouth," [Portsmouth] *New Hampshire Gazette*, July 12, 1777; Ezra Stiles diary, July 4, 1777, in Franklin Dexter, ed., *The Literary Diary of Ezra Stiles, D.D., LL.D.*, Vol. 2 (New York, NY: Charles Scribner's Sons, 1901), 175.

31. *Boston Gazette*, July 7, 1777.

32. "Charles-Town, July 7," *The* [Charleston] *South Carolina Gazette and County Journal*, July 7, 1777.

33. GW to Adam Stephen, July 20, 1776, *PGW* (5), 408-409.

34. Commission to George Washington, https://edu.lva.virginia.gov/oc/stc/entries/commission-to-george-washington-as-commander-in-chief-june-19-1775.

35. "Extract of a letter from London, January 24," [Philadelphia] *Pennsylvania Journal*, April 16, 1777; Mark Anthony to Mr. Towne, December 30, 1776, [Philadelphia] *Pennsylvania Evening Post*, January 7, 1777.

36. Samuel Adams to NG, May 12, 1777, *LDC* (7), 70-71.

37. NG to GW [April 1777], *PNG* (2), 61-62; Council of War, May 2, 1777, *PGW* (9), 324-25.

38. NG to Samuel Adams, May 28, 1777, *PNG* (2), 100.

39. Gerald M. Carbone, *Nathanael Greene: A Biography of the American Revolution* (New York, NY: Palgrave Macmillan, 2008), 4-20.

40. NG to GW, March 25, 1777, *PNG* (2): 46-47.

41. GW to John Rutledge, July 5, 1777, *PGW* (10), 198-99; AH to Gouverneur Morris, July 6, 1777, Henry Cabot Lodge, ed., *The Works of Alexander Hamilton*, Vol. 9 (New York and London: G. P. Putnam's Sons, 1904), 88; Robert Mayers, *Revolutionary New Jersey: Forgotten Towns and Crossroads of the American Revolution* (Staunton, VA: American History Press, 2018), 55-66.

42. Mayers, *Revolutionary New Jersey*, 55-66; Jason R. Wickersty, "A Shocking Havoc: the Plundering of Westfield, New Jersey, June 26, 1777," *JAR* https://allthingsliberty.com/2015/07/a-shocking-havoc-the-plundering-of-westfield-new-jersey-june-26-1777/.

43. Boatner, *Encyclopedia of the American Revolution*, 133-36. GW to JH, July 2, 1777, PGW (10), 168.

44. Ibid.; "The British Campaign for Philadelphia and the Occupation of Valley Forge in 1777," https://www.nps.gov/vafo/learn/historyculture/upload/Philadelphia%20campaign.pdf.

45. "Extract of a letter from Morris Town, July 5," [Baltimore] *Maryland Journal*, July 15, 1777.

46. After Orders, *PGW* (10), 181.

CHAPTER TWO: "AN ARMY OF OBSERVATION"

1. "Extract of a Letter from Camp, at Morris Town, dated July 5th, 1777," [Portsmouth, NH] *Freeman's Journal*, July 26, 1777; "Extract of a letter from camp near Morristown, July 10," *Purdie's Virginia Gazette* [Williamsburg], July 25, 1777.

2. JH to GW, July 8, 1777, *PGW* (10), 227.

3. Boatner, *Encyclopedia*, 1117; Rick Atkinson, *The British Are Coming: The War for America, Lexington to Princeton, 1775-1777* (New York, NY: Henry Holt and Company, 2019), 476-77, 681.
4. Boatner, *Encyclopedia*, 1117; GW to William Heath, June 1, 1777, *PGW* (9), 579.
5. William Williams to Jonathan Trumbull, Sr., July 5, 1777, *LDC* (7), 302-303 (quote at bottom of page 302).
6. Eliphalet Dyer to Joseph Trumbull, July 7, 1777, James Lovell to William Whipple, July 7, 1777, James Lovell to GW, July 24, 1777, *LDC* (7), 312-14, 316, 367-71.
7. AH to Gouvenor Morris, July 6, 1777, in Henry Cabot Lodge, ed., *The Works of Alexander Hamilton*, Volume 9 (New York, NY: Knickerbocker Press, 1904), 86-88.
8. GW to JH, July 10, 1777, *PGW* (10), 240; Philip Schuyler to GW, July 7, 1777, *PGW* (10), 219-20.
9. GW to JH, July 10, 1777, *PGW* (10), 240-41; Persifor Frazer to Polly Frazer, July 18, 1777, Persifor Frazer, *General Persifor Frazer, A Memoir* (Philadelphia, PA: n.p., 1907), 148.
10. Coudray to GW, July 4, 1777, *PGW* (10), 183-87; GW to Coudray, July 13, 1777, *PGW* (10), 268-70.
11. Pickering journal, July 12-20, 1777, *Life of Timothy Pickering* (1), 147.
12. GW to JH, July 22, 1777, PGW (10), 356; GW to Israel Putnam, July 21, 1777, *PGW* (10), 346.
13. NG to Catharine Greene, July 23, 1777, in *PNG* (2), 125.
14. David Forman to Continental Congress, July 23, 1777, in *Pennsylvania Archives*, Vol. 5 (Philadelphia: Joseph Severns & Co., 1853), 439-40. See *PGW* (10), 382, 390-91, 398-401, for numerous letters from GW to his subordinates in response to Forman's observation.
15. GW to Lincoln, July 24, 1777, *PGW* (10), 385.
16. GW to Anthony Wayne, July 24, 1777, *PGW* (1), 401-402; Boatner, *Encyclopedia*, 704-705; General Orders. July 1, 1777, *PGW* (10), 162; General Greene's Orders, October 8, 1776, *PNG* (1), 310; Erna Risch, *Supplying Washington's Army* (Washington, DC: Center of Military History, United States Army, 1981), 67, 101-102.
17. *Pennsylvania Archives* (5), 450-51, 455, 461.
18. Timothy Pickering to his wife, July 26, 1777, in *Life of Timothy Pickering* (1), 147-48; Washington to Putnam, July 25, 1777, *PGW* (10), 414-15. For contents of letter and the circumstances regarding its intercept, see annotations in *PGW* (10), 394-96.
19. Mifflin to GW, July 26, 1777, *PGW* (10), 439; Jacob Hiltzheimer diary, July 27, 1777, "Extracts from the Diary of Jacob Hiltzheimer," *PMHB*, Vol. 16, No. 1 (April 1892), 98.
20. GW to Mifflin, July 28, 1777, *PGW* (10), 449.
21. GW to Gates, July 28, 1777, *PGW* (10), 444-46.
22. David Hackett Fisher, *Washington's Crossing* (New York, NY: Oxford University Press, 2004), 211.
23. GW to Hancock, July 30, 1777, PGW (10), 459; Clement Biddle to James Wilson, July 29, 1777, in *Revolutionary Manuscripts and Portraits* (Philadelphia, PA: Thos. Birch's Sons, Auctioneers, 1892), 72; Pickering journal, July 28, 1777, *Life of Timothy Pickering* (1), 147. Pickering mispronounced and thus misspelled the host's name as "Oakham."
24. GW to JS, July 29, 1777, *PGW* (10), 455; GW to Stirling, July 30, 1777, *PGW* (10), 464; "Journal of Capt. William Beatty," 1776-1781," *Maryland Historical Magazine* 3, no. 2 (1908), 106-107.
25. Persifor Frazer to Polly Frazer, July 29, 1777, *A Memoir*, 151; GW to JH, July 30, 1777,

PGW (10), 459; Clement Biddle to James Wilson, July 29, 1777, in *Revolutionary Manuscripts and Portraits* (Philadelphia, PA: Thos. Birch's Sons, Auctioneers, 1892), 72; GW to JS, July 29, 1777, *PGW* (10), 455; GW to Stirling, July 30, 1777, *PGW* (10), 464; "Journal of Capt. William Beatty," 106-107.

26. Clement Biddle to James Wilson, July 29, 1777, in *Revolutionary Manuscripts and Portraits*, 72.

27. NG to General James M. Varnum, August 14, 1777, *PNG* (2), 140-41.

28. GW to Gates, July 29 and 30, *PGW* (10), 454, 459.

29. GW to Hancock, July 31, 1777, PGW (10), 468; Israel Shreve journal, July 30-31, 1777; Captain John Chilton diary, July 31, 1777, in Michael Cecere, *They Behaved Like Soldiers: Captain John Chilton and the Third Virginia Regiment, 1775-1778* (Westminster, MD: Heritage Books, 2007), 118

30. Pickering journal, July 31, 1777, *Life of Timothy Pickering* (1), 148; Jacob Hiltzheimer diary, July 31, 1777, "Extracts . . . ," 98. (Final two sources both place arrival at City Tavern at 10:00 P.M.) The count of headquarters staff and servants derived from an August 1 breakfast receipt from the City Tavern proprietor. See Daniel Smith to George Washington, August 6, 1777, Revolutionary War Accounts, Vouchers, and Receipted Accounts 1, George Washington Papers, Manuscript Division, LOC. Today, Montgomery County encompasses the Philadelphia County region used by Washington this day.

31. Lafayette Memoir, in Stanley K. Idzerda, ed., *Lafayette in the Age of the American Revolution*, Volume 1 (Ithaca, NY: Cornell University Press, 1977), 9-12, 91.

32. "To 21 Breakfasts for Gentn," August 1, 1777, in Daniel Smith to George Washington, August 6, 1777, Revolutionary War Accounts, Vouchers, and Receipted Accounts 1, George Washington Papers, LOC; GW to NG, August 1, 1777, *PGW* (10), 473. Army strength on August 1 derived from September 3 report in Timothy Pickering Papers, Massachusetts Historical Society, Boston, MA.

33. The forts and other locales of the trip are specified in Marvin Kitman, *George Washington's Expense Account* (New York, NY: Grove Press, 1970), 223-24. "Wilmington" heads a letter to mark the farthest advance. See GW to Anthony Dalton White, August 1, 1777, *PGW* (10), 485. Pennsylvania Arms is speculative as Chester headquarters merely because it had been misidentified as headquarters one month later. After this visit, the hotel was renamed "Washington House." The building survived 222 years until 1959, when it was demolished.

34. Hunn's intelligence annotated to JH's letter to GW, August 1, 1777, in *PGW* (10), 479-80.

35. All these correspondences from Chester generated from 10:00 P.M. and later on August 1. See *PGW* (10), 475-85.

CHAPTER THREE: "IRKSOME STATE OF SUSPENSE"

1. Description excerpted from Rev. Andrew Burnaby's travels in North America, published in 1760, and reproduced in "An Account of Pennsylvania," *Derby Mercury* [Derbyshire, England], March 3, 1775.

2. John W. Jackson, *With the British Army in Philadelphia, 1777-1778* (San Rafael, CA: Presidio Press, 1979), 275-77.

3. "The British Campaign for Philadelphia and the Occupation of Valley Forge in 1777," https://www.nps.gov/vafo/learn/historyculture/upload/Philadelphia%20campaign,pdf; William Howe to George Germain, December 20, 1776, and April 2, 1777, *The Parliamentary Register; or, Proceedings and Debates of the House of Commons* (London: Wilson and Co., 1802), 271-272, 386-387.

4. Michael C. Harris, *Germantown: A Military History of the Battle for Philadelphia, October 4, 1777* (El Dorado Hills, CA: Savas Beatty, LLC, 2020), 18-19.
5. Baker, "The Camp by Schuylkill Falls," 28-41; "Camped on Queen Lane," [Philadelphia] *The Times*, October 19, 1891; McMichael diary, August 1,1777, *PMHB* (16), 146.
6. GW to Horatio Gates, August 4, 1777, *PGW* (10), 499.
7. GW to Richard Peters, August 5, 1777, *PGW* (10), 511.
8. GW to Richard Peters, August 5, 1777, *PGW* (10), 511. The bill delineated "28 Gentn" and "16 Servt." See Daniel Smith to George Washington, August 6, 1777, Revolutionary War Accounts, Vouchers, and Receipted Accounts 1, Washington Papers, LOC.
9. Baker, "The Camp by Schuylkill Falls," 28-41; "Camped on Queen Lane," [Philadelphia] *The Times*, October 19, 1891; McGuire, *The Philadelphia Campaign* (1), 100-101; GW to Daniel Morgan, August 9, 1777, *PGW* (10), 566. Henry Hill's association with Madeira traces to his father, who had been living for thirty-eight years on the Portuguese island famous for its namesake wine.
10. GW to Joseph Reed, November 30, 1776 (including annotation of Reed's disparaging November 21 letter), *PGW* (7), 237-38; F[rancis] B. Heitman, *Historical Register of Officers of the Continental Army During the War of the Revolution, April 1775, to December 1783* (Washington, DC: n.p., 1883), 342.
11. Coudray to GW, July 23, 1777, *PGW* (10), 369; Charles Carroll to Charles Carroll, Sr., June 13, 1777, *LDC* (7), 189-90.
12. "Opinions on the Defense of Philadelphia," *PGW* (10), 518-37. For details of the Invalid Corps, see General Orders, August 6, 1777, *PGW* (10), 516-17.
13. GW to William Heath, August 10-11, 1777, *PGW* (10), 575-76.
14. NG to James Varnum, August 14, 1777, *PNG* (2), 141.
15. Lafayette, "Memoir of 1776," *Lafayette in the Age of the American Revolution* (1), 91. Lafayette emphasized "hunting shirts" within the quote.
16. Pickering journal, August 8, 1777, *Life of Timothy Pickering* (1), 150; McMichael journal, August 8, 1777, PMHB (16), 146-47; Lafayette, "Memoir of 1776," *Lafayette in the Age of the American Revolution*, 91. Temperatures recorded in the [Philadelphia] *Pennsylvania Evening Post*, August 16, 1777, and [Philadelphia] *Dunlap's Pennsylvania Packet*, August 26, 1777.
17. Pickering journal, August 8-10, 1777, *Life of Timothy Pickering* (1), 150-51; McMichael journal, August 8-10, 1777, *PMHB* (16), 146-47.
18. JH to GW, August 10, 1777 (including Col. Zadoc Purnell to JH, August 7, 1777), *PGW* (10), 574-75; GW to William Heath, August 10-11, 1777, *PGW* (10), 575-76.
19. G. Weedon, "Camp, Cross Roads, August 10, 1777," Purdie's *Virginia Gazette*, September 12, 1777; "Old York Road and its Points of Interest," *Chester Times*, August 30, 1918; John C. Patrick, *George Washington's Accounts of Expenses* (Boston, MA: Houghton Mifflin Company, 1917), 48.
20. Kitman, *George Washington's Expense Account*, 221-24.
21. Lefkowitz, *George Washington's Indispensable Men*, 118-22; GW to John Laurens, August 5, 1777, *PGW* (10), 509.
22. Pulaski to GW, July 26, 1777, *PGW* (10), 428-29; William Heath to GW, August 4, 1777, *PGW* (10), 499; GW to John Hancock, August 21, 1777, *PGW* (11), 27. Biographical information and quotation from Franklin in annotations to these sources.

23. Boatner, *Encyclopedia*, 1117; George Frost to Josiah Bartlett, September 8, 1777, *JCC* (7), 630; Heitman, *Historical Register*, 136.

24. Lafayette to JH, August 13, 1777, *Lafayette in the Age of the American Revolution* (1), 103; GW to Benjamin Harrison, August 20, 1777, *PGW* (11), 13.

25. "Memoir by the Chevalier Dubuysson," *Lafayette in the Age of the American Revolution* (1), 81.

26. GW to Benjamin Harrison, August 19, 1777, *PGW* (11), 4.

27. Ibid.; JS to GW, August 7, 1777, *PGW* (10), 547.

28. Pickering journal, August 14, 1777, *Life of Timothy Pickering* (1), 151; John Adams to Abigail Adams, August 14 & 17, 1777 [electronic edition]. *Adams Family Papers: An Electronic Archive.* Massachusetts Historical Society. http://www.masshist.org/digitaladams/. Temperature readings for the first fifteen days of August recorded in the [Philadelphia] *Pennsylvania Evening Post* on August 16, 1777, and [Philadelphia] *Dunlap's Pennsylvania Packet* on August 26, 1777.

29. McMichael diary, August 16,1777, *PMHB* (16), 147.

30. John Laurens to Henry Laurens, August 13, 1777, *Army Correspondence of Colonel John Laurens*, 57.

31. Lafayette, "Memoir of 1776," *Lafayette in the Age of the American Revolution*, 91; NG to James M. Varnum, August 14, 1777; *PNG* (2), 140.

32. GW to John Trumbull, August 4, 1777, *PGW* (10), 506; GW to John Augustine Washington, August 5, 1777, *PGW* (10), 514-15.

33. GW to Horatio Gates, August 20, 1777, *PGW* (11), 12; GW to JH, August 21, 1777, *PGW* (11), 21-23.

34. Council of War, August 21, 1777, *PGW* (11), 19-21.

35. General Orders, August 21, 1777, *PGW* (11), 19.

36. John Page to "Sir," August 15, 1777, *PGW* (10), 623; John Hancock to GW (including enclosure from Thomas Nelson, Jr.), August 21, 1777, *PGW* (11), 25-26. The quote appears in both Page's and Nelson's intelligence reports.

37. GW to John Page, August 21, 1777, *PGW* (11), 28-29.

38. General Orders, August 22, 1777, *PGW* (11), 30-35 (quote on page 34).

39. Ibid.

40. JH to GW, August 22, 1777, *PGW* (11), 41 (see footnote for the enclosed intelligence).

41. Sir William Howe to Lord George Germain, April 2, 1777, in House of Commons, *Parliamentary Register*, Vol. 10 (London: Reprinted for John Stockdale, J. Walker, R. Lea, and J. Nunn, 1802), 387.

42. General Orders, August 22, 1777, *PGW* (11), 30-35 ("After Orders" on pages 34-35).

43. Henry Knox to Lucy Knox, August 25, 1777, Knox Family Papers.

44. NG to Anthony Wayne, August 22, 1777, *PNG* (2), 146.

45. Henry Knox to Lucy Knox, August 25, 1777, Knox Family Papers.

46. GW to Nash, August 22, 1777, *PGW* (11), 43.

47. Greene to James M. Varnum, August 14 & 17, 1777, *PNG* (2), 140-43.

48. Henry Knox to his wife, August 25, 1777, Knox Family Papers. This opening portion of the letter was not included in the published correspondence of Henry and Lucy Knox. He alludes to the first intelligence regarding Howe's possible ascent of the Chesapeake two weeks earlier which halted the Americans' advance to the Hudson by way of Coryell's Ferry, and essentially influenced their encampment at Crossroads. By not mentioning the definitive

intelligence received at headquarters on August 22 in his letter written three days later, Knox demonstrated that he was not privy to this news.
49. GW to JH, August 23, 1777, *PGW* (11), 52-53.
50. "Jerry," *Pittsburgh Press*, May 5, 1907; Sarah Logan Fisher's August 23 diary excerpts in McGuire, *The Philadelphia Campaign* (1), 123.
51. Henry Knox to Lucy Knox, August 25, 1777, Knox Family Papers; General Orders, *PGW* (11), 49-51; "Philadelphia," *Pennsylvania Evening Post*, August 23, 1777.
52. McMichael diary, August 23-24, 1777, *PMHB* (16), 147; John Adams to Abigail Adams, August 24, 1777, *LDC* (7), 538-39; Henry Marchant to Nicholas Cooke, August 24, 1777, *LDC* (7), 540-42; Richard Henry Lee to Thomas Jefferson, August 25, 1777, *LDC* (7), 550-52.
53. Pickering journal, August 24, 1777, *Life of Timothy Pickering* (1), 152; Daniel Smith bill, August 24, 1777, Revolutionary War Accounts, Vouchers and Receipted Accounts (1), LOC.

CHAPTER FOUR: "IF WE BEHAVE LIKE MEN"

1. Henry Knox to his wife, August 25, 1777, Knox Family Papers.
2. General Orders, August 24, 1777, *PGW* (11), 55. Washington called them "bad women." The Delaware County, Pennsylvania town of "Derby" is known today as "Darby." The former spelling will be retained in the narrative except when occasionally presented in the latter form in quotes by campaign participants.
3. The decision to query his commanders was sound but the record is shy of evidence within the *Papers of George Washington.* The source for the council comes from a captured aide of a participant in the meeting. See Friedrich von Münchhausen diary, September 1, 1777, in Ernst Kipping and Samuel Stelle Smith, eds., *At General Howe's Side 1776-1778: The diary of William Howe's aide de camp, Captain Friedrich von Muenchhausen* (Monmouth Beach, NJ: Philip Freneau Press, 1974), 27. The captured aide infers that the council was held on August 25. This is unlikely as with less than half of Washington's army present, he was unlikely to convene such an important meeting. Backdating this event to August 24 is the most reasonable target date. Although it is feasible to consider backdating the council one more day to August 23, the absence of Greene and Knox that earlier date makes this highly unlikely.
4. Ibid. The aide never named the advocates but identified them as the "French generals." Lafayette and Conway met this description.
5. The British landed 18,418 at Head of Elk; this number included non-military men and women, including camp followers. See John W. Jackson, *With the British Army in Philadelphia, 1777-1778* (San Rafael, CA: Presidio Press, 1979), 280.
6. General Orders, August 24, 1777, *PGW* (11), 55.
7. Pickering diary, August 25, 1777, *Life of Timothy Pickering* (1), 152.
8. George Forsyth to George Washington, August 27, 1777, George Washington Papers: Revolutionary War Vouchers and Receipted Accounts, 1776-1780, Manuscript Division, Library of Congress, Washington, D.C.
9. Muhlenberg's Orderly Book, August 29, 1777, 450.
10. GW to JH, August 25, 1777, *PGW* (11), 69.
11. Samuel Chase to GW, August 25, 1777, PGW (11), 65. Jacob Broom's map was completed two days later, evidence that his service was immediate and imperative. Original Broom map is held by Historical Society of Pennsylvania. Credit to Wade Catts for providing the author with information regarding Broom.

12. The estimate of 500 is supported by a witness who spoke of it to a British officer. See Francis Downman journal, August 28, 1777, in F. A. Whinyates, ed., *The Services of Lieut.-Colonel Francis Downman, R.A. in France, North America, and the West Indies, Between the Years 1758 and 1784*. (Woolwich: Royal Artillery Institution, 1898), 30.
13. Washington to Landon Carter, October 27, 1777, *PGW* (12), 25-27; Receipt to Captain Caleb Gibbs and "General Washington's Bill," August 26, 1777, in Harold C. Syett et al., eds. *The Papers of Alexander Hamilton* (New York, NY: Columbia University Press, 1979), Vol. 26, 363. Lanigan is misnamed "Sanigan" by Alexander Hamilton on the receipt. See correct spelling in "Treason in Delaware County," *Delaware Archives: Revolutionary War in Three Volumes*, Vol. 3 (Wilmington, DE: Chas. L. Story Company Press, 1919), 1306.
14. Today, the river is called "Christina." Although 20th and 21st century works label it as a creek in 1777, contemporary newspapers designate it as a river. See "To be Sold on the Premises," [Philadelphia] *Pennsylvania Gazette*, September 4, 1782, and "Christiana Mills For Sale," *Philadelphia Inquirer*, July 5, 1794.
15. "Extract of a letter from a General officer . . ." August 27, 1777, Purdie's [Williamsburg] *Virginia Gazette*, September 5, 1777; GW to JH, August 27, 1777, *PGW* (11), 78. For the importance of Head of Elk as an American magazine, see Risch, *Supplying Washington's Army*, 65, 103-105.
16. "major Forsyth" letter extract, August 27, 1777, Purdie's [Williamsburg] *Virginia Gazette*, September 5, 1777.
17. "A Maryland Loyalist," *Maryland Historical Magazine* Vol 1, No. 4 (December 1906), 321-23; Robert Alexander, Archives of Maryland Biographical Series, MSA SC 3520-17. Timing of rain to late afternoon is taken from Münchhausen journal, August 26, 1777, in *At General Howe's Side*, 26.
18. Receipt to Captain Caleb Gibbs, September 2, 1777, in Harold C. Syett et al., eds. *The Papers of Alexander Hamilton* (New York, NY: Columbia University Press, 1979), Vol. 26, 363. The Gibbs receipt was for expenses "paid at Mr. James in Cecil [County] August 26th." Seth James fits this description as his residence sat between Chestnut Hill and Iron Hill near the state boundary. James later claimed that Washington and a lone servant lodged in his house that night. (See George Johnston, *History of Cecil County, Maryland* [Elkton, MD, published by the author, 1881, 331-32.]) If this had any truth to it, Caleb Smith would not have had to submit a receipt for one boarder that night.
19. Washington to Landon Carter, October 27, 1777, *PGW* (12), 25-27.
20. "Memoir, 1776," *Lafayette in the Age of the American Revolution* (1), 92. Lafayette never identified who owned the home where they slept.
21. "A Maryland Loyalist," *Maryland Historical Magazine* Vol. 1, No. 4 (December 1906), 321-23; Erika Quesenbery Sturgill, "The 'frien-emy' of Friendship in Elkton," May 9, 2015, https://www.cecildaily.com/our_cecil/the-frien-emy-of-friendship-in-elkton/article_2e845e59-4d3a-51dd-bdcb-d040fc2352b7.html.
22. "Fine Tablet Now Marks Historic Old Mansion," [Wilmington, DE] *Evening Journal*, February 24, 1902; "Research Bares New Data on Washington's Quarters," [Wilmington] *Morning News*, February 22, 1957; "To be Sold on the Premises," [Philadelphia] *Pennsylvania Gazette*, September 4, 1782; Records of the Wilmington Monthly Meeting of Friends Committee to Collect and Keep a Record of All Sufferings, 1777-1780. Friends Historical Library, Swarthmore College, Swarthmore, PA.
23. Kitman, *George Washington's Expense Account*, 224; GW to JH, August 27, 1777, *PGW* (11), 78; Jacob Broom map, August 27, 1777, original held by Historical Society of Pennsylvania.
24. Münchhausen journal, September 1, 1777, *At General Howe's Side*, 27. Theodorick Bland

to GW, August 27, 1777, *PGW* (11), 74-75; General Orders, August 27, 1777, *PGW* (11), 73; McMichael diary, August 28, 1777, *PMHB* (16), 148.

25. Hamilton to Gouverneur Morris, September 1, 1777, in Lodge, ed., *Works of Alexander Hamilton* (Vol. 9), 99; Greene, *Life of Nathanael Greene* (vol. 1), 444. Howe's aide mistakenly places Washington on either Iron Hill or Chestnut Hill that day, but he likely spied General Greene instead. See Münchhausen journal, August 26, 1777, in *At General Howe's Side*, 26. Washington confirms he was not at either of those heights that day when he informed Congress he was at White Clay Creek. See GW to JH, August 29, 1777, *PGW* (11), 89.

26. Although frequently branded as a river in modern studies of the colonial era, the Brandywine was exclusively referred to as a creek in contemporary print. See "To Be Let," [Philadelphia] *Dunlap and Claypoole's American Daily Advertiser*, November 8, 1773, for an example of this usage.

27. William Gordon, *The History of the Rise, Progress, and Establishment, of the Independence of the United States of America* (Vol. 2), 494-495. Greene's grandson and biographer, George Washington Greene, cites a letter from Gordon to NG, dated April 5, 1784, as the evidence that General Greene was Gordon's authority. See Greene, *The Life of Nathanael Greene* (Vol. 1), 444 (n#2); NG to Jacob Greene, August 31, 1777, *PNG* (2), 147.

28. General Orders, August 28, 1777, *PGW* (11), 81-82; General Greene's orders, August 28, 1777, *PNG* (2), 147; General Orders, August 30, 1777, *PGW* (11), 91; GW to William Maxwell, August 30, 1777, *PGW* (11), 95.

29. Münchhausen journal, August 31, 1777, in *At General Howe's Side*, 26.

30. Deposition on page 1 of Purdie's [Williamsburg] *Virginia Gazette*, October 3, 1777. Francis Alexander's relationship to the newly declared Loyalist Robert Alexander is unknown by the author.

31. GW to JH, September 1, 1777, *PGW* (11), 108.

32. September 3 returns, Timothy Pickering Papers, Massachusetts Historical Society, Boston, MA. Credit to Michael Harris for notifying the author of this source which has never been referenced before. Previous attempts to derive September numerical strength was estimated from a May 20, 1777, strength returns with proportional estimates of additional regiments not included in those returns, generally estimating that additional troops recruited in the three months since the official return were nearly equally offset by losses. See McGuire, *The Philadelphia Campaign* (1), 169-71 and Harris, *Brandywine*, 168-173.

33. GW to Adam Stephen, July 20, 1776, *PGW* (5), 408-409; Chernow, *Washington: A Life*, 128-129, 275; Boatner, *Encyclopedia*, 1055.

34. Lord Stirling to GW [August-September 1777], *PGW* (11), 105.

35. Thomas Conway to GW, September 1, 1777, *PGW* (11), 106-107.

36. Boatner, *Encyclopedia*, 154-55; Heitman, *Historical Register*, 112; John Cadwalader to GW, September 2, 1777, *PGW* (11), 122-23.

37. General Orders, August 25, 1777, *PGW* (11), 63; GW to JH, August 30, 1777, *PGW* (11), 93; GW to Theodorick Bland [August 1777], *PGW* (11), 104. "Light Horse Harry" is the father of the Confederate general Robert E. Lee.

38. GW to JH, August 8, 1777, PGW (11), 85. Exactly when Pulaski joined the army is unknown. Pulaski may have been accompanying Washington as early as the day of the Philadelphia parade on August 24, or as late as September 10. The date was August 24 or thereabouts.

39. "There were giants in those days," *Sandusky Daily Commercial Register*, October 21, 1854; Heitman, *Historical Register of Officers*, 253; "Return of ordnance stores belonging to the USA, November 16, 1777," reproduced in U.S. Government, National Park Service, *The*

Valley Forge Encyclopedia: Comprehensive History of the Famous American Revolutionary War Winter Continental Army Encampment, 370. This report delineates thirty-nine cannons in November. At least eleven others were captured after the first week of September.

40. NG to Jacob Greene, August 31, 1777, and to Catharine Greene, September 10, 1777, *PNG* (2), 149, 154-55.

41. John Armstrong to Thomas Wharton, September 8, 1777, in Samuel Hazard, *Pennsylvania Archives*, Volume 5 (Philadelphia, PA: Joseph Severns & Co., 1853), 598; General Orders, September 4, 1777, *PGW* (11), 141-43. The identification of regiments and brigades within Armstrong's command is best depicted in Harris, *Brandywine*, 407-408.

42. General Orders, August 31, 1777, *PGW* (11), 99.

43. McGuire, *The Philadelphia Campaign* (1), 156-57.

44. Wright, *Some Notes on the Continental Army*, 10.

45. General Orders, September 5, 1777, *PGW* (11), 147-48.

46. John Adams to Abigail Adams, September 1 & 8, 1777, in *Familiar Letters*, 304-305.

47. Henry Laurens to John Lewis Gervais, September 8, 1777, *LDC* (7), 630.

48. *Pennsylvania Packet*, September 9, 1777; *Pennsylvania Gazette* and *Pennsylvania Post*, September 10, 1777.

49. [Baltimore] *Maryland Journal*, September 16, 1777; [Boston] *Independent Chronicle*, September 18, 1777; [Hartford] *Connecticut Courant*, September 22, 1777, & *Norwich* [Conn.] *Packet*, September 22, 1777; [Portsmouth] *New-Hampshire Gazette*; [Williamsburg] *Purdie's Virginia Gazette*, September 26, 1777; [Williamsburg] *Virginia Gazette*, October 3, 1777; [Charlestown] *South-Carolina and American General Gazette*, October 9, 1777.

50. Quote in Thomas J. McGuire, *The Philadelphia Campaign: Germantown and the Roads to Valley Forge*, Vol. 2 (Mechanicsburg, PA: Stackpole Books, 2007), 44.

CHAPTER FIVE: "MANUVRING APPEARS TO BE THEIR PLAN"

1. "Hale-Byrnes House," http://www.halebyrnes.org/history.html.

2. General Orders, September 6, 1777, *PGW* (11), 157-58.

3. Ibid.

4. GW to William Smallwood, September 9, 177, *PGW* (11), 179-80; McMichael diary, September 8, 1777, *PMHB* (16), 149.

5. Downman diary, September 8, 1777, *The Services of Lieut. Colonel Francis Downman*, 32; Münchhausen diary, September 8, 1777, *At General Howe's Side*, 30.

6. Richard Peters to GW, September 9, 1777, *PGW* (11), 178; "Philadelphia, September 10," [Charlestown] *South-Carolina and American General Gazette*, October 16, 1777; Henry Laurens to John Lewis Gervais, September 9, 1777, *PHL* (11) 511. The letter from headquarters probably was authored by Henry's son, John.

7. Marquis de Lafayette, *Memoirs Correspondence and Manuscripts of General Lafayette, Published by His Family*, Volume 1 (New York, NY: Craighead and Allen, printers, 1837), 22; GW to JH, September 9, 1777, *PGW* (11), 175; McMichael diary, September 9, 1777, *PMHB* (16), 149; GW to William Smallwood, September 9, 1777, *PGW* (11), 180; General Orders, August 31, 1777, *PGW* (11), 99.

8. "Extract of a letter from Camp, Tuesday Morning," [Charlestown] *South-Carolina and American General Gazette*, October 16, 1777.

9. Wade P. Catts, Robert Selig, and Sean Moir, *"Left Newport... Before Daylight and March'd to Chads Ford" Military Terrain Analysis for Two Brandywine Battlefield Strategic Landscapes* (West Chester, PA: Chester County Planning Commission, 2019), 61-65.

10. General Orders, September 9, 1777, *PGW* (11), 174; Harris, *Brandywine*, 166-67.
11. John Armstrong to Thomas Wharton, September 8, 1777, in Samuel Hazard, *Pennsylvania Archives*, Volume 5 (Philadelphia, PA: Joseph Severns & Co., 1853), 598; General Orders, August 31, 1777, *PGW* (11), 99.
12. Robert H. Harrison to JH, September 10, 1777, *PGW* (11), 182.
13. "1777 Chester County Property Atlas," 1777 Chester County Property Atlas (storymaps.arcgis.com).
14. Benjamin Ring receipt, February 9, 1778, Vouchers and Receipts, George Washington Papers, LOC.
15. Thomas Burke to Richard Caswell, September 10, 1777, *LDC* (7), 640.
16. General Orders, September 10, *PGW* (11), 180-82; GW to Richard Peters, ibid., 184-85; GW to Israel Putnam, ibid., 185-86; GW to Caesar Rodney, ibid., 186.
17. GW to Caesar Rodney, *PGW* (11), 186; NG to Catharine Greene, September 10, 1777, *PNG* (2), 154, 156.
18. NG to Catharine Greene, September 10, 1777, in *PNG* (2), 154, 156. The major general of the day was notified of that headquarters duty through the previous day's General Orders. See September 10 assignment of "Green" under September 9 orders in *General Muhlenberg's Orderly Book*, 462.
19. McMichael diary, September 10, 1777, *PMHB* (16), 149.
20. JS to JH, October 6, 1777, *LPJS*, 475-76; GW to JS, October 24, 1777, *LPJS*, 541.
21. Today, Corinne Road closely follows the roadbed of that 1741 road. For this and all other roads on the battlefield in 1777, see "1777 Chester County Property Atlas," 1777 Chester County Property Atlas (storymaps.arcgis.com).
22. JS to JH, October 6, 1777, *LPJS*, 475-76; JS to GW, September 11, 1777, *PGW* (11), 197-98.
23. Harris, *Brandywine*, 223; Robert H. Harrison to JH, September 11, 1777, *PGW* (11), 195-96; George Weedon to John Page, September 11, 1777, Chicago Historical Society, Chicago, IL.
24. Idzerda, ed., *Lafayette in the Age of the American Revolution*, 94; Harris, *Brandywine*, 248; McGuire, *The Philadelphia Campaign* (1), 180 (Ferguson quote).
25. Washington quote in J. Smith Futhey and Gilbert Cope, *History of Chester County, Pennsylvania* (Philadelphia, PA: Louis H. Everts, 1881), 80; Loyalist quote reproduced in Harris, *Brandywine*, 254.
26. JS to JH, October 6, 1777, *LPJS*, 475; Harris, *Brandywine*, 248-49; McGuire, *The Philadelphia Campaign* (1), 185-86.
27. Weedon to Page, September 11, 1777, Chicago Historical Society.
28. James Ross to GW, September 11, 1777, *PGW* (11), 196.
29. GW to Theodorick Bland, September 11, 1777, *PGW* (11), 197. The mutilated heading of the original dispatch gave a partial time of "20 Mints after [ ] O'Clock." The editors interpreted the missing time as 11:00 A.M. This is not possible as Ross timed his report at 11:00 A.M., but from a position nearly six miles from Washington. This eliminates the possibility of Washington crafting an 11:20 A.M. message to Bland, based on "satisfactory information of a body confidently reported [by Ross most likely, not Hazen] to have gone up to a Ford." and points most strongly to a note written at 12:20 P.M., rather than an hour earlier.
30. John Sullivan to JH, October 6, 1777, *LPJS*, 475-76; GW to JS, October 24, 1777, *LPJS*, 541.
31. JS to GW, September 11, 1777, *PGW* (11), 197-98.

32. GW to JS, October 24, 1777, *LPJS*, 541; Weedon to Page, September 11, 1777, Chicago Historical Society.
33. Pickering reminiscence quoted in McGuire, *The Philadelphia Campaign* (1), 197.
34. Theodorick Bland to GW and JS to GW, September 11, 1777, *PGW* (11), 198.
35. Weedon to Page, September 11, 1777, Chicago Historical Society; Pickering reminiscence, Pickering Papers, Reel 52, 184-85. Time is approximated.
36. Harris, *Brandywine*, 286-320.
37. Ibid., 308-310; GW to JS, September 20, 1777, *LPJS*, 453-54; Idzerda, ed., *Lafayette in the Age of the American Revoluntion* (1), 95.
38. Robert Harrison to JH, September 11, 1777, *PGW* (11), 199.
39. Harris, *Brandywine*, 334-65. The measured distance by roads from Greene's position at the Brandywine to his final defensive stand is one mile less than the traditional interpretation of his "having covered four rugged miles in 45-minutes." (See Reed, *Campaign to Valley Forge*, 135-36.)

CHAPTER SIX: A PROSPECT OF SUCCESS

1. Pickering identified the tavern in a post-war letter, excerpted in *Life of Timothy Pickering* (2), 82.
2. Harris, *Brandywine*, 378. The oft-repeated story that Lafayette was taken from Chester is refuted by his own memoir which suggests that he traveled by barge to Philadelphia. He apparently was carried "a distance from" Chester before being placed on the boat. His claim that Washington insisted that the doctors "take care of him as if he were my son, for I love him the same," is suspect as Washington, who had known him less than six weeks, had been irked by the young general's mid-August request to command a division in the field. See *Lafayette in the Age of the American Revolution* (1), 64, 127.
3. GW to JH, September 11, 1777, *PGW* (11), 200-201. The latter page includes the postscript describing Washington's addition to Pickering's letter, described in Pickering, *Life of Timothy Pickering* (1), 156-58.
4. JH to GW, September 12, 1777, *PGW* (11), 207-208.
5. General Orders, September 12, 1777, *PGW* (11), 204-205; McMichael Diary, September 12, 1777, *PMHB* (16), 1, 50; "Orderly Book of Gen. John Peter Gabriel Muhlenberg, March 26–December 20, 1777," *PMHB* (34), 4, 464.
6. McMichael diary, September 13, 1777, *PMHB* (16), 150; Pickering journal, September 12, 1777, *Life of Timothy Pickering* (1), 158.
7. Ibid.; "The Military Journal of George Ewing," in Thomas Ewing, *George Ewing, Gentleman, a Soldier of Valley Forge* (Yonkers, NY: Privately Printed, 1928), 22-23; "Extract of a letter from Philadelphia, dated September 13, 1777, 9 o'clock," [Charleston] *South-Carolina and American General Gazette*, October 16, 1777; GW to Colonel Stephen Moylan, September 13, 1777, *PGW* (11), 218. Washington's secretary headed this letter: "Camp at Mr. Hills," pinpointing the army and Washington's location.
8. Howe to GW, September 12, 1777, *PGW* (11), 208. GW to Howe, September 13, 1777, *PGW* (11), 215. Dating Howe's courier to September 13 as well as the American interpretation can be found in NG to his wife, September 14, 1777, *PNG* (2), 162-63.
9. "Common Sense," "American Crisis No. 4," *Pennsylvania Evening Post*, September 13, 1777. Also see Thomas Paine, *Collected Writings* (New York, NY: Literary Classics of the United States, Inc., 1955), 147-150.
10. "Extract of a letter dated Camp, near Schuylkill Sept. 13," [Charleston] *South-Carolina*

and American General Gazette, October 30, 1777; Samuel Shaw to his father, September 13, 1777, *The Journals of Major Samuel Shaw*, 36.

11. GW to JH, September 19, 1777, *PGW* (11), 268; General Orders, September 14 [13], 1777, *PGW* (11), 223. The only known evidence for this council is a brief but convincing passage relayed ten days later: "... our design of attacking the enemy agreeable to the resolution taken at German Town." It is written by NG and is part of a filed document of a subsequent council. See "Sentiments of a Board of Genl officers taken near Potts grove, Sep.: 1777" excerpted in *PGW* (11), 297.

12. GW to William Heath, September 14, 1777, *PGW* (11), 227.

13. GW to Armstrong, September 14, 1777, *PGW* (11), 224.

14. GW to William Heath, September 14, 177, *PGW* (11), 227. Departure time found in James McMichael diary, September 14, 1777, *PMHB* (16), 150.

15. James McMichael diary, September 14, 1777, *PMHB* (16), 150; General Orders, September 14, 1777, *PGW* (11), 223; "Orderly Book of Gen. John Peter Gabriel Muhlenberg, March 26–December 20, 1777," *PMHB* (34), 4, 467; Wharton to GW, September 12, 1777, *PGW* (11), 210-211. Wharton's official title was "President of the Supreme Executive Council of the Commonwealth of Pennsylvania," akin to Governor of the state.

16. G. D. Scull, ed., "The Montresor Journals." *Collections of the New York Historical Society*, vol. 14 (1881), 419, hereinafter cited as "The Montresor Journals."

17. Pickering journal, September 14, 1777, *Life of Timothy Pickering* (1), 158-59; McMichael diary, September 14, 1777, *PMHB* (16), 150.

18. GW to JH, September 23, 1777, *PGW* (11), 301.

19. John H. Hawkins journal 1779-1782; MS Am. 0765 (Old Manuscript Guide 273), Historical Society of Pennsylvania, Philadelphia; Adam Hubley to William Atlee and Paul Zantzinger, September 15, 1777, Peter Force Collection, LOC; Anthony Wayne to Thomas Mifflin, September 15, 1777, Anthony Wayne Papers, Historical Society of Pennsylvania, Philadelphia.

20. JH to GW, September 14, 1777, *PGW* (11), 226-27; GW to JH, September 15, 1777, *PGW* (11), 236-37; James Lovell to William Whipple, September 17, 1777, *LDC* (7), 687.

21. GW to JH, September 15, 1777, *PGW* (11), 236-37. Also see annotations on page 233 regarding purchases at Sorrel Horse Tavern. Although no primary account places Washington specifically in Malin Hall, that residence is accepted as his headquarters because it is the only site that is supported by at least a contemporary secondary source. Two days after Washington left the area, John Montresor identified the house clearly as Malin Hall: "the Forks of Randel Malins (which was Washington's Headquarters the night before last)" in Scull, ed., "The Montresor Journals," 454. For an alternate location, based on tradition, see K. Varden Leasa, "A Great Valley Legend Examined: Where Did Washington Really Sleep on September 15, 1777?" https://www.tehistory.org/hqda/pdf/v45/v45n2p054.pdf.

22. John Heard to GW, September 15, 1777, *PGW* (11), 240.

23. John Montresor journal, September 15, 1777, "The Montresor Journals," 452. Montresor's identification of the crossing without any additional description of it suggests that he (and Howe) had been aware of Levering's Ford well before the aftermath of Brandywine. Montresor sketched a map of several fords and their distance from Philadelphia in an undated map entitled, "Fords Across the Schuylkill River in 1777 From Potts Grove to Philadelphia," ibid., 419.

24. Ibid., 452-53.

25. GW to JH, September 19, 1777, *PGW* (11), 268.

26. Quotes from Col. Paul Bentalou, *A Reply to Judge Johnson's Remarks to an Article in the North American Review Relating to Count Pulaski* (Baltimore, MD: J. D. Tot, 1825), 19-23; Pickering diary, September 16, 1777, *Life of Pickering* (1), 159; Clement Biddle to [General Mifflin], September 16, 1777, *Providence Gazette*, October 4, 1777. For the date of Pulaski's commission, see Boatner, *Encyclopedia*, 900.
27. "1777 Chester County Property Atlas," storymaps.arcgis.com; S. Smith to Bentalou, April 1, 1826 (see *A Reply to Judge Johnson*, p. 23) places the army's morning encampment to the east of the Lancaster Road. This road generally runs east-west with a dip southwestward, so Smith's comment places the army between the road and the South Valley Hills. Upham, *Life of Timothy Pickering* (2), 83. Today, the roadbed of King Road closely mimics Caln Road.
28. By tradition, Washington's partial force is placed on what is today the campus of Immaculata University, which stands north of West King Road. Based on campus location and the evidence at hand, the traditional location is not refuted.

CHAPTER SEVEN: "PRAY, SIR, DECIDE"

1. "Memoir by the Chevalier Duboysson," *Lafayette in the Age of the American Revolution* (1), 79.
2. Coudray to Samuel Chase, September 15, 1777, https://www.fold3.com/image/462820?terms=coudray,1777,chase; *JCC* (8), 745; James Lovell to William Whipple, September 17, 1777, *LDC* (7), 687-88.
3. Anonymous letter to a friend, September 16, 1777, [New Haven] *Connecticut Journal*, October 8, 1777; McGuire, *The Philadelphia Campaign* (1), 282.
4. Adams diary, September 16, 1777, www.masshist.org/digitaladams/archive/doc?id=D28&bc=%2Fdigitaladams%2Farc.
5. Pickering to Judge Peters, n.d., *Life of Timothy Pickering* (2), 83. Pickering mentions here that his 1808 letter to Governor James Sullivan of Massachusetts, recounting this incident initially included the final, three-word plea, but he did not want to emphasize Washington's indecisiveness at that time, so "I struck them out."
6. County of Chester, *Battle of the Clouds Technical Report*, https://www.chesco.org/DocumentCenter/View/17453/CloudsTechReport?bidId=, 25 (n49).
7. Montresor journal, September 18, 1777, "Montresor Journals," 454.
8. Clement Biddle to [Thomas Mifflin], September 16, 1777, *Boston Gazette*, September 29, 1777; Biddle to GW, September 16, 1777, *PGW* (11), 244-45; Clement Biddle to Dear General, September 16, 1777, [Portsmouth, NH] *Freeman's Journal*, October 4, 1777. Biddle timed the letter at 2:15 P.M. from Howell Tavern. Notwithstanding his debatable psychoanalysis of the troops, Biddle's eyewitness characterization of the men formed on the North Valley Hills likely sixty to seventy-five minutes earlier easily makes his letter the most reliable and unimpeachable account of September 16. No other American witness was able to record any view of this event prior to September 17; most surviving accounts were written days, weeks, months, years, or decades later.
9. Clement Biddle to [Thomas Mifflin], September 16, 1777, [Portsmouth, NH] *Freeman's Journal*, October 4, 1777. According to an anonymous letter from Philadelphia to a friend, on September 17, he wrote: "A letter was received last night from Col. Biddle, by General Mifflin . . ." and then details the exact information from Biddle to "Dear general," thus confirming that Mifflin was the recipient of Biddle's missive. See "Boston, October 2," [New Haven] *Connecticut Journal*, October 8, 1777.
10. County of Chester, *Battle of the Clouds Technical Report*, 5. The report insists Wayne's brigade was on the height; however, the position aligns more with Stephen's division from

the Lancaster Road. General Stephen indicates that Scott's brigade had moved off. See Stephen to GW, October 9, 1777, *PGW* (11), 468-70.
11. Clement Biddle, "P.S. Half after two o'clock," *Providence* [R.I.] *Gazette*, October 4, 1777.
12. Tell-tale evidence for the return to this house can be found in the notation for payment to Malin for use of his house "and trouble—(rainy day)." See Kitman, *George Washington's Expense Account*, 225-26. No rain had fallen at the time they departed headquarters in the morning to scale the South Valley Hills.
13. GW to JH, September 17, 11, *PGW* (11), 253; Joseph Reed to GW, September 16, 1777, *PGW* (11), 251. Reed wrote two dispatches; only this second one, written at 6:00 P.M. exists today. It briefly describes the contents of the first one sent "a few Hours ago."
14. Time of departure estimated from timing of GW receiving Reed dispatch, sent from seventeen miles down the Swede's Ford Road. One source timed the departure at 3:00 P.M. See James McMichael diary, September 16, 1777, *PMHB* (16), 151. Another soldier claimed they departed at 2:00 P.M. See William Beatty journal, September 16, 1777, in "Journal of Capt. William Beatty, 1776-1781," 110.
15. Ibid.; Samuel Shaw to his father, September 30, 1777, in Josiah Quincy, ed., *The Journals of Major Samuel Shaw, The First American Consul at Canton* (Boston, MA: Wm. Crosby and H. P. Nichols, 1847), 37; Henry Knox diary, September 16, 1777, Knox Family Papers.
16. Joseph Reed to GW, September 16, 1777, *PGW* (11), 251.
17. John Laurens to Henry Laurens, November 6, 1777, *PHL* (12), 31.
18. Henry Knox to his wife, September 24, 1777, in Drake, *Life of Henry Knox*, 50; Orders, September 17, 1777, *Muhlenberg's Orderly Book*, 469-70.
19. Clement Biddle to GW, September 16, 1777, *PGW* (11), 244-45 (The list of supplies is found in annotations on pages 245-46); GW to JH, September 17, 1777, *PGW* (11), 253.
20. GW to William Maxwell, September 17, 1777, *PGW* (11), 258; GW to Thomas Mifflin, September 17, 1777, *PGW* (11), 259.
21. GW to JH, September 18, 1777, *PGW* (11), 262; GW to Anthony Wayne, September 18, 1777 (3), *PGW* (11), 265-66.
22. AH to JH, September 18, 1777 (2), *The Works of Alexander Hamilton* (1), 34-36; Henry Lee, *Memoirs of the War in the Southern Department* (1), 19-20.
23. Newton, *Alexander Hamilton, The Formative Years*, 208-209; "Delegates' Testimonial for the Bethlehem Moravians," September 22, 1777, *LDC* (8), 9; James Lovell to Robert Treat Paine, September 24, 1777, *LDC* (8), 15.
24. Lee, *Memoirs of the War in the Southern Department* (1), 21; Alexander Hamilton to JH, September 18, 1777 (2), *The Works of Alexander Hamilton* (1), 34.
25. Anthony Wayne to GW (2), September 19, 1777, *PGW* (11), 273.
26. GW to JH, September 19, 1777, *PGW* (11), 268-70; Enoch Anderson, *Personal Recollections*, 40. John Montresor drew a map of the fords about a week later, noting at Buckwater's "where Washington went last Friday [September 19]." This intelligence likely came from scouts witnessing the wagon's crossing at this ford. See Scull, ed., "The Montresor Journals," 419.
27. Henry Knox diary, September 19, 1777, Knox Family Papers; GW to JH, September 19, 1777, *PGW* (11), 268-70.
28. "Wednesday, September 17, 1777," *JCC* (8), 752.
29. GW to JH, September 19, 1777, *PGW* (11), 268.

30. Ibid.; James McMichael diary, September 19, 1777, *PMHB* (16), 151; Henry Muhlenburg journal, September 19, 1777, *Muhlenberg Journals* (3), 77-78; Scull, ed., "The Montresor Journals," 419.
31. GW to Alexander McDougall, September 19, 1777, *PGW* (11), 271; Henry Muhlenburg journal, September 15, 1777, *Muhlenberg Journals*, (3), 74-75; GW to Thomas Mifflin, September 17, 1777, *PGW* (11), 259; General Orders, September 20, 1777, *PGW* (11), 274-75.
32. "The Thompson Tavern and the Jeffersonville Inn," *Historical Sketches of Montgomery County* (1), 348-49.
33. "John Sullivan," *LPJS*, 1-14.
34. GW to JS, September 20, 1777, *PGW* (11), 277 (bottom of page); "Fords Across the Schuylkill River in 1777," in Scull, ed., "The Montresor Journals," 419.
35. Joseph Reed to my Dearest Sukey, September 21, 1777, Princeton University Library, Princeton, NJ.

CHAPTER EIGHT: "HE DOES NOT KNOW HOW TO IMPROVE UPON THE GROSSEST BLUNDERS OF THE ENEMY"

1. Münchhausen diary, September 21, 1777, *At General Howe's Side*, 34-35; William Howe to GW, September 21, 1777, *PGW* (11), 283. The unrefuted evidence of the miscarry of the message can be found in Washington's response: "Your Favor of this date was received this Evening . . ." See GW to William Howe, September 21, 1777, *PGW* (11), 284.
2. William Howe to George Germain, October 10, 1777, *Parliamentary Register* (10), 429; John Montresor journal, September 21, 1777, "The Montresor Journals," 456; Münchhausen, diary, September 21, 1777, *At General Howe's Side*, 34-35; Tench Tilghman to Alexander McDougall, September 21, 1777, *PGW* (11), 293.
3. James McMichael diary, September 21, 1777, *PMHB* (16), 152; Henry Muhlenberg journal, September 21, 1777, *Muhlenberg Journals* (3), 78.
4. "Wednesday, September 17, 1777," *JCC* (8), 752.
5. Newton, *Alexander Hamilton: The Informative Years*, 209-10; JH to GW, September 17, 1777, *PGW* (11), 254-55; "Instructions to Lieutenant Colonel Alexander Hamilton," *PGW* (11), 282-83. These instructions were written out by Hamilton, likely dictated in large part from Washington.
6. GW to John A. Washington, October 18, 1777, *PGW* (11), 551.
7. John Fitzgerald to JS, September 21, 1777, *PGW* (11), 278.
8. GW to William Howe, September 21, 1777, *PGW* (11), 284.
9. Anthony Wayne to GW, *PGW* (11), 286-87.
10. McMichael diary, September 21, 1777, *PMHB* (16), 152.
11. Ibid.; William Howe to George Germain, October 10, 1777, *Parliamentary Register* (10), 429.
12. Upham, *Life of Timothy Pickering* (2), 83-84; Greene, *Life of Nathanael Greene*, 468-69.
13. General Orders, September 22, 1777, *PGW* (11), 288; GW to George Gibson, September 22, 1777, *PGW* (11), 290-91; Henry Knox diary, September 22, 1777, Knox Family Papers.
14. Traditional interpretation suggests Howe feigned a movement farther upriver to lure the American army away from fords he wished to cross, then adeptly countermarched back to those fords for an uncontested crossing. See Craig L. Symonds, *A Battlefield Atlas of the American Revolution* (Baltimore, MD: Nautical & Aviation Publishing Company of Amer-

ica, Inc., 1986), 54-55. No evidence supports this supposition. See Gary Ecelbarger, "The Feint That Never Happened: Unheralded Turning Point of the Philadelphia Campaign, *JAR*, November 19, 2020, https://allthingsliberty.com/2020/11/the-feint-that-never-happened-unheralded-turning-point-of-the-philadelphia-campaign/.

15. "Henry Antes House, National Register of Historic Places registration papers, https://npgallery.nps.gov/NRHP/GetAsset/NHLS/75001657_text.

16. Münchhausen journal, September 22-23, 1777, *At General Howe's Side*, 35; Council of War, September 23, 1777, *PGW* (11), 294-96.

17. Ibid.; William Howe to George Germain, October 10, 1777, *Parliamentary Register* (10), 429-30.

18. GW to JH, September 23, 1777, *PGW* (11), 301-302.

19. "Council of War," *PGW* (11), 294-96. [Tench Tilghman's version. Stirling's and Greene's versions quoted on pages 296-97].

20. GW to JH, September 23, 1777, *PGW* (11), 301-302; GW to Caesar Rodney, September 24, 1777, *PGW* (11), 315. Henry Knox repeated the feign claim the same day. See Henry Knox to his wife, September 24, 1777, *Life of Henry Knox*, 50.

21. Knox diary, September 22, 1777, Knox Family Papers; GW to JH, September 23, 1777, *PGW* (11), 301.

22. Quote in McGuire, *Philadelphia Campaign* (2), 44.

23. Friedrich Kapp, *The Life of John Kalb: Major-general in the Revolutionary Army* (Bedford, MA: Applewood Book, 1884), 117-18, 123, 127.

24. Samuel Shaw to his father, September 30, 1777, Quincy, ed., *The Journals of Major General Samuel Shaw*, 39; Undated letter to editor, [Purdie's] *Virginia Gazette*, October 17, 1777.

CHAPTER NINE: "THIS HAPPY OPPORTUNITY"

1. Charles Willson Peale diary, September 26-27, 1777, in Lillian B. Miller, ed., *The Selected Papers of Charles Willson Peale and his Family*, Volume 1 (New Haven, CT: Yale University Press, 1983), 245-46.

2. "Life Portraits of George Washington," *George Washington's Mount Vernon*, https://www.mountvernon.org/george-washington/artwork/life-portraits-of-george-washington/.

3. Charles Willson Peale diary, June 26, 1777, in Miller, *Selected Papers of Charles Willson Peale*, Vol. 1, 236-237. This sketch is reproduced on page 237.

4. GW to Thomas Nelson, September 27, 1777, *PGW* (11), 332.

5. Charles Coleman Sellers, a mid-Twentieth Century curator at Dickinson College, produced an essay on the 1776 and 1777 works reflecting an impressive body of detective work to isolate the exact date of the sketch based on what Peale told his son about the sitting being interrupted when Washington first learned of the strong American effort near Saratoga. See Sellers, "Portraits and Miniatures by Charles Willson Peale," in *Transactions of the American Philosophical Society*, Volume 42 (1), 1952, 221-223. Mistakenly believing that Washington first learned the news on September 28, Sellers appears to misplace the true sketch date by one day. Washington first learned of the battle on Saturday evening, September 27, 1777. See GW to Thomas Nelson, September 27, 1777, *PGW* (11), 333.

6. "General Washington from Life, 1777," Portraits in Revolution, https://www.americanrevolution.com/gallery/american_artists/charles_willson_peale/general_washington_sketch_1777. The sketch is reproduced as the frontispiece of this volume.

7. Mark Maloy, "The Battle of Freeman's Farm, September 19, 1777," *American Battlefield Trust*, https://www.battlefields.org/learn/articles/battle-freemans-farm-september-19-1777.

8. GW to Thomas Nelson, September 27, 1777, *PGW* (11), 333; General orders, September 28, 1777, *PGW* (11), 337.
9. Theodore W. Bean, *History of Montgomery County, Pennsylvania* (Philadelphia: Everts & Peck, 1884), 1022-23. Beane's traditional identification of Keeley's house as headquarters is supported by the recollection of Maria Grimly Keeley, who knew the dwelling as a teenaged neighbor to Keeley before marrying into his family. See Alan Keyser, "The Perkiomen and Skippack Township Encampment of the Revolutionary War," goschenhoppen.org/ak-maria-keely/. The Pennypacker house on the east side of the creek has often been identified as Washington's headquarters in campaign histories because that was the name widely used for the encampment on both sides of the creek, but the payment on the day of departure for use of the house "at Paulins mill for Sundries used at the house—& extra trouble" argues against Pennypacker's residence as headquarters. See *PGW* (11), 328 (no. 1, top of page). Pawling's mill stood on the west side of the creek, directly across from Pennypacker's mill.
10. Council of War, September 28, 1777, *PGW* (11), 338-39.
11. Ibid.; Gary Ecelbarger and Michael C. Harris, "The Numerical Strength of George Washington's Army During the 1777 Philadelphia Campaign," *JAR Annual Volume 2022* (Yardley, PA: Westholme Publishing, 2022), 106-10.
12. Council of War, September 28, 1777, *PGW* (11), 338.
13. Ibid., 339.
14. William Williams to Jonathan Trumball, Sr., October 2, 1777, *LDC* (8), 44.
15. GW to JH, September 29, 1777, *PGW* (11), 346-47; William Williams to Jonathan Trumbull, Sr., October 2, 1777, JH to Dorothy Hancock, October 1, 1777, and Nathaniel Folsom to Meshech Weare, October 2, 1777, *LDC* (8), 39, 42, 44.
16. JH to GW, September 30, 1777, *PGW* (11), 349-50.
17. Pickering journal, October 2, 1777, *Life of Timothy Pickering* (1), 166.
18. Thomas J. McGuire, *The Philadelphia Campaign* (2), 46-47. Thomas Livezy was so bothered by how swiftly the story of his deception had spread from the American encampment through the environs of Philadelphia that four weeks later, in an attempt to spin the incident, he wrote to Reed and Cadwalader, claiming that although he first believed they were "English Light horsemen" he realized mid-conversation who they really were. "I then Wanted to Discover to you that I knew you," wrote Livezy, "but in my Surprise did not know how to do it." See Thomas Livezy to Joseph Reed and John Cadwalader, October 29, 1777, John Cadwalader Papers, Historical Society of Pennsylvania, Philadelphia.
19. Ecelbarger and Harris, "The Numerical Strength of George Washington's Army During the 1777 Philadelphia Campaign," 107-108.
20. Montresor journal, September 29, 1777, "Montresor Journals," 460.
21. GW to Patrick Henry, October 3, 1777, *PGW* (11), 382-83.
22. General Orders, October 3, 1777, *PGW* (11), 372-74.
23. GW to JH, October 5 & October 7, 1777, *PGW* (11), 393, 417; "General Orders for Attacking Germantown," October 3, 1777, *PGW* (11), 375-76.
24. Brecht, ed., *The Genealogical Record of the Schwenkfelder Families*, 1441.
25. Ibid., 242-61; "General Orders for Attacking Germantown," *PGW* (11), 375-80.
26. Harris, *Germantown*, 222-225, 237-241, 440-441.
27. Ibid., 242.
28. "Papers of Elias Dayton," *Proceedings of the New Jersey Historical Society*, Volume 10 (Newark, NJ, 1864), "Notes on the Battle of Germantown, with Preceding and Subsequent

Movements," 183-187 (quote on page 185).
29. JS to Meshech Weare, October 25, 1777, *LPJS* (1), 543-44.
30. Ibid., 547.
31. Timothy Pickering [to Jared Sparks], August 23, 1826, [Philadelphia] *Register of Pennsylvania*, January 26, 1828.
32. Dayton, "Notes on the Battle of Germantown," 185; Anthony Wayne to his wife, October 6, 1777, in Charles J. Stille, *Major-General Anthony Wayne and the Pennsylvania Line in the Continental Army* (Philadelphia, PA: J. P. Lippincott Company, 1893), 95-97 (quote on page 96).
33. Harris, *Germantown*, 240, 299, 322.
34. Ibid., 323-25.
35. Pickering to Governor James Sullivan, April 22, 1808, *Interesting Correspondence*, 28; Henry Lee, *Memoirs of the War in the Southern Department*, Lee Family Digital Archive, https://leefamilyarchive.org/papers/books/south/05.html (page 3); Pickering [to Jared Sparks], August 23, 1826, [Philadelphia] *Register of Pennsylvania*, January 26, 1828. Also see *North American Review* Vol. 23 (1826), 427-28, for the original publication of this letter.
36. Charles Pinckney, "The Battles of Brandywine and Germantown," *The Historical Magazine*, Vol. 10 (Morrisania, NY: Henry B. Dawson, 1866), 202-204. Pinckney's 1820 account states that Washington informed him that he "ordered Col. Ogden to remain with his Regiment to watch the house, & to fall on the soldiers in it, if they should attempt to quit it."
37. Pickering, *Life of Timothy Pickering* (1), 173.
38. Gregory D. Massey, *John Laurens and the American Revolution* (Columbia, SC: University of South Carolina Press, 2015), 76-77.
39. Washington Irving, *Life of Washington*, Volume 3 (New York, NY: G. P. Putnam's Sons, 1881), 267.
40. Harris, *Germantown*, 341-43.
41. JS to Meshech Weare, October 25, 1777, *LPJS* (1), 546-47.
42. Harris, *Germantown*, 360-87. For the derogatory reference to "major" Washington, see André Journal, September 30, October 5, and October 6, 1777.
43. "General Greene's Orders," October 7, 1777, *PNG* (2), 171.
44. Irving, *Life of Washington* (3), 305.
45. Major Henry Miller to his family, n.d., in Henry Miller Watts, "Memoir of Henry Miller," *PMHB* (12) (1888), 426-27 [add 7/4/78 on 428]; Anonymous participant to George Clinton, October 5, 1777, in *Public Papers of George Clinton*, volume 2 (New York, NY: Wynkoop Hallenbeck Crawford Co., 1900), 367-73 (quotes on page 372).
46. First two quotes reproduced in Wayne Bodle, *The Valley Forge Winter: Civilians and Soldiers in War* (University Park, PA: Penn State University Press, 2002), 41; Third Quote: Anthony Wayne to family member, October 6, 1777, Samuel Hazard, ed., *The Register of Pennsylvania*, Vol. 3 (June 13, 1829), 375.
47. Anonymous letter excerpt, October 6, 1777, William S. Baker, *Itinerary of George Washington from June 15, 1775 to December 23, 1783* (Philadelphia, PA: J. B. Lippincott Co., 1892), 96; William Heth to Colonel John Lamb, October 12, 1777, Isaac Q. Leake, *Memoir of the Life and Times of General John Lamb* (Albany, NY: Joel Munsell, 1850), 183-84; Richard Parker Jr. to Richard Henry Lee, October 18, 1777, "Selections and Excerpts from the Lee Papers," *The Southern Literary Messenger*, Vol. 27 (November 1858), 327; anonymous letter, October 5, 1777, [Baltimore] *Maryland Gazette*, October 23, 1777.
48. General Orders, October 5, 1777, *PGW* (11), 380-91. GW to JH, October 5, 1777,

PGW (11), 394.

49. GW to JH, October 5, 1777, GW to Benjamin Harrison, October 5, 1777, GW to JH, October 7, 1777, and GW to Israel Putnam, October 8, 1777, *PGW* (11), 393-94, 401-402, 416-419, 446-47.

50. Irving, *Life of Washington* (3), 307; "Olivia" to The President of the State, [Philadelphia] *Pennsylvania Packet*, June 3, 1779.

51. "Wednesday, October 8, 1777," *JCC* (9), 785.

52. GW to William Howe, October 6, 1777 (two letters), *PGW* (11), 409-410. GW to William Howe, October 6, 1777 (two letters), *PGW* (11), 409-410.

53. William Howe to George Germain, October 10, 1777, *Parliamentary Register*, Vol. 10, 424-433.

54. William Howe to George Germain, October 22, 1777, *Parliamentary Register*, Vol. 10, 436-438.

CHAPTER TEN: "WE HAVE A FORCE SUFFICIENT, BY THE FAVOR OF HEAVEN TO CRUSH OUR FOES"

1. Rush revealed in his memoirs that during the battle he "had nearly fallen in the hands of the enemy by my delay in helping out the wounded," only to return a few days later "with a flag from Gen'l. Washington to dress the wounded belonging to the American army . . ." see Benjamin Rush, *A Memorial Containing Travels Through Life or Sundry Incidents in the Life of Dr. Benjamin Rush* (Philadelphia, PA: Louis Alexander Biddle, 1905), 100.

2. "Historical Notes of Dr. Benjamin Rush, 1777," *PMHB*, Vol. 27 (1903), 147.

3. Benjamin Rush diary, October 10, 1777, "Historical Notes of Dr. Benjamin Rush, 1777," *PMHB*, Vol. 27 (1903), 147. Rush's lamentation was edited from the 1905 publication of his memoirs by a descendant but appears in a more complete autobiography. See Benjamin Rush, *The Autobiography of Benjamin Rush, His "Travels Through Life"* (Princeton, NJ: University Press at Princeton, 1948), n.p.

4. Damby, "Camp Towamensing," 116; "Monuments," *Buffalo Courier*, March 19, 1884; Brian Hagey, "The Continental Army at 'Headquarters Towamensing' October 8-16, 1777," https://mhep.org/wp-content/uploads/2020/07/Hagey-The-Continental-Army-at-Towamencin.pdf.

5. [Findings of the Court of Inquiry], October 12, 1777, *LPJS* (1), 531-32.

6. "London," London *Public Advertiser*, December 5, 1777.

7. General Orders, October 15, 1777, *PGW* (11), 512-513.

8. Israel Putnam to GW, October 16, 1777, *PGW* (11), 531-32; GW to John Augustine Washington, October 18, 1777, *PGW* (11), 551-52; GW to Christopher Greene, October 18, 1777, *PGW* (11), 543; General Orders, October 18, 1777, *PGW* (11), 541. As it turned out, the news was accurate by the time Washington received it, but premature for the date on which it claimed the actual surrender terms were finalized.

9. GW to John Hazelwood, November 2, 1777, *PGW* (12), 97. The heading of Washington's November 2 letter ("Whitpin–Morris's") confirms Pickering's October 20 journal entry in *Life of Timothy Pickering* (1), 180.

10. Wade P. Catts, Robert Selig, Elisabeth LaVigne, et al., *"It is Painful for Me to Lose So Many Good People:" Report of an Archeological Survey at Red Bank Battlefield Park (Fort Mercer), National Park, Gloucester County, New Jersey* (West Chester, PA: Commonwealth Heritage Group, Inc., 2017), 30-33.

11. Credit to Michael Harris for providing the October 13 rank and file return. The conversion factor to adjust from rank and file only to also include officers is 1.3 (derived by the

author from a study of 1777-1778 of seven American returns).

12. Catts, Selig, LaVigne, et al., *Report of an Archeological Survey at Red Bank Battlefield Park*, 30-33.

13. Paul Zantzinger to John Clark, October 25, 1777, "Memoir of Major John Clark, of York County, Pennsylvania," *PMHB*, Vol. 20 (1896), 83-84.

14. Clement Biddle to "his lady," October 24, 1777, *Norwich* [Conn.] *Packet,* November 10, 1777.

15. GW to JH, October 24, 1777, *PGW* (11), 596; Joseph Reed to GW, October 24, 1777, *PGW* (11), 599; General Orders, October 25, 1777, *PGW* (11), 604-605.

16. GW to Horatio Gates, October 30, 1777, *PGW* (12), 59-60

17. Council of War, October 29, 1777, *PGW* (12), 46-49.

18. GW to AH, October 30, 1777, *PGW* (12), 60-62.

19. AH to GW, November 2, 1777, and [November 3], 1777; Hamilton to Horatio Gates, November 5, 1777, *Private Correspondences of Alexander Hamilton*, 103-109.

20. AH to GW, [November 3], 1777, *Private Correspondences of Alexander Hamilton*, 106-109.

21. Henry Laurens to John Laurens, October 16, 1777, in "Correspondence Between Hon. Henry Laurens and His Son, John, 1777-1780," *South Carolina Historical and Genealogical Magazine*, Vol. VI (January 1905), 6-7.

22. Benjamin Rush to John Adams, October 21, 1777, *Founders Online,* National Archives, last modified June 29, 2017, http://founders.archives.gov/documents/Adams/06-05-02-0187. [Original source: *The Adams Papers*, Papers of John Adams, vol. 5, *August 1776–March 1778*, ed. Robert J. Taylor. Cambridge, MA: Harvard University Press, 2006, 316–319.]

23. John Adams to Abigail Adams, 26 October 1777, *Founders Online,* National Archives, last modified June 29, 2017, http://founders.archives.gov/documents/Adams/04-02-02-0289. [Original source: *The Adams Papers*, Adams Family Correspondence, vol. 2, *June 1776 –March 1778*, ed. L. H. Butterfield. Cambridge, MA: Harvard University Press, 1963, pp. 360–361.]

24. Benjamin Rush to John Adams, October 21, 1777, https://founders.archives.gov/ documents/Adams/06-05-02-0187.

25. JS to John Adams, November 10, 1777, *LPJS*, (1), 577; Thomas Conway to Board of War, September 25, 1777, https://www.fold3.com/image/4345480.

26. NG to Gouverneur Morris, June 1, 1778, *PNG* (2), 423.

27. GW to Richard Henry Lee, October 16, 1777, *PGW* (11), 529-30.

28. Alexander Graydon, *Memoirs of a Life, Chiefly Passed in Pennsylvania, within the Last Sixty Years* (Harrisburg, PA: John Wyeth, printer, 1811), 279.

29. JL to HL, January 3, 1778, *PHL* (12), 245-46. The date of this letter illustrates that Washington was discussing Cadwalader's accusations two months after the Battle of Germantown, evidence that he never dismissed them.

30. Richard Henry Lee to GW, October 20, 1777, *PGW* (11), 562-63. Smith's death date revealed in *Life of Timothy Pickering* (1), 173.

31. GW to Richard Henry Lee, October 28, 1777, *PGW* (12), 40-42; Timothy Pickering to his wife, December 13, 1777, *Life of Timothy Pickering* (1), 191-92.

32. Pickering quote in Newton, *Alexander Hamilton: The Formative Years*, 228.

CHAPTER ELEVEN: "ONE HEAP OF RUIN"

1. "Washington's Headquarters. Historic Buildings at One Time or Another Occupied by the Revolutionary Leader," *New York Herald*, February 18, 1894; "Emlen Family Geneal-

ogy," https://www.emlen.us.

2. John Laurens to Henry Laurens, November 5, 1777, *Army Correspondence*, 69.

3. GW to Henry Laurens, November 1-3, 1777, *PGW* (12), 78-84. The promotion to Henry Laurens as president on November 1, 1777, can be found in *JCC* (9), 854.

4. Major General Stirling to GW, November 3, 1777, *PGW* (12), 110-11 (quote found in footnote #4). The source of Stirling's injury in James Wilkinson, *Memoirs of my Own Time*, Volume 1 (Philadelphia, PA: Printed by Abraham Small, 1816), 331.

5. Stirling to GW, November 3, 1777, *PGW* (12), 110-11.

6. Wilkinson, *Memoirs of My Own Times*, 331; Mark Edward Lender, *Cabal!: The Plot Against General Washington* (Yardley, PA: Westholme Publishing, 2019), 85-87.

7. "To John Adams from Benjamin Rush, 21 October 1777," *Founders Online*, National Archives, https://founders.archives.gov/documents/Adams/06-05-02-0187. [Original source: *The Adams Papers*, Papers of John Adams, vol. 5, *August 1776–March 1778*, ed. Robert J. Taylor. Cambridge, MA: Harvard University Press, 2006, 316–319.]

8. David Duncan Wallace, *The Life of Henry Laurens With a Sketch of the Life of Lieutenant-Colonel John Laurens* (New York, NY: G. P. Putnam's Sons, 1915), 271-72.

9. Wilkinson, *Memoirs of My Own Times*, 330-331.

10. GW to Thomas Conway, November [5], 1777, *PGW* (12), 129-30; GW to Horatio Gates, January 4, 1778, *PGW* (13), 138-39.

11. Thomas Conway to GW, November 5, 1777, *PGW* (12), 130-31.

12. JL to HL, January 3, 1778, *PHL* (12), 245.

13. Clement Biddle to "his lady," October 24, 1777, *Norwich* [Conn.] *Packet*, November 10, 1777.

14. John Laurens to Henry Laurens, November 5, 1777, *Army Correspondence*, 62-63. Laurens does not mention the spyglass, but it would have been a necessary tool for this mission. Washington owned one (See https://www.rockislandauction.com/detail/66/3084/historic-dolland-brass-spyglass-inscribed-g-washington-mt-ve) and had been painted by John Trumbull in 1792 holding this field telescope.

15. John Laurens to Henry Laurens, November 5, 1777, *Army Correspondence*, 63. The roof of Cliveden today is not the same as it was in 1777. A 1763 drawing of the house distinctly shows the roof walk likely available to Washington and Laurens. See Kim Keister, "History Lesson," *Historic Preservation* (November-December 1993), 52-110.

16. General Orders, November 7, 1777, *PGW* (12), 149.

17. GW to Richard Henry Lee, October 16, 1777, *PGW* (11), 530. GW to John Augustine Washington, October 18, 1777, *PGW* (11), 551-53; Philemon Dickinson to GW, November 6, 1777, *PGW* (12), 140.

18. GW to Thomas Nelson, November 8, 1777, *PGW* (12), 170-71; Council of War, November 8, 1777, *PGW* (12), 163.

19. James Varnum to GW, November 11, 1777, *PGW* (12), 217.

20. GW to General Varnum, November 12, 1777, *PGW*, (12), 232.

21. NG to [Susanna Livingston], November 11, 1777, *PNG* (2), 195.

22. NG to GW, November 14, 1777, *PGW* (12). Greene's report must have assumed that the Middle Ferry bridge spanned the river at the time he viewed it, rather than having been pulled into the Philadelphia side of the river by British forces.

23. Ibid.

24. Anthony Wayne to Richard Peters, November 18, 1777, in Charles J. Stille, *Major-General Anthony Wayne and the Pennsylvania Line in the Continental Army* (Philadelphia, PA: J. B. Lippincott Company, 1893), 105-106.

25. Ibid.
26. Ibid.
27. Ibid.
28. Charles Scott to "Dear Frankey," November 15, 1777, John Reed Collection, Valley Forge National Historic Park, King of Prussia, PA.
29. Samuel Smith to GW, November 15, 1777, *PGW* (12), 271.
30. Anthony Wayne to William Peters, November 18, 1777, *Major-General Anthony Wayne and the Pennsylvania Line,* 105-106.
31. Thomas Conway to GW, November 16, 1777, *PGW* (12), 276-77.
32. The four letters interchanged between Conway and headquarters on November 16 are chronologically found in *PGW* (12), 276-78.
33. General Orders, November 20, 1777, *PGW* (12), 327-28.
34. Henry Laurens to GW, November 7, 1777, *PGW* (12), 155-56.
35. Jonathan Dickinson Sergeant to James Lovell, November 20, 1777, *LDC* (8), 296.
36. NG to George Washington, November 21, 1777, *PGW* (12), 340.
37. Lender, *Cabal!*, 30-31. Credit to Dr. Lender for uncovering this letter, sought for decades, and identifying Mifflin as its author, when snippets of it suggested that James Lovell had written it.
38. Excerpt from November 24, 1777, proceedings, *JCC* (9), 959.

CHAPTER TWELVE: "IT IS IN OUR POWER TO PRODUCE A CONVICTION TO THE WORLD"

1. General Orders, November 22, 1777, *PGW* (12), 344.
2. GW to NG [two letters], November 22, 1777, *PNG* (2), 205-206.
3. NG to Catharine Greene, November [20], 1777, *PNG* (2), 200; "Return of the detachment of the Army, commanded by Major General Greene," November 24, 1777, M246, RG 93, NA (available online at https://www.fold3.com/image/9687328). Extremely misleading in these calculations is a preferred tendency among Continental officers to count only infantry privates. Based on the same return, Greene also had 1,023 healthy and available Continental infantry field and staff officers, sergeants, fife players, and drummers at his immediate disposal, as well as several hundred privates available and "on command" in temporary but readily available detachments. Artillery and dragoon detachments, as well as militia and headquarters officers and other military personnel, swelled Greene's ranks by an additional 300-to-500 men. This meant that on November 24, 1777, Greene's detachment consisted of 7,000 soldiers. Likewise, the 8,200 infantry privates calculated from the Whitemarsh force was barely half of the total soldiery present in that camp.
4. E. W. Spangler, "Memoir of Major John Clark of York County, Pennsylvania," *PMHB* (20), 1896, 77-78; Clark to GW, October 6, 1777, *PGW* (11), 405-407 (two dispatches).
5. Spangler, "Memoir of Major John Clark," 78; John Clark to GW, November 22, 1777 (10:00 A.M. and 6:00 P.M.), *PGW* (12), 345-49.
6. "Return of the detachment of the Army, commanded by Major General Greene," November 24, 1777, M246, RG 93, NA (available online at https://www.fold3.com/image/9687328).
7. "Brigadier General John Cadwalader's Plan for Attacking Philadelphia," [c. 24 November 1777] *PGW* (12), 371-73.
8. GW to Greene, November 25, 1777, *PGW* (12), 389.
9. "General Greene's Orders," November 24 and 25, 1777, *PNG* (2), 206, 212; Greene to

GW, November 26, 1777, *PNG* (2), 218-19.

10. GW to John Augustine Washington, November 26, 1777, *PGW* (12), 426.

11. JS to GW, November 25, 1777, *PGW* (12), 398-402.

12. Anthony Wayne to GW, November 25, 1777, *PGW* (12), 403.

13. All these November 25 responses are found in *PGW* (12), 393-96.

14. Ecelbarger and Harris, "The Numerical Strength of George Washington's Army During the 1777 Philadelphia Campaign," 110-111.

15. GW to Henry Laurens, November 1, 1777, PGW (12), 81.

16. NG to GW, November 26, 1777, *PGW* (12), 408-11.

17. GW to Henry Laurens, November 26-27, 1777, PGW (12), 420-21; General Orders, December 4, 1777, *PGW* (12), 534.

18. "Order of Battle," December 4-5, 1777, *PGW* (12), 535.

19. Claude-Noël-François Romand de Lisle to "My dear Count," November 28, 1777, "Notes and Queries," *PMHB* (35), 1911, 365-68 (excerpt on page 367).

20. John Cadwalader to Joseph Reed, November 30, 1777, Joseph Reed Papers, New York Historical Society, New York; Ichabod Burnett to unknown addressee, November 30, 1777, Etting Collection, Historical Society of Pennsylvania; Ebenezer David to Nicholas Brown, November 24, 1777, in Jeannette D. Black and William G. Roelker, eds., *A Rhode Island Chaplain in the Revolution: Letters of Ebenezer David to Nicholas Brown, 1775-1778* (Providence, RI: The Rhode Island Society of the Cincinnati, 1949), 69.

CHAPTER THIRTEEN: "THEY ARE DETERMINED TO ATTACK YOU WHERE YOU NOW ARE"

1. Ecelbarger and Harris, "The Numerical Strength of George Washington's Army During the 1777 Philadelphia Campaign," 110-112; Ricardo A. Herrera, *Feeding Washington's Army: Surviving the Valley Forge Winter of 1778* (Chapel Hill, NC: University of North Carolina Press, 2022), 34.

2. GW to Joseph Reed, December 2, 1777, *PGW* (12), 500. "Circular to the General Officers of the Continental Army," December 3, 1777, *PGW* (12), 506; Committee to Henry Laurens, December 6, 1777, *LDC* (8), 380-81; Henry Laurens to GW, December 1, 1777, *PGW* (12), 469-70.

3. "Committee at Headquarters to George Washington," December 10, 1777, *LDC* (8), 399-400.

4. Anthony Wayne to GW, December 4, 1777, *PGW* (12), 558.

5. NG to GW, December 3, 1777, *PGW* (12), 516-22; JS to GW, December 4, 1777, 555-58; Joseph Reed to GW, December 4, 1777, *PGW* (12), 548-52. For Washington's preference to personally hear (and see) Reed's response rather than read it, see GW to Joseph Reed, December 2, 1777, *PGW* (12), 500.

6. John Cadwalader to GW, December 3, 1777, *PGW* (12), 507-10.

7. Order of Battle (with diagram), December 4, 1777, *PGW* (12), 534-35; William Dewees to GW, December 4, 1777, *PGW* (12), 538.

8. John W. Jackson, *Whitemarsh 1777: Impregnable Stronghold* (Fort Washington, PA: Historical Society of Fort Washington, 1984), 10-13.

9. Ibid., 27-28 (region map showing Edge Hill spans between these two pages.)

10. Benjamin Tallmadge, *Memoir of Colonel Benjamín Tallmadge* (New York, NY: Thomas Holman, Book and Job Printer, 1858), 35.

11. "Williamsburg, December 19," [Purdie's] *Virginia Gazette*, December 19, 1777.
12. John Armstrong to Thomas Wharton, December 7-9, 1777, reproduced in *PGW* (12), 571-72 (footnote number 1).
13. Münchhausen journal, December 5, 1777, *At General Howe's Side*, 45; General Orders, December 6, 1777, *PGW* (12), 564.
14. Ibid.; Joseph Reed to Thomas Wharton, December 10, 1777, in Reed, *Life and Correspondence of Joseph Reed*, 350. John André, *Major André's Journal: Operations of the British Under Lieutenant Generals Sir William Howe and Sir Henry Clinton. June 1777 to November 1778* (Tarrytown, NY: William Abbatt, 1930), 68.
15. Israel Angell diary, December 6, 1777, in Joseph Lee Boyle, ed., "The Israel Angell Diary, 1 October 1777–28 February 1778," *Rhode Island History* (58):4), 119; Münchhausen journal, December 7, 1777, *At General Howe's Side*, 45; "Extract of a letter from an officer in camp," December 10, 1777, Enoch Edwards to GW, December 7, 1777, *PGW* (12), 568.
16. Isaac Sherman to GW, March 11, 1778, *PGW* (14), 147-50. André, *Journal*, 68-69.
17. James Graham, *The Life of Daniel Morgan of the Virginia Line of the Army of the United States, With Portions of His Correspondence* (New York, NY, 1856), 182-85.
18. Upham, *Life of Timothy Pickering* (2), 85.
19. "Extract of a letter from an officer at camp, dated December 10," *Virginia Gazette*, December 26, 1777; Tallmadge, *Memoir*, 36.
20. Reed, *Life and Correspondence of Joseph Reed* (1), 352.
21. Washington did consult with his generals during the multi-day siege of Yorktown, which is distinguished from a single-day battle.
22. "Morning Post," [London] *Morning Post and Daily Advertiser*, January 19, 1778; Münchhausen journal, December 7, 1777, *At Howe's Side*, 45.
23. "Extract of a Letter received by a Gentleman in the City from his Nephew at Philadelphia," [London] *Public Advertiser*, January 29, 1778.
24. "Extract of a letter from an officer at camp, dated December 10," *Virginia Gazette*, December 26, 1777; Jackson, *Whitemarsh*, 46-47.
25. Jackson, *Whitemarsh 1777*, 47; Ecelbarger and Harris, "The Numerical Strength of George Washington's Army During the 1777 Philadelphia Campaign," 113.
26. Quote from "London, February 10," [London] *St. James Chronicle*, February 7, 1778.
27. Münchhausen journal, December 8-11, 1777, *At Howe's Side*, 45-46; André Diary, December 10-11, 1777.
28. James Lovell to Samuel Adams, December 20, 1777, *LDC* (8), 451.
29. Cornelius Hartnett to Thomas Burke, December 8, 1777, University of North Carolina at Chapel Hill, https://docsouth.unc.edu/csr/index.php/document/csr11-0616.
30. "Committee at Headquarters to George Washington," December 10, 1777, *LDC* (8), 399-400.
31. Washington was the victor at Harlem Heights (September 16, 1776), Trenton (December 26, 1776), Assunpink Creek (January 2, 1777), Princeton (January 3, 1777), and Whitemarsh (December 5-8, 1777). He was the victim at Long Island (August 27, 1776), White Plains (October 3, 1776), Brandywine (September 11, 1777), White Horse Tavern (September 16, 1777), and Germantown (October 4, 1777).
32. Diary entry reproduced in Jackson, *Whitemarsh 1777*, 51.
33. "London," London *Public Advertiser*, December 2, 1777.
34. Ibid.; "London," London *Public Advertiser*, December 5, 1777.

35. "London," *London Evening Post*, December 2, 1777

36. Noailles to Vergennes, October 7, 1777, quote reproduced in Orville T. Murphy, "The Battle of Germantown and the Franco-American Alliance of 1778," *PMHB* Vol. 82 (January 1958), 55-64 (quote on page 55).

37. Orville T. Murphy, *Charles Gravier Comte de Vergennes: French Diplomacy in the Age of Revolution, 1719-1787* (Albany, NY: State University of New York Press, 1982), 245-248.

38. Ibid., 249.

39. Ibid., 249-250.

Bibliography

MANUSCRIPTS

Friends Historical Library, Swarthmore College, Swarthmore, Pennsylvania
Records of the Wilmington Monthly Meeting of Friend Committee to Collect and Keep a Record of All Sufferings, 1777-1780.
Gilder Lehrman Institute of American History, New York
Henry Knox Papers
Historical Society of Pennsylvania. Philadelphia
Anthony Wayne Collection
Ettinger Collection
Jacob Broom Map
John Cadwalader Collection
John H. Hawkins Journal
Library of Congress, Manuscript Division, Washington, D.C.
George Washington Papers
Peter Force Collection
Maryland State Archives, Annapolis
Archives of Maryland Biographical Series
Massachusetts Historical Society, Boston
Adams Family Papers: An Electronic Archive. Massachusetts Historical Society. http://www.masshist.org/digitaladams/.
Timothy Pickering Papers
National Archives, Washington D.C.
General du Coudray to Samuel Chase, September 15, 1777, https://www.fold3.com/image/462820?terms=coudray,1777,chase
Return of the detachment of the Army, commanded by Major General Greene, November 24, 1777, M246, RG 93, NA (available online at https://www.fold3.com/image/9687328).

Thomas Conway to Board of War, September 25, 1777, https://www.fold3.com/image/4345480.
New-York Historical Society, New York
Joseph Reed Papers
Princeton University Library, Princeton, New Jersey
Joseph Reed Letter
University of North Carolina at Chapel Hill
Cornelius Hartnett to Thomas Burke, December 8, 1777, https://docsouth.unc.edu/csr/index.php/document/csr11-0616.
Valley Forge National Historic Park, King of Prussia, Pennsylvania
Joseph Boyle Collection
John Reed Collection
Virginia State Library, Richmond
Commission to George Washington, https://edu.lva.virginia.gov/oc/stc/entries/commission-to-george-washington-as-commander-in-chief-june-19-1775.

PUBLISHED PRIMARY SOURCES

"Historical Notes of Dr. Benjamin Rush, 1777," *Pennsylvania Magazine of History and Biography*, Volume 27, no. 2 (1903), 129-150.

"Journal of Capt. William Beatty, 1776-1781," *Maryland Historical Magazine* 3, no. 2 (1908), 104-119.

"Memoir of Major John Clark, of York County, Pennsylvania," *Pennsylvania Magazine of History and Biography* Vol. 20 (1896), 83-84.

"Notes and Queries," *Pennsylvania Magazine of History and Biography* (35), 1911, 365-68.

"Papers of Elias Dayton," *Proceedings of the New Jersey Historical Society*, Volume 10 (Newark, N.J., 1864), "Notes on the Battle of Germantown, with Preceding and Subsequent Movements," 183-187.

"Selections and Excerpts from the Lee Papers," *The Southern Literary Messenger* Volume 27, no. 5 (November 1858), 324-333.

"Treason in Delaware County," *Delaware Archives: Revolutionary War in Three Volumes*. Wilmington, DE: Chas. L. Story Company Press, 1919.

Abbot, W. W., ed. *The Papers of George Washington*. Charlottesville: University Press of Virginia, 1987–.

Anderson, Enoch. *Personal Recollections of Captain Enoch Anderson, an officer of the Delaware regiments in the revolutionary war*. Wilmington: Historical Society of Delaware, 1896.

André, John. *Major Andre's Journal: Operations of the British Under Lieutenant Generals Sir William Howe and Sir Henry Clinton. June 1777 to November 1778. Recorded by Major John André, Adjutant General*. Tarrytown, NY; William Abbatt, 1930.

Anthony Wayne to family member, October 6, 1777, Samuel Hazard, ed., *The Register of Pennsylvania* Vol. 3 (June 13, 1829), 375.

Baker, William S. *Itinerary of George Washington from June 15, 1775, to December 23, 1783*. Philadelphia, PA: J. B. Lippincott Co., 1892.

Bentalou, Paul. *A Reply to Judge Johnson's Remarks to an Article in the North American Review Relating to Count Pulaski*. Baltimore, MD: J. D. Tot, 1825.

Black, Jeanette D. and Roelker, William G., eds. *A Rhode Island Chaplain in the Revolution: Letters of Ebenezer David to Nicholas Brown, 1775-1778*. Providence, RI: The Rhode Island Society of the Cincinnati, 1949.

Bland, Martha to Frances Bland Randolph, May 12, 1777, *N.J. Hist. Soc. Proceedings* n.s., 51 [1933], 250–53.

Boyle, Joseph Lee, ed. "The Israel Angell Diary, 1 October 1777 — 28 February 1778," *Rhode Island History*. Volume 58, no. 4 (November 2000).

Burnett, Edmund C., ed. *Letters of Members of the Continental Congress*. Vols. 2-3. Washington, D.C.: Carnegie Institute of Washington, 1923-1926.

Cecere, Michael. *They Behaved Like Soldiers: Captain John Chilton and the Third Virginia Regiment, 1775-1778*. Westminster, MD: Heritage Books, 2007.

Chesnutt, David R. and Taylor, C. James., eds. *The Papers of Henry Laurens*. 16 vols. Columbia, SC: University of South Carolina Press, 1968–2002.

Clement Biddle to "his lady," October 24, 1777, *Norwich* [Conn.] *Packet*, November 10, 1777.

Clement Biddle to Dear General, September 16, 1777, *Boston Gazette*, September 29, 1777; [Portsmouth, NH] *Freeman's Journal*, October 4, 1777; *Providence Gazette*, October 4, 1777.

Dexter, Franklin, ed. *The Literary Diary of Ezra Stiles, D.D., LL.D.* 2 vols. New York, NY: Charles Scribner's Sons, 1901.

Drake, Francis S. *Life and Correspondence of Henry Knox, Major-General in the American Revolutionary Army*. Boston: Samuel G. Drake, 1873.

Ewing, Thomas. *George Ewing, Gentleman, a Soldier of Valley Forge*. Yonkers, NY: Privately Printed, 1928.

Ford, Worthington, ed. *Journals of the Continental Congress, 1774–1789*. 34 volumes. Washington, DC: U.S. Government Printing Office, 1904–1937.

Graydon, Alexander. *Memoirs of a Life, Chiefly Passed in Pennsylvania, within the Last Sixty Years*. Harrisburg, PA: John Wyeth, printer, 1811.

Graydon, Alexander. *Memoirs of His Own Time with Reminiscences of the Men and Events of the Revolution*. Philadelphia, PA: Lindsay & Blakiston, 1846.

Hammond, Otis G., ed. *Letters and Papers of Major-General John Sullivan, Continental Army*. 3 volumes. Edited by Otis. G. Hammond. Concord, NH: New Hampshire Historical Society, 1930.

Hazard, Samuel, ed. *Pennsylvania Archives*. 12 vols. Philadelphia, PA: Joseph Severns & Co., 1852-1856.

Henkels, Stan. V. *Revolutionary Manuscripts and Portraits*. Philadelphia, PA: Thos. Birch's Sons, Auctioneers, 1892.

House of Commons. *Parliamentary Register*. 17 volumes. London: Re-printed for John Stockdale, 1802-1803.

Idzerda, Stanley J., ed. *Lafayette in the Age of the American Revolution*, 5 vols. Ithaca, NY: Cornell University Press, 1977-1983.

Kipping, Ernst and Smith, Samuel Stelle, eds. *At General Howe's Side 1776-1778: The diary of William Howe's aide de camp, Captain Friedrich von Muenchhausen*. Monmouth Beach, NJ: Philip Freneau Press, 1974.

Kitman, Marvin. *George Washington's Expense Account*. New York: Grove Press, 1970.

Lafayette, Marquis de. *Memoirs Correspondence and Manuscripts of General Lafayette, Published by His Family*. Volume 1. New York, NY: Craighead and Allen, printers, 1837.

Leake, Isaac Q. *Memoir of the Life and Times of General John Lamb*. Albany, NY: Joel Munsell, 1850.

Lee, Henry. *Memoirs of the War in the Southern Department*, Lee Family Digital Archive, https://leefamilyarchive.org/papers/books/south/05.html.

Lesser, Charles H. *The Sinews of Independence: Monthly Strength Reports of the Continental Army*. Chicago, IL: University of Chicago Press, 1976.

Lodge, Henry Cabot, ed. *The Works of Alexander Hamilton*, 12 volumes. New York, NY: G. P. Putnam's Sons, 1904.

McMichael, William P., ed. "Diary of Lieutenant James McMichael, of the Pennsylvania Line, 1776-1778," *Pennsylvania Magazine of History and Biography*. Volume 16 (July 1, 1892), 129-159.

Miller, Lillian B., ed. *The Selected Papers of Charles Willson Peale and his Family*, Volume 1. New Haven, CT: Yale University Press, 1983.

Muhlenberg, Peter. "Orderly Book of Gen. John Peter Gabriel Muhlenberg, March 26 to December 20, 1777," *Pennsylvania Magazine of History and Biography* Volume 34, no. 4 (1910), 438-477. [covers August 21 to September 29, 1777].

Paine, Thomas. *Collected Writings*. New York, NY: Literary Classics of the United States, Inc., 1955.

Patrick, John C. *George Washington's Accounts of Expenses*. Boston, MA: Houghton Mifflin Company, 1917.

Pickering, Timothy [to Jared Sparks], August 23, 1826, *North American Review* Vol. 23, (1826), 427-28.

Pickering, Timothy. *Interesting Correspondence Between His Excellency Governor Sullivan and Col. Pickering; in which the Latter Vindicates Himself Against the Groundless Charges Made Against Him by the Governor and Others*. Boston, MA: Greenough and Stebbins, 1808.

Pinckney, Charles. "The Battles of Brandywine and Germantown," *The Historical Magazine*, Vol. 10. (Morrisania, N.Y.: Henry B. Dawson, 1866), 202-204.

Quincy, Josiah, ed. *The Journals of Major Samuel Shaw, The First American Consul at Canton*. Boston, MA: Wm. Crosby and H. P. Nichols, 1847.

Reed, William B. *Life and Correspondence of Joseph Reed.* Vols. 1-2. Philadelphia, PA: Lindsay and Blakiston, 1847.

Rush, Benjamin. *A Memorial Containing Travels Through Life or Sundry Incidents in the Life of Dr. Benjamin Rush.* Philadelphia, PA: Louis Alexander Biddle, 1905.

Rush, Benjamin. *The Autobiography of Benjamin Rush, His "Travels Through Life,"* (Princeton, NJ: Princeton University Press, 1948.

Scull, G. D., ed. "The Montresor Journals." *Collections of the New York Historical Society*, vol. 14 (1881). 582 pages.

Showman, Richard and Parks, Roger N., eds. *The Papers of Nathanael Greene.* 13 volumes. Chapel Hill, NC: University of North Carolina Press, for the Rhode Island Historical Society, 1976-2005.

Simms, William G. *The Army Correspondence of Colonel John Laurens in the Years 1777-8.* New York, NY: Bradford Club, 1867.

Smith, Paul H. and Gephart, Ronald M., eds. *Letters of Delegates to Congress,* 1774–1789. 26 volumes. Washington, DC: Library of Congress, 1976–2000.

State of New York. *Public Papers of George Clinton, First Governor of New York,* volume 2. New York, NY: Wynkoop Hallenbeck Crawford Co., 1900.

Syrett, Harold C. and Cooke, Jacob E., eds. *The Papers of Alexander Hamilton.* 27 volumes. New York, NY: Columbia University Press, 1961–87.

Tallmadge, Benjamin. *Memoir of Colonel Benjamín Tallmadge.* New York, NY: Thomas Holman, Book and Job Printer, 1858.

Taylor, Robert, ed. *The Adams Papers, Papers of John Adams*, volume 5. Cambridge, MA: Harvard University Press, 2006.

Watts, Henry Miller, ed. "Memoir of Henry Miller," *Pennsylvania Magazine of History and Biography* Volume 12, no. 4 (1889), 425-31.

Whinyates, F. A., ed. *The Services of Lieut.-Colonel Francis Downman, R.A. in France, North America, and the West Indies, Between the Years 1758 and 1784.* Woolwich: Royal Artillery Institution, 1898.

Wilkinson, James. *Memoirs of My Own Times.* 3 vols. Philadelphia. PA: Printed by Abraham Small, 1816.

LETTERS AND LETTER EXTRACTS PUBLISHED IN NEWSPAPERS

"A Jersusalem Blade" to editors, n.d., *Boston Independent Chronicle*, July 10, 1777.

Anonymous letter to a friend, September 16, 1777, [New Haven] *Connecticut Journal*, October 8, 1777.

Anonymous letter, October 5, 1777, [Baltimore] *Maryland Gazette*, October 23, 1777.

Clement Biddle to [General Mifflin], September 16, 1777, *Providence Gazette*, October 4, 1777.

Clement Biddle to [Thomas Mifflin], September 16, 1777, *Boston Gazette*, September 29, 1777.

Clement Biddle to "his lady," October 24, 1777, *Norwich* [Conn.] *Packet*, November 10, 1777.

Clement Biddle to Dear General, September 16, 1777, [Portsmouth, N.H] *Freeman's Journal*, October 4, 1777.

"Common Sense," "American Crisis No. 4," *Pennsylvania Evening Post*, September 13, 1777.

"Extract of a letter dated Camp, near Schuylkill Sept. 13," [Charleston] *South-Carolina and American General Gazette*, October 30, 1777.

"Extract of a letter from a General officer . . ." August 27, 1777, Purdie's [Williamsburg] *Virginia Gazette*, September 5, 1777.

"Extract of a letter from an officer at camp, dated December 10," *Virginia Gazette*, December 26, 1777.

"Extract of a letter from camp near Morristown, July 10," *Purdie's Virginia Gazette* [Williamsburg], July 25, 1777.

"Extract of a Letter from Camp, at Morris Town, dated July 5th, 1777," [Portsmouth, NH] *Freeman's Journal*, July 26, 1777.

"Extract of a letter from Camp, Tuesday Morning," [Charleston] *South-Carolina and American General Gazette*, October 16, 1777.

"Extract of a letter from London, January 24," [Philadelphia] *Pennsylvania Journal*, April 16, 1777.

"Extract of a letter from Morris Town, July 5," [Baltimore] *Maryland Journal*, July 15, 1777.

"Extract of a letter from Philadelphia, dated September 13, 1777, 9 o'clock," [Charleston] *South-Carolina and American General Gazette*, October 16, 1777.

"Extract of a Letter received by a Gentleman in the City from his Nephew at Philadelphia," [London] *Public Advertiser*, January 29, 1778.

"Jerry," *Pittsburgh Press*, May 5, 1907.

Mark Anthony to Mr. Towne, December 30, 1776, [Philadelphia] *Pennsylvania Evening Post*, January 7, 1777.

"Olivia" to The President of the State, [Philadelphia] *Pennsylvania Packet*, June 3, 1779.

Timothy Pickering [to Jared Sparks], August 23, 1826, [Philadelphia] *Register of Pennsylvania*, January 26, 1828.

Undated letter to editor, [Purdie's] *Virginia Gazette*, October 17, 1777.

G. Weedon, "Camp, Cross Roads, August 10, 1777," Purdie's *Virginia Gazette*, September 12, 1777.

NEWSPAPER ARTICLES

"An Account of Pennsylvania," *Derby Mercury* [Derbyshire, England], March 3, 1775.

[Baltimore] *Maryland Journal*, September 16, 1777.

Boston Gazette, July 7, 1777.

[Boston] *Independent Chronicle*, September 18, 1777.
"Boston, October 2," [New Haven] *Connecticut Journal*, October 8, 1777.
"Camped on Queen Lane," [Philadelphia] *The Times*, October 19, 1891.
"Charles-Town, July 7," *The* [Charleston] *South Carolina Gazette and County Journal*, July 7, 1777.
[Charleston] *South-Carolina and American General Gazette*, October 9, 1777.
[Charlestown] *South-Carolina and American General Gazette*, October 16, 1777.
"Christiana Mills For Sale," *Philadelphia Inquirer*, July 5, 1794.
"Fine Tablet Now Marks Historic Old Mansion," [Wilmington, Del.] *Evening Journal*, February 24, 1902.
[Hartford] *Connecticut Courant*, September 22, 1777.
Leeds Intelligencer and Yorkshire General Advertiser, July 8, 1777.
London Public Advertiser, August 27, 1777.
"London, February 10," [London] *St. James Chronicle*, February 7, 1778.
"London," *London Evening Post*, December 2, 1777.
"London," London *Public Advertiser*, December 2, 1777.
"London," London *Public Advertiser*, December 5, 1777.
"London," London *Public Advertiser*, December 5, 1777.
"Masquerade," *Ipswich Journa*l, July 12, 1777.
"Monuments," *Buffalo Courier*, March 19, 1884.
"Morning Post," [London] *Morning Post and Daily Advertiser*, January 19, 1778.
Newcastle Weekly Courant, May 10, 1777.
"Old York Road and its Points of Interest," *Chester Times*, August 30, 1918.
[Philadelphia] *Dunlap's Pennsylvania Packet*, August 26, 1777.
[Philadelphia] *Pennsylvania Gazette* and *Pennsylvania Post*, September 10, 1777.
[Philadelphia] *Pennsylvania Evening Post*, August 16, 1777.
[Philadelphia] *Pennsylvania Packet*, September 9, 1777.
"Philadelphia, July 10, 1777," [Baltimore] *Maryland Journal*, July 15, 1777.
"Philadelphia, July 8, 1777," *Boston Gazette*, July 28, 1777.
"Philadelphia," *Pennsylvania Evening Post*, August 23, 1777.
"Portsmouth," [Portsmouth] *New Hampshire Gazette*, July 12, 1777.
"Research Bares New Data on Washington's Quarters," [Wilmington] *Morning News*, February 22, 1957.
"There were giants in those days," *Sandusky Daily Commercial Register*, October 21, 1854.
"To Be Let," [Philadelphia] *Dunlap and Claypoole's American Daily Advertiser*, November 8, 1773.
"To be Sold on the Premises," [Philadelphia] *Pennsylvania Gazette*, September 4, 1782.
"To Mark a Spot Now Held Sacred," *Philadelphia Inquirer*, November 10, 1895.

"Washington's Headquarters. Historic Buildings at One Time or Another Occupied by the Revolutionary Leader," *New York Herald*, February 18, 1894.
"Williamsburg, December 19," [Purdie's] *Virginia Gazette*, December 19, 1777.
[Williamsburg] *Purdie's Virginia Gazette*, September 26, 1777.
[Williamsburg] *Virginia Gazette*, October 3, 1777.

SECONDARY SOURCES

Anderson, Troyer Steele. *The Command of the Howe Brothers During the American Revolution.* New York, NY: Oxford University Press, 1936.
Atkinson, Rick. *The British Are Coming: The War for America, Lexington to Princeton, 1775-1777.* New York, NY: Henry Holt and Company, 2019.
Baker, William S. "The Camp by Schuylkill Falls," *Pennsylvania Magazine of History and Biography* Volume 16 (1892), 28-41.
Bancroft, George. *History of the United States, From the Discovery of the American Continent.* Boston, MA: Little, Brown, & Company, 1866.
Bean, Theodore W. *History of Montgomery County, Pennsylvania.* Philadelphia, PA: Everts & Peck, 1884.
Boatner, Mark M. *Encyclopedia of the American Revolution.* Mechanicsburg, PA: Stackpole Books, 1994.
Bodle, Wayne. *The Valley Forge Winter: Civilians and Soldiers in War.* University Park, PA: Penn State University Press, 2002.
Brecht, Samuel K., ed. *The Genealogical Record of the Schwenkfelder Families.* New York, NY: Rand McNally & Company, 1923.
"The British Campaign for Philadelphia and the Occupation of Valley Forge in 1777," https://www.nps.gov/vafo/learn/historyculture/upload/Philadelphia%20campaign.pdf.
Carbone, Gerald M. *Nathanael Greene: A Biography of the American Revolution.* New York, NY: Palgrave Macmillan, 2008.
Catts, Wade P., Selig, Robert and Moir, Sean. *"Left Newport...Before Daylight and March'd to Chads Ford" Military Terrain Analysis for Two Brandywine Battlefield Strategic Landscapes.* West Chester, PA: Chester County Planning Commission, 2019.
Catts, Wade P., Selig, Robert, LaVigne, Elisabeth et al. *"It is Painful for Me to Lose So Many Good People:" Report of an Archeological Survey at Red Bank Battlefield Park (Fort Mercer), National Park, Gloucester County, New Jersey.* West Chester, PA: Commonwealth Heritage Group, Inc., 1917.
Chernow, Ron. *Washington: A Life.* New York, NY: Penguin Books, 2010.
Chervinsky, Lindsay M. *The Cabinet: George Washington and the Creation of an American Institution.* Cambridge, MA: Harvard University Press, 2020.
Colles, Julia K. Colles. *Authors and Writers Associated with Morristown, with a Chapter on Historic Morristown.* Morristown, NJ: Vogt Bros., 1895.
County of Chester, *Battle of the Clouds Technical Report*, https://www.chesco.org/DocumentCenter/View/17453/CloudsTechReport?bidId=

Dorwart, Jeffery M. *Fort Mifflin of Philadelphia: An Illustrated History*. Philadelphia, PA: University of Pennsylvania Press, 1998.

Ecelbarger, Gary. "The Feint That Never Happened: Unheralded Turning Point of the Philadelphia Campaign," *Journal of the American Revolution*, November 19, 2020, https://allthingsliberty.com/2020/11/the-feint-that-never-happened-unheralded-turning-point-of-the-philadelphia-campaign/

Ecelbarger, Gary and Harris, Michael C. "The Numerical Strength of George Washington's Army During the 1777 Philadelphia Campaign," *JAR Annual Volume 2022*. Yardley, PA: Westholme Publishing Co., 2022, 101-114.

Ellis, Joseph J. *His Excellency: George Washington*. New York, NY: Alfred A. Knopf, 2004.

"Emlen Family Genealogy," https://www.emlen.us.

Fischer, David Hackett. *Washington's Crossing*. New York, NY: Oxford University Press, 2004.

Flavell, Julie. *The Howe Dynasty: The Untold Story of a Military Family and the Women Behind Britain's Wars for America*. New York, NY: Liveright, 2021.

Ford, Worthington Chauncey. *British Officers Serving in the American Revolution, 1774-1783*. Brooklyn, NY: Historical Print Club, 1897.

Frantz, John B., and William Pencak, eds. *Beyond Philadelphia: The American Revolution in the Pennsylvania Hinterland*. University Park, PA: The Pennsylvania State University Press, 1998.

Freeman, Douglas Southall. *George Washington: A Biography*. Volume 4. New York, NY: Charles Scribner's Sons, 1951.

Futhey, J. Smith and Cope, Gilbert. *History of Chester County, Pennsylvania*. Philadelphia, PA: Louis H. Everts, 1881.

"George Johnston," https://www.mountvernon.org/library/digitalhistory/digital-encyclopedia/article/george-johnston/

"George Washington's Marquee Tent," https://www.mountvernon.org/library/digitalhistory/digital-encyclopedia/article/george-washingtons-marquee-tent/

"General Washington from Life, 1777," Portraits in Revolution, https://www.americanrevolution.com/gallery/american_artists/charles_willson_peale/gen eral_washington_sketch_1777.

Gillett, Mary C. *The Army Medical Department 1775-1818*. Honolulu, HI: University Press of the Pacific, 2002.

Gordon, William. *The History of the Rise, Progress, and Establishment, of the Independence of the United States of America*. 3 vols. New York, NY: Hodge, Allen, and Campbell, 1789.

Graham, James. *The Life of Daniel Morgan of the Virginia Line of the Army of the United States, With Portions of His Correspondence*. New York, 1856.

Greene, George Washington. *The Life of Nathanael Greene*. 3 vols. New York, NY: Hurd and Houghton, 1867-1871.

Greenwalt, Phillip S. *The Winter that Won the War: The Winter Encampment at Valley Forge, 1777-1778*. El Dorado Hills, CA: Savas Beatie, 2021.

Gruber, Ira D. *The Howe Brothers & the American Revolution*. New York, NY: Atheneum, 1972.

Hagey, Brian. "The Continental Army at 'Headquarters Towamensing' October 8-16, 1777," https://mhep.org/wp-content/uploads/2020/07/Hagey-The-Continental-Army-at-Towamencin.pdf.

Hagist, Don N. *Noble Volunteers: The British Soldiers Who Fought the American Revolution*. Yardley, PA: Westholme Publishing, 2020.

"Hale-Byrnes House," http://www.halebyrnes.org/history.html.

Harris, Michael C. *Brandywine: A Military History of the Battle that Lost Philadelphia but Saved America, September 11, 1777*. El Dorado Hills, CA: Savas Beatie, 2014.

Harris, Michael C. *Germantown: A Military History of the Battle for Philadelphia, October 4, 1777*. El Dorado Hills, CA: Savas Beatty, 2020.

Hasselgren, Per-Olof. "The Smallpox Epidemics in America in the 1700s and the Role of the Surgeons: Lessons to be Learned During the Global Outbreak of COVID-19." *World Journal of Surgery* 2020, 44(9): 2837-2841.

Heitman, Francis B. *Historical Register of Officers of the Continental Army During the War of the Revolution, April 1775, to December, 1783*. Washington, DC, n.p., 1898.

"Henry Antes House, National Register of Historic Places registration papers, https://npgallery.nps.gov/NRHP/GetAsset/NHLS/75001657_text.

Herrera, Ricardo A. *Feeding Washington's Army: Surviving the Valley Forge Winter of 1778*. Chapel Hil, NY1: University of North Carolina Press, 2022.

Hibbert, Christopher. *Recoats and Rebels*. New York, NY: W.W. Norton & Company, 1990.

Irving, Washington. *Life of Washington*, 5 volumes. New York, NY: G. P. Putnam's Sons, 1881.

Jackson, John W. *The Delaware Bay and River Defenses of Philadelphia 1775-1777*. Philadelphia, PA: Philadelphia Maritime Museum, 1977.

Jackson, John W. *Whitemarsh 1777: Impregnable Stronghold*. Fort Washington, PA: Historical Society of Fort Washington, 1984.

Jackson, John W. *With the British Army in Philadelphia, 1777-1778*. San Rafael, CA: Presidio Press, 1979.

"John Fitzgerald," https://www.mountvernon.org/library/digitalhistory/digital-encyclopedia/article/john-fitzgerald/.

Johnson, Donald. *Occupied America: British Military Rule and the Experience of the Revolution*. Philadelphia, PA: University of Pennsylvania Press, 2020.

Johnston, George. *History of Cecil County, Maryland*. Elkton, Published by the Author, 1881.

Kapp, Friedrich. *The Life of John Kalb: Major-general in the Revolutionary Army*. Bedford, MA: Applewood Books, 1884.

Katcher, Philip R.N. *Encyclopedia of British, Provincial, and German Army Units 1775-1783*. Harrisburg, PA: Stackpole Books, 1973.

Keister, Kim. "History Lesson." *Historic Preservation* (November-December 1993), 52-110.

Ketchum, Richard M. *Saratoga: Turning Point of America's Revolutionary War*. New York, NY: Henry Holt and Company, 1997.

Keyser, Alan, "The Perkiomen and Skippack Township Encampment of the Revolutionary War," goschenhoppen.org/ak-maria-keely/.

Knouff, Gregory T. *The Soldiers' Revolution: Pennsylvanians in Arms and the Forging of Early American Identity*. University Park, PA: Pennsylvania State University Press, 2004.

Leasa, K. Varden. "A Great Valley Legend Examined: Where Did Washington Really Sleep on September 15, 1777?" https://www.tehistory.org/hqda/pdf/v45/v45n2p054.pdf.

Lefkowitz, Arthur S. *George Washington's Indispensable Men: The 32 Aides-de-Camp Who Helped Win American Independence*. Mechanicsburg, PA: Stackpole Books, 2003.

Lender, Mark Edward. *Cabal!: The Plot Against George Washington*. Yardley, PA: Westholme Publishing, 2019.

Lengel, Edward. *General George Washington: A Military Life*. New York, NY: Random House, 2005.

"Life Guards," https://www.mountvernon.org/library/digitalhistory/digital-encyclopedia/article/life-guards/.

"Life Portraits of George Washington," *George Washington's Mount Vernon*, https://www.mountvernon.org/george-washington/artwork/life-portraits-of-george-washington/.

Lossing, Benjamin J. *The Pictorial Field-Book of the American Revolution*. New York: Harper and Brothers, 1852.

Maloy, Mark. "The Battle of Freeman's Farm, September 19, 1777," *American Battlefield Trust*, https://www.battlefields.org/learn/articles/battle-freemans-farm-september-19-1777.

"A Maryland Loyalist," *Maryland Historical Magazine* Vol 1, No. 4 (December 1906), 321-23.

Massey, Gregory D. *John Laurens and the American Revolution*. Columbia, SC: University of South Carolina Press, 2015.

Mayers, Robert. *Revolutionary New Jersey: Forgotten Towns and Crossroads of the American Revolution*. Staunton, VA: American History Press, 2018.

McGuire, Thomas J. *Battle of Paoli*. Mechanicsburg, PA: Stackpole Books, 2000.

McGuire, Thomas J. T*he Philadelphia Campaign: Brandywine and the Fall of Philadelphia*. Mechanicsburg, PA: Stackpole Books, 2006.

McGuire, Thomas J. *The Philadelphia Campaign: Germantown and the Roads to Valley Forge*. Mechanicsburg, PA: Stackpole Books, 2007.

"Military Departments in the Continental Army," https://revolutionarywar.us/continental-army/military-departments/.

Murphy, Orville T. *Charles Gravier Comte de Vergennes: French Diplomacy in the Age of Revolution, 1719-1787.* Albany, NY: State University of New York Press, 1982.

Murphy, Orville T. "The Battle of Germantown and the Franco-American Alliance of 1778." *Pennsylvania Magazine of History and Biography* Vol. 82 (January 1958), 55-64.

Newton, Michael E. *Alexander Hamilton: The Formative Years.* Phoenix, AZ: Eleftheria Publishing, 2015.

Newton, Michael E. *Discovering Hamilton.* Phoenix, AZ: Eleftheria Publishing, 2019.

Olson, Eric, "Weight of a War, or The 'Big Men' of the Continental Army," https://www.nps.gov/fost/blogs/weight-of-a-war-or-the-big-men-of-the-continental-army.htm.

O'Shaughnessy, Andrew Jackson. *The Men Who Lost America: British Leadership, the American Revolution, and the Fate of the Empire.* New Haven, CT: Yale University Press, 2013.

Pancake, John S. *1777: The Year of the Hangman.* Tuscaloosa, AL.: University of Alabama Press, 1977.

Parsons, Eugene. *George Washington: A Character Sketch.* Dansville, NY: Instructor Publishing Co., 1898.

Peckham, Howard H., ed. *The Toll of Independence: Engagements & Battle Casualties of the American Revolution.* Chicago, IL: The University of Chicago Press, 1974.

Pickering, Octavius. *The Life of Timothy Pickering.* 2 vols. Boston, MA: Little, Brown, and Company, 1867.

Reed, John F. *Campaign to Valley Forge: July 1, 1777-December 19, 1777.* Philadelphia, PA: Pioneer Press, 1965.

"Richard Kidder Meade," https://www.mountvernon.org/library/digitalhistory/digital-encyclopedia/article/richard-kidder-meade/

Risch, Erna. *Supplying Washington's Army.* Washington, DC: Center of Military History, United States Army, 1981.

Ruppert, Bob. "His Excellency's Guards," *Journal of the American Revolution,* August 18, 2014, https://allthingsliberty.com/2014/08/his-excellencys-guards/.

Sellers, Charles Coleman. *Charles Willson Peale: Early Life: 1741-1790,* vol. 1. Philadelphia, PA: The American Philosophical Society, 1947.

Sellers, Charles Coleman. "Portraits and Miniatures by Charles Willson Peale," in *Transactions of the American Philosophical Society.* Volume 42 (1), 1952.

"1777 Chester County Property Atlas," 1777 Chester County Property Atlas (storymaps.arcgis.com).

Smith, Samuel Steele. *Fight for the Delaware 1777*. Monmouth Beach, NJ: Philip Freneau Press, 1970.

Soltis, Carol Eaton. *The Art of the Peales in the Philadelphia Museum of Art: Adaptions and Innovations*. New Haven, CT: Yale University Press, 2017.

Spears, John R. *Anthony Wayne, Sometimes Called "Mad Anthony."* New York, NY: D. Appleton and Company, 1903.

Spring, Matthew H. *With Zeal and With Bayonets Only: The British Army on Campaign in North America, 1775-1783*. Norman, OK: University of Oklahoma Press, 2008.

Stewart, Frank H. *History of the Battle of Red Bank: With Events Prior and Subsequent Thereto*. Woodbury, NJ: Board of Chosen Freeholders of Gloucester County, 1927.

Stille, Charles J. *Major-General Anthony Wayne and the Pennsylvania Line in the Continental Army*. Philadelphia, PA: J. P. Lippincott Company, 1893.

Stone, Garry Wheeler & Paul W. Schopp. *The Battle of Gloucester 1777*. Yardley, PA: Westholme Publishing, 2022.

Stryker, William S. *The Forts on the Delaware in the Revolutionary War*. Trenton, NJ: The John L. Murphy Publishing Co., 1901.

Sturgill, Erika Quesenbery. "The 'frien-emy' of Friendship in Elkton," May 9, 2015, https://www.cecildaily.com/our_cecil/the-frien-emy-of-friendship-in-elkton/article_2e845e59-4d3a-51dd-bdcb-d040fc2352b7.html.

Symonds, Craig L. *A Battlefield Atlas of the American Revolution*. Baltimore, MD: Nautical & Aviation Publishing Company of America, Inc., 1986.

"The Thompson Tavern and the Jeffersonville Inn," *Historical Sketches of Montgomery County* (1), 348-49.

Upham, Charles W. The *Life of Timothy Pickering*. Volume 2. Boston, MA: Little, Brown, and Company, 1873.

U.S. Government, National Park Service. *The Valley Forge Encyclopedia: Comprehensive History of the Famous American Revolutionary War Winter Continental Army Encampment*. Wilmington, DE: n.p., 2019.

Wallace, David Duncan. *The Life of Henry Laurens With a Sketch of the Life of Lieutenant-Colonel John Laurens*. New York, NY: G. P. Putnam's Sons, 1915.

Wickersty, Jason R. "A Shocking Havoc: the Plundering of Westfield, New Jersey, June 26, 1777." *Journal of the American Revolution* https://allthingsliberty.com/2015/07/a-shocking-havoc-the-plundering-of-westfield-new-jersey-june-26-1777/.

Wright, John W. *Some Notes on the Continental Army*. Vails Gate, NY: Temple Hill Association, 1963.

Wright, Robert K., Jr. *The Continental Army*. Washington, DC: Government Printing Office, 1983.

Acknowledgments

My cadre of friends, diverse experts of military history and the Revolutionary War, have aided me immensely throughout the creation of this volume. They have been instrumental sounding boards in field trips and correspondences to either support or vanquish my theories, while offering advice and direction and oftentimes providing me with wonderful primary source material. This includes—in no particular order—Bill Welsch, Doug Bonforte, Scott Patchan, Christian McBurney, Tom McAndrew, Jim Christ, Glenn F. Williams, Kim Burdick, Bob Fanelli, Justin Clement, and Rich Rosenthal. I also wish to credit National Park historians Eric Olsen (Morristown) and Jennifer Bolton (Valley Forge) for sharing their expertise and sources with me. I also thank Wade Catts for providing me information related to his archaeological work specific to this campaign.

A special acknowledgment is extended to Mike Harris, a campaign expert, good friend, and a writing partner for contributions to the *Journal of the American Revolution* (JAR). Mike's knowledge of the Philadelphia Campaign is incomparable; his generosity in sharing it with me has proven to be invaluable to this volume. Speaking of JAR, I thank its managing editor, Don N. Hagist, for accepting all my contributions over the past four years for publication in this outstanding online journal. This proved to be a valuable test for critiques of several of my newest discoveries and hypotheses related to this book.

Historians of the Philadelphia Campaign, past and present, deserve special commendation for their efforts to accurately document these crucial months of the Revolutionary War. This includes John Reed, Stephen Taaffe, John W. Jackson, Thomas McGuire and Michael Harris. Additionally, those who focused on George Washington during this period, particularly Douglas Southall Freeman and Edward G. Lengel, as well as Thomas Fleming and Mark E. Lender (both dissected the Cabal which began late in this campaign) all earn my respect and gratitude for their contributions. Although my analyses of campaign events and decisions oftentimes differ from theirs, the depth of understanding I acquired from their research provided me the ability to confidently develop and portray a unique interpretation of both rare and oft-told events.

I also wish to thank Bruce H. Franklin, the founder of Westholme Publishing. No book project I have developed over the past thirty years was more dependent on one publisher than *George Washington's Momentous Year* has been with Westholme. The concept of a single-year, military campaign biography could only come to fruition due to Bruce, who not only understood and appreciated this author's premise, but also encouraged me and provided the leeway to develop and expand the topic into two volumes.

I also thank the staff and consultants at Westholme for their contributions to this volume. My editors strove to make my manuscript a strong historical narrative as well as a crisp, engaging story. This includes Michael Dolan, my copy editor, and Glenn Williams, my historical editor. Credit is also extended to Sarah Ferguson, who "red inked" an early version of the manuscript to present it for fine tuning. Tracy Dungan created eleven outstanding maps to best represent George Washington's movements as well as those of his and his and his opponent's armies on battlefields and within contested theaters. Not to be overlooked at Westholme is Trudi Gershenov, who created a superlative cover that makes me regret the adage of not judging the book by it.

Carolyn Ecelbarger earns, as always, my warmest acknowledgment. Her patience and personal sacrifices made to support my history obsession has spanned thirty-five years, the past four on this project. For her unwavering support, I am eternally grateful to her.

Index